Part-Time For All

 *Heretical Thought*

HERETICAL THOUGHT

Series editor: Ruth O'Brien,
The Graduate Center, City University of
New York

Part-Time For All

A Care Manifesto

JENNIFER NEDELSKY AND
TOM MALLESON

Oxford University Press is a department of the University of Oxford. It furthers
the University's objective of excellence in research, scholarship, and education
by publishing worldwide. Oxford is a registered trade mark of Oxford University
Press in the UK and certain other countries.

Published in the United States of America by Oxford University Press
198 Madison Avenue, New York, NY 10016, United States of America.

© Oxford University Press 2023

Library of Congress Cataloging-in-Publication Data
Names: Nedelsky, Jennifer, author. | Malleson, Tom, author.
Title: Part-time for all : a care manifesto / Jennifer Nedelsky and Tom Malleson.
Description: New York, NY : Oxford University Press, [2023] |
Includes bibliographical references and index.
Identifiers: LCCN 2022047928 (print) | LCCN 2022047929 (ebook) |
ISBN 9780190642754 (hardback) | ISBN 9780190642778 (epub)
Subjects: LCSH: Caregivers—Social conditions. | Caregivers—Economic
conditions. | Work-life balance. | Part-time employment. | Hours of labor.
Classification: LCC HV65 .N434 2023 (print) | LCC HV65 (ebook) |
DDC 362.0425—dc23/eng/20230109
LC record available at https://lccn.loc.gov/2022047928
LC ebook record available at https://lccn.loc.gov/2022047929

DOI: 10.1093/oso/9780190642754.001.0001

Printed by Sheridan Books, Inc., United States of America

For Joe Carens, who models care at work and male care in the household.
And for Roey Malleson, caregiver par excellence.

Contents

Preface

One of the most important insights I (J.N.) got from having my children was the importance of routine physical caretaking for forming the basic bonds of connection . . . [that] initial insight . . . broadened into a belief that physical caretaking is part of what roots us in the world and permits us to feel a connection with the material foundations of life, from the care the earth requires to respect for the labor that permits us to live as we do.

The dominant culture of North America treats virtually all forms of physical caretaking with contempt. Until there is a shift in this basic stance, those who do the caretaking will be treated with contempt: They will be paid little and defined as unsuccessful. If caretaking were actually valued, there would be a revolution in the structure of our society.[1]

Jenny Nedelsky wrote those sentences in 1998. Now Jenny and Tom Malleson offer a path to that transformation. This book is about new norms that could restructure our lives so that *everyone* (no matter how "important" their work) experiences the joy and connection of care giving (both physical and emotional). The norm would be that all who are able should provide roughly 20–25 hours of unpaid care every week, an amount sufficient for them to acquire the knowledge and connection that care brings. The need to learn from care grounds our argument that everyone needs to do it. In addition, roughly 30 hours a week would be the upper end of the norm for paid work. We think these profound changes could have vitally important impacts: ending the unsustainable stress on families and the gross inequality for those who provide care. It could ensure that high level decision-makers know something about care, and those who know something about care could become policymakers. Even if care givers were respected and well-compensated, if one group of people makes the policy (in corporations and government) and a *different* group does the care, we will continue to have dangerously ignorant policymakers.

Part-Time for All could end the long-standing degradation of care and those who do it, as well as the policy distortions that flow from failing to recognize the value of care.

As we were completing this book, the global pandemic struck. COVID-19 has made it brutally obvious that people cannot get their work done unless *someone* is available to provide care. When schools and daycares close it becomes hard to ignore the fact that the economy, and our society more generally, depend on people providing care for those who need it (not just children, of course). COVID-19 has even helped people see that women and the less well-off disproportionately bear this responsibility. The pandemic has made it impossible to ignore the fact that both the benefits and burdens of care (given and received) are extremely unevenly distributed. The pandemic has also revealed how painful it can be when those we love are not receiving adequate care (such as elderly people isolated from loved ones in inadequate care homes). Given all of this, there is no better time than now to pose the fundamental question: What happens to care when the demands of the workplace ignore the need for care? Getting people back to work as we knew it will not address this vital question. Work relies on care, but care is becoming unsustainable—because of the structure of work and the ongoing failure to value care.

Who is supposed to provide care for those who need it when the "ideal worker" is still someone whose top priority is work? There are many forms of family, but few with someone at home to provide full-time care. Many workers (disproportionately women) have to provide care on top of their work hours. Increasingly, someone outside the family (usually female, often racialized and/or an immigrant) is paid, badly, to do at least some of the care. Men in heterosexual couples are "helping" a little more than they used to, but doing nowhere near 50 percent of the care. Better publicly funded care for children, the elderly, and people with disabilities is urgently needed, but will not solve the underlying problems of workplace demands that are incompatible with care responsibilities and a pervasive degradation of care and those who do it.

This book presents the argument that the problems of care—its low status and its unequal distribution—cannot be fixed without changing the structure of work. By reducing work hours across the board (with no exceptions for "important" jobs at the top), individuals, families, and societies will reap the benefits of a revaluation of care and a population who has learned the joys, the skills, and dispositions of care by doing it.

COVID-19 has highlighted the ongoing crisis in care. Now we need to see its connections to the structure of work. Fundamental change is necessary, but there is reason for optimism. The pandemic has proven that given sufficient political will, there can be rapid, radical, and deep change in how work and care is structured. Change is possible. We can hear it coming.

Acknowledgments

Part time for All had its origins in an essay Sara Ruddick invited me to contribute to the book *Mother Troubles (1998)*. That invitation gave me space to work out ideas that I had thought I could never find a place to publish. It is a pleasure to be able to offer my gratitude and return to her work here.

Once I started on this book, I found help and support in many places. The first time I presented a version at the American Political Science Association, Joan Tronto asked a question about guaranteed annual income, and I replied that I did not have the expertise for the political economy side of the issues. Tom Malleson was in the audience and introduced himself to me after the panel saying he had that expertise. That was the beginning of a wonderful collaboration. In addition to providing that vital contribution, he edited the entire manuscript down from an unwieldly size. And he provides a living model of someone who resists over identification with "work," thus freeing himself from the usual academic hang ups and becoming available for generosity, care, responsibility, and activism, as well as "work" that advances equality.

I have been extremely fortunate in the institutional support I have had. In 2016–17 I held a research fellowship at the Jackman Humanities Institute at the University of Toronto, which gave me a year off teaching. The theme that year was "time" and there was an exceptional group of people from many disciplines who helped me think through the puzzles of time. Between 2014 and 2018, I spent six weeks each Spring at the Institute for Social Justice in Sydney, Australia. Nick Kompridis and Allison Weir had gathered an extraordinary group of scholars who provided some of my most important conversations as the project unfolded. The visits also allowed me to participate in multiple forums of the wonderful Australian feminist community.

Osgoode Hall Law School at York University offered a special opportunity by creating a part time job for me. Although it turns out that neither they nor I anticipated some of the complications (the work world is not set up for equal status for part-time workers), Osgoode has provided a great environment for me to teach and write while finishing the book.

I am grateful for thoughtful feedback from students at both the University of Toronto and Osgoode.

Libraries at the University of Toronto and Osgoode Hall have provided important support, but I am particularly grateful for all the help I have received as a retired faculty member from the University of Toronto law library and would like to thank Sufei Xu in particular.

It has been a tremendous help to have been able to present these ideas at many different forums, with different kinds of audiences, and in different parts of the world, both in person (pre-COVID) and virtually. I am not going to try to name them all. But I do want to mention the Care Forum run by Dan Engster at the University of Huston, which provides a great virtual space for conversations about care, and the wonderfully innovative series of events, including Epistemologies of Care, Visualizing Care, and Revaluing Care in the Global Economy, organized by Jocelyn Olcott and her colleagues at Duke and around the world

In addition, I was able to discuss my ideas with nonacademic audiences thanks to Bathurst Street and College Street United Churches, and to the generosity of Sarah Polley in convening a wonderful group of women in my kitchen and in offering her living room for a session on *Part Time for All* as part of Joanna Polley's Plutarch's Table Salon.

There are so many individuals who have offered comments, advice, encouragement, and new perspectives that it is a risk to mention any given that omission is the norm here. Nevertheless, I want to mention Judith Resnick who read a very early draft and was one of the first to make clear to me that revaluing care was really a central objective of the project. I was honored to get some early encouragement from Nancy Fraser, whose work is so foundational to this project. Joan Tronto has been an important interlocutor throughout. My oldest friend, Carlin Meyer, offered an early warning about *Part Time for All* being seen as a form of privatization. Another early warning about middle class bias and preoccupation came from Clare Huntington. At an Osgoode reading group, where I got great feedback, Adrian Smith provided a crucial heads up about the way I was distinguishing activism and care. Rainer Forst, who allowed himself to serve as the voice of "liberal reason," helped me articulate why I believe *Part Time for All* does not unreasonably impose a vison of the good life on others. Finally, Paul Raynor, of Hobart, Tasmania, Australia gave me great encouragement and very helpful insights as someone who had already adopted the norms of Part Time for All (and great hospitality).

Osgoode has an excellent system of supporting its faculty and students by funding research assistants. Both Maria Arabella Robles and Jen Laws provided excellent research, suggestions, editing, and manuscript preparation.

In sum, I am incredibly grateful for the many conversations over the years that have enriched this work. Some of these took place in the context of "work," but almost always in a spirit of care. Care about the project and my engagement with it became part of the "work" of others. The foundation for all of this was the care my husband, Joe, provided me and our family, which enabled me to share with others my ongoing efforts to enable everyone to blend, mix, and balance work and care in a life sustaining way.

Of course, despite all this help and support, limitations remain. I know I did not sufficiently meet every valid objection and errors have no doubt remained for which I am responsible. I hope transformation gets started nevertheless, and future efforts will carry us all forward.

Introduction

Among the critical problems that confront contemporary societies, there are four that we think we have a solution to: unsustainable stress on families, persistent inequality for women and others who do care work, policymakers who are ignorant about the care that life requires, and time scarcity.[1] These problems arise out of destructive norms around work and care. By norms, we mean the widespread expectations of how adult men and women should contribute to society and fulfill their responsibilities to one another.[2] This book is about the transformation of those norms. It is about rethinking what is important by talking together about how we want to work, how we want to provide care, in short how we want to live. What is needed is not small improvements like flexible hours, but the kind of fundamental change that can actually address these pressing problems. The book presents a proposal, Part-Time for All (PTfA), for reshaping the existing conversations about "work-family balance."[3] The proposal is that all capable (preretirement) adults are expected to do paid work part-time (i.e., what we would now call part-time), no less than 10 and no more than 30 hours a week, and to do significant unpaid care regularly, which for most people will be between 20 and 25 hours a week. For those who are able to provide this level of care, we use the idea of "22 hours" a week as a shorthand for the minimum most people should treat as a norm. Our hope is that this proposal will spark an urgently needed conversation that will radically change existing beliefs and practices around work and care. Solving the problems of family stress, inequality, the ignorance of policymakers, and time scarcity makes this urgent.

Part-Time For All. Jennifer Nedelsky and Tom Malleson, Oxford University Press.
© Oxford University Press 2023. DOI: 10.1093/oso/9780190642754.003.0001

I. The Problems

A. Stressed Families

We begin by briefly identifying each problem that the new norms of work and care are meant to address. The first is the unsustainable structure of work and family life that puts enormous stress on families, and forces workers (at all levels) into untenable choices between work and family. The stress has serious consequences (including health and autonomy) for all, and almost certainly harms children with long term, intergenerational consequences.

Almost all families experience this stress, although they experience it very differently.[4] Women's workforce participation is increasing around the world.[5] The increase puts pressure on families that have long been organized around unpaid care by women in the home, especially since few countries have responded with either changes in the demands from the workplace or good alternative sources of care. Indeed, instead of accommodating to women's decreased availability for care, workplaces, especially in the Anglo world, are increasing the number of hours they require. Of course, this varies greatly from elite jobs requiring 60–70 hour weeks to the millions of people surviving on multiple precarious jobs and racking up long (often unpredictable) hours of work and commuting, and trying to fit childcare and elder care into that mix.[6] Although the stresses of these two groups are extremely different, stressed families are a common result.

The popular press in North America tends to focus on the challenges faced by families where both parents work (i.e., dual income families), and where at least one of the parents does professional or managerial work.[7] The working elite in the rich countries have in many instances traded leisure (for centuries a privilege of the wealthy) for very large salaries and very long hours. About 62 percent of high earning Americans work more than 50 hours a week, 35 percent work more than 60 hours a week, and 10 percent more than 80 hours a week. Other countries have similar trends.[8] At the very top, the scale of salaries is relatively new and disturbing. In 1965, the ratio between the income of CEOs and their average workers in the United States was 20 to 1. Now it is approximately 300 to 1.[9] The norms around what kinds of salaries are "appropriate" have changed drastically. These norms are relevant to family stress because they mean that the people who get elite jobs usually need to work very long hours, while the people at the lower end have to work long hours to make ends meet and to keep their jobs. Moreover, the hours required at elite jobs reinforce a problematic association between long hours and "success."

In discussions of the work-family tensions of the professional and managerial class, the focus is often on women, as if the problems of "work-family balance" (as it is often called) are primarily a women's issue. Of course, there is some reason for this. Women still do most of the care for children, elderly, and household maintenance.[10] And women more commonly put family ahead of work and so pay financial and career advancement penalties, in addition to stress. Women who want to compete for top-level positions face huge hurdles, especially the incompatibility of long hours with the family commitments they often want to maintain.[11]

At the elite level, people have money to buy care and thus to relieve some of the stresses of competing time demands from work and family. High earning women (and, in principle, men and nonbinary people) often have the option of leaving their successful careers to stay home and rely on their partner's high income (and long hours). Stress at this elite level does not include anxiety about whether children will have enough to eat or be apprehended by state authorities because they were left alone or looking after younger children when childcare was unavailable.[12] Nevertheless, the stress is real and approximately 65 percent of families have parents working a combined 80 hours a week, and 12 percent working more than 100.[13] For many people, the work they have trained for, the most interesting jobs, are only available if they are willing to work manic hours putting a huge strain on their family life.[14] Many of these workers would like to work fewer hours.

While the popular "work-family balance" articles tend to focus on the fully employed, dual income families, everyone knows that there are also many people who are struggling to find enough work. They, of course, want more hours of work. Other people, doing multiple, precarious jobs often need more money, but they do not actually want to spend more hours working, searching, and commuting. What they need is stable, decently paid work. (There is evidence that increasing the stability of work is even more important than increasing income for the well-being of families.[15]) People who are trying to raise families while stuck in precarious work with no security, no benefits, and unpredictable hours face extraordinary levels of stress, as do their children.[16] For them, the existing structure of work is deeply corrosive of satisfying family life that provides the time and security for nurturing relationships.

Finally, when we talk about family stress, we recognize that family forms are changing. The rise of single parent families in North America and Europe is one part of the rapid change in the structure of families.[17] An increasing number of children are born to parents who are not married, a pattern that in the United States is heavily shaped by class.[18] There are also increasing numbers of families formed by queer couples, and by more than two parents, as well as by extended families where children are cared for by grandparents, other relatives, or collectives of friends. Rethinking the structures of work and care to relieve family stress needs to be done in light of the evolving formations of family. We believe that PTfA will support greater freedom in the choice of family formation and will make life better for all family forms.

B.   Equality

The second problem is equality. Providing care is not highly valued, and this low status, low paid activity is not equally distributed. Not everyone takes a turn providing the care that their children, parents, spouses, or friends need. On the contrary, care is organized on the basis of status hierarchies. Those on the top—rich, white men—do very little of it. They get others to do it for them. And those "others" are not random; they are people whose gender, race, class, ethnicity, and citizenship status mark them as less important, less valuable, or lower status. One need only look around to see who takes care of children, tends the elderly, or assists the disabled to see this inequality at work. The patterns are so obvious that it should be clear that they are not simply the result of individual preferences. Gender norms sustain the patterns, because both men and women have been socialized to believe that women have a responsibility (and sometimes a natural aptitude) for care. Long histories of exclusion from opportunity and advantage shape this pattern, as low paid care jobs are often the only ones available to people marked by intersecting hierarchies of gender, race, class, and citizenship. Economic and social coercion are, therefore, central to the organization of care.[19]

Until these long-standing links between care and hierarchy are broken, care cannot be organized in a way consistent with equality, and thus *equality itself will be unattainable*. The long history of linking care with subordination is such that as long as only a subset of the population provides care, both care and the people who do it will be devalued. The fact that people seen as "lesser" (on the basis of race, class, gender, citizenship) provide care, which is seen as a lowly form of work (when recognized as work at all), reinforces the appropriateness of the low status of both the people and the care they provide.[20] When whole groups of people, such as those who provide care, are seen as "lesser," the resulting society will inevitably be systematically unequal.

It is also true that a just system of care will be impossible as long as power and advantage are organized around hierarchies such as gender, race, citizenship, and class. As long as there are systemic inequalities there will be powerful incentives to get people at the bottom to do low-paid (or unpaid) care. Thus, societies can only achieve equality when the distribution of care is just, *and* they can only achieve a fully just distribution of care when there is equality.

Of course, the most obvious category around which care is organized is gender. Around the world and throughout history, women have been the primary care providers. Yet today it is increasingly obvious that gender intersects with other categories, such as race, class, and citizenship status. Care givers in wealthy countries are not just predominantly female, but are also racialized women and immigrant women. And while women around the world are increasingly entering the paid labor force, they are hiring poorer women from elsewhere to provide care through the global care chain.[21]

Despite some modest changes in the past few decades, the shift in gender norms and the inequality of women improves at a glacial pace (or what a glacial pace used to be before global warming), leaving women with less pay, less economic security, vulnerability to poverty, less leisure time, and less access to top jobs and other advantages such as high-quality health care. This inequality is tied to (although, of course, not exclusively caused by) women's unequal share of care responsibilities.[22] The failure to achieve equitable care arrangements also affects both autonomy and democracy.[23] Women who come home from a full day of work to another four to six hours of care work have little time for either personal reflection or political action to change the conditions of their lives.

As women increasingly enter the paid labor force, much of the care work they used to do for free becomes part of the market economy.[24] The global care chain of imported care workers is a big part of this marketization of care, and it includes racialized and immigrant men. They mark some shift in the historic link between gender and care but maintain the connection between the low status of care and those who do it. The global care chain provides economic opportunity for people in low-income countries, but it does little to shift either global inequality or the inequality in the receiving countries where the imported workers join other low-paid and stigmatized workers in the care sector.[25]

The link between gender and the degradation of care is part of the bigger picture that gender inequality is incredibly resistant to change. According to the International Labor Organization, "between 1997 and 2012, the gender gap in time spent in unpaid care declined by only 7 minutes (from 1 hour and 49 minutes to 1 hour and 42 minutes) in the 23 countries with available time series data. At this pace, it will take 210 years (i.e., until 2228) to close the gender gap in unpaid care work in these countries."[26] A central contention of this book is that we will *never* obtain gender equality until we rearrange the distribution of care, which itself requires the transformation of paid work. In other words, it's important to see that the central reason why gender inequality has proven so resilient and difficult to overcome is that the problems are not rooted in any one place. Rather, gender inequality is the result of a number of causal processes, both institutional and cultural, that feed off each other and sustain each other, resulting in a relatively stable social system that gets reproduced again and again. This is important to appreciate because it means that changing gender relations requires making changes to cultural norms *and* economic workplaces simultaneously; it requires changing negative feedback loops into positive ones.

Consider the following mix of norms and economic structures which together reinforce gender inequality:

(i) Gendered norms of women as inherently and "naturally" care givers put immense pressure on women to do the bulk of caring and housework, resulting in unequal sharing of caregiving responsibilities,[27] as well as unequal success in the labor market: over a 15-year period, women earn only 49-cents to the dollar that men earn.[28]

(ii) Gendered norms of men as inherently and "naturally" breadwinners put immense pressure on men to prioritize their jobs over care concerns. Long hours of full-time work prevent men from spending substantial amounts of time caregiving. This both reinforces the pressure on women to do such work and de-skills and undermines male capacities for care and nurturance, so that women are overworked, and men are underdeveloped. At present the conventional and old-fashioned norms of women as primary care givers and men as primary breadwinners continue with force. These are zombie norms; no matter how many times they are killed with evidence or counter-example, they continue marching on.[29]

(iii) Once heterosexual couples have children, the gendered wage gap makes it economically rational for them to divide work in traditional ways, thereby reproducing gendered lives. The family decision to maximize earning potential by having the man work has longstanding effects on gender equality. It reduces women's skills and experience, deepens the pay gap, and reinforces gender stereotypes of women as primarily care givers and men as primarily workers.

(iv) Inflexible workplaces make it hard for care givers to move fluidly in and out of work. A number of important consequences flow from this inflexibility. First, it means that women who stay in the workforce find themselves working a double-shift of long hours at work combined with long hours at home.[30] Second, it leads to a number of women dropping out of the labor force altogether, which hurts their economic independence and their cultural status. The conclusion of Pamela Stone's study on why professional women leave their careers is that these women are not "opting out," rather the inflexible structure of workplaces means they are essentially being shut out.[31]

(v) The norm that a career requires full-time, continuous work is penalizing to care givers. The consequence being that women must choose between work or family, and invariably cannot "have it all".[32] Moreover, this means that women, and mothers in particular, are deprived of the best jobs and the highest earnings since these tend to be tied not only to full-time work, but to work with particularly long hours.[33] This again perpetuates the gender earnings gap.

(vi) The lack of affordable and accessible childcare makes it hard for women to balance work and care, again constricting women's access to the labor market and reinforcing norms of female care givers.

(vii) Part-time jobs are often unattractive because they offer lower wages and worse benefits than full-time work. The consequence is that it reinforces the desire of men to work full-time, which then means they are unavailable for caregiving, which again sustains the pressure on women to do such work. A second important consequence is that part-time work can reinforce gender inequalities by channeling women into low-paid jobs or confining them to the lower rungs of career ladders, again reinforcing gender divisions.[34]

(viii) Unregulated market competition means that firms can generally make more profit by extending working hours. Competitive pressure makes it harder for firms to introduce family-friendly policies if their competitors are not doing so.[35] And, of course, the longer the required working hours, the greater the gender imbalance in terms of who is willing to work them. Arlie Hochschild puts it this way, "The long hours men devote to work and recovering from work are often taken from the untold stories, the unthrown balls, and uncuddled children left behind at home."[36]

(ix) The centrality of wealth and consumption to the contemporary ideal of a good life makes full-time work seem vitally important. This makes it harder for men or women to opt out of the full-time rat race and puts indirect cultural stigma on those who prioritize unremunerated caregiving.

The bottom line is that gender inequality is sustained by the mutually reinforcing nature of norms and workplace structures. Hence, the only way that we will ever reach true gender equality is by changing *both* cultural norms and workplace structures in tandem. Part-Time for All, we believe, is the only feasible way to achieve this.

C. The Care/Policy Divide

Of our four concerns, this third problem is the least commented on in the now extensive literature on care. We call it the care/policy divide. This means that those in top policymaking positions—those in government, managers, and CEOs of firms, as well as the private investors and financiers who exert so much control over our collective future—are almost always people with very little experience of the demands, satisfactions, or importance of care taking. In our view, this means that policymakers are, for the most part, ignorant of a core dimension of human life. This renders them unfit for the job. We should no more consider electing someone without substantial experience in caregiving to public office, or appointing them CEO of a corporation, than we would someone who had never held a job. Those who *do* have the requisite knowledge and experience (primarily women) have very limited access to high-level policymaking positions. Our claim is that knowledge of care is essential to good policymaking, and the necessary knowledge can only be acquired by hands-on experience. Reading reports, or novels, or talking to one's mother, while useful, is no substitute. To ensure that everyone has the capacity to make and evaluate policy, everyone needs substantial experience in providing care.

It is probably obvious why people who are making decisions about childcare (whether a national childcare policy, or a decision about on-site childcare at a corporation, or how to license in-home care) need to have some understanding of both the specific issues around quality care and the nature of families' needs. Something similar could be said about after-school programs, early childhood education, and aid for families caring for the sick and elderly. But there are many other policy fields—health care, social assistance, labor and employment, housing and city planning, communications (including access to the internet), transportation, finance and taxation, parks and recreation, human rights, foreign aid, democratic participation, immigration, pensions, support for the elderly—which require knowledge of the centrality and significance of care for individual, family, and community well-being. Without such knowledge, policymakers will not only be without the information they need to implement good care, but they will not recognize when a policy (like inadequate public transit) will have an important impact on care—and thus on families and communities. At the deepest level, they will not have the knowledge of the value of care, which is necessary for wise judgment in the face of inevitable trade-offs between competing policy objectives and costs.

Many efforts to make the gendered division of care compatible with gender equality fail to address the problem of policymakers who are ignorant about care. For example, Wages for Housework, or well-paid and long-term maternity leave, or part-time work that is overwhelmingly taken up by women, or pensions for homemakers—none of these will solve the care/policy divide. Indeed, even fixing the gendered division of care would not be sufficient, although it is necessary. Only breaking the link between care and hierarchy can do it. As long as one group of people does the policymaking and a different group provides care, society will still suffer from ignorant policymakers. This would remain true even if the care givers were better protected and compensated than they currently are, and it would remain true even if women gain access to high-level policymaking by leaving care to be done by others.

D. Time

The problems of family stress, inequality, and the care/policy divide all intersect with the issue of time: time scarcity and the warping of the experience of time.[37]

It is not just women who suffer the loss of autonomy and judgment that comes from the acute time scarcity of the current structure of work and care. When people are constantly stressed by long hours of work, multiple competing demands, and compounded by anxiety about the future of their jobs, they do not have time for reflection or the habits of receptive thoughtfulness. At a personal level, reflection and a stance of openness to perception and possibility are necessary for people to figure out what matters most to them, how they want to live their lives, what relationships most nourish them, how they can best foster such relationships, and how they can best share their gifts. At the social and political level, the current structures of work and care are a recipe not only for a wide variety of social ills, but for a population too stressed and exhausted to protest them.

Some of the most important forms of human connection—playing with children, caring for the sick, cooking food for loved ones—are experienced as chores for which people do not have the time. They need to be done quickly and efficiently so that people can get to their other chores and try to get enough sleep so that they can get through long hours of work. There is no time for the slow rhythms of care with its often vital attention to the details of the moment. Forcing that rhythm into haste makes the tasks stressful and unpleasant instead of connecting and sustaining. Not only do people lose the pleasure of care but rushing erodes their knowledge of its potential for connection and thus its core importance for human well-being. This loss affects not only individual but societal understanding of the value of care and thus compounds the ignorance of high-level policymakers who have virtually no experience of care.

These high-level policymakers (in both government and corporate contexts) work under the extreme time pressure of long hours and urgent deadlines. All of us are likely to suffer the consequences. As Rosa Brookes put it in the Washington Post, "When did we come to believe that crucial national security decisions are best made by people too tired to think straight?"[38]

Not only is people's judgment impaired by time scarcity, but there is increasing evidence that their creativity, indeed their basic efficacy, is undermined by long hours.[39] Even people's health is affected by time scarcity, with its complex links to the structures of work and care.[40]

Moreover, the commonly proposed solutions to pressures of work and care, flextime, and working from home, create their own time problems. Brigid Schulte writes eloquently about the harms of "fractured time," where there are always multiple, competing commitments.[41] And "flexibility" has, notoriously come to mean that employers can change their employees' hours of work on a whim and at the last minute.

Finally, consider the invocation to "stop and smell the roses."[42] The phrase points to another harm of the current structures of work and care: the difficulty of finding time to enjoy nature and the connection with the earth. The image of stopping to smell the roses suggests that this connection, too, requires the slow pace that fosters receptivity, openness to our bodily senses, and attention to the detail of the moment. Indeed, speed and time scarcity foster not just a remove from the earth, but from one's own body (at least until pain signals become urgent). We increasingly become like James Joyce's Mr. Duffy, who "lived at a little distance from his body."[43]

In sum, our claim is that the (integrated) problems of family stress, equality, the care/policy divide, and time scarcity cannot be fixed until everyone, no matter how high their status, participates in part-time unpaid care and part-time paid work.

E. Scope and Context

We believe that versions of these problems are present all over the world, although they can of course take very different forms. For example, the need to emigrate to find work is not one that characterizes rich societies, although they rely heavily on the work of immigrants, particularly for care work. The impact on family life is very different for "sending" and "receiving" countries. The importance of a *conversation* about norms of employment and care applies everywhere, but our particular proposal may not be applicable in counties with widespread poverty.

We address our particular recommendations to high income societies, and the examples we draw on come largely from Europe and the "Anglo countries," the United States, Canada, the United Kingdom, Ireland, Australia, and New Zealand. But given the realities of the global care chain, the common practice of hiring poorer women to provide care as wealthier women increasingly enter the paid workforce, we believe that the topics of this book are relevant everywhere, even if the particulars of the solutions will necessarily be different for different contexts.

The degradation of care is a very old problem. But the particular exacerbation of the tensions between work and care in the contemporary society is relatively new. There are many causes and consequences of the current structure of work, with its long hours for the elite, and the precarity and insecurity for almost everyone. But one piece of the story is that large numbers of women have joined the paid workforce, and there is a move all over the world to get more women into full-time employment. It is as though there has been an unspoken collusion: women wanting gender equality demand access to full-time jobs because they rightly see that part-time employment has not been a path to real equality; governments think that women working full time will increase their country's economic output; employers get access to relatively cheap labor. But no one has figured out a new way to organize care and work once the women who had been providing free care began spending long hours in the paid workforce. So, women now do both.[44] Work remains organized around an assumption that someone other than the worker is looking after their care needs and those of their family. The "ideal worker" is still someone who shows their commitment by putting their job first and putting in long hours to prove it.[45] Women are forced into the impossible situation of trying to meet those standards as well as providing the care at home. Men are encouraged to identify with work and neglect care. Everyone is taught that work is more valuable.

Perhaps the failure to take account of the impact on care of bringing women into the workforce is itself part of the degradation of care: the widespread failure to pay attention to care, to recognize the value of care as essential to human life and well-being. It is as though the common failure of individual men to notice the care they are dependent on has been mirrored in a collective failure: blindness to the need to change both work and care now that the traditional care providers are expected to be out of the home earning money.[46] The effects of this massive policy lapse are played out in stressed households, rising health problems, including an epidemic of anxiety and depression, and costs to employers. The harms are unevenly distributed—a single mother's anxiety over how to make enough money to pay the rent and make sure her child is well cared for is not the same as the stressed finance worker who takes cocaine to make it through 10-hour days and has a six-figure income. But the suffering is widespread, and the harms are pervasive.

This failure to address new ways to provide care and reasonable expectations at work also arises out of the "care–policy divide." The people who are making high-level policy in corporations and governments are overwhelmingly men who have almost no experience of providing care, and thus are ignorant about both its demands and its importance.

Hence, we start to see that there are four interlocking failures of the prevailing system of work and care. The first is the pervasive failure to recognize the value of care and the second is care's fundamental role in structuring inequality. When a hierarchical society devalues care, it is unsurprising that care will be relegated to those low down in the hierarchy. The degradation of care and of those who do it become mutually reinforcing, making both seem "natural."[47] Hierarchies of inequality are then further cemented, perversely tied to what should be a core value, care. In such a context (all the societies we are addressing), the third problem, the care/policy divide, arises: some groups (historically white men) are the decision-makers and *different* groups (women, racialized people, and immigrants) provide the care, resulting in high-status, ignorant policymakers and subordinated care givers excluded from high-level decision-making. Fourth, contemporary high-income societies face the pressing problems of stressed families (as well as stressed workplaces) due to the unsustainable demands of work and care—which ill-informed policymakers fail to respond to.

A real solution must address all the core problems. We think that the heart of the solution must be that *everyone* is responsible for providing care, regardless of how "important" their work is. A society committed to equality, to respect for care, to good public policy, and to thriving families cannot assign care to only a subset of the population.

An equal, well-governed society, requires a population all of whom know about care from the experience of doing it. *Everyone is a care provider, just as everyone is a care receiver, and everyone identifies as both.* Everyone acquires the skills, disposition, and knowledge that come from doing sustained care giving. Everyone builds the relationships that care fosters and sustains. Everyone comes to recognize the care they receive.[48] Care givers are not looked down on because everyone is one, and individually and collectively everyone recognizes the real value of care. And everyone recognizes the full diversity of capacities to provide care as well as the huge range of needs for care. Everyone learns what they need to know about care to make good policy and, as community members, to assess that policy.

To transform a structure of care so that everyone does it, will, of course, involve transforming the structure of work. (Otherwise, we would create a new version of the existing policy failure.) If everyone is going to have time to provide care, most people will have to do less paid work. Work has to be restructured so that *good* part-time work becomes the norm. Everyone becomes a part-time paid worker and a part-time unpaid care giver. This would, of course, be a huge cultural shift affecting people's sense of identity, and the way care is connected to family, to the state, and to the market. It would also require a profound economic shift, redistributing significant resources to the bottom of the income distribution so that everyone is able to live well, with all their basic needs met, so as to be able to lead a comfortable, indeed a flourishing life, while working only part-time.

Finally, although this book is focused on new norms around human-to-human care, there is, one great additional issue of care: care for the earth. The earth—with all its vast interdependent complexity of life forms, geological formations, air, and water—provides humans with the necessities of life and the gifts of beauty, awe, and wonder. We think it makes sense to see this as care from the earth, requiring care in return.[49] We see care for the earth as distinct from prudent resource management. A relationship of mutual care is not a relationship based on extraction or exploitation, even if well "managed" for long-term availability. In a caring relationship with the earth community, humans no longer sit at the top of some hierarchy of moral significance. We are one (often destructive) part of a vast web of interdependence.

As we turn now to outline the details of the solution, it is important to see that Part-Time for All would do more than remove the harms. It would bring joy, pleasure, and satisfaction into human lives and, ultimately, improve the well-being of the earth community we are part of. People would enjoy the pleasure in giving and receiving care, the satisfaction of working for a living wage for 30 hours a week, with time left to enjoy family, friends, leisure, art, and to connect to community and nature. The pleasures of enjoying life when there is routinely enough time for what matters would compensate for the reduction in consumption that (for the well-off) would follow from reduced work hours. And living in a society with vastly reduced urges for consumption would itself be a relief, together with the benefit of knowing that those of us in wealthy countries are no longer gobbling up many times our share of the world's increasingly scarce natural resources.[50]

II. Part-Time for All: The Short Version of the Solution

Our objective is to challenge the inevitability of existing norms of work and care, and to invite people to imagine how they would really like to live. We hope for widespread, small and large-scale discussions where people examine everyday expectations about who should do what kind of work, for how many hours, and who should be providing the care everyone needs. These basic norms shape people's lives and should be subject to democratic deliberation. To foster this deliberation, we are proposing new norms that would be socially sanctioned like the old ones, but not enforced as law—although supporting state law and policy will be necessary. As with current gender norms, people would feel pressure to conform, but there would be no bureaucracy to define and measure care; no one would go to jail for working more than 30 hours or be fined for failing to change their fair share of diapers. We hope that individuals, families, and communities will reflect on the PTfA model and debate about how it might best be implemented.

For these new norms to be effective they need to be reinforced by and sustained within new kinds of public infrastructure. We might call these the "infrastructures of care," which are absolutely central to the project of PTfA.[51] These infrastructures of care include things like guaranteed economic security, affordable housing, living wages, high-quality universally available daycare, top-notch eldercare facilities, and so on. All of which will be discussed at length. PTfA is in no way a call for privatization, for shifting care responsibilities from the state onto already overburdened families. Quite the opposite. Our vision is of creating the cultural and material conditions, underpinned by extensively resourced infrastructures of care, that will allow for all of us, young and old, disabled and temporarily able-bodied, to have enough freedom from economic worry to be able to participate fully in the joys and labors of care.

For PTfA to be feasible the central economic requirement is that everyone has access to good part-time jobs. By this we mean jobs that are *secure, flexible, and high quality* (in the sense that they provide pay and benefits that are proportional to full-time work). Unfortunately, this is far from the case in many rich countries today, particularly the United States, where part-time work is typically inferior, unattractive work. In many places, part-time work pays proportionally less than full-time work, provides fewer benefits, and offers fewer opportunities for career advancement.

Moreover, the meagerness of state supports means that it is often not possible to achieve basic economic security on part-time work. For instance, a single mother in New York City working 30 hours per week at a minimum wage job, will earn only $19,500.[52] This is in brutal contrast to a living wage, which for such a person is more than three-times greater, at $71,400. As a matter of principle, we insist on the right of every person to receive a living wage, that is, a wage sufficient to acquire economic security—the basic necessities of food, healthcare, housing, transportation, childcare, and other needs (such as clothing and personal care items) required to live a modest but dignified life. Since PTfA requires that everyone, even the poorest, be able to survive adequately on part-time work, it is not currently possible in the US. Things are similar but not quite so dire in other Anglo countries. For instance, in the UK, a person on part-time minimum wage will make £13,900, whereas the living wage is, roughly, £18,500.

Hence a fundamental perquisite for PTfA is economic security. This could be accomplished in various ways, through robust public services, an unconditional basic income, a job guarantee, or some combination thereof. In many parts of Europe, such security already exists. For instance, in the Netherlands, a single mother working 30 hours per week on minimum wage would earn about €17,000, whereas a living wage is, roughly, €13,700. In Denmark she would earn earns €22,500, whereas a living wage is only €14,200. The major difference between these European countries and the Anglo ones in that the living wage is much lower due to the fact that the guaranteed public services—healthcare, childcare, housing, and so on—are much better. So while PTfA does not require revolutionary changes to the economy, it does require significant redistribution, to at least social democratic levels. (Beyond this, we think that more equality would be desirable in many ways, but it is not strictly necessary for PTfA).

Are such changes feasible? Chapters 3 and 4 address this question head-on. Chapter 3 examines the possibilities of transitioning our economies to PTfA—this requires not only creating more options for good part-time work, but also increasing people's desire (particularly men's) to take up such jobs.

Chapter 4 examines the question of economic feasibility—would an economy based on part-time jobs actually function? We will see that PTfA does indeed impose some costs. For instance, it requires higher taxes to pay for economic security; requiring firms to provide flexitime may slightly increase their costs (though as we will see the evidence here is mixed); and if rich individuals voluntarily reduce their hours (as we advocate) this would reduce tax revenues. On the other hand, the shift to part-time work has the potential to create additional employment, and the evidence is strong that reduced hours typically increases productivity (due to reduced fatigue, boredom, burnout, and so on).

The most powerful evidence for the feasibility of PTfA comes from a number of Western European countries, which already possess the perquisite institutions. For instance, the Netherlands and Denmark (and other places) demonstrate the feasibility of having large numbers of quality part-time jobs. In the Netherlands (as of 2019), a massive 47 percent of the labor force was engaged in part-time work (compared to the EU27 average of 18 percent)[53]; it is the world's first "part-time economy."[54] In other words, part-time work is no longer a marginal phenomenon but has become fully mainstream employment. Moreover, part-time jobs in these countries are not usually inferior jobs; they typically pay proportionally just as well as full-time jobs, as well as offering benefits and career advancement opportunities. Compared to the United States and the United Kingdom, the Nordic countries in particular have significantly higher taxes, better economic security, and substantially lower average hours of work. Yet they are highly productive and robust. Their welfare states have existed for decades, and as we will see, appear strongly resilient to globalization. Should these countries desire to implement PTfA, it would be perfectly feasible to do so.

We will argue that a society of PTfA could be viably built on four main pillars: quality part-time work, flexibility (or what we prefer to call "time sovereignty") economic security, and care-friendly policies (including but not limited to: antidiscrimination; fatherhood friendly parental leave, such as a use-it-or-lose-it policy and bonuses for equal sharing of leave; rights for parents to switch to part-time work for the five years after the birth of a child with specific incentives for fathers or other minority care givers to do so; quotas of women on corporate boards and in parliament, and of men in caring professions; and public prizes for feminist role models). Such a society does not currently exist anywhere in the world. Yet we will demonstrate that each and every one of these components do. We know that each pillar is feasible, as it already exists in some form, and we see no reason why the pillars could not be combined. This is the essential realism of the project. We are not advocating institutions that are unknown or untried. Rather the task before us is to weave together the best practices that already exist in various parts of Western Europe into a coherent whole. That is, of course, no easy task, and we do not want to minimize the obstacles. But if we can overcome the standard political difficulties of electing care-friendly governments into office, PTfA is an entirely practical project: it is institutionally sound, economically affordable, ecologically sustainable, and capable of withstanding the pressures of globalization.

In our proposal, paid work (between 10 and 30 hours per week) would continue to be a central way in which people contribute to society, and commitment to doing one's work well would be a respected value. But work would become just one among other important sources of identity and contribution. Everyone would also contribute unpaid care part-time, about 22 hours a week—which includes time spent caring for oneself. The shorthand of "22 hours" is intended to serve as a guideline as people get used to the new norms, as they get a sense of the time it takes to meet care needs and to make a significant contribution. During the transition, minimum target hours may make it easier to get a realistic sense of how one's contribution compares both to that of others and to the needs around one.

When the demands of friends and family are high (children are young, parents aging, or friends in need), most of this care would be provided within those intimate circles. But the care responsibility is constant. When those immediate needs recede, people would provide care within their chosen "communities of care." They would form serious commitments to mutual care among people they know and care about—such as neighbors, faith communities, clubs, sports groups, or those they share a park with. People are not caring for strangers, but the communities of care are not primarily family or close friends. Thus, care responsibilities extend beyond family, and the solution to degradation and inequality is not paying for the care (e.g., Wages for Housework), but *everyone* offering unpaid, personally connected care. The objective is to recognize the forms of interconnection possible within the vast human diversity of talents, temperaments, and needs, and to encourage everyone to participate in ways suited to their particular needs and capacities.

Mutual care within communities of care would, among its other benefits, disrupt the deep patterns of people of lower status providing care for those with more privilege (by gender, race, class, income, ethnicity, and/or immigration status). Of course, there would still be a variety of challenges of continuing inequalities, oversight, training, and meeting the needs of the "hard to serve." But we will argue that there is good reason to believe that in the presence of strong norms of equality and of contribution,[55] the great diversity of capacities can be matched with the great range of needs. We expect the quality of care for most people will improve under these new norms.

Part-Time for All is a proposal about part-time work and care. But its outcome would be *time* for all. As the pace and stress of life recedes, health, peace, and daily pleasures expand.[56] There is time for reflection about what matters.

This is not a utopia. These transformations are possible within the parameters of the economic systems of the current Global North (as outlined in Chapters 3 and 4). PTfA will not solve all the problems of either stress or injustice, but we also do not have to wait for all those problems to be solved to bring about vast improvements in quality of life, greater equality, and better governance.

Norms around work and care can change and indeed have changed hugely over the past few hundred years. Think about these examples: ideas about how many hours a workday should be—from 12 hours a day to the successful battle for the eight hours a day to current norms of 60–70 hour work weeks in the financial sector; who should do care work (should female aristocrats nurse their own babies?); whether the elite should be unemployed (the definition of a gentleman); whether children should work; whether it is ideal for women to be home when their children are young. Many of these issues are still contested while some (like the unemployed gentleman) seem like ancient history.

Consider an example of a recent change in norms that captures the kind of change we propose: a friend asked a young male colleague at a Swedish university whether he would be taking the full paternity leave available to him when his wife had their first child, or whether he would feel career pressure not to take the leave. He answered, "Are you kidding? If I *didn't* take the leave all my colleagues would be saying, 'Who knew he was such a money-grubbing careerist?!'" From concern about undermining one's career by taking paternal leave (a story one hears every day in North America), the norms had so changed that to *fail* to take the leave would subject one to the disapproval of one's colleagues.[57]

That is the kind of change we are looking for. Our project here is to radically change the kinds of things that generate approval and disapproval among one's colleagues, friends, family, neighbors, and society in general. People would encourage one another to resist the pressure of taking on more work, and support and appreciate the care they do, as well as the leisure time they take and the ways they contribute to their communities. Although we picture the new norms being fostered more by support and encouragement than by disapproval, it is in the nature of norms that failure to comply brings some kind of censure. Thus, the failure to meet these norms by working long hours or refusing to participate in care would generate the sort of concern, disapproval, embarrassment, pity, or unease that currently would arise if a competent adult male announced at a party that he had never held a job. One might, for example, offer a "workaholic" advice on where to get help. But whether the response was kindly or disapproving, it would be clear that an important norm was being violated.

Thus, new norms of work and care would be enforced not by state law, but (like most norms) by the complex power of social expectation and the socialization that happens in families, communities, workplaces, and schools—just as is now the case with the norms that men should "earn a living" and "support their families." One difference would be in levels of consciousness—and deliberation—around the norms. The norm around "supporting one's family" is so deeply internalized that most men do not think of their behavior as governed by a societal norm. By contrast, we would expect some level of ongoing deliberation in communities of care on the norms of PTfA. While the core value of everyone having a responsibility for care might become similarly deeply embedded, the many questions of how best to implement it would remain a subject of conscious reflection. Thus, democratic deliberation on norms, not just law and policy, would itself become part of the norms of PTfA.

Finally, when daunted by the depth of the norm changes involved in Part-Time for All, it can be helpful to remember five recent and important norm changes, all begun by grassroots conversations and organizing. The first example is the feminist transformations initiated by thousands of women's meetings throughout the "consciousness raising" conversations of the 1970s and 1980s. Although many of the best-known groups were limited by racial homogeneity and exclusion, as well as conflict around heterosexuality, they were part of a very diverse and widespread movement that transformed common understandings of "women's place" and female capacities. This was a major transformation, even if an "incomplete revolution"—especially with respect to who does the care work and its related issues of inequality. Although laws were not necessarily the target of the early "consciousness-raising" groups, some parts of that feminist agenda ultimately became state law, such as laws against gender discrimination and sexual harassment. Second, as Brigid Schulte points out, in Sweden and Denmark and elsewhere, we have seen truly massive norm shifts in only one generation: men went from being aloof breadwinners to engaged fathers present in delivery rooms, taking parental leave, and pushing strollers. Today 70 percent of Danish women and 60 percent of Danish men say they prefer to divide work and childcare equally.[58] Third, is the major shift in norms around drinking and driving. Again, the norms that permitted otherwise responsible adults to drive while intoxicated (generally violating existing state law) caused huge harm and were transformed significantly by civil society groups, then later backed by more serious law enforcement. Norms around smoking are a similar example. The state entered in slowly with laws restricting smoke in public places and restricting advertisements, but the civil society movements aimed at changing norms, while spreading education about harm. Finally, the huge change in norms around the acceptability of LGBTQ relationships is a scope of change that almost no one could have predicted 50 years ago. Again, ultimately the state entered in with various forms of protection against discrimination and the legal right of marriage. But this was largely in response to the huge shift in norms. Like the transformation in norms we are calling for, the norms around women's roles and queer relationships touched deeply held values, beliefs, and feelings that go to the core of people's identities.

In these examples, changes in norms preceded state action, which in turn strengthened the changes in norms. Sometimes state action, like the recognition of same-sex marriage by the Supreme Court of Canada in 1999, made a particularly big impact in furthering changes in a society's norms.[59] Another well-known example is the Swedish introduction of "Daddy days," parental leave aimed at fathers, which the family loses if the father does not take it. Of course, there had to be sufficient public commitment to shifting patterns of care responsibilities for the legislature to pass the law. But that change in the law brought a significant change in the number of men who took the paid parental leave they were entitled to. As the example above of the young Swedish professor shows, in some sectors, the norms around fathers taking leave became very strong. There is often a complex interplay of norm change and state action, but there has to be some acceptance of new norms before governments will see it as in their interest to implement them in public policy.

There are several different kinds of reasons to be optimistic about the possibility of the norm transformations we are advocating. While moving to a norm of part-time work might once have seemed impossible,[60] there is already considerable experimentation with it. The Netherlands, France, Germany, and other countries have already reduced hours to an average of roughly 35 hours per week (though significant gender inequality in work hours remains), and many companies today are trying (on their own initiative) to shorten work weeks, sometimes reporting great improvements in productivity.[61] Perhaps most importantly, technology is expected to eliminate as many as 40 percent of existing jobs in rich countries. Instead of trying to figure out how full-time employment can remain the norm in the face of such change, technology can be an added incentive to restructure work around a "part-time" norm of 30 hours or less a week. In addition, the reduction in resource extraction and consumption demanded by climate change can be relatively painlessly assisted by a reduction in work hours and income at least for those in the top third of the income bracket.

In sum, we should not underestimate either the possibility of changing norms or their power to shape beliefs, behavior, and policy. Part-Time for All aims at fostering conversations that will shift norms, and thus make the powerfully constraining norms that exist today—that men have to work, women have to care *and* work—the subject of democratic deliberation. Our focus here is on the kind of norm change that can grow out of millions of conversations about existing harms and visions of better structures of work and care. We hope to persuade our readers to initiate those conversations because they have come to share our belief that Part-Time for All would bring many benefits and that without such norm transformation, we cannot hope to solve pressing problems—stressed families, inequality, ignorant policymakers, and time scarcity—that afflict all high-income societies. The norms of PTfA would also foster the care and collective responsibility for the Earth necessary to respond to our climate emergency. We see our hoped for conversations as starting points for a positive interaction of norm change and policy transformation.

In Chapter 1, the Care Chapter, we delve into the details and nuances of what it would really mean for everyone to engage in significant amounts of care work. We discuss what "care work" entails and for whom we should care. We explain the profound learning that can come from the experience of providing care, and we extend the issue of human-to-human care to the broader issue of the importance of care for the earth. We also engage with the most common objections to our proposal. These include (but are not limited to) the worry that expecting everyone to care is an authoritarian imposition of values (Shouldn't people be free to devote themselves to care or work as they see individually see fit? Isn't it best for families to divide care internally however they so choose?) Another set of concerns is whether it is really necessary for *everyone* to care (Can't we just pay taxes to fund public care workers and professionals instead of having to do it ourselves? And does everyone really have the ability to be perform care well?).

Chapter 2, the Work Chapter, examines the other side of the coin: what would the new norms of work have to be for everyone to be a care giver? We elaborate on the idea of good part-time work for all, and describe how the new work norms might look in practice. We discuss the expected benefits of good part-time work for all, and contrast our vision with other well-known feminist proposals (such as those of Anne Marie Slaughter, universal breadwinning, and Wages for Housework). We also respond to the major concerns that our interlocutors typically have, such as the worry that reducing work hours to part-time will undermine creative work and excellence (doesn't excellence require a full-throttled, single-minded devotion to one project, which will be terribly undermined by forcing such experts to care?), as well as the frequent worry that "my job couldn't possibly be done part-time. I'm barely managing as it is!"

As already mentioned, Chapters 3 and 4 move from questions of cultural norms to focus on the economic institutions needed to underlie PTfA. Chapter 3 investigates what would be required for rich societies to slowly but surely transition toward an economy of part-time work for all. This involves the difficult question of how we can shift desires, in particular, how can we persuade men to reduce their working time (which currently provides them with both money and status) in order to do more of a kind of work, care work, which is not only unpaid but widely devalued. Chapter 4 examines the feasibility of having a whole economy based on good part-time jobs for all. We examine the four pillars that would be necessary for this new kind of economy to function well: quality part-time jobs, time sovereignty, economic security, and care-friendly public policies, in each case examining the empirical record from around the world of constraints, limitations, and best practices.

The conclusion sums up the big picture of our argument, and considers the political prospects for PTfA in the near future. We are optimistic about the possibilities for seeing profound changes in the structures of care and work in our lifetimes. Small steps can be taken immediately. Our hope is that by the end of this book, you find yourself more hopeful too.

1
Care

I. Introduction

This chapter presents the heart of our argument: part-time care for all. We frame that argument with a brief statement of the importance of care and some of the most pressing failures of care. We begin with human-to-human care.

Everyone needs care. It is essential to human life and well-being, to well-functioning communities, and to the productive enterprises all societies require—which in the modern world we generally organize through paid work. A great deal of what follows is about the importance of care and of learning from care. While we often focus on the practicalities of care, we want to highlight the point that care builds the relationships that matter most to people. Under current conditions care is often a burden, but providing care is also a source of joy and connection. The ability to take delight in those one is caring for will be one of the most important benefits of PTfA.

The need for care is obvious in the case of infants, the sick or injured, the elderly, and those with disabilities. But everyone needs care throughout their lives. There is the daily bodily maintenance requiring food, shelter, and clothing—almost no one can single-handedly provide this for themselves. Then there is the need for love, attention, respect, sympathy, and play that requires emotional care, and the education, stimulation, and reciprocal engagement that forms a kind of mental care. Adults isolated from caring relationships do not thrive and often have difficulty in being "productive members of society."

Children need multiple forms of care to grow into adulthood. New generations need to be raised from infancy, educated, and socialized to participate in the productive practices of their societies. They need to learn social norms, modes of play and of respect. They need to develop their own skills and talents and figure out how they want to live

Part-Time For All. Jennifer Nedelsky and Tom Malleson, Oxford University Press.
© Oxford University Press 2023. DOI: 10.1093/oso/9780190642754.003.0002

their lives. Some of the necessary reproductive labor (raising new generations to become functioning members of society) is done by the paid work of people such as teachers, counselors, and health care workers, but much of it is done in families, among neighbors, within communities. The idea that "it takes a village to raise a child" is an expression of the many forms of unpaid contributions it takes to bring a child to satisfying adulthood.

For many years, childcare was the primary focus of concern for those interested in "work-family balance" and equitable care arrangements. However, as Duxbury and Higgins put it, "eldercare is the new childcare." The number of people with elder care responsibilities is expected to "increase dramatically over the next several decades, while the number of people able to provide such care is likely to shrink."[1] Good care for the elderly, like childcare, has many components beyond the complex material needs of aging bodies. Emotional skills and a supportive community are important to support a sense of dignity and ease in the face of shifting capacities.

Economists like Nancy Folbre have carefully demonstrated the economic value of the unpaid care done in families (disproportionately by women) and have made it clear that what has been traditionally counted as economic productivity relies on often hidden contributions of unpaid reproductive labor and care.[2] The interdependence between economic productivity and care is slowly becoming more widely recognized as both employers and workers see the costs at work of the stress caused by the current demands of work and family. It seems likely that this stress is also one of the causes of the epidemic of depression and anxiety in North America that has overwhelmed schools, universities, professions (such as law), and health care systems. Thus, the failures of the current structures generate yet further care needs, which are also unmet. It is increasingly clear that societies with high levels of economic insecurity and deep social divisions have become collectively unable to provide their members with the care they need.

This chapter explores the ways new norms of care can redress the four core problems outlined in the introduction: unsustainable stress on families, inequality for care givers, policy makers who are ignorant about care, and time scarcity—while fostering a recognition of the value of care. We use the following questions to guide us: (1)

What is the best system for providing the different kinds of care that allow people to thrive? (2) How can care be organized in ways that ensure that the people who provide care realize the benefits of caring? (3) How can care be provided fairly, in ways that enhance equality for all? This includes ensuring that all those who need care receive it and that both the benefits and burdens of providing care are shared equitably. (4) What forms of restructuring care will foster a widespread understanding of the value of care, and thus a collective revaluing of care? (5) What organization of care will foster good governance, strong communities, and the conditions for democracy?

As we said in the introduction, equality cannot be achieved without a fair distribution of care, and care can neither be fairly distributed nor properly valued until the hierarchies that it relies on are dismantled. As we will discuss more fully later, as long as care is disproportionately done by people of color, women, immigrants, or other denigrated groups, the degradation of care and of those who do it will be mutually reinforcing. While the full project of removing discrimination, stigma, and degradation according to categories like race is, of course, beyond the scope of this book, it must always inform the questions about how to restructure care.

II. Failures of Care

Our starting point is the chronic stress of so many households who are trying to meet both their care needs and the demands of workplaces. This stress has very real costs in terms of health, well-being, and economic productivity. In extreme cases, people trying to meet high care needs at home can lose their jobs and then their homes. The harms are pervasive and amount to a colossal and systematic failure in the current structure of work and care.[3]

Those who provide paid care often suffer bad working conditions, poor pay and benefits, and the experience of low status.[4]

Children are a group who obviously need care. Provision of this care varies greatly in its form: unpaid care at home or with other family members, paid care at home, informal paid care outside the home, paid care in formal care settings. In Anglo countries, there is a serious problem of access to affordable (state supported) care centers, and there is particular concern about whether children from low-income families receive adequate care. In the United States, women from low-income families, as well as single mothers, generally do not have the option of staying home to care for their children, *and* do not have adequate access to affordable, high-quality childcare. Low-income neighborhoods are less likely to have local childcare centers or good parks for children to play in. Low wage and part-time work are now increasingly characterized by unpredictable hours, making childcare arrangements very difficult. Low-income women end up having to commute long distances to both work and childcare, adding to their long hours of work and care. Current structures of work are thus exacerbating the demands of care, especially for the poor.

Children suffer from the stresses their parents' experience. One stress is the sense of time scarcity. This sense of scarcity arises from the competing demands of work and care for both high-income earners who work very long hours and believe in intensive parenting, and for low-income earners trying to manage childcare along with precarious work, unpredictable work times, hours spent looking for work, and commuting time. At the low-income end, the stress of time scarcity is exacerbated by anxiety about economic insecurity. Children are surrounded by stresses at both the high and the low end of the income spectrum. Parents—and the care givers they hire—usually provide adequate care. But relaxed time to take delight in their children is scarce. For a child to feel like one more task on a tired parent's long list is not a comforting feeling, even if the task gets done.

It is worth noting that in the United States the "super elite" may be a partial exception. Although the super elite often work very long hours, they can afford to create more time for care at home: "Roughly half of female Harvard and Chicago MBAs with two or more children . . . leave the workforce or work part-time in order to care for their children." Super elite parents are very focused on giving their children competitive advantages, including "concerted cultivation specifically designed to promote . . . children's adult achievement."[5] The result is part of the staggering inequality in life prospects between the children of the poor and of the American elite and middle class. Of course, the success of the super-elite in ensuring that their children remain among the elite, does not tell us that those children were spared stress in their childhood.

Almost everyone recognizes that the elderly will need care, yet they are increasingly at risk of inadequate care. The current inadequacy has been tragically highlighted during the COVID-19 pandemic. And virtually no wealthy country has adequate structures in place for the looming demands of the increasing percentage of elderly in the population. Already countries such as Australia, the United Kingdom, and Canada have commissioned inquiries into complaints of inadequate care. Often governments respond to these inquiries with more regulations, which do not solve the problems of poor design and inadequate resources.[6]

People with disabilities and with mental health problems routinely face both discrimination in workplaces and inadequate care. The poverty resulting from discrimination exacerbates the lack of care. The care problems lie both with inadequate institutions and inadequate support for those trying to provide care at home.

In sum, children, the elderly, people with disabilities, and those with mental health problems frequently do not have reliably adequate care. That is a large—and growing—percent of the population. Whether care is provided by family members or by institutions, there is widespread anxiety about the availability and quality of care, and insufficient collective concern about the burdens borne by those providing the care, paid and unpaid. These harms are particularly widespread in the Anglo countries. But even in the context of much better social services (and labor law), no country has solved the problem of the work–care tension, adequate care for and integration of people with disabilities, the gendered structure of care, and the rising demands of aging populations. Although the problems of care take different forms in different sectors and different countries, there is good reason why people who study care so often refer to a "crisis."

Finally, we want to highlight in advance one way in which much of the discussion around the crisis in care has a somewhat different emphasis from ours: it highlights the failures and the burdens. The argument we are making, that everyone should care, will stress not only the equal sharing of such burdens, but the many *benefits* associated with care. The revaluing of care is really about the fundamental significance of care, and thus, primarily, its benefits. Of course, one of the consequences of understanding its significance is to understand the true costs of a failed system of care—to both care givers and care receivers. But one of our objectives is ultimately to shift the emphasis from burden to benefit. The burdens now are very real, for both paid and unpaid carers, as well as for the recipients of care. Our hope is that with a radically different distribution of responsibility for care, together with a collective revaluation of care, those burdens will be much decreased.

III. The New Norms: What Do We Mean by Care and Who Does It?

Everyone who is able should contribute to the care of themselves, others, and the earth. Most adults should provide at least "22 hours" of unpaid care a week.[7] In an optimal adoption of these norms, neither individual households nor societies at large would rely on a division of labor where some people (or groups of people, like women) are primarily responsible for unpaid care and others are primarily responsible for earning money through paid work. Both forms of contribution would be seen as something society requires and everyone normally participates in. This norm of care from all holds regardless of the "importance" accorded to the paid work someone does. One foundation for these norms is that everyone needs care, and everyone should share in providing it. We should all be both givers and receivers of care, so that both the benefits and the burdens of care are shared among all. Under the new norms, everyone learns to be competent, thoughtful, and respectful in providing care, and graceful and respectful in receiving it. Acquiring the complex skills of both giving and receiving care is an important benefit of PTfA. When some are excluded from either giving or receiving care, both the individuals and their communities are harmed.

We now turn to the basics of our approach to care: What do we mean by care and who cares? In the discussion that follows, readers should remember that the issues we take up are ones we expect every "community of care" would try to grapple with. Here, we present the identification of key issues, how we have thought about them, and the conclusions we have come to—in the hopes that these discussions will be of help to others as they make judgments about implementing Part-Time for All.

A. What Do We Mean by Care?

Scholars have invoked many different definitions of care for their different purposes. Here we want a definition for the purposes of understanding what everyone's responsibilities are under the new norms. In other words, what "counts" as care for assessing whether one is doing one's fair share. We find Evelyn Glenn's definition of human-to-human care helpful: "Caring can be defined most simply as the relationships and activities involved in maintaining people on a daily basis and intergenerationally." This includes direct caring for the person, maintaining the immediate physical surroundings/milieu in which people live, and fostering people's relationships and social connections.[8] For the purpose of what should count as part of one's obligation to provide unpaid care, we add the requirement that care *builds personal relationships*.

Like Glenn, we include all the basic forms of labor that are necessary to sustain a household and the people who inhabit it. This includes acquiring food (often by shopping), cooking, serving, cleaning, as well ensuring people are clean, clothed, and entertained (children especially), and the material maintenance that sustains the physical structure of the household (which might include keeping sidewalks and roofs clear of snow). Providing care in sickness or injury will be routinely, though not constantly, required. Enabling access to education is part of care for children, as is supporting it through help with homework and facilitating participation at school. Storytelling and reading to children aids education and is also an important part of emotional connection and attention. All members of a household will need, and need to provide, the emotional care of attention, listening, playing together, and loving. This brief description includes both intimate, personal care like playing with a child and material care like cleaning and repairing. We think it is important to recognize the full range of care that people need to thrive, and to avoid treating some forms of care as more important than others.

For the purposes of changing the norms of both paid work and unpaid care, we do not include doing *paid* care as part of one's responsibility to contribute *unpaid* care. There are a set of nuances around the issue of when care in the context of paid work (like spending time talking to a student or colleague in distress) should count as work and when it should count as part of one's care contribution. We return to those later.

The main criterion we use to define the unpaid care that counts toward the obligation of 22 hours is that it builds personal relationships. One way of putting it is that when a person receives the kind of care we have in mind, it makes her feel valued. It affirms her sense of worth. It makes her feel cared about. It allows both care giver and receiver to feel a mutual appreciation and satisfaction. It is important here that the norms we propose would foster patterns in which almost everybody is both a care giver and a care receiver—and recognizes themselves as such. It is in part experiencing the link between care and relationship, as well as the links between care and well-being, that is the basis for the knowledge a carer acquires about the demands, the rewards, and the human significance of care.

B. Who Provides Care Under PTfA? And the Puzzle of Devaluation

People will continue to provide unpaid care within families and to close friends, except that now everyone will do it. And when those immediate demands are low, people's care responsibilities will extend to their chosen communities of care (which we discuss in Section IV).

The question of shaping norms about who *should* provide care needs to be addressed in the context of who *does* provide care. That is, the explanation of the claim that everyone who can should care begins with the issue of the degradation of care and of those who do it. As we have said, in most high-income countries care is organized around status hierarchies. (Indeed, this is true virtually all over the world.) That means that, for the reasonably well-off, care is done by "others," lesser others. This poses a central puzzle, as well as the problems of inequality and the care/policy divide.

The puzzle is how does it happen that a practice—the provision of quality care—that is so vital to the well-being of those we love, is relegated to the people who society treats as the least valuable, the lowliest, the least skilled or talented? The practice of assigning care to lesser others—whether women, racialized people, immigrants, or anyone who is poor—is so nearly universal that its deeply puzzling nature disappears into convention.

It is essential to understand this puzzle and transform this practice. No society can achieve either equality or the proper valuing of care as long as care is systematically relegated to lesser others. Indeed, a central argument of this book is that as long as a society uses hierarchies—like race, class, and gender—to organize care, that society will be unable to achieve equality. The distribution of the benefits and burdens of care shapes individual lives, families, and societies. As long as that distribution is unequal, inequality will be a central feature of the society. As long as certain groups are seen as fit only to provide care (or other denigrated work), they will not have the same opportunities as others.[9] Until care is fully valued, it will be relegated to subordinated groups in society. And as long as that subordination is understood in terms of categories like race and gender, the distribution of a devalued task according to those categories will reinforce the categories themselves. The daily experience of seeing (devalued) care provided by subordinated people will reinforce the "naturalness" of both the low status of care and the categories of subordination.

The norms of PTfA make unpaid care the responsibility of everyone, and thus resist the pattern of assigning it to lowly others. Nevertheless, we do not think this particular disruption of hierarchy will, in itself, be sufficient to overcome deeply ingrained categories of hierarchy (like race and gender) that organize economic and social inequality as well as reinforce the degradation of care. There are many forces that sustain inequality, and as long as there are people "at the bottom," there will be powerful pressures to assign care to them—at least until care has been fully revalued.

With this invocation of what is at stake in shifting the links between the degradation of care and the complex beliefs about inferiority and superiority that sustain categories of hierarchy, we want to return briefly to the puzzle noted above. We offer a personal note to invite readers to reflect on their own experiences of the crucial importance of quality care.

My (J. N.'s) mother died on September 4, 2018, two days after her 100th birthday. I was with her for the last week and she was in a lot of distress off and on. This experience of caregiving—mine as well as that of the professionals (aides from her retirement home, her doctor, nurses, social workers) helping her, and the professionals helping *me*—has shaped my reflections in this book. It has framed with a new poignancy the puzzle that has been at the back of my mind for years: virtually everyone has had some experience of how important care is, for their children, their elderly parents, their sick or disabled partner or friends, if not for themselves. They must, therefore, know at some level how important good, skillful, attentive, concerned care is, and how scary and upsetting unskilled, unkind, thoughtless, or neglectful care is. In these contexts, the idea that care is unskilled labor makes no sense.[10] How is it then that this most vital, often delicate and complex human function, the care of those who need it, is left to groups of people who are considered lesser, low down on hierarchies of importance, value, and abilities? Many people have come to take it for granted that care is accorded low status and value, as are the people who do it. But how is this possible, given what must be widespread experience of the crucial value of care? And then, how is it possible to transform such deeply mistaken, but deeply embedded beliefs and practices around the devaluation of care and those who do it?

It helps to understand some of details of the links between the categories of hierarchy and degradation of care.[11] For example, in *Every Day Transgressions: Domestic Workers' Transnational Challenge to International Labor Law*, Adelle Blackett reveals these links in the context of racialization and paid domestic labor.[12] We see Blackett's work as particularly relevant for our argument because the degradation of paid domestic labor is closely tied to the degradation of care more generally. Blackett adroitly traces the way law treats domestic workers in ways that build in subordination and often the particular subordination of racialization. She shows how domestic work retains its historical link to servitude and slavery. That is, the degradation of the work is closely tied to its enduring connection to the degradation of the people who do it—through intersecting categories of race, class, and gender. She carefully demonstrates (in Chapter 3, "Subordination or Servitude in the Law of the Household Workplace") that ethnographic studies of domestic labor show that "race, class, and gender are not simply factors of identity. They are structuring factors that mark the bodies of Indigenous, postcolonial, and Black women as those who undertake domestic work." The denigrated status of these women "makes sense" of the degradation of the work, and vice versa. The puzzle of the low status of care is obscured by the apparent naturalness, or self-evident quality, of the subordination of the people and the work they are fit for. And even as some of this subordination of people is increasingly challenged, Blackett offers a warning in the context of legal reform that is equally apt for the normative transformation PTfA aspires to: "The risk is that recurring hierarchies will continue to reassert themselves, inscribed on historically subordinated bodies or on newly emerging ones. Regulatory frameworks must look specifically at how to correct inequality."[13]

Beyond this, we suspect that there is an even deeper, more hidden reason for the devaluation of care. We begin to see this by asking what the powerful get out of a system that insulates them from care by ensuring that those who are "other" do it.

The reason we offer here is that the degradation of care has some-thing to do with the basic existential vulnerability that underlies the necessity and importance of care. To provide care in a sustained way is inevitably to confront bodily vulnerability head on, and deal with the fear it gives rise to.[14] It helps to avoid facing this fear by ensuring that "others," lesser "others" do the care. One aspect of the existential threat that care can pose is in terms of autonomy. Autonomy is a highly cherished value in liberal societies (perhaps in all societies if we understand the value in relational rather than individualistic terms). In liberal societies, particularly the Anglo countries, autonomy is widely understood as independence and control of one's life. But to routinely engage in hands-on care of others, is to recognize the dependence that all human beings have on other human beings. The illusion of independence is likely to be shattered.

The issue of control may run even deeper than independence. In many cases, providing care to those who need it confronts one with the basic inability to control our lives and our bodies. We cannot control whether we get sick, or have a disabling accident, and ultimately, of course, we cannot control the fact that we will die or even when or how we will die. We cannot ensure that our loved ones will not suffer illness or accident. In a culture that worships power and control, such recognition can be terrifying. This may be especially true for powerful men who have persuaded themselves that their lives are characterized by the ability to control. Of course, everyone thinks they already know that they cannot control death, disease, or accident. But truly confronting the essential vulnerability of our embodied lives through care is viscerally different and is likely to be experienced as an existential threat. Being involved with regular care makes it harder to ignore the reality that many try to keep at a distance. Hence the powerful devalue care and care givers because doing so creates a powerful barrier insulating them from the pain and discomfort of having to stare into the face of mortality and inexorable decrepitude.

In sum, if only some subset of people provides care, the subordination of both people and care will endure. Correcting inequality and revaluing care have to go together.

C. Who Is "Able"?

We have said several times that everyone "who is able" should contribute unpaid care. In using this language, we mean to highlight two things. First, care involves skill, effort, and responsibility which, in turn involve physical, intellectual, and emotional abilities. People have these abilities in a wide variety of forms, making them able to provide some kinds of care and not others. Second, this means that people's care contributions can take a wide variety of forms and no one should be seen as failing to meet the norms of PTfA because (of course) their contributions are limited by their abilities. It would be a failure indeed if the new norms of care from all served to add one more burden of "inadequacy" to those whose abilities are seen as diverging from some presumed norm of competence.

Part of the point of the new norms of care for and from all is that
we would all become more creative about how to meet care needs.
Children from a very young age would learn how they could do things
to help others—thus participating in a core norm of society. They
would all see their parents actively participating in various forms of
care, rather than observing that important people don't do it. Thus,
their relation to care would not be disdain and resistance. Learning to
provide care would be seen as part of the process of becoming a full,
respected member of society. Developing the skills of care would be
an integral part of every child's upbringing. And in keeping with the
idea that care obligations extend beyond the family, children would
very early help in bringing food to a sick neighbor, feeding a cat whose
family is on vacation, raking leaves, delivering groceries to an elder,
and reading to the sick or frail. They would, of course, also be building
a network of relationships that would make them a respected, competent part of a community of care—not just dependents in need of
care and supervision. Their sense of security, an ability to count on care
and attention, would not be limited to their family. Both care givers
and care recipients of all ages might become friends, thus expanding
the range of adult-child relationships both can benefit from. Children
would come to understand the links between relationship, security,
and the care responsibility they share in. Of course, the new norms
would not allow such responsibility to undermine the need for play
and leisure (as is sometimes necessary in low-income families who
need to rely on older children to care for younger ones).

We also expect a great deal more creativity about involving the elderly in care for others. Many older people spend years feeling useless
and dependent, when in fact they have the ability to be sharing in the
care of others, even as they receive care themselves. When people have
spent a lifetime giving and receiving care, their recognition that aging
has brought shifts in their needs and abilities will not make them feel
that they have fallen out of the category of the competent and productive. They can use the skills of a life time to figure out how they can
continue to care for others, at the same time that they can gracefully
accept the additional care they need—without feeling humiliated as
unproductive dependents. Similarly, when adults with high care needs
(such as those with disabilities) have those needs well served, they will

be in a better position to figure out how they can contribute in both the paid work context and in the context of participating in communities of unpaid care.[15]

When everyone recognizes themselves as both a care giver and receiver, one other form of degradation would also be removed: the degradation of people with high care needs (people with disabilities, the elderly, and people with mental health problems) who are looked down on as "dependents" and thus vaguely incompetent.[16] To be seen as dependent is to fail to meet the criteria of the (illusory) model of the independent, autonomous, adult. As a colleague, Chloe Atkins, reminds us, not only are care and those who do it denigrated, but so are those who need care.[17] PTfA should provide redress for that as well. Everyone will be more fully integrated into communities and reap the benefits of relationships sustained by care.

D. Professional Care, "Arms-Length" Care, and the Ethics of Giving and Receiving Care

Our call for everyone to contribute to the care of those around them is based on the view that there is a great deal of care that most people can learn how to do. This does not mean, however, that we see no place for professional care. Indeed, one of the dangers of the saying that everyone should be a care giver is that it might be seen to imply that anyone can provide care because there is no skill involved. (This, of course, is one of the justifications for the low wages and low status for paid care givers, to which we will return later.) The question is not whether care requires skill, but who can learn it and when professional care is important.

Current practices and assumptions foster the risk of assuming that some forms of care, like injections, can only be done by a professional when in fact thousands of people have learned to give injections to themselves and their family members. The fact that some training is needed does not mean that the task can only be done by a professional. Communities of care will need to decide how much training is realistic, for some or all of their members. At the same time, people in need of the specialized care of professionals often fail to get it either because they don't have the money, or they are in institutions where they have no choice about who provides their care.[18] Implementing the norms of PTfA will require careful attention in assessing when professional care is required, including, of course, the preferences of those in need of the care.

Some of the reasons we have heard for why people would prefer paid care givers to the kind of unpaid relationships we are proposing are not so much about the special skills of professionals as about the differences between an employment relationship and relationships with friends or neighbors. In one account from someone who actually did have a "care collective" to help her while she was bedridden with pain, she appreciated the way working with the collective built relationships, but she found it very hard to sustain the amount of work needed on a purely friend/volunteer basis. It became exhausting to always have to be asking for help, and "guilt-tripping" friends to come over to cook. In her case, relying on friends led to guilt, self-hatred, and self-imposed isolation. What this person most wanted was state support so that she would be able to buy consistent, reliable care and have it supplemented with care from friends.

This example tells us many things. First, sometimes part of the care that is needed is the organization of that care. This is an example of how providing care that is not "face to face" will need to be part of the care that communities provide. It meets the criteria of relationship building because the organizer knows the person she is helping and talks to her about what it is she wants, and the care recipient knows from whom she is receiving the care of organization. Second, sometimes the sheer magnitude of care required will exceed the capacity of a given community of care. Then state funding for hiring care givers will be important. Of course, this would also be the case if professional expertise were required. Sometimes communities of care will make state support unnecessary, and sometimes they won't. They are not a blanket substitute for state responsibility. Indeed, we expect the new norms would foster an increased awareness (as everyone is involved with care) of the need for significant state resources that would enable disabled people to pay for (and choose) their care, as well as for group homes and independent living centers. Exactly how the state should fund and provide such services is a policy decision, which, under the new norms would be made by people with extensive knowledge and experience of care—as recipients as well as providers.

There is also another kind of concern we have heard: the care recipient's ability to ask for what she wants from her care giver. In one case, the care recipient wanted tasks, like feeding her, done slowly. She felt that if she had a paid care giver, she could make that clear and feel entitled to ask for patience. But if it was a friend or family member (perhaps seeing them as doing her a favor), she would not feel entitled to express her preferences. A rather different example is the kind of irritation, even rudeness, a tired, stressed care recipient (perhaps also in pain) feels entitled to express to a paid care giver. By contrast she might feel more constrained (even if she felt just as irritated) if the care were being offered by a "volunteer," whether close family member or somewhat more distant member of community of care.

Finally, there is the concern that sometimes people would prefer intimate care to be offered by someone with whom there is an arms-length relationship. One person gave the example that both she and her elderly mother preferred a paid care giver to help her with her toileting. This seems like the kind of preference that should be accommodated, but it also seems possible that some of the relationships within a community of care could be sufficiently distant. As people become accustomed to, and skilled at, such routine care, we think the need for professional paid care will decrease—but not disappear. What matters here is that an arms-length relationship need not be a paid one.

The employment relationship currently seems to stand in for distance, for control, and sometimes even for license. As communities work out the details of the new norms, they will need to think through the kinds of distance, control, and predictable excess that care relationships should foster and/or tolerate, and what role paid care should play. Part of what matters here is that care is a relationship which should be characterized by mutual respect and often a mutual concern for care of the other. There has been such a long history of disregarding the preferences of the elderly and people with disabilities that the legitimate demand for autonomy in managing one's own care can sometimes spill over to a desire for control that seems to leave little space for a mutuality of caring respect between care giver and receiver. Perhaps at some point there will be help from robots available that will remove this requirement. But until then, the new norms need to foster a careful attention to how to enact mutual care and respect in all the varied contexts of care, paid and unpaid.

The discussion above takes for granted that some kinds of paid care will continue under PTfA. That is, indeed, our expectation. Even when people are drawing on the support of their communities of care, they may want additional help with things such as childcare and house cleaning and repair. Here, we just want to make clear that as we see it, the new norms will not preclude people's choice to use some paid care to supplement their own care contribution and that of their communities of care. (We support this scope for choice even though it means families with more money will have an easier time providing care than those with fewer economic resources.)

E. The Role of the State in Providing Care

It should be clear from the brief references above that we expect the state to play an important role in providing care with direct or indirect funding. The state is necessary for building (and often running) critical care infrastructures, from hospitals, to schools, to community centres, to training facilities, to social housing, public parks and other communal spaces, care facilities, and so on. The state will also have a role in licensing care professionals, although some of the existing regulations might be re-thought as large numbers of people come to have increasing skills in care. Ensuring that the voices of those with care needs are heard will be important in thinking through regulations. Governments may also have a role in implementing new laws and regulations governing liability in communities of care (see the next section).

Moreover, governments—from towns and cities to national legislatures—can encourage other kinds of infrastructure that support care communities. It can encourage and support co-housing ventures; it can encourage (by regulation or tax incentive) apartment building developers to build shared kitchens with children's play areas adjoining them to make shared meals and childcare easier. Developers could be encouraged to experiment with evening sleep over rooms, allowing shared babysitting while parents are out. The state can offer incentives for all kinds of imaginative responses to a new reality that everyone is routinely involved in care. Our project here focuses on the interconnection between part-time work and part-time care. But part-time higher education should also become more easily accessible. It is important to remember that some important contributions can be made at a very local level—like hours for city employees and municipal housing regulation.

F. The Care Norms of Part-Time for All Are Not a Form of Privatization

People have good reason to worry about whether PTfA amounts to a form of privatizing care. First of all, throughout the Anglo countries there has been a trend toward shifting responsibility for care from the state to private individuals.[19] In practice this means that families, and in particular women, assume the responsibility for unpaid care. (And poor people without family support often end up without adequate care.) For people whose relatives need long-term care, this often results in serious loss of income, health, leisure, and even friendships when carers have no time for themselves or their friends.

A current example of the harms of badly conceived state regulation of care is provided by Rosie Harding's analysis of the *UK Care Act, 2014.* The issue of privatization arises because,

> where an adult is assessed as having needs that are met by a carer, the local authority no longer has a duty to meet those needs, nor provide a personal budget to allow the adult with care and support needs to meet their needs independently of their carer. It seems, therefore, that the Care Act 2014 recognizes that care is founded in relationships, but then uses everyday interpersonal relationships of care and support to reduce the support available for community resources. . . . [The Act thus] privatizes responsibility for meeting care needs . . . exacerbating vulnerabilities of both carers and cared for.[20]

It is vital that as communities develop new norms of everyone contributing to unpaid care, these norms do not become grounds for removing publicly supported care. Public support will remain necessary for providing professional care (e.g., for children, people with disabilities, the elderly), often through formal care centers, as well as respite care for people with very heavy care responsibilities, and financial support for people whose care needs will exceed what can be expected to be provided by their informal communities of care.

In sum, the increase in unpaid care would relieve some of the demand on public resources. The new norms would increase the contexts in which people can give and receive care from those with whom they have a personal connection. These are important benefits of PTfA. The new norms would not, however, eliminate the need for publicly funded care.

G. Summing Up

The answer to who cares is, then, everyone who is able, with the expectation of much greater creativity in finding ways for virtually everyone to participate in care. Everyone will be conscious that they need care, and everyone will learn to provide care as they are able. There will still be professional care, and many forms of paid care, although we expect the demand for it to be considerably reduced in individual households. The unpaid care that everyone takes up may reduce the demands on publicly funded care, but there will remain important responsibility on the part of governments at all levels to facilitate community care, to provide needed institutions from childcare to eldercare, and to provide support for people providing care in their homes for those with heavy care needs. In (widespread) contexts where there is a serious deficit in publicly funded care, there would be a need for an increase, even with the additional unpaid care provided under the new norms.

IV. For Whom Do We Care?

A. Family

We begin with care in the family even though a central part of PTfA is that care obligations extend beyond the family. And we want to remind our readers that when we refer to family, we are bearing in mind that family forms are fluid and changing.[21] We expect the new norms of care to facilitate care in a wide variety of families, thus making life easier for people in relationships other than the once traditional heterosexual, two parent family. So, when we say "family" we include families in whatever way people have chosen to constitute them.

We begin with family for two reasons that highlight the tensions surrounding fair and sustainable norms about care. First, a huge amount of care currently does take place in families. Around the world, it is overwhelmingly done by women, and most of it is unpaid. In wealthy countries where large numbers of women engage in paid work, they still do a disproportionate amount of the care-work at home. In poorer countries, women routinely engage in productive labor such as small scale farming and selling in local markets, and still are responsible for care. Social policies, such as those that are supposed to address the care needs of people with disabilities—particularly those with high support needs—still rely on a great deal of that labor being done by unpaid family members, usually women. So, the family remains a central site of unjust norms and practices of care.

At the same time, there are particularly compelling care responsibilities within families, and very often—though not always—family members are particularly well suited to provide the care that is needed. Families have traditionally been, and probably should remain, one of the main places where people get the care they need and thus where people learn about care.

One of the important things one learns when one does care (and often fails to understand when one doesn't) is that it matters who does it. Care givers are frequently not interchangeable. People most often learn this in the family. A sick or sad child often wants a parent, even a particular parent, for comfort. And particular individuals urgently want to be able to be there for a child, a spouse, a sibling, or an elderly parent who is suffering and needs care. Care builds bonds: when people are cared for by a loved one, they are often able to feel, recognize, appreciate and believe in the love they receive. And their own love develops and is also recognized and appreciated by the care giver. Bonds call for care; if that call cannot be met, it causes suffering for both the one who needs care and the one who wants to provide it. For example, J. N. had a friend who wanted to take time off from work to be with her six-year old who was in pain with a broken leg. Her colleagues seemed not to understand that, at that time, hiring a care giver would not provide an adequate substitute for the loving comfort both mother and child wanted.[22] (Of course, there can come a point where both mother and child might have to accept a second-best solution.) In sum, the family is a location where people learn the link between connection and care, and the importance of who does the care.

Ideally, one also learns in families about the links between mundane, material care and the connection that arises from feeling cared for and from providing that care. When everyone participates in care (as they are able), everyone experiences the links between a good conversation around a tasty meal and the shopping, chopping, cooking, and cleaning that make that meal possible. Similarly, even children (who share in the material care) come to know the link between the comfort of "coming home" and the work of keeping the home a pleasure to be in. (Norms of repair, cleanliness, tidiness, and the aesthetics of attractiveness will vary a lot.) The work of cleaning is not invisible because everyone shares in it, and thus in the satisfactions of creating and sustaining a comfortable, welcoming home. People will come to know and feel the link between intimate and material care, and the well-being both bring. And if one family member is too sick, tired, or busy on a given day to do their share, someone else's doing it for them will be received as a gift.

We have heard suggestions that some material care is so mundane, so disconnected in its nature from who does it, that it makes no sense to treat it as part of the shared project we describe above. For example, we have frequently heard the objection that cleaning toilets does not build relationships. We think this comment reveals several things. First of all, clean toilets can seem separated for the experience of care if one can ignore how they got that way, or when that gift of care is treated as an (unconscious) entitlement by the recipient. Second, a person responsible for hiring someone else to do the cleaning (and thus not ignorant about how it gets done) may still experience the characteristic of care disappearing into an employment relationship: the clean toilet is the product of paid work, not an act of care. This may indeed characterize the experience of both the paid worker and the employer, while the rest of the family may be happily ignorant. So, we can acknowledge that care can be transformed into paid work, changing its relational nature. But this transformation is not a necessary part of paying for care, although it might be very common if certain tasks, like cleaning toilets, are routinely delegated to paid others.

We will return to this question of paying for care later in this chapter. Here, the point is that clean toilets are part of what makes a home comfortable, and when everyone shares in those tasks and knows what they entail, the mundane task need not cease being part of care and its network of relationships. It is not the material requirements of a clean toilet that make it experienced as the result of care or as the result of a financial transaction. (Of course, in principle it is possible to be both. Paid care can be experienced as care by both those who do it and those who pay for it. It is a question of consciousness and of the nature and pattern of the relationships.) The point here is that mutual obligations of care within families are part of how the norms of care are learned. The knowledge that material, mundane care is an essential component of the experience of both being cared for and providing care is one of the most important things one can learn in the shared care of family or communal life. Of course, when women do most of the care (both intimate and material), and paid "help" does a lot of the material work of cleaning, then instead of these lessons, children learn, and adults are confirmed in, beliefs about the low value of care (especially material care) and those who do it.

Another thing people learn in families, if they are lucky, is the link between a sense of security and the reliability of care. Children learn it, and their care givers learn it as they see children develop a sense of security together with confidence in the reliability of care. The reverse is also true. When care is not reliable—whether because of poverty, warfare, bad foster care systems, or parents' mental health or addiction problems—it is very difficult for children to develop a sense of security. Under the norms of PTfA, the people whom children (and others) can count on for care will extend beyond family members (as is already the case in many communities).

Care obligations in families are, of course, important in part because families are often experienced as the source of demands for care. For people with young children, the time demands of care within their family may cover most of their care responsibilities. Many people, however, will also have care responsibilities for their aging relatives and perhaps for friends with (physical or mental) health problems. Under the new norms, where there is a need for care, there should be someone with a responsibility for meeting it (sometimes from publicly funded institutions, sometimes from care networks). For people whose responsibilities for family and friends are not too demanding, the expectation would be that they would form wider communities of care in which they would meet their care responsibilities.

Finally, there will be many people who routinely need help with care of their own children. There will be single parents and people whose partners need intensive periods of work or travel that make them unavailable at times. Under PTfA, those partners would then have equally long stretches without work when they can make up for the missed care time. But, of course, that won't meet the immediate needs, especially of young children. Part of the new norms of care would be that neighbors and members of communities of care would be aware of such needs, and it would become routine for people to share in the care. Something similar could happen with care of the sick and elderly. No one should find themselves shouldering the burdens and responsibilities (as well as the benefits) of care alone.

B. Communities of Care

In the discussion above, we note that we expect that people would continue to give priority to the care needs of family and friends. In this section, we outline how the norms of PTfA would extend one's care responsibilities beyond that realm by asking everyone to join a community of care with whom they share mutual care responsibilities. The basic point is that in periods of people's lives when the needs of the immediate family and friends do not take up "22 hours" of their time each week, they would not reduce their care-work, but transfer it to their chosen community (or communities) of care.

Of course, communities of care have long existed in many contexts. The familiar phrase, "it takes a village to raise a child," expresses the idea that everyone in the village shares in the responsibilities for raising children. Even in modern urban environments many poor communities, immigrant communities, single parents, and faith groups have created networks of mutual care that are quite close to what we have in mind. Some "co-housing" projects have norms around mutual care.[23] Our picture of communities of care would extend norms of mutual care to include everyone.

The new norms of PTfA would generate expectations of caring attention to the needs of one's neighbors and one's chosen community of care. This is, of course, a demanding norm. In particular, it means that one's care obligations would not simply be defined by the arc of an individual life: intense obligations when one's children are young or one's parents are in ill health, with the expectation that these intense obligations would decrease over time. Another way of highlighting the demanding nature of what we propose is this: *one can never retire from care* (though one can take vacations). That said, the norms must of course allow for fluidity, as people's own health, as well as that of family and friends, leads to shifts in the hours they devote to direct care (assuming they will sometimes exceed the minimum of "22 hours") and to whom they provide care.

How would people choose and create communities of care? We picture a wide variety of communities. For some, their geographical neighborhood, the people who live close to them, would form the community within which they create norms of mutual care. These norms would be reciprocal in the widest sense that everyone in the community is expected to participate and to benefit, but not in the quid pro quo sense that I will repay the care you give me with similar care. It would involve patterns of attention to who has what needs and who has which abilities and inclinations. In many cases spontaneous responses to need by those who become aware of it may provide what is necessary. It seems likely, however, that to ensure that no one slips through the cracks there will be a need not only for developing new norms of letting people know when one needs help, but some forms of responsibility for checking in with people and for co-ordination of care giving. In addition, as we noted in the discussion of disability, people who have high care needs may need both professional help and someone to coordinate the care from those in their community of care. We picture fairly small communities of say 10–40 people so that the demands for co-ordination would not be great.

In addition to neighborhoods, we envision that some will choose faith communities as their communities of care.[24] These are often communities that already have practices of mutual care worked out, that could be expanded as everyone takes up additional care responsibilities. Others still might find that the community with which they have, and want to sustain, the closest bonds are communities of shared interest, in arts, politics or sports, for example, like one's choir, soccer club, or environmental action group. Such communities would need to work out ways of letting each other know about their care needs and abilities to meet care needs. Both things can be quite challenging, as the strong norms around competence and independence make it difficult for many people to reveal their needs. (This is even true in faith communities with long-standing practices of mutual care.) And there can also be habits of anxiety about taking on responsibilities of care. Addressing these anxieties would be part of the ongoing process of norm transformation. And communities of care would be central to that process.

The constitution of communities of care, which will become part of what every (capable) adult needs to do, will not just be a choice of the people with whom one wants to create mutual obligations and bonds of care. It will also be a choice about the community in which one wants to take up the inevitable and ongoing conversations about issues such as those we discuss in this chapter: what constitutes care, how to accommodate preferences, what are appropriate minimum hours, and when is professional care desirable. Similarly, communities of care will provide a primary locus for the development of new norms about what are respectful forms of interaction between care givers and receivers, how to learn to ask for help and receive it graciously, and how to build confidence about one's care capacities. We do not picture conversations about these issues as constant, but we do see them as recurring over and over as conditions and people change. As we will discuss more in the conclusion, the implementation of new norms requires ongoing judgment, and honing one's skills at taking the perspectives of others is both necessary for good judgment[25] and facilitated by the exercise of care. Happily, these two vital life skills are mutually supporting. Communities of care will become one of the most important communities of judgment people participate in.

There are several challenges that we can already anticipate. The first is to ensure that no one is left out. Communities organized around neighborhood or shared interests and commitments may replicate social and economic hierarchies. So, the objective is both not to leave any one out because they are already isolated in ways that make it difficult to join communities of care, and to ensure some diversity within communities so that there are not large disparities in capacity to care between one community and the next. (Such disparities are found, for example, in North American public schools, with some parent groups able to raise large funds to supplement state support as well contribute time to extra-curricular activities.)

Thus, one task for every community is to reflect on issues of diversity and ways of reaching out to the isolated and vulnerable. People with care needs are not just those who are ill or injured, but those who deal with addiction, chronic underemployment, discrimination and harassment, and vulnerability to violence (like women in abusive relationships, sex workers, and trans people). Remember that by care we mean direct care responsive to particular needs, not more general activism—essential as it is. So, what we mean here is being alert to the particular needs for care of people with particular vulnerabilities. And this will mean finding ways to provide care for those initially outside of one's networks of family, friends, and communities of care—as well as finding ways for those networks to become more inclusive. Because of the important link between care and relationship, it seems likely to us that this kind of care is also best provided in consistent, continuous ways. The key is to ensure a mutuality of relationship, so that the care for the vulnerable does not primarily take the form of charity.

We want to offer two quite different examples of existing communities of care that respond to the needs of the vulnerable. The first comes from a moving documentary, *Blue Roses*,[26] that offers a view of a successful community of care for people living in rooming houses in Ottawa's inner city. The community members "face poverty, addiction and mental illness that often leads to their premature death alone in their rooms or on the street." Ottawa Inner City Health teamed up with Somerset West and Centretown community health centers to create a "palliative care" program designed and run collaboratively by people who have experienced these conditions together with professionals such as publicly funded nurses. This is a program aimed not at getting people off drugs, but meeting them where they are, providing the care they need. What makes it an important example of a "community of care" is that many of the people who are providing the care are or were in situations like those they serve. This is a picture of mutual care for and by people facing extreme challenges, aided by space provided by churches and public funding for professionals. The collaborative nature of the work and decision-making, the lived experience of the participants, demonstrates the possibility of even those in quite dire circumstances forming communities of mutual care. Vulnerable communities may often need additional help, but it does not mean that they cannot form their own communities of care. It will be the responsibility of both state actors and caring "neighbors" to provide the help that is wanted.

Another example is Moms Stop the Harm (MSTH), a network of Canadian families whose loved ones have died from drug related harms or who struggle with substance use.[27] MSTH call for an end to the failed war on drugs and the criminalization of people who use drugs (PWUD). Calling for compassion and respect, they embrace harm reduction. MSTH mothers have established a "care railroad" to respond to the gaps in state care required by PWUD in the opioid crisis. Care needs arise out of overdoses that are serially survived and a range of other serious drug injuries (brain damage, heart infections, and so on). MSTH put out calls in their private online member groups requesting assistance in care provision when a teen/youth/young adult is far from family and sitting in an emergency room, has just been just discharged from an ER, or is alone on an Intensive Care Unit or alone on an infectious disease or internal medicine ward. "We are keenly aware that time matters in these situations as does care and support. When we find out, we get to them as fast as we can." Sheila Jennings offers this example:

> A young person who overdosed in Vancouver and was immediately discharged from that Vancouver ER after the overdose was reversed. He was reached when a Quebec Mom and an Ontario Mom who heard about his plight contacted a Vancouver Mom to seek out the youth so that he could receive personal attention and try to access a

detox bed and or medically assisted treatment. These mothers were all bereaved, having lost a child to this public health crisis. I was asked by an Ontario mother to visit her son on a hospital ward in Toronto as she was in Asia (she'd already lost one son to overdose) and I agreed to do that. I know a rural Ontario mother whose now late son received care from a hospital volunteer in Oshawa, and that volunteer went on to become a family friend.[28]

The mothers at Moms Stop the Harm also provide support to one another. Members will arrange to meet with mothers who have a very recent loss, or whose "child" is overdosing, or have a child (teenager, young adult, or even older adult children) who has just survived their first overdose. Members have also stepped in and prevented fellow-mothers from self-harm and even suicide in the wake of highly stigmatized and sudden child death. They provide care for one another in multiple ways in a society that often treats their children (and their losses) with ignorance and contempt.[29]

We see MSTH as an example of a functioning community of mutual care for people in need, spread out across Canada. There is a strong sense of mutual aid, responsibility, and appreciation even though the next person one offers care to may be someone one has never met. As is often the case, some of the dire need arises out of failure of state responsibility and widespread prejudice. Thus, MSTH engages in advocacy as well as trying to meet the vital need for personal care and attention.

Finally, one more example of mutual care. There used to be a drop-in center in Toronto where people could go to have lunch with, and serve lunch to, people in poverty, many with substance use problems. There was no clear dividing line between those who came (at least in the beginning) primarily to give help and those who came looking for food, support, and companionship. Everyone shared in the tasks and in the eating together. In addition to time to help clean up, there was also usually a session after lunch of sharing stories and poems. Lots of people shared. These practices fostered a sense of mutual care and became a kind of community of care, from which everyone learned and benefited. We think the ongoing sharing and learning was an important part of what created a mutuality that was genuine despite obvious differences in material resources, life circumstances, and health. The desire to create such bonds in sustainable ways might encourage institutions—such as schools, faith communities, recreation centers—to work to ensure that their membership is diverse. That would provide additional opportunities for creating diverse communities of care.

There is nevertheless likely to be some tension between the goal of diversity and the goal of cohesive, committed communities among people who share enough to feel themselves bonded to one another. It may be that given deeply entrenched patterns (in Anglo countries in particular) of income differences between neighborhoods (and thus schools, places of worship, and recreational facilities), differences in resources—of time, energy, and money—between communities of care will persist. Long-standing patterns of class differences, as well as attachments to communities of national origin or ethnicity may also generate differences in resources among chosen communities of care. It may therefore be important to figure out ways to share material and financial resources across communities. Of course, attention to these differences can be hoped to foster greater commitment of public resources to making access to health care, housing, transportation, and education more equitable.

The second challenge might be seen as another dimension of diversity. Of course, we anticipate resistance to the new norms from people who think their work is too important to waste their time on care, as well as from people who see PTfA as intrusive and coercive. We offer arguments to meet these concerns. But in addition, there may be people who belong to communities with strong religious or cultural commitments to gendered divisions of labor around work and care. Our arguments may seem irrelevant to these allegiances. People in such communities may already feel excluded by the dominant norms, and the norms of PTfA may make that exclusion worse. All forms of exclusion from the norms and communities of PTfA, or indeed from a wider sense of inclusion in social citizenship, are a sad loss in our view. For better and for worse, members of such alternative communities are likely to be insulated from the influence of the new norms.

There is another set of challenges that arise from existing hierarchies and prejudices, which may be in tension with the choice emphasized above. We have already mentioned the degradation of people with high care needs. We might add here the fear many feel around people whose disabilities remind them of their own vulnerability. There is a long, shameful, and continuing history of neglect and abuse of people with disabilities.[30] One of the great fears of many people whose disabilities mean they require regular care from others is that at some point they will have to move into an institution—where they are particularly likely to have their preferences around care ignored and be subject to neglect and abuse. Communities of care can help to provide the care that is needed so that such a move can be avoided or at least delayed. And when members of a community do need to move to residential care, their fellow members can visit them regularly, helping to ensure that they are receiving the respectful care they deserve. In many (but of course not all) cases, people with disabilities will also be able to contribute care to others in their communities. This would be one important way in which people with disabilities would be integrated into communities: like everyone else they would be both care recipients and care givers, and everyone would know them as such. Indeed, as everyone becomes more conscious of their own care needs and limitations, they may come to see "disability" as a vast continuum on which we all have a (shifting) place.[31]

One of the things we hope everyone will learn from the norms of PTfA is that the now existing degradation of care and those in need of it is tied to a valorization of independence that denies the basic interdependence of all human beings. Part of the fear around old age and disability is a very real vulnerability to abuse and neglect, compounded by a sense of failure to meet the (impossible) standard of independence held out as the marker of competent adulthood. Under the new norms, in well-functioning communities of care people will learn how to give and receive care with mutual respect and attentiveness. People will come to know in a visceral way that autonomy does not mean independence. Autonomy must be fostered by respect and by material scope for discovering, expressing, and enacting what one wants in life. All of that is made possible by constructive relationship, not by a fantasy of "independence."[32]

Given both the current legacy of degradation and the potential for abuse, it will be essential that all communities of care attend to the need to develop the ability to listen carefully to the preferences and desires of those one is caring for. And the *mutuality* of respect and a caring disposition remains essential. Care has been so shaped by hierarchy and disrespect that both those in need of care and those providing it will, especially in the transition period, be vulnerable to many layers of harm. We think that the norms of PTfA, and the experience and *self-perception* of everyone as both care giver and receiver are promising ways to overcome the long-standing and deeply embedded practices of degradation. But the vulnerabilities will never simply disappear, so alertness to the potential for abuse will always be necessary. In ways similar to the (now quite imperfectly implemented) model of intervention in families with abuse of children and/or intimate partners, we envision that in the normal course of events communities of care will be able to self-monitor and to call in state authority when abuse is suspected. Indeed, we expect the norms of mutual care to increase everyone's willingness to intervene in all forms of abuse, including that of children and intimate partners—where there is still widespread reluctance to acknowledge, intervene, or report.

V. Learning from Care

Here we focus on what one learns from care, and how this learning underpins our argument that everyone should care, as well as the more specific claim that care giving from all is essential for good policy.

A. Personal Reflection

To connect back to my (J. N.) reflections in the context of my mother's death, I want to begin with some of the things I learned from being with her for the last 9 days of her life. She was in her own bed in her apartment at her retirement home in Santa Cruz, CA. I had asked Viara, one of her regular care givers, to call me if there were any important changes in how my mom was doing. I received her call in Toronto late on the evening of August 26, 2018. She told me my mother had stopped eating and drinking for the last 48 hours. I was scheduled to fly to Boston the next day to arrive early for a conference, and then six days later to fly to California for my mom's 100th birthday. I was able to change my flight (with caring assistance from both my husband and Air Canada) to fly to California the next morning. Thanks to Viara, I was able to arrive while my mom was still very lucid and not in much distress and be with her during her stressful last days. Here are some of the things I learned.

Sometimes professionals don't know best. The care givers insisted (as they had been trained to do) on checking and changing my mother's diaper every four hours even though she was not eating and barely drinking. It distressed her greatly, driving her to yelling and kicking. Finally, I invoked the medical hierarchy and asked her doctor to give an order that this was not necessary.

Often what matters most is just being emotionally connected. I needed to be tuned in (as well as I could) to what my mom was feeling. Trying to *manage* things well could be a distraction from that attunement and connection. And it was not possible to fix everything.

It was all so much harder than I expected. I wasn't prepared for the wild fluctuation of distress and calm. I wasn't prepared for her suddenly sitting up in bed and repeating, "I am scared." Not since my first child almost died at birth had I experienced the acute pain of watching someone I loved in serious distress, distress that I could not prevent. Mental anguish can be as terrifying as physical pain, and sometimes hard to distinguish. Care givers often speak of how exhausting it is. In my case this was true even though I had excellent support and actually very little material responsibility. I slept in the room next to my mom and so my sleep was regularly disturbed even though there was a care giver there all night. I was emotionally drained, which interfered with the openness that might have allowed me to comfort my mom better.

I learned about the importance of compassion and the responsiveness it enables. For example, Phoebe, one of the care givers came by to say goodbye. She held my mom's hand, and she told me my mother was only angry and hostile when she was in pain. Otherwise, Phoebe said, my mom always said thank you. One of the servers in the dining room came by to say Happy Birthday and brought a small flower she had picked, which delighted my mother. One of the all-night care givers, who had never met my mother before, was a young woman of great kindness and compassion. One night when my mother woke in distress, she was able to calm her down with kind words and touch, thoughtfully applied. She said my mother didn't want her hands to be touched but was happy to have her legs stroked. Another care giver would have immediately called for meds when my mother woke distressed, which would have caused further distress as she hated having to take anything. I wished I had more of the calm compassion of that young woman.

I also had a couple of experiences of the importance of caring for the care givers.[33] This same compassionate young woman had been in a hurry to get there on time and had not had time for dinner or even to pick something up—and was facing a twelve-hour shift. Fortunately, I had a lot of tasty leftovers from a dinner out with my brother. She was delighted to have them. On another occasion, an overnight care giver did bring dinner. I set a place for her at the table and offered the use of the microwave. She was grateful, saying some people treated her like a servant and would never have thought of sitting at the table with her. I find this last story a particularly shocking version of the puzzle of how people can denigrate care givers when they (should) know how vital their care is.

Is any of this the kind of knowledge that matters? It certainly feels like after writing about care for several years, I still had a lot to learn. Even things I thought I knew—like it is hard, it is exhausting, it is painful—took on an entirely new meaning. I think of this as my own visceral, embodied experience of our claim that reading or even hearing stories is not a substitute for the experiential knowledge of care. Similarly, the special competence of a compassionate young woman able to tune in to what my mother needed, gave a concreteness to the idea that good care requires a set of very important skills that belie that idea that the basic care of a nighttime attendant is unskilled labor. And finally, care givers are doing hard work, often including demanding emotional labor, that should earn them not only fair wages, but compassionate care from the family members of those they are helping. This cannot be boiled down to (nevertheless essential) "decent working conditions," and is undermined by a culture that denigrates care. How can people expect the sort of caring, compassionate people they (should) hope are caring for their loved ones, if care givers can expect disrespect and disregard? I could not have learned all this if my role had only been to interview some care agencies, selected an appropriate one, and arrange for payment. I learned because I participated in giving and receiving care for nine crucial days in my life and in the life of my mother. I believe it is the sort of knowledge that not only can make people better care givers but can help them make decisions both in their own households and in public policy based on a better understanding of the demands of care, the benefits of good care, the connections care brings, and the skills it entails.

B. Control, Rhythms of Care, and the Hierarchy of Freedom and Necessity

Next in our exploration of learning from care is the contested issue of control, so central to contemporary management culture. We then turn to the distinct rhythms of care and their challenge to the norms of "productivity." Experience with the repetitive quality of many dimensions of care provides a basis for understanding and rejecting a key to the degradation of care: care is held in contempt because of its association with necessity, contrasted with freedom and its higher creations.

In interviews with young women without children, Daphne de Marneffe found that fears around control was one of the themes that emerged: "They flinch from the notion of losing control over their bodies and emotions and time and feel a bit sorry for the harried moms ('stroller-tethered people,' as one called them)."[34] They are right in the sense that care challenges the conventional notion that one should be in control of one's life. In caring for the people one loves, the carer can learn about the complexities of seeking control. When caring for an uncooperative toddler or sullen adolescent or scared and angry elderly parent, the desire to exert control can be overwhelming, and easy to see as being for the benefit of the one cared for. But with the sort of reflective attention to both self and other (advocated particularly clearly by de Marneffe) that is essential to caring well, one learns that control is not a respectful form of relationship. It is also in many ways impossible (for example to stop the deterioration of the mind of one's parent) as well as fundamentally undesirable.[35] To recognize both the power of the urge and the undesirability of attaining it, can help to shift the powerful role of control in contemporary life. Bureaucrats, teachers, and managers of all kinds are trained to aim at controlling their subordinates, in order to achieve the results those in charge are aiming at. Life-long experience with providing care can help people to see that the growth and development not just of children but of employees or clients is not best accomplished by the apparent short cut of control (or manipulation). The capacities and accomplishments hoped for require attention, reflection, guidance, and nurture—not control.[36]

Carers learn about the rhythms of care, which are part of the rhythms of life and of growth, as well their counterparts: the rhythms of death, of decline, and recovery. The rhythms of care are not the rhythms of "productive labor." Care is characterized by actions that have to be performed over and over again repetitively, but also with unpredictable variation. Children have to be fed over and over, but what and when they want to eat can vary and requires the attention of the carer. When they have been fed, a need has been met, but nothing has been "produced" (except perhaps the contents of diapers which also have to be repetitively, but tenderly changed). Repetitive, attentive care enables a child's growth, a sick person's recovery, or comfort for one approaching death. The carer's attention to both self and others build bonds of relationship that are themselves vital to the development, healing, and ease the material care facilitates. But there is no product to be pointed to, and the process may go on for a long time with only the subtle (though powerful) benefits of human connection. This pattern is part of what underlies the old refrain about the "housewife": what does she *do* all day?

Part of what one learns by regular, life-long engagement with care is that the current focus on "productivity" and the understanding of time associated with it is, at best, only one dimension of life, and at worst, in its dominance, a distortion of core values of life, of what sustains human survival as well as happiness, fulfillment, and well-being. Starla Hargita highlights the contrasting conceptions of time and productivity this way:

> The immediacy of care needs operates outside the dominant normative time of productivism and financialized processes. The

temporality of the everyday prioritizes the present . . . as each act operates independently of financialized outputs or incentivized clock-time. The child in need of soothing, food, napping, or changing does not adhere to a regimented schedule, but demands instead the undulated unpredictability of the presently-situated body in flux. Care needs are not easily absorbed into the time-discipline of waged labor hours and clock-time. This orientation to the present, as seen from the body of the child, is demanding and immediate; from the perspective of the carer it can be simultaneously disruptive and transformative. The act of caring for a child disrupts the worker, ideal or otherwise, and transforms that worker into an agent of reproductive and unremunerated labors, in opposition to productive and waged labor.[37]

Sustained engagement with care allows people to understand in a visceral way the dark side of the long-standing contrast between the repetitive practices characteristic of care and the model of productive (and creative) work: it rests on a dangerous hierarchy that has sustained the degradation of care for centuries. The hierarchy of work over care is connected (through a complex history) to the hierarchy of freedom over necessity in Western political thought. Of course, most people don't think in terms of freedom vs. necessity, but virtually everyone knows and feels the hierarchy that flows from that dichotomy: important (paid) work that is a serious contribution to society versus the demeaned work of care, tending to the human needs that sustain life, relationship, and well-being. This hierarchy is so central both to everyday norms and to traditions of Western thought that we think it is worth a brief indication of what is at stake.

The once common contrast between productive and reproductive labor is helpful in many ways. But it is also oddly anachronistic, since the kind of work that is valorized (and financially rewarded) in rich societies today is no longer the work of material production. Today, serious, "important" work manages the finances and the legal regimes that organize production (often taking place elsewhere) or it manages the huge bureaucracies of government and corporations. Such work is, notionally, an exercise of freedom. Material production and manual labor, by contrast, sinks back to the realm of necessity. The realm of freedom is where high-level decision-making, power, and (also notionally) real creativity and joy reside. Thus the realm of "productive work" has always had its own, shifting, hierarchies with different rankings for, say, coal mining, farming, carpentry, law, and banking. Whatever is seen as closest to material necessity, is likely to be coded as lowly. The "reproductive labor" of care has also had (shifting) class differentiation, but it is always linked to necessity and virtually always at the bottom, even below lowly forms of male manual labor.

In the Western tradition, the opposite of freedom is necessity. Being bodily creatures, humans have needs that place them in the realm of necessity. Meeting these needs has exactly the sort of repetitive, nonproductive quality we just described in the context of care. In the dominant Western tradition, the objective from the Greeks onward has been to free oneself as much as possible from necessity, so as to live in the realm of freedom. "Others"—women, slaves, the working class—should do the inevitable work of necessity so that those with higher abilities can devote themselves to free creativity, and the sort of valuable, lasting creations freedom can generate. A related value is participating in the political realm; having the freedom to do so is also enabled by being lifted above the realm of necessity by the labor of others.[38]

Caring labor is the (often) repetitive labor of meeting human needs (most often physical and emotional). In the freedom vs. necessity framework, care lies squarely in the realm of necessity. It is what anyone with aspirations to the highest human capacities should avoid. Not to do so when one could, would be a terrible waste not just of, say, an expensive education, but of one's most valuable, most truly "human" abilities. It is an abdication of freedom to mire oneself in necessity. This is a basic part of the framing that underlies the degradation of care.

What is fundamentally wrong with this hierarchy and how can the sustained practice of care help people unlearn it? At the heart of what is wrong is that care builds and sustains human relationships and it is those relationships that make life possible, valuable, and rewarding. Care is a necessity, *and* the choices people make about relationships and care are among the most important exercises of human freedom. There is extensive evidence (now regularly available in the news media) that happiness is most reliably achieved through positive, enduring relationship. At some level, most people know that, yet that knowledge has to compete with powerful pressures and incentives to "succeed," to excel, to advance, to consume. Human beings are social creatures and when recognition flows toward what is defined as success while care is consistently denigrated, it is difficult to hold onto and act on the knowledge about the importance of human relationships and the care they require.

Of course, as noted above, the dominant framework acknowledges that the demands of the realm of necessity must be met in order for the higher activities of freedom to take place. One might argue that in an era of at least lip service commitment to equality, everyone should have a chance at the higher realms, so everyone should take a turn in the realm of necessity, making sure needs are met. This is where arguments about differing natural abilities (or sometimes temperament and preference)—which happen to correspond to categories like gender, race and class—enter in to make sure that those with the "higher" talents and skills do not waste their time on the low skilled work of "reproductive labor," which simply repetitively provides the basis for the higher work and its continuance into the next generation.

The problem of equal turns in "productive" and "reproductive" work is, however, not the most basic problem. The most basic problem is a misunderstanding of the contribution of each. The dominant framework might concede that no society can survive without both kinds of contribution, but continue to insist on a hierarchy of value between them. After all, acknowledging necessity does not, in itself, change the hierarchy between necessity and freedom. It is that hierarchy itself that needs to be dismantled through an understanding of exactly what the realm of necessity consists in. And it is that understanding that the experience of care can facilitate.

When parents feed, shelter, soothe, play with, and love their infants, they create a bond between them that shapes the lives and capacities of both parent and child. Both learn the importance of love and the ways material care and security are linked to that love. They learn the ways the capacity to tune into another is connected to the ability to tune into oneself, and that both enable the kind of care that fosters growth and joy. In short, the most basic, necessary forms of care (which are emotional as well as material) are completely entangled with the

development of the capacities for imagination, concentration, commitment, responsiveness, perseverance, creativity, and perception—
which are necessary for the relationships essential to human thriving
as well as for what is seen as the higher, creative, important forms of
work. The importance of positive human relationships for all these
(and other) abilities does not end at 18 or 21 or 30 years of age. It
continues throughout life. Thus, honing these abilities is not simply
some initial prerequisite for adult, high-level functioning, but part of
the life-long work of human development and well-being.

The work of caring for adults in need requires many of the same
skills and involves similar, though not identical, demands and
satisfactions of caring for children. And the mutual work of sustaining
intimate relationships between adults also shares many of these
features: the importance of tuning into the other and to oneself, to be
attentive and receptive, to tolerate ambivalence and celebrate fleeting
joy, to persevere when one is tired, distracted and disinclined. Indeed,
sustaining constructive adult relationships of all kinds, including work
relationships, requires similar skills. Here, as I noted above, learning
(and re-learning) the importance of relinquishing control as a model
of relationship is vital.

Of course, as we said at the outset, not everyone thinks about the
abstractions of freedom vs. necessity. But virtually everyone knows
and feels the work over care hierarchy that we see as interwoven with
the dichotomy. This hierarchy is so pervasive as to seem self-evident.
Rejecting it is vital to equality, to well informed public policy, and to the
reframing of the core values that should govern people's life choices.

C. What People Learn from Care

The argument above claims that the practice of caring teaches people
basic skills, such as tuning into the other and to oneself, attentiveness,
and receptivity. People learn these skills because good care requires
them, and people want to do a good job of caring for people they care
about. They thus also learn that care requires skill. They experience the
ways the care they provide builds relationships with those they care
for, relationships they experience as providing joy, satisfaction, and

the incomparable reward of mutual love. They also experience that these benefits are inseparable from hard work, frustration, ambivalence, anger. That is, they learn vital lessons about the nature of human relationships and what sustains them. The ongoing, evolving, sum of this learning allows them to understand the nature and value of care and its essential link to human well-being.

Of course, a basic part of our argument here is that people need to learn these skills and develop these understandings not primarily by reading good arguments, but through the practice of care. Fortunately for the purpose of persuading people to undertake that practice, a wide variety of authors have tried to explain how this learning from care works. The evidence we offer for these claims is drawn from research based on a combination of personal experience,[39] small scale empirical work backed by larger scale secondary research, together with a set of analytic claims about what good care entails and thus what must be learned in order to do care well. We also include an example from neuroscience. Our purpose here is not to provide dispositive proof, but to give a sense of the available evidence and argument—sufficient to take seriously the idea that learning from care is vital for human well-being and survival. In all societies, enough people (usually women) have learned what is necessary for survival. We advocate spreading this learning to all in the name of well-being, of equality, and in this era of environmental crisis, of survival.

The next set of resources are reflections on what one learns from "mothering." In 1989 Sara Ruddick wrote a wonderful book, *Maternal Thinking: Towards a Politics of Peace*, that argued that caring for children fosters a certain kind of thinking. She makes clear that it is not only women who can engage in maternal practice, although both historically and currently it is overwhelmingly women who have done so.[40] She also distinguishes "maternal practice" from other forms of care, so the kind of learning she helps us understand cannot be expected from all the kinds of care that would count under PTfA norms. Nevertheless, we expect childcare to be something most people will contribute to—whether they have their "own" children or not. Indeed, creating these connections with children for almost everyone is one of the benefits of PTfA. (As one of J. N.'s friends put it, the way North American society is now organized, "in order to have an intimate relationship with a child, you have to own one."[41] This is a loss to both children and adults.)

For Ruddick, the responsibility of childcare is defined by "demands" in the sense of "the requirements imposed on anyone doing maternal work." The key three demands are for preservation, growth, and social acceptance, and they must be met by works of "preservative love, nurturance, and training."[42] There are variants of these demands and responses in other forms of nurturing care, such as for the elderly, people with disabilities (mental and physical) and people recovering from sickness or injury. Ruddick argues that one must develop certain kinds of skills at thinking in order to meet these demands.[43] The first is to *see* vulnerability, and then to choose to respond, and learn to respond with care. These capacities are as relevant to other forms of nurturance as to childcare, even though the demands are not identical.

The capacity to recognize vulnerability and be moved to respond with care is, of course, an extremely important skill, especially in a world with enormous pressures to look the other way in the face of overwhelming vulnerability all around us, near and far. And, of course, extending one's concern with one's own children to vulnerable others is not automatic. Toward the end of the book Ruddick turns to the examples of the mothers of the disappeared in Chile and Argentina who resisted military dictatorship, "specifically the polic[ies] of kidnapping, imprisonment, torture and murder of the 'disappeared.'"[44] She notes that "as in many women's politics of resistance, the Argentinian and Chilean women emphasize mothering among women's many relations."[45] She does not suggest that every woman in Argentinian and Chilean protest movements "extended concern from her own children to all the disappeared then to all of the nation and finally to all victims everywhere."

Yet many of these women did so extend themselves—intellectually, politically, emotionally. They did not 'transcend' their particular loss and love; particularity was the emotional root and source of their protest. It's through acting on that particularity that they extended mothering to include sustaining and protecting any people whose lives are blighted by violence.[46]

She offers a further statement of the ways having learned to think through the demands of maternal practice, mothers can transform the way politics is understood and enacted. She concludes that, "whatever their personal timidities, [these women] publicly announce that they take responsibility for protecting the world in which they and their children must live":

> they mock dichotomies that still riddle political thought. There is no contradiction between "playing the role of victim" and taking responsibility for public policies. It is possible to act powerfully while standing with those who are hurt. It is neither weak nor passive to reveal one's own suffering while refusing to damage or mutilate in return. The Latin American mater dolorosa has learned how to fight as a victim for victims, not by joining the strong, but by resisting them.[47]

These reflections link back to her discussions of how maternal practice involves understanding the complexities, even contradictions of power. Mothers have enormous power over their children but often feel powerless. They bear huge responsibilities but are faced with contempt as mere mothers over and over again—from teachers, doctors, and other professionals their children must work with. Ruddick also notes that the work of maternal practice inevitably involves another complexity: feelings of ambivalence. "What we are pleased to call 'mother-love' is intermixed with hate, sorrow, impatience, resentment, and despair; thought-provoking ambivalence is a hallmark of mothering."[48] Learning to welcome ambivalence as an invitation to thought is surely an advantage to adults navigating both work and intimate relationships, as well as to teachers, doctors and front-line bureaucrats.

Ruddick also explains how the work of mothering teaches people to understand the role of feelings in cognition (long before the now widely recognized neuroscience on the subject[49]):

> It is not possible to understand preservative love "purely" intellectually, nor can protective mothers understand themselves and their children without calling on and understanding feelings. . . . In maternal

thinking, feelings are at best complex but sturdy instruments of work quite unlike the simple and separate hates, fears, and loves that are usually put aside and put down in philosophical analysis. . . . In protective work, feeling, thinking, and action are conceptually linked; feelings demand reflection, which is in turn tested by action, which is in turn tested by the feelings it provokes. Thoughtful feeling, passionate thought, and protective acts together test, even as they reveal, the effectiveness of preservative love.[50]

In the course of care for their children mothers also learn the virtue of humility, "when they recognize in themselves the delusive, compulsive efforts to see everywhere and control everything so that a child will be safe. With 'humility,' a mother respects the limits of her will and the independent, uncontrollable, and increasingly separate existences she seeks to preserve. A mother without humility would become frantic in her efforts to protect." I would add here that Ruddick (unlike our argument above) does not reject the language of control. She treats control as necessary and warns that mothers can be tempted "to give up the patient work of control and resort to domination."

In her chapter on "Fostering Growth," Ruddick talks about nurturing the development, the unfolding, of a child's spirit. Here one of the things maternal practice teaches is the complex intertwining of body, mind and spirit:

To speak paradoxically, from a maternal perspective the spirit is material. A child's body, from its birth, is enspirited. A primary experience of preservative love is an admiring wonder at what a new body does. An enspirited body is, in turn, a source and focus of mental life. From children's perspective, "bodies," both their own and others' provide some of the most poignant features and puzzles of mental life. As children name, desire, avoid, or touch bodies, the bodies become resonant with "spiritual" significance.[51]

Dealing with the inherent complexity of fostering growth, requires that mothers constantly exercise judgment. For example, a mother has to judge "whether intervention is called for and, if so, whether she should attempt to change her child or the forces upsetting him or both."[52] The dangers of making the wrong judgment can be profound. Exercising judgment requires attentiveness and responsiveness, as well as the ability sometimes to step aside and wait. Judgments require being attuned to the particularities of the child as well as the, generally uncontrollable, social context. This, as we will return to, is a central feature of all judgment—a skill required throughout life. Judgments about children also take place in the context of constant change. Ruddick says that "the work of fostering growth provokes or requires a welcoming response to change." She cites Alice Miller who argues that:

> [T]hose who change with change and welcome its challenges acquire a special kind of learning. . . . Miller believes that maternal experience with change and the kind of learning it provokes will help us to understand the changing nature of all peoples and communities. It is not only children who change, grow and need help growing. We all might grow—as opposed to simply growing older—if we could learn how.[53]

In the contemporary world of the early twenty-first century the demanding rate of change—from the economy to the planetary environment—is surely a context in which the skills for dealing well with the inevitability of change are essential.

Ruddick's point here, and throughout the book, is that most mothers do learn the lessons of maternal practice because it is so urgent for the well-being of their children and themselves that they do so. Maternal practice is not the only way of learning attentiveness, responsiveness, humility, good judgment, the centrality of relationships and their connection to care, and the welcoming of change—perhaps Mindfulness Meditation can teach similar things—but one can easily drop one's meditation practice, while the demands of maternal practice are vital and unremitting. Few mothers walk away, and even under quite desperate conditions most mothers learn some of this wisdom, mode of thinking, and skills of life.

Ruddick's insights are complemented by an excellent book on care and masculinity by Niall Hanlon, *Masculinities, Care, and Equality: Identity and Nurture in Men's Lives*.[54] He offers persuasive empirical evidence and acute analysis about the links between gender identity and care. While that is, of course, relevant to the project of PTfA, here we want to focus on his findings about the way men learn and change from the practice of caring. At the most basic level, for our purposes here, his findings support the idea that "maternal thinking" [Ruddick's term] is something men can learn and that they learn it by doing care. They change their understanding of gender, they come to recognize the value and demands of care, and they develop skills and capacities such as "a more other-centered and caring personality," the ability to understand others' perspectives, relational skills, and the ability to express emotions.[55]

In short, the practice of care can be transformative. The stories from his interviews show how "doing caring work helps men to develop a more nurturing and compassionate masculinity." Even though many men initially resist having to share in care-work, many of his subjects concluded that having to do this work was the most important way for them to learn its value.[56] As they came to see the value of care, to experience the skill it involved and the connections it enabled, many came to recognize the traditional male entitlement to be "carefree" and to reject it.

In transforming their understanding of masculinity, the practice of care challenges deeply engrained societal values of power, success, and, indeed understandings of humanity:

> The intersection between masculinity and caring confronts men with a contradiction; to be a valuable man is to be powerful, and to be human is to be vulnerable. How can men acknowledge their masculinity when feeling vulnerable and how can men acknowledge their vulnerability when feeling masculine? Whilst we cannot do anything about our human vulnerability except to deny it, we can change the script of what it means to be a man. Caring helps to resolve these internal and external tensions and contradictions. . . . Equality in caring can create opportunities for men to deepen caring relations with others and create a healthier and caring society. . . . *The relational gain men can experience as a result of becoming caring . . . can help to compensate men for the loss of power.*[57]

We now turn briefly to the question of the extent to which the particular forms of learning that we have highlighted can be expected to be provided by the kind of care people would engage in under the new norms of PTfA. First, of course, those who are providing care within their families (of whatever formation), would find it much easier to learn from care because a significant part of the current stress over competing demands of "work" and "family" would be much reduced. Good jobs would no longer be characterized by long hours, forcing choices between time with children and decently paid, satisfying work. And for those in jobs with few intrinsic rewards, people would not come home drained and exhausted from 8 or 9 hours on the job. The availability of good part-time work would vastly decrease the number of people trying to patch together a living wage from multiple, precarious jobs. In addition, as everyone would be actively engaged in care, the routine degradation care givers have to suffer would be increasingly reduced. This, itself, would be an important reduction in stress, allowing a greater capacity for the joy of childcare and family care more generally. And many families would find they were supported by help in their ongoing care responsibilities by their communities of care, again reducing the stress and increasing the joy.

The qualities of care that seem central to the kind of learning Ruddick, Hanlon, and others identify include: an intense concern for and interest in the person receiving the care (the child, in the case of parenting), a deep commitment to providing that care despite difficulties, participation in care day in and day out, encountering all the ups and downs of an intimate relationship of dependency, sustained participation over time so that one sees the rewards and challenges of change, care that involves hard work (physical and emotional) and that regularly, if intermittently, provides joy not just through the satisfaction of the child's thriving, but the mutual joy of play and sharing of delight. All of these dimensions could be part of the kind of care that we envision taking place in communities of care.

The key is that there has to be sustained commitment to care for particular people so that there can be a version of the features outlined above. One can imagine people organizing forms of short-term care in order to get to know different people, different families, to find compatibility. But in order for people to get the full benefits of learning from care, the relationship must be committed rather than casual. The people and families receiving care must be able to count on it (with the usual need to accommodate illness, travel, etc.) and the one providing the care must know that they should expect difficulty, frustration, even resentment as normal parts of the relationship, not a signal that it's time to move on. This is a high level of commitment, that will be harder for some than others. It seems possible, however, and not just in sharing in the care for children. Children provide special joys and challenges. Usually, they develop much faster than do adults, and so may be more rewarding to care for. But most of the practices of attunement and balancing of needs between care givers and receivers would be present in the context of care for adults, who are elderly, sick, or injured. Of course, in most cases, people who are sick or injured get better and no longer need the same care. So, the relationships forged in those contexts may not have the enduring quality of childcare or elder care. But they could be embedded in other sharing of care, so that the relationships can be sustained in more intermittent shared childcare or shopping, cooking, or other household care. The kinds of relationships, and thus the kinds of learning enabled in the communities of care will vary. But the objective would be to foster norms that everyone tries to be part of sustained, regular, committed relationships of care for significant parts of their life.

Another important dimension of the learning that Ruddick and Hanlon[58] discuss is the embodied nature of the learning and of the relationship with children. One of the pleasures of caring for children is that body contact is normal, often spontaneous, and enjoyed by both the children and those who care for them. Body contact between adults is much more complicated. (Of course, bodily contact can be abused with children as with adults.) But caring for the elderly, the sick, or injured often involves body contact, and to the extent that it is done well, it is part of the bonding and part of the learning about the role of touch in human well-being. The embodied dimension will be different from childcare, but much of the benefit and the learning is available in the adult context of community care.

We want to close this part of the discussion with an extrapolation of some of the points that Ruddick, Hanlon, and other care theorists raise. In learning to care well, one learns that dependency and inequalities of capacity, advantage, and power need not take the form of exploitation, domination, disrespect, or harm. In the context of parenting/familial care, the inequalities of power and capacity can simply be seen as a natural fact of life. However, when "mothers" take up the responsibilities Ruddick identifies of protective love, nurturance for growth, and social acceptance they commit themselves (imperfectly) to use their power to promote these ends, even when they are in short term conflict with their own goals or preferences. Sustained relationships of care in communities of care will (imperfectly) share a less demanding form of commitment from carers to use their position and abilities for the well-being of the other. The point here is that both those giving and receiving care will experience inequality of power and capacity that are the source of bonds of care, compassion, respect, and appreciation. The inequalities become the context for the vital capacity of coming to truly see another person, to try to understand their perspective, and so to know oneself better. In such a caring relationship, people see that bonds formed in inequality can become the basis for deeper knowledge—indeed as we will turn to next—a deeper capacity for knowledge and judgment, of self, others, of people, and practices in the world. It is, of course, an important form of judgment to distinguish between necessary (e.g., parent and child) forms of inequality and unnecessary (race, gender, and class-based) inequalities. But there are many and varying forms of inequality that are likely to continue to exist (e.g., student-teacher, employer-employee), and that can be constructive or destructive. One of the lessons of care is how to develop and sustain constructive relations in the context of inequalities.

Finally, as we turn away from these reflections based on familial care, we want to state the obvious: under the norms of PTfA one does not have to become a parent in order to reap the rewards of caring.

We now turn from some of the specifics of what and how one learns from care, to a more general claim about how the practice of care contributes to the capacities for knowledge and judgment—not just when used in the context of care, but in all contexts. In *Caring to Know,* Vrinda Dalmiya argues that contrary to the enlightenment tradition, in which the knower strives to be objective and thus not to *care* for the object of knowledge, "caring is not the 'other' of reason and . . . our lived experience of caring and being cared for can be useful resources for truth seeking. Care, then, lies at the heart of not only ethical relationships but also successful cognitive enquiry."[59] According to

Dalmiya, we learn to know well by learning to care well. (Later we will extrapolate that claim from knowledge to judgment.) For Dalmiya, the claim is closely linked to the point above about inequality:

> [W]ith the knower as an embodied self, knowing no longer remains a lonely, isolated activity. Truth-seeking takes place in and through relations of dependence that come along with embodiment.... This foregrounds the need for normative strategies to regulate these dependency relations so that knowledge does not become the exclusive property of some.
>
> caring necessarily functions in a realm of unevenness and dependencies . . . the challenge . . . lies in showing how care giving/ receiving lives with . . . inequalities without sliding into paternalism of the cared for or into domination of the care giver.[60]

One of the general points that Dalmiya makes is a challenge to conventional models of knowledge: good knowing is not necessarily about distance.[61] The knowledge one needs to care well is a knowledge of connection, not a form of objectivity for which affectless distance is seen as essential. Learning the value of this form of knowledge comes from the experience of realizing that to care well one must be able to know, to tune into, to connect with the one for whom one is caring. Otherwise, one runs the risk of projecting one's own needs and desires or imagining that one knows the needs and preferences of another and meeting them paternalistically. (For example, nondisabled people often project their own fears in regard to disability when they imagine what a person with disabilities wants.[62]) Rethinking how to know well comes from learning through years of doing, of not just seeing, but feeling the rewards of good care and its connections –as well as the distress of failure.

Dalmiya puts it this way:

> [W]e cannot attend to the needs of a person without understanding who she is and what she wants. Moreover, our desire to satisfy her needs also tells us something about the kind of persons we ourselves are. The practice of good care and the mode of knowing that is part of it are inseparable: . . . this cognitive moment of understanding

the other or oneself is not prior to or independent of the process of our addressing the needs of others. The practice of taking care of someone is *at the same time* a process of discerning what she wants and why we want to respond. Thus, we know people in and through caring for them.[63]

This capacity learned through care becomes important for the stance one takes to others, and to knowledge, more generally. She highlights the importance of recognizing the limits of one's own perspective and taking seriously the perspectives (including knowledge and approach to knowledge) of those who are marginalized.[64]

In ways similar to Ruddick and Hanlon she also emphasizes the importance of the embodied experience of giving and receiving care (as seen in the first quote above), and the ways that teaches a human reality of mutual dependence. Another similarity is her emphasis on humility: "[A] care based epistemology speaks of humility as necessary not only for successful mothering, but for good knowing in general". Her approach to humility, in turn, points to one of the most important parts of her argument for our purposes here, the focus on character traits as key to both good caring and good knowing: "the character trait of relational humility is found to be the root from which both good caring and good knowing flow."[65]

Dalmiya helps us see that in the practice of care one not only learns particular skills, but develops enduring character traits and dispositions. She argues that caring helps to develop a disposition to take the perspectives of others, and skill in doing so (for example avoiding the danger of projecting one's own ideas and fantasies onto others), as well as the habit of questioning one's own certainties. These dispositions, habits, and character traits are important for people's capacity to know well. We see this insight as extremely important for two reasons. First, the capacity to take the perspectives of others is also at the heart of the capacity for judgment.[66] Second, the idea that care creates dispositions helps people see why it is important that everyone should do sustained care over the course of their life. It is also part of why the first-hand experience of care is so important. It is not just that one gains particular kinds of knowledge from doing care (although one does), it is that a disposition is cultivated, and requires sustained cultivation. This is part of the reason why one cannot learn what needs to be learned by reading reports, novels, or talking to one's mother. *The disposition comes from practice; it cannot be acquired second hand.* The idea of sustained cultivation is also a reason why we do not embrace the idea of "care conscription" for a few years as an alternative to life-long engagement.

This, in turn, is part of why it is so important that *everyone* practices care giving. If only the least powerful people in society have the kind of sustained experience of care necessary to cultivate the skills and character traits of good knowers, then those in power are likely to look with disdain and incomprehension on the perspectives of those who bring their experience of care to bear on their judgments and demands. The argument for the special importance for those in high-level policy making positions to have this experience, is (in part) that those in power are particularly likely to insulate themselves from the perspectives of others unlike them, and thus to be ignorant of the range of perspectives necessary for good judgment. This holds true even if many of the particular practices and relationships that policy makers and bureaucratic service providers engage in are quite different from the more intimate relationships of carers. The disposition to take the perspective of others, and the skill in doing so is important to all forms of decision-making, from those of ordinary citizens to high-level policy makers. We emphasize the ignorance of policy makers because their power allows them to give wide effect to their dangerous igno-rance, and because under the current structure, people in power are particularly likely to have failed to acquire the skills and dispositions of carers.

A final insight that we can expect people to acquire from caring is greater awareness of the terrible demands currently faced by parents raising their children in impoverished neighborhoods. The authors we have discussed make claims for learning from care in full awareness of how hard the work of care can be under the best of circumstances. One can admire the vast resilience of parents (usually mothers) facing poverty, discrimination, and terrible working conditions. But one has to hope that if all the policy makers were spending many hours a week providing care, they would recognize the urgency of redressing these conditions.

We offer one more, quite different, source on what and how one learns from care: suggestions from neuroscience about the effects of care on the brain. Here we draw on an interesting synthesis by Riane Eisler and Daniel S. Levine. The core of the argument is that human beings have three different responses to stress: "the "flight or fight" response, the dissociative response, and the tend-and-befriend response, the latter of which involves caring and caregiving rather than aggressive or escapist behaviors." They also argue that the response which becomes habitual is shaped by experience, which, in turn, is shaped by social structures.[67]

They frame their argument (which contains a great deal of technical detail omitted here) with arguments about the centrality of care for human well-being and the relationship between the role of care and the social structures of different societies. We offer the following lengthy quotations which capture these links, as well as the link between hierarchy and the relation to care that we have also highlighted:

Receiving and giving caring are pleasurable experiences for all life forms. Sharing with others is among the most empowering and pleasurable experiences for humans. It enables us to remain open to seize opportunity, express creativity, and draw the best from others and ourselves. By contrast uncaring, violent, or abusive experiences are stressful for all life forms. For humans, powerlessness, poverty, events such as the loss of a job or a significant relationship, and other experiences that cause pain are also stress-inducing.[68]

One of us . . . argues that throughout human history there has been a conflict between those who would inhibit uncaring behavior and promote mutually respectful and caring relations, and those who would inhibit caring behavior in order to protect social hierarchies. Rigid hierarchies—whether man over woman, man over man, race over race, religion over religion, or nation over nation—require the inhibition of caring and empathy. In earlier times, these rankings were considered normal. And even today, beliefs, institutions, and behaviors required to maintain hierarchies of control are often seen as normal . . . In the neuroscience framework of this article, such beliefs, institutions, and behaviors are not viewed as normal. Rather, they are seen as the results of interactions among large numbers of people whose prefrontal-subcortical loops have been disrupted by the chronic stresses inherent in establishing and maintaining hierarchies of domination that are ultimately backed up by fear and force.[69]

Part of what makes their argument helpful here is their articulation of the social and individual costs and benefits of a system in which only some routinely participate in care:

> if men continue to be socialized to suppress their caring capacity, this deprives men of the mutual emotional support that aids in solving complex problems in both work and interpersonal settings. The resulting prevalence of fight-or-flight behaviors also has much to do with the high incidence of violent deaths and other injuries males have historically suffered at each other's hands, both in war and in street crime.[70]

In addition, they specifically endorse societal restructuring to engage everyone in care. Following the point above about the harmful biochemical balance now treated as normal, they urge the importance of a readjustment of that balance and argue that "the most efficient way of making that readjustment is changing the level of caring or noncaring behavior by both men and women that is supported by the social institutions of a society."[71]

Their argument is based on strong scientific evidence about brain chemistry and the kinds of things that affect it. Some of their extrapolations to the restructuring of society are, of course, speculative. Nevertheless, their arguments mesh in interesting and encouraging ways with the very different sources on learning from care discussed above.

Let us wrap up this section by highlighting three ways in which caring provides vitally useful learning, especially for men. The first point is that knowing how to care—to empathize, tune into the needs of others, comfort, nurture, etc.—is a fundamental prerequisite for *any* person to count as a good, decent human being. People who do not know how to care are severely impaired. They are low-level quotidian sociopaths. To the extent that men do not have long experience with caring, they are deprived of the immense cognitive benefits that come from it, in particular, the skills of empathy and emotional intelligence. Empathy—the ability to put yourself in another's shoes—is like any other skill, one that is learned. You get better at it the more you practice; and you get worse the less your practice. So it is no surprise that men tend to be significantly worse than women at empathizing.[72] By emotional intelligence we mean the skills of understanding one's emotions, being familiar with their roots and triggers, and being skillful in responding to them. Of particular importance here is the ability to restrain one's anger and work through one's emotions (of anger, but also shame, fear, disgust, and so on) so that they do not erupt into violence. The point is that in seeking to avoid care responsibilities on the grounds that they are stigmatizing or financially worthless, men are actually causing themselves to suffer a severe loss of these crucial cognitive skills (and basic human virtues). Indeed, the cognitive deficits that come from a life of avoiding care is a central way in which patriarchy harms and impairs men. Of course, the major harms of patriarchy are to women and nonbinary people, whereas the major beneficiaries are men; nevertheless, we must never forget that in certain respects men too are brutalized by the reigning gender norms.

Second, one of the biggest problems in the world today is the deep association between mainstream masculinity and violence. Virtually every violent extremist and terrorist, regardless of their religion or race or nationality or creed, is male.[73] Seventy-one percent of assaults in the United States are perpetrated by men, and 98 percent of the mass shootings.[74] Across the world, the homicide rate among young adults (15 to 29) is nearly six times higher for men than for women.[75] It is also well-known that the inability to regulate emotions is a major driver of violent crime.[76] The essential problem is that (hegemonic) masculinity *means* toughness, competitiveness, nonvulnerability, independence, denial of softness—all of which are antithetical to wanting to care and to identifying as a care giver. In other words, transforming men into people who strongly identify as *care givers*—who see themselves as carers, just as many women do today—would likely go a long way toward diminishing the daily terrors of male violence (rape, assault, domestic abuse, bar fights, gangs, terrorism, state-terrorism in the form of armies, war, and so on). Indeed, the evidence demonstrates that as men become more involved with care of their children, their involvement in violence (particularly violence against women) decreases.[77] For instance, according to Van der Gaag et al., "Greater involvement by men in daily care-work . . . can be linked with a reduction in rates of men's violence against women. . . . Research shows that men themselves benefit from greater engagement in caregiving, including improved physical, mental, and sexual health and reduced risk-taking. Fathers who are involved in the home and with their children say it's one of their most important sources of well-being and happiness."[78]

The final and related point is that although the care-work expected of men will bring some costs, it also brings profound benefits. In addition to the cognitive abilities and the reduction in violence, becoming adept carers offers men the irreplaceable joys of emotional intimacy and friendship. It is widely recognized that men, on average, have far less numerous, and far shallower relationships than women.[79] This is because women, as care givers, are trained from day one to be empathetic and have emotional intelligence, and so are frequently able to achieve deep levels of *emotional intimacy* with others, while men are not. Groups of female friends, for instance, frequently talk about their hopes and joys, their private ruminations and intimate fears; they can be vulnerable with each other in ways that build connection, whereas the norms of male friendship, joking about sports and work, maintain relationships at far more superficial levels. Most men have few deep friendships (or deep relationships of any kind) in large part because they have been so emotionally deskilled that they have no ability to communicate about anything real—about hopes, dreams, fears, vulnerabilities, insecurities. One poignant illustration of this is the fact that when a man's wife dies, he often dies very soon after; whereas this happens much less frequently the other way around because women typically have greater support networks and so suffer less isolation.[80] In other words, learning how to care can literally prolong men's lives. Beyond this, we know that one of the most common and poignant regrets that men express as they reach the end of their lives is the regret of not having had more friends.[81] Hence what PTfA offers is not simply equality with women, important as that is, but the deep emotional connection with others that is among the most beautiful and meaningful aspects of human existence.

VI. Learning to Care

Under the norms of PTfA, the most important form of learning to care would be the daily, routine provision of care everyone engages in. Children would begin learning how to share in care responsibilities in their families from the age of two or three. In communities of care, people would learn from those they care for, those who care for them, and the shared exchange of knowledge and experience with one another. However, this daily informal learning could also be supplemented with more formal training. Skills training and practical experience could be built into the school curriculum, from preschool through higher education. At a more abstract level, as the value of care becomes more widely recognized, we would expect the history of the structures of care to be an important field of both research and teaching. Similarly, as the role of care in work becomes more obvious, fields from sociology to labor law would grow to include more comprehensive investigations of the ways workplaces benefit from or are hostile to caring norms and practices.

In the transition, community workshops and pairing of paid careworkers with those newly acquiring the skills could help people—both care givers and receivers—gain confidence. Indeed, ongoing practices of skill sharing could become regular parts of communities of care. Also in the transition, we encourage particular attention to sharing skills with those who have been treated as care recipients, incapable of being care-providers. This would include many of the elderly, young children, and many disabled people. It will require the creative energy of families, communities of care, schools, and government agencies to rethink the ways almost everyone can enjoy the benefits of being a care provider.

Another suggestion we have heard would be to create a publicly funded "Care Corps," which people could perhaps join after high school or university to spend a year volunteering in areas with acute care needs, thereby learning additional skills as well as responding to pressing needs.

While various forms of formal training could be very helpful, we do not see any of them as an alternative to the norm that everyone engage (as they are able) in significant care giving throughout their lives.

In general, as the skills of care gain greater recognition and respect, those who have those skills will be sought after, and presumably many will be eager to engage in both informal and formal knowledge exchange.

VII. Care for the Earth, Learning from the Earth, and Learning from Care

While the norms of PTfA are directed at human-to-human relationships, it is our hope—and we think reasonable expectation—that the transformation brought about by everyone engaging in sustained care and the reduction in "time scarcity" will also yield a deeper sense that human life and well-being is shaped not just by interdependence with other humans, but with the earth. However, reflections during the COIVD-19 pandemic have led me (J. N.) to believe that hoping for this link is not enough.[82] Here, I can only scratch the surface of what it means to care for the earth, how one learns *from* that care, and how one *learns how to* care for the earth. But I see these issues as both pressing in the context of climate change and closely linked to our core project of revaluing care. So, I am offering the following thoughts on learning to and from care for the earth.

A. Why Care for the Earth?

I begin with a discussion of why care for the earth should be part of everyone's care obligation. Originally, I asked the question whether people who choose to spend time caring for the earth could treat that time as part of their "22 hours" of care. I have now arrived at the view that just as everyone should participate in human-to-human care, everyone should share in care for the earth. The reasons are similar. Care is urgently needed and the basic, life sustaining responsibility of care for the earth should be shared by all. But as with care for humans, equity (everyone doing one's fair share), is not the only consideration. People need to learn what can be learned from caring for the earth.

A full revaluation of care will only be possible if it includes care for the earth. At the most basic level, I believe the degradation of care is connected to the disregard for the earth and the care this living system requires.[83] Caring for the earth (as with human-to-human care) builds the relationship, the capacity to love the earth and to recognize the true mutuality of human-earth care.[84] Without that, I do not see how basic assumptions about the earth can be realigned, assumptions that have been the basis for the catastrophic harm humans are inflicting on the earth community. And if we cannot transform our relationship to the natural world from one based on extraction, exploitation, and the priority of human preferences, then we will destroy the habitability of our planet—and no other kind of reform, however important, will matter very much.

I see this transformation of the relationship to the earth as the heart of what care for the earth means. When I say earth, I mean to include the interdependent multitude of life forms and geological formations that together constitute the whole earth, which, in turn, is in relationship with the wider universe. The language of relationship, mutual responsibility, and mutual care is found in many writings by Indigenous authors. This language is echoed in many, but by no means all, non-Indigenous writers urging attention to a sustainable economy or to climate change. Some of these authors make arguments about the need to use the resources of the earth wisely so that they will last and be able to sustain human beings for a long time to come. This advocacy for prudent resource management (while important) seems quite different from a call to attend to our relationship with the earth and the mutual care and responsibility entailed in that relationship.

To seriously respond to climate change, mass extinctions, depletion of ground water, poisoning of rivers (among other forms of harm to the planet) will take a vast change in people's affect, philosophy of life, core values, and spirituality,[85] as well as conceptions of the economy and appropriate forms of collective decision-making and distribution of power (politics). I do not think that this shift can be accomplished simply by encouraging prudent resource management. The sorts of cost-benefit analyses that might accompany decisions about what counts as prudent, how to weigh short and long-term benefits, may make sense if the earth is viewed as a resource to be managed and divided up among humans according to current metrics of economy and politics. But such calculus will not make sense if the earth is seen as a living entity in which humans are one among others who live in relations of interdependence with each other—all of whom deserve respect and require care.

The ancient and world-wide language of "Mother Earth" captures a sense of the earth as nurturer, who gives us life and sustains us, and to whom not just respect, but love and responsive care is called for.[86] Human beings need to come to see themselves in an entirely different relation to the earth and the other beings we share it with. I do not see how we can fully understand the nature of the harm we are engaged in if the calculus is entirely managerial and human centric, even if it were a better, more far-seeing kind of calculus than what seems to be prevailing at the moment. We should make judgments about how to care for the earth the way we would for a beloved parent in urgent need of complex care, not with the cost-benefit analysis that resource management is likely to yield. Trade-offs that might seem acceptable in a cost-benefit analysis (economic growth vs. species extinction) would become unimaginable in the context of care for a loved one. (Of course, I say all this knowing there can still be difficult choices and that, collectively, most rich countries have chosen to underfund care for the elderly to an alarming extent that has become obvious during the COVID-19 crisis. It turns out we are quite capable of making cost-benefit choices for the care of our elderly in ways that are every bit as callous and destructive as our treatment of the planet. The same degradation of care received, and care required is at stake.)

What is needed for the human relation to the earth is, thus, a stance of care, not just resource management. Of course, as we have argued throughout, care requires skill, knowledge, perception, receptivity, and wisdom. One cannot provide good care if one is unable to perceive the needs, preferences, and desires of the one cared for. The carer needs to take the perspective of the cared for, and then needs to acquire and use all the relevant skill and knowledge and use it wisely on behalf of the cared for. Just what this means in the context of caring for the earth is not at all simple. But to recognize that complexity and the limitation of the understanding many of us have, does not mean we cannot identify obvious harms, and begin to recognize that something more than harm reduction is called for. We need, collectively, to envision what "right relations" with the earth community would look like.

Of course, even the resource management approach can recognize harms. But it does not seem to be able to generate the motivation for change that is required. Attending to that motivation and to the scope and content of change necessary to reverse current practices leads me to the language of care for the earth and the need for so many to learn about it by doing it.

Reading authors like Thomas Berry[87] and Joanna Macy[88] helps in understanding the intellectual and spiritual frameworks that have shaped and justified the destructive practices humans are engaged in. These authors have been raising their clarion calls for decades and are now joined by thousands of scientists making pressing and per-suasive sound resource management arguments. It doesn't seem to be working. In part, I think people need to move from an awareness of the harm, to the "intimacy with the earth" Berry invoked, or the "wild love of world" associated with Macy. Most people are too disconnected from the earth to have actual experience of either being nurtured by the earth or being capable of providing care in return. I think small, regular, sustained practices of active care could help shift this, together with practices of patient, attentive, responsive observation. It may be that learning about harm is not sufficient when it is not supported by experiencing mutual human–earth care.

I would venture to say that most Westerners without connections to Indigenous traditions would find the idea of actively caring for the earth (as opposed to sound resource management) at least unfamiliar, and perhaps silly, and certainly not an obligation. Many people in the urban centers of rich countries do not feel a connection to the earth. They do not experience themselves as the recipients of earth's care for them and they do not feel the caring about—in the sense of an affective connection—that would lead them to be caring, as opposed to being more prudent in their use of Earth's resources. An insight from Robin Wall Kimmerer helps explain how it is that even though everyone "knows" that their food comes from the earth and her creatures, they do not experience that food as a gift from the earth. They do not expe-rience the food as a form of loving care from the earth, care that should inspire reciprocity.

Of course, much of what fills our mouths is taken forcibly from the earth. That form of taking does no honor to the farmer, to the plants, or to the disappearing soil. It's hard to recognize food that is mummified in plastic, bought and sold, as a gift anymore. Everybody knows you can't buy love. In a garden, food arises from partnership. If I don't pick rocks and pull weeds, I'm not fulfilling my end of the bargain. I can do these things with my handy opposable thumb and capacity to use tools, to shovel manure. But I can no more create a tomato or embroider a trellis in beans than I can turn lead into gold. That is the plants' responsibility and their gift: animating the inanimate. Now there is a gift.[89]

B. What to Learn and How to Learn

To recognize the *importance* of care for the earth does not explain *what* one needs to learn in order to care for the earth, *how* to learn what one needs to know, or how one *learns from* providing care to the earth (the answers to each are interconnected). I tried to find answers to these questions by reading Indigenous writers,[90] educators interested in teaching children about the natural world,[91] and people interested in the differences and overlaps between mainstream science and Indigenous approaches to nature.[92] What I kept finding was stories of paying close, attentive, receptive attention to whatever part of the earth community one was engaged with[93]. Sometimes, this attention was part of direct care, as in gardening, but sometimes it was not. So, I have tried to integrate receptive attention more fully into my understanding of care.

Let us begin with what (most) people need to learn. First, they need to unlearn a human centric vision of the earth. They need to unlearn a confident, unquestioned sense of the superiority of human beings that yields ignorance and disinterest in the capacities for responsiveness of other living beings. They need a visceral sense of interdependence; they need to recognize (and, ideally, marvel at) the intricacies of different forms of life by engaging with them close up.[94] As I noted above, these are profound transformations connected to core ideas about life, identity, success, and responsibility, as well as property and the economy. But I see the transformation as possible. Ideally, starting in childhood, people would have the experience of being cared for by the earth, or receiving gifts from the earth—whether food, play, joy, inspiration, or the excitement of curiosity followed by knowledge. And then they need to learn how to care for the earth in return, whether by feeding depleted soil in community gardens, or cleaning up parks or waterways, or planting native plants to encourage pollinators, or raising monarch butterflies, or keeping bees in their backyards. (I have chosen examples available to urban dwellers.) Such forms of experiential care do not, of course, replace the need for working for policy changes to mitigate global warming. But I see them as a necessary complement, even if they seem (like most forms of care) time intensive with small scale impact. They are ways of caring, attending, and learning from care.

I have spent time looking for resources that will articulate for me *how* as well as what people learn from being in nature and caring for nature. There is an interesting literature about the importance of nature for children's well-being as well as for their capacity to understand the need to protect and care for nature. So far, I have found that detailed accounts of the process of the learning are scarce. There is also a moving and interesting literature about the importance of land-based education for Indigenous children as well as for non-Indigenous adults who want to understand Indigenous law.[95] Both call for lots of embodied experience, and neither body of literature tries to condense that experience into a nice summary I could quote. I think this is because neither the process of experiential learning nor what is learned is easily condensed.[96]

There seems to be a wide consensus that being in nature is important for human well-being and that in Westernized countries urbanized populations get less and less of that. And our children get much less than their parents' generation had. Many commentators connect the physical, emotional, and spiritual harms of the loss of connection with nature to the inability to know how to be responsible in relation to nature. (There is an interesting connection here to my discussion of knowledge of harm vs. experience of mutual care. Louv comments that children today know a lot about acid rain, but very little about the joys of playing in wilderness.[97]) What interests me most in the literature is often implicit: it takes active, embodied experience of connecting to nature to go beyond abstract knowledge of our material dependence, to feeling ourselves as receiving the gifts, the care of nature and wanting to learn how to care in return. It is the difference, as I suggested above, between being a prudent manager of an important resource, and being in a loving reciprocal relationship.

Kimmerer offers a concrete example of how to learn and its relation to care:

> People often ask me what one thing I would recommend to restore relationship between land and people. My answer is almost always, "Plant a garden." It's good for the health of the earth and it's good for the health of people. A garden is a nursery for nurturing connection, the soil for cultivation of practical reverence. And its power goes far beyond the garden gate—once you develop a relationship with a little patch of earth, it becomes a seed itself. Something essential happens in a vegetable garden. It's a place where if you can't say "I love you" out loud, you can say it in seeds. And the land will reciprocate, in beans.[98]

The language of love appears regularly in the various sources I have looked at.[99] It is what often happens when people become connected to the earth through care. There is a cycle of learning. People take up gardening and learn about what the soil needs, what the plants like, what makes them thrive, not just survive. People become more curious, more attentive to the amazing distinctiveness of the life they are carefully tending. In the process, they care more and more, until it feels like love. And they are rewarded with tomatoes, or beans, or visits from butterflies, or the beauty of flowers. The care feels reciprocal. People want to learn more.

It is this mutuality that makes care for the earth fit so clearly into the definition of care we offered in the beginning—even if the mutual human–earth relationship is not self-evident to those who have not experienced it. Coming to know that relationship is at the very heart of what needs to be learned. Even with human-to-human care there is a question about how to get the positive cycle started. How will people be persuaded that taking on (what will initially look like the burdens of) care will bring them joy, love, and knowledge that will help them live better (as in the capacity to take the perspective of others)? This is where the gentle pressure of norms, supported by friends, family, and colleagues can help. As there is a growing consensus that everyone should provide care, and that care for the earth is included, more and more people will respond to that call, and to the gentle disapprobation when they fail to.

Of course, there can be practical tensions between time spent in human-to-human care and in care for the earth, as well as the urgent need for advocacy. (We address the relation between care and activism in section IX.) There will always be difficult judgments about balance, especially in a time of climate crisis.

I think these judgments should be made in the context of awareness about the deep connections between these forms of care. I have come to see care for the earth as literally and symbolically foundational. We are all embodied and embedded in a complex ecology most of us barely understand, and *the well-being and moral legitimacy of human relational structures depends on a sustainable, respectful relationship with the rest of the natural world.*

But I think the reverse is also true: if people aim to bring respectful care to nature without attending to how daily care for people gets done, then that effort at transformation is likely to be based on abstractions, and is unlikely to be either equitable or sustainable. People with good ideas have done a lot of harm when they are disconnected from care. Having everyone engaged in and learning from the daily practices of care (human and more than human) is a foundation for transforming all our relationships.[100]

Finally, in closing this section that owes so much to Indigenous writers, I want to just note a vital issue that is beyond the scope of this book. It is obvious that among the most important resources for rethinking (Western/Northern/urban/wealthy) human relationship to the earth are the legal, cultural, and spiritual traditions of Indigenous peoples.[101] It should be equally obvious that settlers cannot imagine that we can "take" and absorb the knowledge of the deep connection between the land and Indigenous peoples without acting to redress the massive wrongs of dispossession of their land. For settler societies like the United States, Canada, Australia, and New Zealand, creating a just and caring relationship with the earth and with each other will have to entail a serious redress of these wrongs.

VIII. Why Does Everyone Have to Care?

We have argued so far that sustained, regular experience of direct care offers the opportunity to learn things vital to living well as individuals and communities. The knowledge about human care ranges from important particulars such as the way it often matters *who* provides care, the complexities of control, the way care has its own rhythms, to the broader knowledge that material, mundane care is an essential component of the experience of both being cared for and providing care. One learns about the demands of care, how hard it can be, physically and emotionally, and one learns the satisfactions of providing for the needs and desires of others.[102] The experience of care invites a deep reevaluation of care and the way it has been embedded in false hierarchies of necessity and freedom. Because providing good care requires the capacity to take the perspective of others, in the experience of care one learns a skill that is essential for exercising judgment and, as Vrinda Dalmiya[103] argues, for knowledge itself. Like care for humans, care for the earth community builds relationships—with animals, with plants, with the earth itself—and teaches the link between care and relationship. The experience of the connections of care similarly disrupts hierarchies of value, and teaches the creative dimension of repetitive, time consuming, attentive care. Care for the earth brings vital knowledge about the nature of interdependence in our shared world, as well as skills in acquiring further knowledge.

Following these arguments, it is easy to see why it is important that people in power, whose decisions influence the lives of many, are not ignorant of the knowledge and lacking the skills and dispositions that come with the sustained practice of care. There remain, however, some important questions, all of which revolve around our claim that *everyone* has to participate in care. The following section turns to these questions.

IX. Experiential Learning

We begin with a brief reminder of the familiar idea of experiential learning, in part because it follows well from the previous discussion of how people learn from care, and in part because it is a good way of addressing the question of why we claim everyone needs to learn from care by doing it. We also start by thinking about human-to-human care.

Of course, common examples of experiential learning are not precise analogies to the nature of our claim about care. People might be willing to accept that in order to learn to become good carers they have to practice care, just like they have to practice the violin, or law, in order to learn to be a good violinist or lawyer. The issue for PTfA is that many may not *want* to become carers because they think that the "work" they are doing is more important, more rewarding, more suited to their talents, or better recognized as valuable. The claim they are resisting is that they *should* become carers because they need to learn things that can only be learned by caring. So, our claim is both that everybody needs to learn these things and that the best (perhaps the only) way to learn them is to engage in a sustained practice of care. Part of what will become clear is that the idea that everyone needs to know what one learns from care is not primarily about individual choice of knowledge acquisition; it is about the importance of a kind of collective knowledge (and ongoing practice) of the value of care for individual and societal well-being. Just as democracies cannot thrive without some widespread understanding of the values of equality, freedom, and free speech (which are, notionally, taught in schools as well as families and communities), well-functioning societies need a widespread understanding of the value of care.[104] The experiential learning discussion is directed at the part of our claim that says one must learn by doing.

People often seem dubious about our strong claims that everyone needs to do care in order to learn what one needs to know. This doubt arises despite the fact that there are many forms of learning in which direct experience is recognized as a requirement. No one thinks one can learn to become a surgeon, a violinist, a dentist, or an accomplished tennis player without directly practicing the craft in question. Books, observation, and explanation can all assist, but they cannot replace direct experience. In addition, practitioners are generally thought to gain in skill over time and with consistent practice. Most patients do not want their heart surgery performed by a doctor who only does heart surgery occasionally. In these contexts, no one is surprised that to learn what one needs to know (knowledge, skills, honing of talent, development of dispositions), to be good at these practices, one needs to do them in a sustained way, consistently over time. The examples that come most easily to mind entail physical skills, but so does a great deal of care. In addition, the physical skills are intertwined with capacities for observation, for quick, intuitive responses, for good judgment, and for attention to context. As much of the discussion above points to, the physical and emotional dimensions of care are also closely intertwined, as they are also with the cognitive capacities for reflection, attunement, and self-awareness. The need to practice care to know how to do it well and to learn its many lessons should not be a surprise.

While the embodied dimension of care is important, it is also worth noting that it is widely recognized that the qualification for other professions, like being a lawyer or a teacher, cannot simply be learned from books and lectures. Practice is essential. (Oddly, and to the detriment of their students, university professors often do not receive any training in teaching.)

We think part of the resistance to the idea that everyone needs to know what can (only) be learned from care is based on the tenacious idea that care is low skilled. After all, that is the widespread justification for why it is low paid, or not paid at all. Anyone can do it.[105] In short, there just isn't that much to learn. It is true that no formal training is required to become a biological parent. And most first-time parents who have not grown up in extended families that involved them in childcare feel terrified before the birth of their first child. And most of them (disproportionately women) manage to learn to care reasonably well. But none of that constitutes a denial of the arguments above about what caring well entails and what one can learn from it. Almost everyone who studies care feels called upon to note that the claim that it is unskilled labor is false. It is a convenient myth that serves to support unjust and unwise practices that ensure that only some practice and thus learn from care. It is, of course, unjust that the privileged get the care they need at low cost. But our point here is that there is a cost, both to those in power who are cut off from the connections and the knowledge that comes with providing care, and to society at large that has to live with decision-makers ignorant about care and its diverse skills, knowledge, and dispositions.

It is worth noting that it is true that (virtually) anyone can do it, otherwise it would not make sense to argue that everyone should do it. Anyone can provide care because the range of forms of care and kinds of skills are wide enough that anyone willing to learn can learn. This doesn't mean that there is not also a range of talents and aptitudes which will make some people more highly gifted at care than others. Different people will excel at different dimensions of what one learns from care as well as at the practice of care itself. This diversity is consistent with the claim that everyone should practice care because everyone needs to learn what care teaches.

There is also substantive knowledge one gains from practicing care, knowledge that is important for policy makers and for the ordinary citizens who elect public policy makers. People engaged in routine care, and people who know lots of other people engaged in a range of care—for children, for the elderly, for people with injuries, illness, and disabilities—learn about the kinds of policies that support care or make it more difficult than it needs to be. They learn, for example, that some areas of a city like Toronto are day care deserts,[106] requiring anyone living there to spend long hours commuting to day care. They learn that well-functioning public transit makes a huge difference to how many hours must be devoted to getting to and from work and childcare, and thus to family well-being. They learn about whether there are adequate supports—both financial and in terms of respite care—for family members caring for people with very high care needs. They learn about the importance of flexibility from employers when employees have sudden changes in care responsibilities. They learn how physically demanding some forms of care are, and what kinds of supports (both mechanical and human) could ease those demands. They can learn about the different preferences the elderly and their families have about living arrangements, and how public support could help. They can learn about the importance of imagination in creating housing for people with a range of care needs.[107] In short, there is a very wide range of policy that affects whether people can provide care without great personal and financial costs. People who have this knowledge will be able to make better informed choices about where public resources should go and what kinds of government incentives or requirements can make workplaces more accommodating to people providing care.

If everyone needs to care because everyone needs the knowledge that caring brings, there is an obvious question about whether the people who care *will* acquire the knowledge they could acquire. Nothing that Ruddick, Hanlon, or Dalmiya say suggests that the learning is guaranteed or automatic. What each of their arguments relies on is that if one wants to care well, one has to learn the skills, develop the dispositions, and integrate the knowledge that is available from the practice of care. Thus, the motivation is that it matters to the carer to be able to care well. Even with that motivation, poverty, ill health (mental or physical), addiction, exhaustion, neighborhood violence, or living in a war zone or refugee camp can seriously impair one's capacity to learn even if one cares desperately about providing good care for a loved one.

These are important cautions. In the context of PTfA, it means that the new norms should include information and encouragement about the need to learn. Many years ago, a colleague told one of us (J. N.) that he had discovered the pleasures of audiobooks when looking after his two-year-old. There is, he said, a lot of "dead time" looking after a toddler. I was shocked, though I did not say so. I have come to see this as a story of someone who did not know that he needed to learn to care, to engage, to attend in order to get the pleasure of connection with his child. I am sure that the child was physically safe; he was not being negligent. But he was bored because he was not connecting and learning from caring engagement. As people who never expected to spend much time caring start to take up the practice, they will need to learn that neither good care nor learning from care is automatic. Many will need encouragement and a collective recognition that learning will, inevitably, come more easily to some than others.[108] If those used to success, and to being the recipient of care they often do not even notice, find that learning to care does not come easily, they may be tempted to abandon it as not worth their time. There needs to be collective support in place: recognizing the difficulties some may have is as important as recognizing the importance of the learning itself. There will be a learning curve for everyone, but it will vary from person to person—as with all forms of learning. A norm of compassion is important.

X. Potential Harm

Perhaps more disturbingly, in implementing the new norms people need to recognize that some people will fail to learn to care well and fail to reap the benefits of learning from care. There are always people who do not comply with norms. Virtually every relationship in which one can help another is also a relationship in which one can harm the other. This is true of parents, foster parents, bureaucrats, teachers, doctors, psychotherapists, and meditation teachers. Everyone will have heard some story of lasting harm done by people in positions of power and trust. Taking on the role of a care giver to someone whose need renders them dependent on the help of the carer is inevitably a position of relative power and trust (even if there are other, countervailing relations of power between the two people, such as class and gender). For example, Ruth Fletcher says,

> Care practices can be significant sites of harm, not only when care goes spectacularly wrong, but also through mundane experiences of othering. The asymmetry of care . . . may be expressed by treating people as if they cannot look after themselves, as if they are victims in need of rescue, or trouble waiting to happen.[109]

Recognizing the potential for harm in the inevitable asymmetries of care has to be part of the development of new norms about reasonable expectations and courtesies between care givers and receivers, whether paid or unpaid. But in thinking about the potential pitfalls of PTfA, it is also important to remember the many widespread harms that are now routine parts of unsupported care. Elizabeth Peel studied people caring for parents with dementia. She concluded that "the overarching message from this literature has been summarized as 'care giving often results in chronic stress, which compromises care givers physical and psychological health. Depression is one of the common negative effects of caregiving.'" She also notes that these care givers suffer strains in relationships with partners and that friendships can be lost due to lack of time. She quotes one person as saying, "no, I would say there's no pleasure in it whatsoever. No, no."[110]

In short, the learned benefits of care cannot be guaranteed and the potential for harm must always play a role in the development of the norms and their implementation. Our conclusion, of course, is that these concerns are not arguments against the widespread, mutually beneficial relations of care that PTfA envisages. Nevertheless, we often hear the question: do norms *requiring* everyone to participate in care increase the likelihood of people failing to learn to care well and thus also failing to learn the lessons caring well is said to teach? Put most bluntly, if people only care because they feel they have to, will they do it badly—thus endangering others and learning little?

XI. Norms That Require Care from All

If one restates the question above in more general terms it would sound like this: will care that comes from complying with norms be bad care (with bad learning)? Or perhaps, what is really meant is, if people do not accept the norms, but feel compelled by social pressure to comply, will they resist and provide care badly? Those are quite different questions.

The answer to the broad question about care that is generated by norms cannot be that it is doomed to be bad care. Virtually all the care provided around the world is driven by norms that women should care. This is so even if one also believes that women have some instinctual drive to care. If instinct alone were sufficient, societies would not need socially sanctioned norms that attach care to being a true, proper, or responsible woman. Virtually all societies have such norms. In contemporary societies, it is impossible to determine how much women's willingness and desire to care arise from the norms surrounding them since birth and how much is something inherent in "female nature," whatever that means. Whatever the (at present) irretrievable answer turned out to be, one can still recognize the harms of the existing norm structure and assess the potential benefits of a change in the direction of equality, thriving families and communities, and good governance.

One can, of course, also recognize that the sort of transformation in norms we are calling for is a huge social experiment. But there are several things one needs to be conscious of in assessing its potential. First, we are already in the midst of a huge social experiment of bringing large numbers of women away from the home into the paid workforce without making substantial changes in either the norms of the workplace or of care in the home. We see this as a decisively failed experiment, requiring urgent redress. And, of course, we reject the idea of returning to the "good old days" of gender and class inequality where poor women did both paid work and unpaid care, and of a long-standing care/policy divide (where most of the policy makers were not only men ignorant of care, but white, well-off men).

We also recognize that the new norms call for deep changes not only in people's habits and patterns of life (itself not trivial) but in identity. And while the changes would take place, as just noted, in the context of existing change (women becoming paid workers as well as unpaid carers), norms that call on men to become unpaid carers as well as "workers" or "providers" is a deep change in a long-standing and very widespread set of norms. When norms change, those comfortable with the old system are likely to experience the new norms as demanding, constraining, even coercive. We see some of the challenges to norms requiring care and limiting work, including the question whether the result would be bad care, as versions of this response to change. (This is in addition to the understandable anxiety of people with disabilities about whether these new practices of care would replicate some of the existing harms of degradation and disregard.)

We think it is important to put these concerns about the demands of the new norms in the context of the very serious constraints, indeed coercion, that mark the existing structures of care.

Contemporary norms tell us that women should have children and then take up the primary responsibility for caring for them. There are still social sanctions for women who refuse to comply with these norms. (Some of these women may be among those who resist the idea of more norms demanding care from them.) There are also strong norms that women should provide care for sick, injured, disabled, or elderly family members. For example, because no one else is going to do it and there is inadequate public support, many women feel driven to provide care for elderly parents even at the cost of reducing their income and jeopardizing relations with spouses and friends. Particularly tragically, their reduction in income and thus pension will, in turn, often make these women dependent on others for care in their old age.[111] This care may or may not be forthcoming.

In addition to thousands of women who feel they have no alternative (that is, no decent choice) but to provide unpaid care for sick, disabled, or elderly relatives, there is the powerful economic coercion at work in the organization of paid care: it relies heavily on the discrimination that makes low paid care the only employment opportunity for many from disadvantaged groups. Indeed, we think it makes sense to say that coercion is central to the current organization of care.[112]

Part of our objective is to dismantle these unjust coercive structures. It is, however, worth noting that even though they produce pain and hardship and thwarted opportunity, they do not always produce bad care. And not everyone who suffers pain and hardship regrets having provided the care.

We think it is important to distinguish this kind of coercion from the constraints we envision from the new norms of PTfA. If someone opts out of their care responsibilities, they will suffer some social disapproval, but no one close to them will go without the care they need. The combination of communities of care and improved publicly funded care would ensure decent care. And no one will be reduced to poverty and hunger if they resist either the care or the work norms.

Nevertheless, the whole premise of our argument is that social norms are powerful. Bad ones cause serious harm, and all effective norms shape beliefs and behavior. As we have noted, the (destructive) gendered norms of care currently generate millions of hours of unpaid care from women all over the world. (Of course, sometimes these norms are enforced by violence, exclusion, or other sanctions that amount to coercion beyond the social influence of norms.) Some women are happy providing that care, some not, but to say it is simply a choice would be an implausible denial of the power of social norms. If the norms of PTfA were adopted, we would expect millions of people to make choices about work and care that are shaped by the new norms.

In theory, one could perhaps aim to eliminate all social norms with respect to care and work, leaving it entirely up to individual preference and choice (which after several generations could, *in principle*, be freed from the hierarchies embedded in historic norms). But since care from infancy to old age is a human requirement, every society has had norms about how to meet that requirement. Similarly, every society needs to have food, shelter, and other material needs met by "productive" labor, and that too has always been organized by social norms. In the modern world, property laws enforce the norm that if you don't work you don't eat (mitigated by the welfare state). Neither work nor care is organized around simple individual preference. It is hard to imagine a society without any norms and expectations about how members should contribute to care and to producing both material and nonmaterial goods (e.g., education, art, law) of society.

If there are to be social norms governing the organization of care and work (remembering that the organization of one will inevitably affect the other), these norms will shape behavior in ways that are not captured by the idea of individual choice—as is the case with all basic forms of social values and organization. One might say that individual choices always take place in the context of shared (even if contested) social norms. The objective should be to foster democratic deliberation around norms and to advocate norms that would be just, beneficial, and respectful of individual freedom. We think that some of the worst forms of coercion that shape existing structures of care would be removed with PTfA, and, overall, the scope of people's freedom would be increased. As we will discuss in much detail later on, robust economic security and guarantees of good part-time jobs would remove much of the coercion around work.

With these reminders about the inevitable influence of norms and the coercion in the existing structure of care, let us return to the question whether resistance to the new norms might result in bad care and failure to learn. We see resistance arising in two contexts: (1) People (probably disproportionately men) who would feel socially pressured to spend more time caring for family (and less time working) than they might initially choose to; and (2) People feeling obliged to join communities of care when their obligations to immediate family and friends have receded—and thus under current norms they would have few care responsibilities.

Let us begin with the family context (remembering that we envision a wide variety of family forms). For Ruddick, mothers' motivation to learn comes from a desire to care well for children they love. And this is in contexts in which not every mother has chosen the circumstances of her care or the amount of time she has to devote to it. Ruddick treats frustration, anger, and resentment as common companions to care. Recent data suggests that many fathers say they would prefer to have more time with their children. Is there reason to believe that, in the transition, the adjustment to less paid work (*sometimes* along with less power, recognition, fulfillment) and more care would prevent men from deepening their attachment to their children and learning the skills of attunement, engagement, receptivity and, perspective-taking which would allow them to learn to care well (and further hone those skills which are of great value in many contexts)? The same question could be asked of women who currently "choose" to spend 70 hours a week at paid work. In the long run, there will probably always be people who feel a strong pull toward paid work, even find it more satisfying than care. Should we expect that a social norm of "22 hours" a week of care will be so burdensome that their resistance or resentment will make them fail to learn to be good carers and thus to acquire the skills, knowledge, and dispositions of good carers? Perhaps their preference for work will mean they are not the best carers, but is there reason to believe that they will not be good enough—as most mothers are even in very difficult circumstances? We think that the presence of social coercion to spend at least "22 hours" a week providing unpaid care will not be likely to generate bad care. Indeed, we think that the combined effects of PTfA—reduced paid work, massive improvements in the public infrastructures of care, increased support from communities of care, more equal division of care in the household, and increased recognition of the value of care—will significantly improve the quality of care most recipients get as well increasing the joy that care givers experience.

The context of communities of care raises somewhat different questions. We do not expect the bonds that form within these communities to be quite as deep or intense as in families (at least in most instances). But we know that friends, extended family members, and paid care givers form powerful connections when caring for children and for the elderly, sometimes seeing them through to their death. Their sense of a powerful, positive bond is part of their learned capacity to provide care. People act as "aunties" (biological or chosen) to troubled teenagers and form lasting, satisfying bonds on the basis of the care—whether mentoring, sheltering, or feeding them. Often people choose to provide care to those they are already connected to, but it is also frequently the case that people find themselves in a position to provide care when it is needed, and they step up to the responsibility— and find that bonds form.

The point here is that there are many complex forms of "chosenness" in relationships of care. Some are more deliberate, some more circumstantial. Under the norms of PTfA, people will have chosen their communities of care, and will have some significant choice about exactly how to carry out their responsibilities within those communities. Of course, (as with norms generally) they will not have exactly chosen the broad social norm of responsibility to spend a chunk (at least "22 hours") of each week devoted to providing care for others. They will, however, participate within their communities in discussing how to implement the norms, so they will actually have more direct participation in how the norms will affect them than is usually the case with powerful social norms. Norms are by their nature collective, and while we are particularly interested in rendering them subject to democratic deliberation, it is in their nature to exercise a kind of collective force or pressure. Some people are more conscious than others about the extent to which their behavior is governed by collective norms (many people are still quite oblivious to the ways gender norms shape their preferences, choices, and actions). Some may chafe under the demands that they participate in care, or even the demands of community conversation about norms, and refuse to join a community of care. The main consequence would be a degree of isolation and some (one hopes, compassionate) disapproval. Some may find other ways of contributing care—keeping it within family, friends, or colleagues in ways distinct from the (sustained, reciprocal, and diverse) relations we envision in the communities of care. Perhaps these alternate forms of contribution will be more sporadic, more under the control of the shifting preferences of the carer. These could still provide important (though different) bonds and learning. They would generate less isolation and little disapproval if some significant amount of care was provided. Maybe over time, such choices would generate other models of complying with the norm of providing care in ways that some would experience as providing greater freedom. If these models provided less reciprocity, they would not do as much to contribute to the experience of everyone being both a care provider and receiver, and thus perhaps run a greater risk of perpetuating the asymmetries of care.

For the purposes of the discussion here, we think that there would be sufficient bonding in communities of care to generate good (enough) care and thus good (enough) learning. Those so hostile to joining communities as to risk providing bad care could, as noted above, find alternative ways of contributing. In the most extreme cases, the fact that only social (not legal) coercion is at work, should allow people to opt out completely, thus protecting the vulnerable from bad care by those most fiercely resistant to the norms. Another, second best, option would be for some members of communities to opt consistently for the least intimate forms of care—grocery shopping, cleaning, shoveling snow. (We will return to the limitations of this option shortly.)

This last option raises the question of the potential exclusion of those who find it very difficult to form relationships, including the relationships that are the foundation and the reward of caring. Finding ways to include everyone would be a reason for having the second-best option of mostly nonintimate care. Of course, every community of care could try to work out other alternatives while trying to welcome everyone who is (even hesitantly) interested in joining.

XII. Why "22 Hours"?

There remains the question of why the choice of "22 hours" from everyone. This recommended minimum is in part a calculation built on estimates of hours of care needed in a family with two adults and two children.[113] If there are two adults to share the care roughly equally, they will each need to do at least 22 hours a week.[114] The same generally holds true for other family and care arrangements.[115] A further time estimate would look something like this:

(24 hours x 7 days = 168 total hours in a week)

56 hours sleep
30 hours work
22 hours care
7 hours self-care
3 hours community work
32 hours leisure

=

150 hours

That list accounts for 150 hours out of a total 168 hours in a week. So, on this model there are 18 hours to account for individual variation in need. For example, some people need more than eight hours of sleep, and people with various kinds of health problems will need more hours of self-care (including time-consuming medical appointments), and so on. One might also see these extra hours as available for leisure, free from any norms or expectations (other than the most general ones of not causing harm).

Perhaps most importantly, "22 hours" is an amount that is substantial enough to (1) gain the experiential knowledge of care necessary for participation in policy deliberation; (2) sustain the bonds of relationship necessary for a fulfilling life; and (3) contribute to a fair distribution of the care needs in their society.

We think it is probably a low estimate for learning from care and for the corresponding deep bonding between care givers and receivers. We think an ideal would be equal amount of paid work and unpaid care, about 25 hours per week of each. The overlap of care and shared leisure time might often bring the hours of care higher.

In any case, we see the proposed hours as a necessary guideline, but a guideline only. It is meant to give everyone a sense that a serious, ongoing commitment is necessary if the goals of PTfA are to be achieved. It is not intended to foster obsessive time accounting, as if the whole population became like lawyers tracking billable hours.[116] But particularly in the transition, it is useful for people to have guidelines in order to check if their intuitive sense of engaging in a serious ongoing commitment is actually accurate. (We know that people's estimates of the time they spend on care are not entirely reliable. Time use studies often show significant differences between spouses' assessments of the hours each spends.)

In short, everyone needs to care in order to achieve the goals of PTfA. In this section, we have focused on those who are providing care. But, of course, among the goals is that everyone who needs care receives good care and that the true value of care is widely recognized. If one's only concern were good quality care for those who need it, one could, in principle, focus on advocating a great deal of public support for well-paid care for all those who need it—and for the increasing number of elderly people who are going to need it in the near future. In many of the rich countries today, this is extremely unlikely to be achieved. Indeed, it seems impossible given the widespread degradation of care and ignorance about its demands, rewards, or significance to well-being. Thus, the revaluation of care seems a requirement for adequate public support. If good arguments and good evidence alone could accomplish this revaluation, it would have been accomplished by now. A norm of everyone providing substantial care is crucial for the revaluation of care and for undoing the link between hierarchy and care that ties the structure of care to an underlying structure of inequality. In terms of care recipients, of course, growing inequality has meant that the poor often do not get the care they need, and are forced to see huge burdens imposed on family members trying to provide that care.

There is one further dimension to the quality of care people receive that we want to draw attention to here. Under the new norms of PTfA, there will be far less stress around providing care because people will have more time and more support. One of the important consequences of these changes would be that far more people will be able to take delight in those they care for. We envision PTfA as not just solving pressing problems, overcoming serious harms, but bringing more joy and pleasure into the daily lives of those engaged in the basic connection of care. Of course, if everyone cares, everyone is so engaged. Not only are the burdens of care distributed fairly, but the benefits are as well—both of which help ensure that everyone who needs care receives good care.

XIII. Puzzles and Challenges

A. It's Not Desirable: Restriction and Intrusion

The most common, and powerful, objection we hear to the proposal is that these new norms are too restrictive and intrusive. At the heart of these concerns is the question of why everyone has to limit their paid work and do unpaid care, regardless of their preference, inclination, talent, or contribution through paid work.

First, note that complaints about "restriction" and "interference" are common in the face of social change such as norms around "interfering with family life" in terms of intimate partner violence,[117] or the acceptability of making racist and sexist jokes. For much of this interference, the correct response is surely: so much the better. Interfering with violence and coercion is no sin, quite the opposite. We argue that, like all norms, the new norms of PTfA will indeed shape choices. So, some people whose existing preferences (shaped by earlier norms) conflict with the new norms may experience constraint. And the new norms around the distribution of household labor may be experienced as intruding into private realms (as is the case with preventing intimate partner violence). But these new norms will not, in fact, be more coercive or constraining than the existing (gendered and racialized) norms around who should do care and work. In fact, they will be much less violent or coercive. Another way of putting this is that intimate decisions around who does what kind of care in the household and work in the paid labor force are *always and already* heavily influenced by social norms. Such norms place continued constraint on people's ability to make choices both in their households and their workplaces. So, the real issue is not "norms or not," but *which norms* should we embrace. Our goal is to replace the destructive constraints of existing gendered and racialized norms with norms that shape belief and action in the direction of equality and the multiple benefits of a society in which everyone participates in care.

B. Why Everyone Has to Care (and so work less)

There are many reasons for limiting work hours, but the main driver here is the need to enable everyone to participate in care. Therefore, we return to the two overlapping reasons why everyone has to care. First, everyone needs to know about the value of care, as well as its demands and satisfactions, in order to be able to exercise good democratic judgment as a member of society and as a policymaker, as well as to shift the collective valuation of care. The second reason is to avoid the harms of having only a subset of the population doing care. Those harms are the undermining of equality, the maintenance of the care/policy divide, and the ongoing devaluation of care. Although they overlap, it is important to bear both reasons—knowledge and equality—in mind.

Earlier we elaborated on the claims about what people need to know and how they can learn it. Here we want to highlight the role of care in relationships: how care builds relationships; how relationships require care; and how a lack of care, attention, and availability can harm relationships. People need to understand the importance of care and relationship and the link between them. This understanding is essential to individual and collective well-being for without it people will make poor choices—about how to design their institutions, how to use their time and resources, and about what norms and practices to support, foster, and facilitate. This collective failure is exacerbated when those who make policy decisions affecting the lives of others are especially ignorant due to their very limited experience of care.

Deborah Stone offers an example of the kind of understanding that we think care can teach. She uses John Steinbeck's story *Of Mice and Men*, about Lennie, who is strong, goodhearted, and with cognitive limitations, and his friend George, who tries to look out for him. One day while looking for work, the boss asks George why he speaks for Lennie when the boss asks him questions.

"Say—what you sellin'? he asks George. "What stake you got in this guy? You takin' his pay from him?"

Stone comments,

> What stake you got in this guy? The question sounds the clash
> of self-interest and altruism, two ways of understanding human
> relationships and two ways of being in relationships. George does
> have a stake in Lennie, it's true, but devotion is not the kind of stake
> the boss can grasp.
>
> When doctors advise parents to put their profoundly disabled
> children in an institution, when friends suggest to full-time care-
> givers that they ought to pack their loved one in a nursing home and
> get a life, when supervisors refuse to accommodate an employee's
> caregiving schedule—these are all ways that altruism and self-
> interest collide in contemporary life, and people's stakes in each
> other are met with the ranch boss's dim bewilderment.[118]

It is this dim bewilderment that PTfA hopes to redress through a revaluation of care. Stone reminds us that this ignorance of care and
relationship is often dressed up in the rhetoric of the "rational, self-
interested actor," which is the dominant language of so much of contemporary economics, law, and politics. The knowledge we believe
people can acquire through care can start to cut through this dominant
frame of analysis.

The overlapping second reason, the harms to equality and the
valuing of care, is what makes it essential that there is not some
subset of capable people who claim to be exceptions to the need to
know about care first-hand. Such a subset would almost certainly
re-establish a hierarchy between work and care, between those "especially talented and important" people and the rest whose time is
not so valuable and thus can be spent providing care. This would,
of course, reinforce a care/policy divide. If the important people,
the people with public and private decision-making power, are not
doing the care, then the revaluing of care that would dispel the "dim
bewilderment" could not take place. The hierarchy of work and care
would be matched by a hierarchy of the people who are too important to do care over those deemed suitable for both paid and unpaid
care. PTfA aims to dismantle the hierarchies around which care has
been organized.

C. Preferences and Freedom

With the knowledge and equality arguments as background, we will briefly link them to the concerns we have heard. One version is just about preference: some people would prefer to do paid work 40 or 50 (or even 60 or 70) hours a week. Work is exciting, meaningful, an important way to contribute to large numbers of people, maybe even to change institutions or the world, and draws on their particular talents. For some people, person-to-person care seems to have none of these characteristics. Why should those who are drawn to work long hours be forced to feel that they are failing a social norm if they exercise those preferences?

Perhaps our resistance to exceptions is really only necessary during the transition to the full embrace of these norms (maybe a generation). Maybe once care was highly valued throughout society, and a corresponding understanding of the centrality of relationship had taken hold, society could tolerate a small percentage of people who refused care responsibilities in favor of paid work. Maybe they could just seem quirky, and not the object of deep social censure—like the proverbial surfers who get by on occasional work and contributions from friends and family. But during the transition, any carving out of categories of exception runs the strong risks noted above of recreating hierarchies of work and care, prestige and degradation.

The danger of recreating hierarchy is even greater for exceptions based on exceptional talent and training, like doctors. This is in part because during the transition many people would still be ignorant about the exceptional talent that can be involved in basic care.

We have also heard the view that PTfA has a disturbingly authoritarian, or "Maoist re-education" tone to it.[119] The concern is that it would foster a culture that is highly regimented, requiring a high level of consensus about intimate matters like how people organize their household labor, and reducing diversity in the ways people run their lives. It is true that we are after a cultural revolution (as, in a broad sense, all feminist, socialist, anti-racist, anti-colonial projects are) in the sense that the proposal aims at deep changes in people's values and norms. But we do not of course envision a totalitarian social regime or a shame culture. As we have said, the new norms would be no more constraining than the current (highly gendered and racialized) norms around who does what kind of work and care. We also think the new norms would facilitate the continuing emergence of multiple family forms as well as new forms of housing. In many ways, we expect people's choices about how to live to expand, not contract, as paid work loses its dominant role in people's lives and time for community participation and leisure (as well as care) increases.

Why not aim, instead, at freeing up of all norms around work and care, so everyone could simply follow their preferences? First, it is important to remember that few people believe that everyone should just be able to work or not work according to their preference. The idea that only those who feel inclined to provide care should be asked to do so simply does not carry over to the sphere of work. It is hard to imagine giving weight to a statement like "Work is just not really what I am suited to. I am not the kind of person who makes a good employee or entrepreneur. People should respect my temperament and choice, and not ask me to work." Yet if you replace "work" with "care," this a view often heard. People accept a requirement to work because everyone recognizes that societies need people to produce things (food, clothing, housing). Both the social and the economic coercion behind work seem natural. But there is not the same recognition that societies could not survive if no one provided care—to children, the elderly, the sick, the disabled. The coercion of social norms around women providing care seems similarly natural—but unnatural when expanded to men. (Although it is not only men who resist the norm that everyone contributes care and limits work.)

What is commonly called work and what we are calling care are both essential, and, as we noted above, all societies have norms about who should make these necessary contributions. The norms of PTfA are, we think, preferable and more just norms: that both men and women contribute to both work and care—with the main constraints being a maximum of work hours and a basic contribution of care from everyone. Of course, one could imagine a society which simply relied on everyone to contribute as they felt inclined to. A generous guaranteed annual income could reduce the economic coercion around work and the removal of social expectations around women to care could end the existing social coercion most societies rely on for care. To substitute individual preference for social and economic norms to generate the work and care societies need would be a far more radical proposal than what we are presenting. It's possible, perhaps, to imagine a future society, after several generations had come to fully internalize the importance of both work and care, allowing for greater individual variation in how people chose to contribute to work and care. Even so we would expect there to remain norms that avoided a division of labor that would replicate the dangers of having significant numbers of people ignorant of care or devalued classes of people responsible for care.

For the purposes of considering the constraints entailed in PTfA, we are assuming a society with norms around contributions to both work and care (rather than a radical reliance on individual preference). It is within that assumption that we try to take seriously the existing preferences we observe. Both of us have had serious conversations with professional women who say they want to organize their lives so that they do not have to personally provide care. They want care workers to be well paid, and they would take financial responsibility for paying someone to look after an elderly parent if that became necessary. But by choosing not to have children, and assuming financial responsibilities for parents, they want to free themselves from direct care obligations and would oppose the norms of PTfA. Should there be exceptions for people with such carefully considered preferences?

Of course, one important reason not to rely on personal preference with respect to care is that existing preferences are so deeply shaped by the norms that underpin our current hierarchical structure of work and care. One can see by the examples of the women above that these preferences are not always shaped by gender norms around care. But those are not the only norms at play. One of the most important is that work is more valuable and rewarding than care.

What would be the harm of accommodating these women by allowing for virtually all care to become paid care, as long as it were well paid and regulated? That way everyone could count on paid care for family and friends who needed it, and only those who wanted to personally provide care would do so.

Of course, there are different ways this could be accomplished. Let us first consider a privatized model that would provide an exception to the norms of PTfA. As long as everyone understood that they had care obligations, it would be up to them whether they met them through their own personal care or hired others to meet them. If this were the approach to care, what would happen to the norms around work? One might get a modification of the proposed hours of work. Perhaps the idea would be that there should be a large number of good part-time jobs available for those who wanted to directly participate in care. But for those who didn't, they could continue to work something like their current hours. Of course, there are other reasons to advocate hours that allow for leisure, friendship, and community participation, so perhaps the new norms would be something like 40-50 hours a week— still a very big departure from norms in the legal and financial sector, as well as in high-level government jobs.

If it were widely taken up, such an option of relying on paid care would almost certainly reinforce the existing hierarchies of work and care. Care (and work) involving physical labor would be at the bottom. Care involving emotional care, such as comforting and playing with children would be higher up, but below most forms of paid work.[120] Professional and managerial work would be the high end of the hierarchy. If significant numbers of people took up the option of contracting out their care obligations, the revaluation of care would not take place—thus making it likely that significant numbers of people *would* opt to buy care if they had the money.

Reinforcing existing hierarchies would thus fail to address the problems of equality in the distribution of care. Care and those who do it would continue to be devalued. Even decent wages for care-providers would not dismantle the hierarchy.

And, of course, only the well-off could take advantage of such "contracting out" of their care responsibilities. The norms of PTfA would become highly differentiated by income.

Equally obviously, norms that accept paying someone else to fulfill one's care obligations would not redress the care/policy divide, unless only a very small number of people chose that option. People who are buying rather than performing care are not learning about it experientially—although even taking on the role of helping to find, select, supervise, and pay someone to care for one's aging parent would, if done conscientiously, involve learning something about the kind of care that matters to the parent and why. Often, however, it is in part being relieved of such commitments that makes retirement residences and nursing homes desirable options for the children of the elderly who need care. Some of the problems that arise in such institutions grow out of the lack of such ongoing oversight. Those who do not want to do the care may also want to purchase care in ways that minimize their ongoing involvement—and thus knowledge of care. (One of the complaints of women in dual-earner marriages where a lot of care is purchased, is that it is the women who end up organizing the care— and thus learning at least something about it.)

Of the basic issues PTfA is aimed at, the issue of family stress seems not as directly salient here, since in the examples of women who do not want care responsibilities, they also opt not to have children. So, then another kind of inequality arises between those who do and those who do not have children. It is already the case that in the United States almost all of the wage differential between men and women is really between men and *women who have children*. Once that is accounted for, the wage differential is only about 5 percent.[121] One could imagine a hierarchical world in which gender was not the big divide between commitment to work and to care; the divide might be between those who had children and those who did not—and perhaps also between those who took personal, hands-on responsibility for sick, elderly or disabled relatives, friends, and neighbors and those whose commitment was financial only. Even if one could imagine communities of care, which, like some co-op childcare centers, allowed "buyouts" of members' care responsibilities through financial contribution, this would still sustain the care/policy divide and some considerable devaluation of care. This category of "care-free" people would then intersect with other hierarchies such as race to shape who got the best paid, most prestigious work and who ended up lower down in the work world.

The other, far more egalitarian, form of relying on paid care rather than personal care responsibilities would be a vast increase in the availability of publicly funded formal care for those who need it: children, the elderly, the sick or injured, those with disabilities. Well-paid professionals could (together with public schools) provide 8 or more hours a day of care for children. Full time care facilities, together with visiting professionals, could manage a great deal of care for the elderly.

Care givers could come to homes to care for sick children, people who have suffered injuries, and help those with disabilities.

Such a publicly funded alternative is likely to have almost all the above limitations of the privatized version in terms of the core goals of PTfA. It would not solve the care/policy divide, it would not challenge the hierarchy of work over care, it is very unlikely to foster a revaluation of the importance of care (and absent such a revaluation it is unlikely to be adequate funded), it is unlikely to generate real equality for care-givers, even if they receive decent wages. On its own, it is unlikely to challenge the pattern of low status people doing the care.

In addition, a huge increase in formal care is not likely to be welcomed by the recipients of that care. Evidence of the benefits of formal childcare do not extend to long hours. Many elderly people would rather stay in their own homes, and would like time and care from family members. The sick and injured often want comfort from people they know care about them, not just highly competent strangers. Many disabled people have a horror of ending up in institutions, which might often be seen as the efficient way to provide publicly funded care.

The costs of high-quality care that could replace most of the current unpaid care would be huge, and the difficulties of generating the political will for such financing equally large.

In addition, unless there were also a huge move to communal housing where all the cooking, cleaning, shopping, etc. were also done by paid care labor, there would still be a great deal of care labor left over. In the context of a European seminar on PTfA, one questioner was advocating the alternative of publicly funded care-providers, and offered a story of the excellent care he received from a visiting nurse for several days after he was released from hospital. I asked who had done the cooking, the shopping, the clothes and dish washing during those days, and he seemed nonplussed. It seemed that he was simply not factoring that mundane care into his argument.

Of course, there could be strong norms of everyone sharing in the care "left over" from the paid care—though for the well off there would be (absent a revaluing of care) strong urges to keep adding more paid care. (For example, the workday, the evening, and the weekend nannies currently necessary to support the work of high-powered urban lawyers with children.) But this norm transformation would have to take place outside the larger framework of support that would be provided by PTfA. There is good evidence that there is only *very* slow improvement in the current sharing of such labor in high-income countries.

As we have said, under the new norms there would continue to be a place for professional care and for a well-funded public infrastructure of care. But this would not be a solution for the woman who wants to manage all her care responsibilities by having them done by paid labor.

Despite the constraints on preferences, we think the norms of PTfA—*everyone provides care*—bring far more benefits than trying to rely primarily on paid care, whether paid by individuals or by the state. We would, however, expect variations across jurisdictions about what kind of care is best provided by publicly funded paid care givers, whether in the context of formal care institutions or home visits.

D. Activism and Community Participation

"Every time the world needs saving, there's a nappy needs changing. And I have some bills need paying."[122]

One of the most important implications of our emphasis on building personal relationships is that many forms of community activism or political organizing would not count toward an individual's care obligation. We come to this conclusion (and recommend it to communities of care) despite the fact that people express care through various forms of activism. We recognize that there are important forms of care that extend beyond the kinds of personal connection we have in mind. Examples are advocating for better childcare facilities, or for using locally grown food, or supporting activists in other parts of the globe who are fighting for better health care. This kind of work—often unpaid— is an expression of care and is often motivated by a feeling of "caring for."[123] In many contexts, therefore, it makes perfect sense to call this work care. Nevertheless, in our scheme we treat such contributions as community participation or activism—which are highly valued and encouraged for everyone—but not as part of everyone's obligation to care for those in one's community of care. Communities of care build personal bonds on the basis of mutual care commitments. Our main reason for urging this distinction is a concern that there are many kinds of work involved in caring activism that do not build personal bonds between those who provide and those who receive the care. Caring activism is often characterized by asymmetrical rather than mutual care, and it usually does not involve the kinds of "hands on" care from which one learns the important lessons of direct care. We do not advocate creating a group of well-intentioned people who are excluded from the direct, interpersonal networks of care because they think that their larger scale projects of care are more important. We also do not want to foster the idea that anyone's work—whether as a doctor, a physicist, or the head of an environmental organization—is so important that it should "give them a pass"[124] on their care obligations.

Unfortunately, NGOs do not have a particularly good reputation for paying attention to the value of care. They often expect both employees and volunteers to work long hours, treating their projects as more important than the care obligations of their workers. J. N. came of age in the 1960s and 1970s when left-wing political organizations were notoriously male led, relying on women to make the coffee, phone calls, and all other "lowly" maintenance work. Good causes are no guarantee that those promoting them will respect care or those who do it. Expressing care by doing unpaid work for activist organizations cannot, in itself, be a substitute for direct, mutual relations of care. Of course, the more NGOs focus on learning from and working with those they aim to help, the more they are likely to attend to the relationships they are building, including those within their organization. Care is, then, more likely to be respected and fostered in their work.

As we noted in the introduction, another way to think about this question of what counts as care for the purposes of the "22 hour" obligation, or what kinds of contribution should give one "a pass," is to ask oneself who shouldn't have to pick up their own socks (or wash their children's) because they are spending their time on important causes—such as reducing poverty or protecting the environment. We highlight the issue of activism because we think that some who might remain unmoved by the claims that a surgeon or CEO is too important to be distracted by the demands of care, might be inclined to make an exception for activists for causes they care about. Indeed, there might be people who advocate for publicly supported day care, or better care for the elderly who could claim that they make their contribution to the care of others—and indeed to the social recognition of the importance of care—through their activism. And here too time presses, even if not from the external demands of an organization. There are issues that need urgent attention: both the global urgency of climate change and more local matters such as fighting to end racism in a school system. For activists responding to these needs, just as for the high-powered lawyer or financier, there are never enough hours in the day to do what needs doing. Should some of those precious hours be taken for direct care?

As we will see in the section on work, the norms we propose should allow for periods of intense paid work. The emergency aid worker in a war zone might need to be totally devoted to her work for weeks, perhaps even months at a time. One could imagine something similar for unpaid activists when an urgent national demonstration means they have to be away from home. In the work context, we propose that the intense period is to be compensated by paid time off work so that there is time to make up for missed care obligations. We propose something similar for unpaid activism.

Of course, many activist organizations also facilitate direct care, such as bringing refugees into people's homes or organizing rotating care for people with disabilities. When this care has the feature of building relationships, of course it "counts." Indeed, some people might belong to a faith community that does a lot of community work as well as reciprocal care among its members. One difficult example is the important contribution of cooking and serving community meals to those in need. Often this is done for fairly large numbers, and it is direct and often urgently needed care. But if it is organized so that no personal bonds between those offering and those receiving the care are formed, and no relations of reciprocity are formed, then it does not quite meet our definition. This seems a valuable act of care that would fall under the heading of community participation rather than meeting individual care obligation. The new norms would promote community participation, encourage people to use some of the time freed up from long hours of work to contribute in that way, but not to expect it to replace their personal care contributions in their families or communities of care. Of course, this is one of many judgments communities of care would reflect on.

It is worth adding here that a realization of the goals of PTfA will require intense and dedicated political activism, to elect care-friendly politicians, to demand new infrastructures of care, and so on. Moreover, the structures of work and care we are concerned about have global dimensions to them which cannot be transformed through the local norms and personal connections of PTfA. As is often the case, there is a difference between the scale of the problem of the structures of work and care (global, international) and the scale of significant solutions.[125] Local communities can move toward adopting the norms of PTfA, city governments can commit themselves to a living wage for shorter hours (or a gradual move toward that), individual businesses can create good part-time jobs. But global economic inequality (as well as climate change disasters) will continue to bring poorer people to richer countries seeking employment and willing to take low paying care jobs. The transformations needed require engagement at all levels, but not all of the engagement should count as care (for the purposes of each person's obligation of "22 hours").

Finally, we want to acknowledge that activism and community work are usually forms of indirect care, and they are also important forms of building social and political relationships. The generation of new norms of work and care, and the ongoing processes of developing them, will require the sort of habits of collective engagement that have traditionally been fostered by activism and community work. Indeed, they are essential for the kind of thriving democracy that will be necessary for ongoing innovation in work and care in a society adapting to norms of environmental sustainability. Our conclusion, then, is that the new norms should encourage people to divide their (nonleisure) time not only between work and care, but community work and activism as well.[126] This would require, of course, attention to the dangers of slipping back into old patterns of treating direct care as of less value than "important," "public" contributions, as well as the dangers of reverting to gendered division of labor.

In sum, even people who are doing vital work in promoting care in the world through their activism should not be encouraged to disregard the immediate care needs around them that will shape the core relationships in their lives. Similarly, if we are ever to have a just distribution of care-work, we must resist all forms of the argument that important people (or people doing important work) don't need to do care-work. Finally, no one should be excluded from the complex set of benefits that flow from being embedded in care networks. Under general norms of care by all, people so isolated would in some ways be excluded not just from satisfactions and capacities, but from a kind of social citizenship.

E. Paid Care and Unpaid Care at Work

The issue of exclusion from social citizenship also applies to our view that people whose paid work is a form of care should still contribute their minimum of "22 hours" of unpaid care. We hold to this even though some forms of paid care will involve the same kind of learning and sometimes even the same kind of bonding as unpaid care. Thus the "everyone needs to learn from care" argument would not be a reason to expect care from them. The exclusionary consequences of not being part of communities of care are. The argument about social citizenship does not apply as clearly in the family context, but in some ways the issue of being embedded in care networks does. Relations with one's children and one's partner(s) would certainly be affected if the fact that one person did paid work outside the home were treated as a reason why they should provide little or no care at home. In sum, people who do paid care-work should be included in communities of care, with similar responsibilities, and both equitable relations among adults and bonding within families suggests that people's paid care-work should not exempt them from contributing the minimum hours of care to their families.

There is another related issue: unpaid care in the context of paid work. People (again disproportionately women) routinely provide care as part of their work. Often it is not recognized, and therefore, not compensated. Would such care count toward one's weekly obligation? And what sorts of things should communities count as care? Consider an example from the university context. Faculty often provide mentoring to junior colleagues and students, advising them about professional participation, career advancement, and decisions about further education. We suggest calling this "work," despite its care-like dimensions of concern and nurture. Mentoring is in fact fairly widespread (though unevenly practiced), draws on professional expertise, and advances the goals of the university. Academics might well try to draw attention to its importance and seek recognition in, say, required yearly reports of professional activity. In that way it might be (minimally) compensated. By contrast, faculty (disproportionately female and racialized faculty) often spend time with anxious students, helping them deal with issues in their personal life that are interfering with their ability to do their school work. While there are professionals at most universities whose job it is to help in these ways, many students first seek out faculty they know and trust. Even if the faculty direct them to other professionals, they may spend hours supporting their students. At most universities there is no effort to recognize this care-work.[127] We would call it care, and suggest that this compassionate, person-to-person comfort and nurture does count toward one's weekly unpaid care—even though it also helps the student perform academically. Even though it is also the kind of care that ordinarily can only be reciprocated by paying it forward, it is a kind of care that often forms long-term bonds.

Of course, these distinctions are somewhat arbitrary. What matters is not whether everyone shares our judgment calls, but the process of collective thinking about the role of care in the workplace. Community deliberation about what counts as care will be an ongoing process in our model. Such reflection, especially about grey areas, will bring more and more to consciousness the fact that care is important everywhere. And as people recognize the many ways in which care is necessary for good work, it may become recognized as part of the work and compensated accordingly. In many cases this will be a good thing, and the work (like doctors taking time to listen to their patients concerns) that once counted as part of one's care obligation will then be counted as work.[128]

F. Self-Care

In thinking about what counts toward one's contribution of at least "22 hours," we believe that self-care should be a separate, and thus protected, category. Our concern is that at least during a transition to the new norms, women might carry on with strong habits of giving their own self-care low priority. Even in a world less stressed by time pressures, they might find themselves devoting all available care time to others. Self-care can be both particularly challenging and particularly urgent for racialized women. As Audre Lorde famously said, "Caring for myself is not self-indulgence, it is self-preservation, and that is an act of political warfare."[129] Hence we suggest a norm of at least seven hours of self-care per week. This might take the form of exercise, meditation, enjoyment of nature, spiritual practices, massage, music, art, and so on—though we also envision substantial additional time for leisure activities. Sometimes leisure activities and self-care will overlap, as in a family bike ride, but often (for women) it requires great discipline to claim time for self-care since both women and those around them are likely to see it as an indulgence.[130]

We suggest at least seven hours a week for self-care (outside basic maintenance), and we envision people encouraging each other in their self-care. Of course, for some people, their health will require considerably more time than that.

G. Fostering People's Relationships and Social Connections: "Weaving and Re-Weaving the Social Fabric"

Glenn's phrase captures well forms of care that are often unrecognized as such, although all communities, including families, rely on it. Examples are organizing family reunions, birthday parties, weddings, and funerals. In a semi-work context, women who host potlucks for a social gathering of colleagues are providing this kind of care. Lots of the work of connecting people in activism and political organizing straddles the line around this kind of care. Working together as a community requires this kind of care, whether it takes the form of organizing block parties or fundraisers or meetings to discuss the availability of day care or public transit. Making the communities of care we envision work to be the cooperative, responsible, and deliberative bodies we hope for will require this kind of care. Because it so often straddles lines of work, activism, logistics, or gendered family responsibility, the people who perform this care (disproportionately women) may experience it as unrecognized *and* as an obligation—even though they think they should also be doing other things. In the current context, lots of care has this quality: women often feel they have to provide it and feel that doing so means they are failing to do something else that is also an obligation. In our terms, this sort of "weaving the social fabric" should generally count as part of one's unpaid care responsibility.[131]

H. Division of Labor in Families and Care Communities

The idea of division of labor as an efficient tool of organization is widely accepted. Yet we resist it in the context of PTfA. Perhaps the most important kind in families is the division of labor between an adult who is the primary income earner and the adult who is the primary care giver. Here we want to argue that this division is undesirable because it generates economic dependence and undermines equal status of work and care.

In households, the pattern of care (physical, emotional, mental) routinely assigns some to one adult and different tasks to others. The division is often described as a matter of personal preference, but also often follows gendered patterns. There can be complicated hierarchies of care at work in these divisions, such that activities such as cleaning toilets, mowing the lawn, and playing with the children are unevenly divided. In the transition to the new norms, existing preferences will, of course, be heavily shaped by existing gender roles and hierarchies of care—in which cleaning toilets is low down and playing with children is high up. Thus, existing preferences should not be encouraged to determine the allocation of care. In addition, different kinds of care will teach different kinds of things, so there is a benefit to having everyone—including the children—do as many of the different kinds of care as possible. At least for some significant time for transition, we advocate a norm that has all tasks rotate among those capable of doing them. This would help dismantle both gender norms and hierarchies of care, as well as spreading the learning.

We have a slightly different intuition about the distribution of care in communities of care. In principle, it would be best, for the same reasons, to have everyone take turns doing all the different kinds of care that arise. Here, however, we think that more accommodation for people's capacities and preferences might be necessary. Without the starting point of family ties, it is important that people providing face-to-face care feel reasonably comfortable with it so that recipients can be confident about receiving good care.

Especially in the transition, we want to be confident that there will be meaningful contributions for everyone regardless of whether they find the idea of intimate care difficult. It is important to recognize that temperament as well and gender and cultural norms will mean that some people will feel a great deal less comfortable than others providing intimate care such as helping people dress themselves, get ready for bed, helping with transfers from wheelchair to toilet, or even less "private" care such as helping someone to eat. For such people, it is important both to find forms of care that still allow some personal connection—such as shopping and helping put away groceries at the direction of the care recipient—and to help them acquire the competence, confidence, and comfort in more intimate care. For some, it may be important to begin with contributions—like shoveling snow, fixing a light fixture, putting out the garbage, or walking the dog—that involve little face to face contact. Even these should allow a brief encounter for the recipient to express their appreciation. Others may find face-to-face care like reading to a child or elderly person to be within their comfort zone as long as no other responsibility is involved. (With a child that might mean that another adult has to be around, even if freed to do other things.) Rides to libraries, grocery stores, and faith communities are other important face-to-face but not necessarily intimate forms of care. There are so many forms of care necessary to human physical and emotional well-being that we feel confident that communities of care will be able to find meaningful contributions for everyone.

Over time, it is important that everyone find ways of providing care within their communities in ways that foster bonds between care givers and recipients. Experiencing the link between care and relationship is, after all, one of the key forms of knowledge that we see as arising from giving care. The goals of communities of care cannot be fully met if some people remain on the margins by always contributing care in ways that do not connect them with other members of the community. It will be important for communities of care to find ways of helping people develop competence and confidence, such as working alongside those who have the skills of intimate care.

There may also be those who need care who find receiving it from nonfamily members (or indeed from anyone) difficult. They, too, may need accommodation such as finding community members they know best to provide face to face care, or those who are especially skilled in reaching out to resistant recipients.

Especially during the transition to the new norms, it is important to recognize the range of temperaments, beliefs, and experiences of people in the community. The preferences of those perceived to be in need of care need to be respected, even as everyone gradually comes to believe that all human beings need care and all are capable of proving some form of it, even if it's just a smile, a cup of coffee, or a hummed tune.[132]

I. Purchasing Care: Equal Status for Personal and Material Care

As the discussion about respectful relations between care givers and receiver suggests, we envision the new norms allowing for people to choose to buy some care by hiring others to do it. Even after one meets one's commitment to "22 hours" of unpaid care, one might want to hire someone to, say, do the house cleaning, freeing up one's time for family, friends, leisure and community participation. We choose the example of house cleaning because it raises a particularly contentious issue around the distinctions between forms of care. We think the new norms should strongly encourage people to resist the temptation to buy material care such as house cleaning and use their own hours only for more personal or intimate care such as playing with children or even doing homework with them. This section explores the reasons why.

One of the issues that we see as important for revaluing care is to disrupt the long-standing hierarchy between intimate, face-to-face, care (sometimes called nurturant care[133]) on the one hand, and "non-nurturant" care involved in activities like cleaning. We believe that under the new norms people should *not* do what J. N.'s generation of professional women so heavily relied on: hire other people (typically working-class women, often racialized) to do the impersonal care in order to free up scarce time for more enjoyable face-to-face care, particularly of our children. We urge this position to help overcome the very long-standing link between hierarchies of care and social categories of hierarchy such as race, class, and immigration status. We now have excellent histories and analysis of the division of care labor into the personal care appropriate for middle class women, and the heavy labor that was to be delegated to racialized and lower-class women.[134] Despite the fact the twenty-first century household no longer has the amount of heavy labor of the nineteenth century (bringing in coal, building fires, washing clothes by hand), the division has sustained itself. Even after children are old enough to be in school so that they don't need nannies or day care, many women who can afford it hire other women to clean their houses for them. Our position is not that under the new norms, no one should ever hire anyone to help clean their house, but rather that everyone should do enough cleaning themselves that the care they do and the care they pay for does not divide along traditional lines of personal/material, thus reinforcing the long-standing hierarchies associated with that divide. (Although the terms "personal" and "material" are not really ideal, we have chosen not to embrace the language of nurturant/nonnurturant because it risks reinforcing the idea that the material, sometimes heavy, labor is not part of the nurture that people need.)[135]

Somewhat to our surprise, we have heard resistance to this idea from senior feminist scholars. These are women who, like J. N., have relied on this division of labor for most of their professional lives. It seems that some women who work full time find it very difficult to embrace the idea of taking on some significant part of the material care they have paid others to do. We are guessing that this is because they constantly feel they are barely managing as it is. If they had some relief from the demands of work, they would want to use those hours for intimate time with family and friends, and maybe for community work, not for cleaning the bathroom. We suspect this reaction is probably not so different from men's reactions. They might be persuaded to give up some income to have more time for the pleasures of life, including the connections of intimate care—but not for scrubbing toilets. What underlies both reactions is the powerful sense that it would surely be wasting one's precious time to be cleaning the house when *someone else* (who—as people like to point out—needs the work) can be paid to do it. One suggestion, from a feminist scholar who has spent decades working on issues of work and care, was "well, we will come to that last. First cut the hours of work, then get people (men) to do more unpaid intimate care, and then get people to take up more of the material care." We resist both this sequential approach and the temptation to make an exception for material care in the norm that everybody does unpaid care. Care and work are integrally connected and the norms around both need to change simultaneously. And the distinction between intimate and material care would reinforce long-standing hierarchies within care and the people who do it.

Here we want to explore a bit why we think there is this resistance. Let's begin with another form of the resistance that we recently heard. Part of the definition of care we provide (for the purposes of what counts for one's obligation to provide unpaid care) is that the care builds relationships, the one who receives it feels valued. One person who heard our talk on PTfA objected that cleaning toilets does not build relationships, does not make one feel cared for. As we mentioned earlier, we think that is only true if the person who receives that gift of care doesn't think that otherwise they will have to do it themselves or go without it being done. (Of course, that is often the case when people are oblivious of the material care that they take for granted.) Personally, I (J. N.) have felt profoundly grateful to the care my husband has given me when he cleans up the kitchen at night when I am (often) too tired to help. I experience it as being cared for, and it provides me with a sense of security.

The response to the toilets question addresses the importance of care, its role in relationship, even its value in the sense that its absence would be sorely felt. But we are not sure it would persuade one who wants to recognize its importance, but doesn't want to have to do it herself. There, we think there is a dual problem: (1) believing that as long as the toilet gets adequately cleaned it doesn't matter who does it (as long as they are properly compensated and properly treated)—unlike caring for a sick child or reading a bedtime story; and (2) believing that cleaning really is a less valuable use of one's time than personal care, and thus a waste of precious, scarce time. Even if the sense of time scarcity were significantly changed under the new norms of PTfA, leisure, community work, and personal care could continue to seem like better uses of one's time. The resister might point out that until there are radical changes in the global economy, there will always be someone who wants the cleaning jobs—so why not use one's money to provide those jobs and use one's time in keeping with one's talents, preferences, and personal relationships?

First, we think it is probably true that in terms of the benefits provided by a clean toilet, it doesn't matter who does it. One of the things we say people will learn by providing care is that it very often is not fungible, it *does* matter who does it. Many forms of cleaning might be an exception to this in terms of the experience of the recipient of the care. But that is not the only reason why it matters who does it. It matters for equality reasons, for the project of revaluing care, and for widespread knowledge about the demands and satisfactions of care.

If it were to become routine under the new norms that wealthier people did not do their own cleaning because they hired other people to do it, this would (as noted above) reinforce the hierarchy within care. One of the powerful existing norms is that important people whose time is valuable (even if they are not very rich) provide little care. The more important and wealthy, the less care they provide. Having others provide the care one needs (and one's family needs) is a major indicator of one's success and importance. Care cannot be revalued as long as such a norm remains in place. The question then becomes: can this norm be dismantled if material care like cleaning is treated as an exception to the norm that everyone cares?

One might say, in defense of the sequential model we heard proposed above that just as the definitions of work and care might shift over time as we recognize the importance of care in work, we might expect shifting norms around people's willingness to devote their time to cleaning. As all care becomes more valued, as the hierarchy between work and care shifts, people might become increasingly uncomfortable with hiring others to provide care that they are fully able to provide themselves. Thus, over time, the full incorporation of material care could happen without having to make such contested demands at the very outset of norm change.

Or one might imagine that just as people will continue to hire editors to help them with their writing, they will want to hire well paid, skilled people to clean their houses for them. Perhaps if the status (as well as the wages) of those jobs improved significantly, the equality costs would be reduced of having some (relatively wealthy) people hire others to provide that kind of care. After all, PTfA does not purport to end all hierarchies of work, even though it does aspire to increase the remuneration of paid care as care comes to be more highly valued.

We also think that as time pressure is reduced people will come to change their affect around a lot of care-work, particularly the more mundane. When not pressed for time, people might come to experience the satisfaction of chopping vegetables, cleaning up the kitchen after a meal, producing a sparkling bathroom, or successfully tidying the mess of a well-used family play area. Differences in preferences for such activities that are not organized around traditional hierarchy might emerge in ways that can be accommodated without undermining the commitment that everyone shares in the care everyone needs.

Nevertheless, we doubt that the status (and remuneration) of material care can be significantly shifted if we retain the hierarchy of "personal" over "material" care in the new norms of PTfA. Even though there may be resistance to this dimension of the recommended norms, it is important to remember that these are norms not state-enforced law. We think that our proposal should continue to advocate for norms encouraging everyone to take up both personal and material care, to foster conversations with "resisters" about why it matters for equality reasons, for reasons of revaluing care, and for experiential knowledge of all dimensions of care being shared by virtually everyone.

There is also the additional issue of the messages that would be sent to children about both hierarchy and the value of care if they see that cleaning is something their parents tacitly treat as beneath them—because they have too many other important things to do, including playing with their children. That last (or versions of it) has always been my (J. N.) excuse for hiring other people to do the cleaning, so that I can have a bit more time for family. People who have spent their whole lives being too busy will have a hard time adjusting to the idea that time is no longer so scarce. Indeed, they may reconstruct their busyness around reduced paid work and increased unpaid care or activism, so that they replicate the earlier time scarcity. This is something people who advocate the new norms will have to try to help people with. I anticipate (given responses that I have heard as well as my own long-standing patterns) that discussions around hiring others to do the fungible care-work like cleaning will be an important part of the transition.

Finally, as we have noted above, sometimes it is important to have professionally trained care givers. This would, of course, be a form of purchased care. For instance, it would be ideal for pre-school for children to become incorporated into the public school system, available on a flexible part-time basis. In that case, individual families would not be purchasing it, and all the (potential) benefits of community and diversity that come with universal, accessible services would follow.

XIV. Conclusion

A. Relational Care: The Links Between Direct Care and Just Structures

Many of the issues we have discussed in this chapter have to do with the links we see between care and relationship. At its most foundational, care builds relationships and relationships require care. This is as true for human relationships with the earth community as it is for human-to-human relationships. This is one of the basic things we think people need to learn from doing care. We also use the requirement of building personal relationships as part of the definition of what counts as care for everyone's obligation under the new norms. This, of course, raises the question of why personal relationships should have a special status, such that people should always make time (at least "22 hours" a week) for direct care regardless of the hours they devote to people or places far away, or to transforming structures that will improve the lives, and indeed the capacity to care, of others they do not know.

The most important point here is that our insistence that the new norms should call on everyone to participate in direct care for the earth, for themselves (instead of always having others do it for them), and for their families, friends and communities is *not* a claim that direct caring relationships are of some higher moral value than, say, relationships with distant people that foster fair trade, or clean water, or respect for Indigenous rights or other projects of justice, sustainability, dignity or care. It is a claim about the foundational nature of direct care.

The relational foundation of our project here is that just and caring relationships with one's immediate community or with the people one knows are ultimately inseparable from just and caring relationships with people we will never meet and with a just and caring structure of relationships with earth and all her inhabitants. This is ultimately why we think it is so important for people to develop a caring disposition and a deep embodied knowledge of the nature and importance of care.

In this context, we also want to acknowledge another tacit priority in our vision. As we said in introducing communities of care, we expect that people would continue to give priority to the care needs of family and friends. We do not suggest trying to resist or transform that priority (unlike other habits and preferences around care). One reason for this is that we think that people who receive love from those close to them usually experience it as something special to them. They feel loved distinctly for who they are, not as one human being among others whose equality entitles them to respect and care. We think this "specialness" that attaches to intimate relationships is important to human well-being, and indeed to the capacity to care, and should be cherished. An acceptance of priority given to care in those relationships reflects the value we accord to that kind of personal love.

This position is also a version of our understanding of the links between care, knowledge of care, and relationship. The intimacy of family and close friendship (usually) brings with it an intense "caring about" friends and family and not just a willingness, but a desire to be able to care for them. We think this affect is part of what makes people want to care well and open to learning what it takes to do so—including developing a caring disposition. The desire to care is, for many, a foundation for their ongoing knowledge and practice of care. Of course, there are some people who seem to develop it, or at least enact it, outside of close relationships. There are probably many unheralded "saints" in the world who offer hands on care to strangers, usually spontaneously in in the face of dire immediate need and much more rarely as a regular practice. But we see this as exceptional. (We do not primarily have in mind professional care by, say, doctors.) Recognizing and validating a priority for care for people one loves can be a foundation for a wider form of care. Of course, as we noted in the Learning from Care section, when a preference for "one's own" becomes a barrier to the extension of a caring disposition to others, that undermines our project. While we do not have a prescription for preventing that, we think building on rather than resisting the common priority accorded to family and friends forms a useful combination with communities of care.

We also expect that the embodied knowledge of human-to-human interdependence and the direct, embodied experience of mutual human–earth care will expand into an awareness of interdependence with distant places and communities, wider social and political structures, and the sort of global practices and policies that generate dangerous climate change. We also expect the reduction in "time scarcity" to enable the sort of reflection that fosters such awareness.

Our insistence, then, that more distant kinds of care should not be a *substitute* for the direct care of PTfA, is not a claim about the superior moral value of direct care. It is a claim about how people learn what they need to about care, including a caring disposition. It reflects a wariness about abstract commitments to justice that are not grounded in the experience of care and a caring disposition (backed by observations about the degradation of care promoted by people in power with little experience of care).

Finally, the requirement of "22 hours" of care leaves ample time for both work and activism aimed at the forms of care that are not about personal relationships.

B. Why Is Care Foundational?

There is another question about the kind of priority we accord to care: why is experiential learning from care more important than say, experiential learning about poverty, or the desertification of the earth, or what drives refugees to leave their homes? First, if it is really experiential learning, not just some kind of brief observational visit, it almost certainly involves caring interaction. And if one is not just dropping in to extend some charity (not likely to be deep experiential learning), there will be some kind of reciprocal relation developed. So, the commitment to regular, mutual care need not preclude learning (in part through care) far outside one's familiar terrain. And while one might learn something important even from a brief observational visit, it is not likely to take the kind of time that would interfere with one's primary care commitments.

Of course, there might be particular circumstances where traveling for distant learning requires one to ensure that the care they have been providing can be provided by someone else. Leaving a family of young children would normally require consultation (and ideally agreement) by other responsible adults. But as a general matter, we do not expect participation in a care community to prohibit mobility—either for a job or for this kind of educational or activist pursuit. Ideally, however, people would be able to carry their care norms with them. They would continue to provide care for themselves and others because that is the responsible, equality-oriented thing to do. (Of course, the care might have to be carried out very differently than at home.)

In part, then, the answer is similar to the answer about activism or care for the earth: we do not really see the commitment of "22 hours" of care for oneself and others as forcing a choice. In most instances, people will be able to abide by the care norms *and* participate and learn in other ways. Still, we acknowledge that if one left one's own care entirely to others and contributed no care to anyone else, one would, in principle, have an additional 22 hours to devote to other valuable and educational pursuits. On some calculations, if one is capable of earning a lot of money, the best way to contribute to welfare in the world would be to use those hours earning money and then donating it where it can generate the greatest benefit. By rejecting those options, we do claim a priority for participation in care. The reason for that is that we see care, and a caring disposition, as foundational to just and sustainable relations among human beings and with the rest of the natural world. Not to participate in care is to be ignorant of an essential dimension of life (human and nonhuman). Not to participate in care is to exclude oneself from some of the most important bonds of relationship, and from the knowledge about the connection between care and relationship, and about the importance of both for the well-being of humans and the planet. The kind of learning that takes place in providing care is, as we have argued, important not just for understanding the central significance of care, but for humility and the capacity for judgment, and for an enduring and evolving caring disposition. This argument is another piece of our rejection of division of labor as a sound approach to how care should be done. The costs of ignorance about care (and exclusion from the relationships of care) are too high to agree that those who have other special skills—as doctors, money makers, physicists, or entrepreneurs—should devote all their time to those skills to the exclusion of care.

C. Publicly Funded Care and the Global Care Chain

In most "Anglo" countries today, institutions of care do not receive adequate public funding, far from it. There are not enough of them and many of them are not adequately staffed. This is true of hospitals, clinics, childcare centers, nursing homes, retirement homes, elder care drop off centers, rehabilitation centers, and group homes. (Of course, the rich can access excellent care institutions.[136]) Even European countries with better social welfare supports are facing challenges to provide adequate childcare, adequate support for people with disabilities, and provisions for the increasing number of elderly in their populations.[137] What this means is that if good care is to be provided for all, there will continue to be a need for publicly funded care—even with the increase in the unpaid care available to people in their families and communities of care. If there are to be enough well-staffed places for people who need the support of institutional care, more people will need to be hired to provide that care. For example, even people well supported in their communities will, from time to time, need quality hospitals and rehabilitation centers. People with disabilities will often benefit from group homes, even if they also receive unpaid care from community members. Similarly, some elderly people will choose retirement communities and some will come to need round the clock care that is best provided in some kind of group context with paid staff. Those who are able to care for people with high care needs in their homes will need support sometimes with professional skills, sometimes with respite options. Some of this support will need to come from publicly funded care.

One of the objectives of PTfA is that a widespread commitment to publicly funded care would flow from the increased recognition of the value of care by all, including people with high levels of decision-making power. Of course, the total need for public care would be less than what it would have been without the new norms. But depending on how underfunded existing public care is, there will be contexts in which public funding would still need to increase. In particular, while we expect that the increased availability of unpaid care will ease the rising demands around elder care, additional public funding is likely to be necessary. (The COVID-19 pandemic tragically revealed the worldwide inadequacy of long-term care homes.) There is also reason to hope that some of the currently escalating needs around mental health would be reduced as the vast stress of the current structures of work and care are transformed. But, again, given the current inadequacy of public support, redressing the deficit will require ongoing, and in some cases, increased publicly funded care.

One important consequence of this is that the demand for paid care that has fueled the global care chain will not disappear. There are, of course, many harms associated with the global care chain. Exporting care from low-income countries to high-income ones cannot really be a good way to organize care. As countries all over the world think about how to restructure work and care, we can hope that the need to leave one's home and family in order to earn a living will decrease. But since we do not expect the norms of PTfA to be able to solve the problem of global inequality, we expect that the pressure to travel to rich countries to find work will continue (and be exacerbated by climate change). If the norms of PTfA take hold in rich countries, there will be both more unpaid care available and a greater value placed on care. If that value is enacted in publicly funded care, then the need for quality care will continue to generate jobs. If those jobs are paid well and treated with respect, it is possible that more residents of the rich countries will come to want them. The impact on the demand for immigrants to do that work is hard to predict. What does seem clear is that the norms of PTfA would not simply replace the current paid work of immigrants with unpaid care. The care jobs for immigrants are, however, likely to shift from private homes to institutional settings—and thus be more reliably compensated and better legally protected.

Although we cannot engage here in any kind of comprehensive analysis of the problems facing the global poor, it is absolutely clear that much needs to be done on this score. We are acutely aware that any account of social justice which fails to focus on the global poor is inherently partial and incomplete. Rich countries adopting PTfA must, at the very least, commit to helping poor countries develop their own care infrastructures. There are many potential avenues to do this, including cancellation of poor country debts, more equitable terms of trade, cracking down on tax havens (which are an even more substantial problem for poor countries than rich ones in depriving governments of desperately needed revenue[138]), and enhancing global aid, perhaps supplemented with some form of annual "solidarity care grants."[139] The key point is that the principles of PTfA cannot stop at the borders of the rich countries. The values of care and equality that ground PTfA must also be embedded in principles of international solidarity with the global poor (particularly women and care givers), and a corresponding commitment to reduction in global inequality, including reparations for centuries of underdevelopment, slavery, and colonial exploitation.

2
Work

I. Introduction to Work

As we have seen in the previous chapter, everyone needs to have a life-long experience of the benefits, demands, and significance of providing (and receiving) care. Yet neither this experience nor the revaluation of care can happen without a radical restructuring of work; more flexible hours (while important) will not do the job. The kind of restructuring advocated by Part-Time for All (PTfA) entails, in turn, a deep revaluation of work. We need to not just understand the true value of care and its connections for human thriving, but to put work in its proper place. Under the norms of PTfA, work (paid or market-based work) is, and would continue to be, a source of identity, contribution, status, and dignity. But it would be only one such source. Care, community participation/activism, and leisure pursuits would be additional, and sometimes more important, sources.[1]

The new norms of PTfA thus involve deep transformations: of the role people expect work to play in their lives; of the kinds of contributions society expects of competent, responsible adults; and of what employers see as the ideal worker.

Most of the discussion of transforming the practical functioning of the workplace will be in the chapters on transition and feasibility. This chapter is about the desirability of new societal norms around work: why everyone who can, should contribute by doing paid work, at least 10 hours but no more than 30 hours per week. The new norms are not just about hours, of course. But hours are the tool most easily available to describe and guide the transformation. The objective of this chapter is to persuade readers that such a transformation is desirable.

We begin with the background of the existing norms around work and the harms they cause. Next, we provide the basics of the new structures and norms of work, followed by some examples of how

Part-Time For All. Jennifer Nedelsky and Tom Malleson, Oxford University Press.
© Oxford University Press 2023. DOI: 10.1093/oso/9780190642754.003.0003

different people might work within those norms. With the context and basics in place, we present the main benefits we see flowing from a new approach to work. We then compare our approach to prominent feminist alternatives, focusing on the ideas of Anne Marie Slaughter as well as the proposal for universal breadwinning. Finally, we close by considering the various challenges that our proposal faces.

This chapter will provide examples of how people might choose to organize their lives around the new norms, but it will not provide examples of the transformation of an economy based on full-time work to part-time. That discussion will be taken up in the next chapter.

It is useful to begin by situating the new work norms in terms of both our aspirations for them and their limits. The norms that we advocate are driven first by the objective of enabling everyone to participate in unpaid care giving (with all the benefits outlined in the previous chapter), and then by the multiple benefits of reduced work time and the decentering of work in people's lives. But while the scope of the benefits is great, these norms alone cannot solve all the problems of just and satisfying work. There are lots of complex problems that PTfA does not try to address: what it would mean to have a just organization of work, how much income differential is desirable, how much fulfillment should be expected, what should be done about undesirable work? Nevertheless, there is reason to believe that PTfA, with a foundation of robust economic security, would bring significant indirect benefits to the problems of just and fulfilling work. PTfA will not itself ensure a "connection between work and the human spirit,"[2] but it should encourage more creativity about how jobs are defined, increase the total number of jobs available, increase the respect and remuneration for paid care, and lower the hours people in bad jobs would have to spend working.

More basically, norms of PTfA will not by themselves end poverty or inequality and cannot alone solve the problems of work and care faced by the poorest in highly unequal countries like the United States. This is why some form of economic security is absolutely crucial for the norms of PTfA to take root, indeed for them to look desirable or even plausible for the poorest. We discuss the economic prerequisites of PTfA in much more detail in Chapter 4.

One last caveat: although we begin with general claims about problems with work in contemporary high-income countries, it is obvious that there are significant variations by country, by geographic region within countries, and by people's place in structures of hierarchy, such as gender, race, and immigration status. The challenges facing a female, Latin American immigrant in New York City are not the same as those facing the son of a working-class family in Naples, Italy. These variations are present for virtually all the issues we discuss: the extent to which long hours are the norm for professions, the prevalence of precarious work, the strength of a "work ethic" as a common norm, the centrality of work for identity, the increasing struggle to find work that provides "a living wage," good benefits, and the possibility of buying a house. Despite these variations, there are global economic pressures felt everywhere and powerful norms and ideas about "efficiency," and the (ostensibly necessary and therefore legitimate) demands of global competitiveness. Although these forces play themselves out very differently for the people working 70 hours a week in the New York financial sector and unemployed youth in Spain, there are shared patterns in the structures and norms of work that shape these particulars.

Finally, while we address primarily high-income countries, countries all over the world are aiming to increase women's participation in the labor force, without changing the existing structures of work. Women need full equality, including economic equality, but the way to achieve that is not to insert more women into a structure of work that ignores the demands, satisfactions, and human importance of care. In addition, there are important international efforts to envision new forms of economies that will be more just and environmentally sustainable.[3] These are aimed at low-income as well as high-income countries. It is vital that as people rethink their economies, they recognize the ways the structures of care and of work are intertwined. As they reenvision economic enterprise, they need to ask how care is going to be provided. Otherwise, they will replicate the inequalities, the care/policy divide, and the stressed families that characterize high-income countries. Low-income countries may not be able to implement the PTfA model in the same way as high-income countries. But those countries can learn from the mistakes of high-income countries—the human and environmental costs of expanding material production through unjust and unsustainable systems of work and care.

II. Norms, Harms, and Existing Transformations

We begin by reminding readers of one of the most serious harms of the existing degradation of care: the terrible working conditions of so many who do paid care. This is a worldwide pattern, present in high-income as well as low-income countries.

As well as doing care work for free at home, many poor women also work providing care for others, for example as domestic workers, who are among the most exploited workers in the world. Just 10% of domestic workers are covered by general labor laws to the same extent as other workers, and only around half enjoy equal minimum wage protection. More than half of all domestic workers have no limits on work hours under national law. In the most extreme cases of forced labor and trafficking, domestic workers find themselves trapped in people's homes with every aspect of their lives controlled, rendering them invisible and unprotected. It is estimated that globally, the 3.4 million domestic workers in forced labor are being robbed of $8bn every year, equating to 60% of their due wages.[4]

In Chapter 2 on Care, we discussed the ways the degradation of care and of those who do it are mutually reinforcing. We also noted that there has been some important improvement with the International Labour Organization's Domestic Workers Convention and the Domestic Workers Recommendation, which mandates inclusion of "domestic work" in labor law regulation.[5] But the Oxfam summary cited in the note above is from 2020, so there is still a long way to go. One of the aspirations of PTfA is that with a revaluing of care, the conditions of those who provide both paid and unpaid care will improve.

Many of the harms that flow from the existing structure of work are the result of norms not laws. Perhaps the most pernicious and tenacious is the norm of the ideal worker—a person for whom work is always the first priority, unencumbered by care responsibilities. The ideal worker can count on someone else being responsible for care of the home and family. This norm is enforced by the complementary norm that a good way of deciding who is a good worker is by measuring who devotes the most hours to the job. (This, despite repeated arguments by management specialists that this crude measurement brings with it more harm—in the form of stress, fatigue, inefficiency, illness, and absenteeism—than good.) Workers all across the income scale feel the pressure to demonstrate their quality and commitment through long hours.

The health risks of long hours are now well documented. For example, a recent review of studies from Europe, the United States, and Australia found that "those working 55 hours or more per week had a 33 percent greater risk of stroke than those working a more balanced 35–40 hour work week. Working the longer set of hours also brings with it a 13 percent increased risk of developing coronary heart disease."[6]

There are also shifting norms about what kinds of work practices are acceptable. Over the past 50 years, there has been a dramatic shift in who reaps the benefits of productivity, particularly in the Anglo countries. In the United States, the ratio of CEO to worker income has gone from 20 to 1 to 300 to 1.[7] There are similar shifts in who bears the risks of enterprise. For example, there has been a rise of precarious work with no benefits, poor pay, and no predictability either about schedules in the short term or long-term employment.[8] In the United States, it is widely recognized by workers (again at all levels) that the demand that they demonstrate their commitment through long hours will not be matched by any sense of loyalty on the part of their employers.[9]

In the Anglo countries, there is an increasing move to part-time work, but *bad* part-time work.[10] Part-time workers are generally paid less, have fewer benefits, less opportunity for career advancement, and have increasingly unpredictable schedules. The combination of short shifts and unpredictability is, of course, particularly hard for parents trying to make childcare arrangements.

The long hours, insecurity, and unpredictability of contemporary work brings stress, ill health, and hardship to millions.[11] Our focus here is on how those harms intersect with the difficulties of providing care under these conditions. At its worst, poor parents (especially single mothers) juggling precarious jobs, are in a constant, exhausting struggle to care for their children.

It is important to recognize that our proposal arises not only out of the harms but out of the odd reality of rapid transformation in some spheres juxtaposed with rigid adherence to workplace time and gender norms (like the ideal worker), which it should be obvious are outmoded:

> Dual-earner, single-parent, and same-sex couple homes now greatly outnumber the once-ascendant homemaker-breadwinner family. Legions of work- and career-committed women, including married and single women with and without children, have taken their place alongside and now outnumber home-centered mothers. The "traditional" career, where male workers of all classes (though not all races) could gain economic security through loyalty to their employers and earn enough to support wives and children, has been supplanted by a myriad of time-demanding but insecure jobs. The life course has become more fluid and unpredictable as people travel new paths through work and family in adulthood.
>
> Yet these intertwined social shifts—revolutions in family life, gender arrangements, work trajectories, and life-course patterns— face great resistance from institutions rooted in earlier eras. At the workplace, employers reward "ideal workers" who provide uninterrupted full-time—often overtime—commitment, an ideal that workers now perceive as not just a requirement to move up but even to keep their place. In the home, privatized caretaking leaves parents, especially mothers, facing the seemingly endless demands of "intensive parenting."[12]

The context for our proposal is, thus, that high-income societies are facing serious problems as well as undergoing major transformations in the patterns of both work and care. We are, therefore, not arguing for a radical transformation of a stable, well-functioning system. We are arguing for the recognition of the harms of the current structures of work and care and the urgent need to redress them together by a new set of norms and economic structures.

In looking at the context for the transformation needed, let us begin with the existing transformation of a huge amount of unpaid care into paid work. As Susan Thistle points out, "about one-quarter of employment in the service-producing sector involves tasks that were once a central part of women's house-hold work."[13] She documents this in the United States as part of what she sees as the abandonment of the support for care—by husbands (with the move to a norm of dual-income families), by the state (the elimination of Aid to Families with Dependent Children), and by employers (with the abandonment of a family wage and benefits).[14] Thistle notes in 1960, that one-half of African American women and two-thirds of white women "earned their living" at home: "In a few short decades, the gender division of labor, or men's support for the domestic tasks done by women, had all but disappeared, and women had turned instead to wages to meet their basic needs."[15] Of course, this did lead to an increase in women's economic independence, as well as benefits to the economy. But Thistle finds that "few of the gains in productivity and profits have come to women or their families."[16] In addition, the marketization of care has often led to bad jobs, a poor quality of care substituted for what had once been provided at home, and ecologically unsustainable practices—think about frozen dinners and the fast-food industry as examples.

Women's entry into the paid labor market can thus be seen as both driven by and enabling the abandonment of a mid-twentieth century wage deal:

> The social contract won by [white] male workers in the first half of the twentieth century committed employers to paying some of the costs of household and domestic tasks, primarily through the family wage and a package of health care and retirement benefits. The abandonment of this contract has released employers from many of their old obligations.[17]

Large numbers of families in North America now feel they require two incomes to meet their needs, meaning that women disproportionately provide both unpaid care and income from (often poor) employment.

Women (disproportionately white and middle-class) have gained access to the professions, but women with children remain at an economic disadvantage. As Joan Williams put it in 2010, "Mothers earn only 67 cents for every dollar earned by fathers. Not one news article noted that two out of three of the elderly poor are women or that only 32% of retired women have pensions (compared with 55% of men)."[18] Almost one-quarter of children in the United Kingdom and North America live in single parent families,[19] the vast majority of which are headed by women. Thus, the consequences for the combined demands of work and care rest especially heavily on (the rising number of) single mothers and their children.[20] In short, increased access to the labor market has reduced women's economic dependence on men but has been a mixed blessing when considering the quality of the jobs many women have, their long term economic prospects, and the burden they bear (at all economic levels) for both work and care.

Another part of the context of the transformations in work and care is the global care chain: "There is a world-wide movement toward full time employment for women, with poorer women from elsewhere taking up the care work."[21] Many see this as both the necessary price for women's increased labor force participation and a source of income for the global poor. But, as we noted, it has serious costs for the women who are forced to leave their families behind as well as for those families. The increasing scope of this practice expands the norm that care is something one should pay someone else (someone poorer, with fewer options) to do. Such a norm is, of course, part of what PTfA means to challenge.

All over the world, the burdens of combining work and care fall heavily on women. But men have long borne a different kind of burden: the responsibility to earn an income and support their families. This is so, even though women often end up supporting their children financially when absent fathers do not provide child support. The connections between one's identity as a man and an earner and "provider" remain powerful.[22] And the changes in some men's capacity to earn has left a now widely recognized cohort of angry and depressed men in former industrial regions. Some of their distress and despair is connected to an inability to adapt either to a significant role as a provider of unpaid care or to other forms of work, in particular work connected to paid care—and thus seen as properly belonging not to men, but to women.[23] This is yet another example of the context of rapid change combined with tenacious norms. These men would stand to benefit a great deal from the new norms of PTfA, but their understanding of masculinity is likely to make it particularly difficult for them to embrace these norms.

On a somewhat more optimistic note, there is reason to believe that attitudes toward gender, work, and care are changing, even if institutions are not keeping up. Jacobs and Gerson carried out a very illuminating study that suggested that some of the common findings on attitudes towards working mothers (and other related topics) are shaped by the limited options that questionnaires provide their subjects. When provided with contextual information about financial need and about how happy a parent is with their work and with their childcare arrangements, people provide more nuanced responses. Of particular interest to PTfA is the finding that "[w]hen the option to work part-time is added to the mix of options, people express nearly universal support for the employment of single mothers and more than 90 percent support for married mothers."[24] Overall, they conclude that

> Everyone is most supportive of parental employment—for married mothers, single mothers, and fathers—when they know these parents have access to satisfying work and good childcare. Such support points to a cultural shift in favor of employed mothers and caregiving fathers that has outpaced the arrival of institutional structures that would enable parents to enact these more flexible gender strategies. Our findings highlight the widespread, if latent, public support for providing the kinds of supports, such as paid parental leave, high-quality, affordable childcare, and flexible job structures, that would ease the conflicts facing contemporary mothers and fathers.[25]

An earlier study of young American men and women highlights what some of those conflicts are. The study suggests that aspirations and expectations with respect to work and care are shifting. These shifts are promising in that both men and women hope for an egalitarian relationship, with responsibilities for care and paid work shared. They also reveal conflicting approaches to what the "fall back" position should be if a couple cannot find jobs that make these equal responsibilities possible:

In contrast to the popular argument that young women are "opting out" of the workplace, almost three-quarters of the women are preparing to fall back on "self-reliance." They see work as essential to their survival and marriage as an appropriate option only if and when they can find the right partner. Men, however, worry that equal parenting will cost them at work, which they believe must remain their first priority. Seventy percent of men are planning to fall back on a neotraditional arrangement that leaves room for their partner to work but reserves the status of primary breadwinner for themselves. These fall-back strategies are not only different but also at odds. Despite the shared desire to strike a balance between work and caretaking in the context of an egalitarian relationship, "self-reliant" women and "neotraditional" men are on a collision course.[26]

Existing norms are shifting without having yet clearly settled, and institutions and policy have failed to find constructive adaptations. Men struggle to figure out new meanings of masculinity as expectations around their role as care givers shift and their realistic options as "breadwinners" continue to change. And women are faced with transforming their own ideals of "attractive masculinity," in ways that fit with their shifting aspirations as well economic transformation. Even women preparing themselves for high-level employment often find themselves caught in a no-win situation as norms around "working mothers" shift. In J. N.'s conversations in Toronto with both female undergraduates and law students, they say that they fear that if they stay home to take care of children, they will be seen to have wasted their education, and if they have children and go to work, they will be seen as (and maybe even feel themselves to be) bad mothers. And the sense that that is the choice they face is shaped by a perception of workplace norms as inhospitable to family responsibilities. While these conversations are hardly a scientific study, they are consistent with an array of studies that find norms are shifting and conflicting, leaving men and women with anxiety, uncertainty, and potential conflict with one another.

The new norms of PTfA would greatly ease the existing situation. They are consistent with the increasing aspiration of young people for egalitarian relationships, and would generate actual structures of work that would make those aspirations attainable.[27] PTfA would carry the norms forward into a consistent system of beliefs about men's and women's equal capacities and responsibilities for both care and contribution to the economy, and guide public policy and employment practices toward structures that would enable all human beings, at all ages, to thrive via multiples forms of contribution.

III. The Basics of Work Under Part-Time for All

Of course, the first basic point is that part-time work would be good work—that is, secure, flexible, and high-quality—the opposite of what part-time work has come to mean in many parts of the world. The details of the kinds of policies and practices needed to ensure good part-time work are elaborated in Chapter 4. They include "time sovereignty," which is not just flexible work, but flexibility that is largely in the hands of employees.[28] Many social benefits such as health care and pensions should be delinked from employment. This is important first so that everyone has basic security regardless of one's employment situation, and also so that there are no bureaucratic barriers to easy shifts in the number of hours someone works. Constantly trying to figure out proportional benefits would be administratively burdensome, and thus expensive. And entitlement to health care and pensions should not depend on whether one's contribution to society is primarily in the form of paid work or unpaid care, or, as we hope, ultimately equal amounts of both.

The basic underlying requirement for PTfA is economic security. There are different paths to creating economic security, such as living wages, universal basic services, unconditional basic income, and a jobs guarantee (or some combination thereof). Different countries are likely to choose different combinations of policies. But there must be economic security in order for people to fully opt in to the new norms. Of course, the transition to PTfA can also take different forms, and one should expect differing and reciprocal interactions of norm change and institutional and policy change. (Sometimes policies will promote norm change, sometimes popular adoption of new norms will provide the political will for policy change.)

One of the most common objections to PTfA is the insistence that "my job couldn't possibly be done part-time; it's just not possible." We hear this all the time, particularly from managers who feel they need to keep an eye on many moving pieces, but also doctors, lawyers, and academics. And while it's true that it will require creativity to rearrange job packages—and it's also true that many organizations and bosses will be fiercely resistant—we completely disagree that it's not possible. Practically every job can be made part-time.

Of course, many jobs *as they currently exist* could not be done in fewer hours. This is what we suspect is behind most people's belief that part-time work is impossible: a certainty that *their current full-time, 40+ hour job* couldn't possibly be done in 30 hours. That is true; we don't deny it. But the key point is that any job can always be redesigned, chopped, and parceled in myriad different ways. It's not a question of doing 100 percent of the work in 75 percent of the time; it's about doing 75 percent of the work in 75 percent of the time. There is nothing impossible about that.

The fundamental point is this: at its most basic level, what a "job" *is* is nothing more than a bundle of discrete tasks. Some of these tasks are done individually, some with others, some are short-term, and some are long-term. But there is no inexorable God-given reason why the bundle of tasks that currently constitute one job could not be parceled differently into several. For example, if a team currently contains six people working full-time, then moving to part-time might well require a new team of eight or nine people. If the team is already fifteen people, it might be best to be divided up into two teams. If an employee's current work bundle involves ten regular tasks, it might need to be reduced to seven (with the other three transferred to someone else, or simply not done right away). All of this is completely possible.

The problem is not any inherent rigidity about the jobs themselves, it's the conservatism of doing things the way they're typically done. What makes it hard to imagine part-time work has little to do with the work itself; it's rather the fact that most workplaces and industries have strong norms and traditions of how things are done, and at what speed, feeding a belief that "it's what we've always done" and "nothing else would work." The crucial thing to realize is that just because work tasks have been divided one way for a long time (even if it's across a whole industry), doesn't mean that they can't change.

Does competitive pressure in the market make part-time jobs impossible? As we discuss in more detail next chapter, it is true that firms are sometimes resistant to hiring more workers for shorter hours because they don't want to pay for the costs of hiring and training, or undertake the logistical headaches of rearranging work/production schedules, so there may well be costs of transitioning to part-time. But once transition is accomplished there is no reason why a firm with, say, 100 employees working 40 hours each is going to be significantly more or less productive than a firm with 133 employees working 30 hours each. The part-time firm may well have marginally higher costs for things like office space, but it will also likely have somewhat more productive workers, given the well-known evidence that reducing hours increases productivity (due to reduced fatigue, stress, boredom, etc.), not to mention that it may be better able to attract highly skilled female employees who are only willing to work part-time.

Indeed, as soon as one takes a broader view of the matter, one sees that work bundles are constantly changing and being assembled in very different ways in different places and times. Average working hours in Europe in the mid-nineteenth century were 50 or 60 hours. In the Nordic countries today, they are 30.[29] The average workweek in North America is around 40 hours. But this average does not capture the full range of existing practices; many jobs offer fewer hours (often requiring people to work multiple precarious jobs) while others require longer hours with overtime that is not really optional or the 50–70-hour weeks in the legal and financial sector. Indeed, many of the "bad" jobs have become part-time (with no benefits) and most of the well paid, prestigious jobs require more than 40 hours a week. So, a 30-hour workweek seems like a big departure from a 40-hour norm, but that norm is already widely ignored.

Consider what happened in places like England during World War II. With the mass exodus of men to the front lines, businesses did not simply shut down. Women became much more involved, but they didn't do the jobs in the same way. Women had unmovable family responsibilities, so their new work responsibilities had to fit around these. So, with the clear and apparent need for it, much of the English economy was quickly reorganized. For example, the engineering industry was reorganized so that production processes were broken down into smaller constituent parts so that they could be done by women with less training, and who required shorter hours.[30] Of course, some things changed back after the war, but the speed and depth with which work practices changed reminds us of the important truth that jobs are fundamentally malleable.

We mentioned earlier the dramatic example of finance. Bankers today often work incredibly long hours, though it was not too long ago when it was regularly assumed that those people doing essentially the same job as they are today, would be on the golf course by 3 p.m. Similarly with the law. Many lawyers feel that their workplaces couldn't possibly function differently than they currently do, but we have careful studies of how to transform the time norms of legal firms.[31]

To take a final example, Perlow found that software engineers doing essentially the same work in China, India, and Hungary worked substantially different hours depending on where they were based.[32] This shows that it is not the nature of the work that determines working hours, but the country-specific norms and practices about work organization.[33]

Ultimately, what counts as a "job" or a "career," even the very distinction between part-time and full-time, is nothing but a social construct.[34] What is required is the reimagining of many existing jobs since the vast majority of tasks can be chopped and parceled and rearranged into an infinitely different number of jobs.

Of course, there are many jobs including lawyers, nongovernmental organization (NGO) aid workers, and some scientists, which do require periods of intense work that exceed the 30-hour maximum. We talk more about this in Section VIII. But the short version of our position is this: Intense periods of paid work that preclude care work are acceptable as long as they are followed by comparable periods of focus on unpaid care, on leave from paid work.

Finally, a brief note on paid care. PTfA revolves around removing a significant amount of care from the market, and organizing its provision around unpaid, voluntary care—but now free from the hierarchies (gender, race, class, citizenship status) that have organized it for centuries. Quite a bit of paid care will, however, remain. First, there is the kind of care work that we are not counting as care for the purposes of everyone's responsibility to care—because it does not have the central feature of building relationships. Examples are cleaning office buildings and doing laundry in hospitals. Some of this work could and should be restructured so that there is a greater relational component, so that the recipients of the care are more aware of the work being done for them and of who is doing it. Such knowledge, and expressions of appreciation, could create relationships as well as a better understanding on the part of the recipients of the daily work that makes their lives comfortable. This would also fit with the enhanced status of care and thus of the paid care that, of course, constitutes paid "work." (One could also imagine greater creativity in the kinds of daily responsibility that might shift to the current care recipients, like emptying their own office trash.) But such transformations would not eliminate paid care. In addition, even in highly personal care, the need for professionally trained people will remain. One of the most obvious roles for trained professionals would be in formal, publicly supported centers for the care of children, the elderly, and the disabled. Their work will be paid care. And even with reduced work hours, parents may wish to carve out more time for leisure activities or for community work, and thus to hire people to look after their children for some hours each week. The same would be true for people caring for elderly parents or disabled adult children.

Thus, despite the importance of distinguishing between unpaid care and paid work to generate new norms, it will remain important to recognize paid care as real work that should be well compensated and protected.[35] This would include paid care work in people's homes, which should be governed by norms like a living wage. Indeed, it is our belief that as the value of care comes to be fully recognized with the new norms, paid care will become better compensated—thus benefiting some of the workers with the lowest incomes.

IV. What Would the New Norms Look Like? Allocating Hours of Work (and Care, Community, and Leisure)

The norm of a minimum of 10 hours of paid work was proposed to meet a basic democratic requirement that everyone has at least some sustained experience of paid work, so that they have some knowledge of a fundamental part of society. The norm of a maximum of 30 hours was chosen for two reasons. First, we thought that 30 hours a week could be compatible with the kind of universal responsibility for care we were advocating. In fact, we think that something more like 25 hours would be better, with the ideal being about 25 hours of work and 25 of care each week. But right now, there are too many places in which people could not earn a living wage at 25 hours a week. So we propose 30 and hope that gradually the norm would be reduced as wages and social benefits increased.

As we discussed in Chapter 2 on Care, another way we have thought about the norms is in terms of an average implementation for two parents with young children. That was how we arrived at the norm of "22 hours" of care.

To get a sense of different ways people might implement the new norms (of "22 hours" a week of care and a maximum of 30 hours of paid work), we offer a few examples. The examples highlight some key parts of the new norms: (1) paid care work continues to be part of the system; (2) intense periods of paid work that preclude care work are possible, they are followed by leave from paid work to catch up on unpaid care; (3) there will be considerable variation both among people and across peoples' life times in how they allocate work and care; and (4) for some people (like artists) their "vocation" will not be their primary paid work; for some, vocation will overlap with paid work (like activists working in NGOs).

Example 1. Desmond is a single young man of 25 without children. He is eager to acquire the knowledge and skills of the work he is hoping to do, and he works over the norm of 30 hours, say 40 hours. He has no intense care commitments, though he may be experimenting with developing intimate relationships, perhaps with the hope of finding a life partner. He is healthy, has a lot of energy, and feels able to devote 17 hours a week to care, 8 of those to the care of others or participation in collective obligations of a household. (He is now at 57 hours of combined work and care, 5 over the norm of PTfA, and allocating more to work and less to care than those norms suggest.) He still is able to spend a couple of hours a week in some community work or advocacy. If his friends and family share his interests in community work and care, his contributions may overlap with recreation and intimacy.

Still, this is a fairly intense life, and those close to him are likely to suggest that he soon cut back on the work hours. But perhaps this is a stage of life when the intensity is not stressful, but invigorating. If it went on like this for more than a year or two, friends and colleagues would become concerned.

Example 2. Maria, a woman of 40 who is "mid-career," having finished professional training by 27 or so, has been working in her field for 10 or more years. Her partner, Rana, is in a similar position. They have young children, having had their two kids when they were 37 and 40. Neither wants to quit her job, but each wants a lot of time with her children. They each take a nine-month parental leave, with the first six weeks after each birth a time when both are off, so they both can bond with the baby and support each other. After the first six weeks, Maria (not the birth mother) goes back to work for seven months and then takes the rest of her parental leave. Rana goes back to work after nine months. Both are then working 20 hours a week. As professionals, they both earn a good income and have decided that while they could afford a larger house if they worked longer hours, they are happy with the modest, but more than adequate, income they earn together. They are each doing at least 22 hours of care, almost all of it within their own household. They each spend a couple hours a week helping neighbors and sharing childcare with other parents of young children. After the birth of their second child, they find they are not very active in other community activities, but they expect to return to greater participation when the kids are a bit older.

Example 3. Scout is a 30-year-old artist who sells the occasional painting but cannot support themself from their art despite the fact that they work 30 hours a week at their painting. Each year they sell a bit more and still hope to support themself from their art. They have no children yet. They do paid employment 15 hours a week (remember that a living wage should support a person and a child on 30 hours a week) and live in an art collective with three other artists, two of whom each have one child. They spend 15 hours a week on shared child-care and shopping, cooking, cleaning, and decorating for the collective. They use a bicycle to get to work and their studio and for errands whenever weather permits, and they work out three hours a week. They read novels and go to art exhibits, plays, and the occasional movie, but often prefer to use their leisure time to paint. Their total work on art and paid employment is 45 hours a week. This is significantly higher than the recommended norm of 30 hours a week of work. They are hoping to gradually reduce their paid work. If they have a child of their own, they expect their care responsibilities to increase. At that point, they expect that they may have to cut back on their painting if they have not been able to reduce their paid employment. They were able to cut back their work hours from 18 to 15 by participating in online crowdfunding for artists. They also spend a few hours a week working to advocate for an artists' allowance for any artist able to show that they make at least the yearly equivalent of 15 hours a week at minimum wage. The allowance would then match that. The members of their collective feel satisfied with Scout's care contribution, given the hours they all feel Scout needs for their art and paid work.

Example 4. Aruna is a 45-year-old activist. She works 35 hours a week in an environmental NGO, but only 15 of those hours are treated as paid employment. She thinks of the other 20 hours as a combination of activism and care for the earth (she spends at least five hours a week doing "hands-on work" like helping to build and tend community gardens). Her partner works 30 hours a week. They have two teenage children, who work summers and about six hours a week during the school year. They live in a large collective house, with separate bedrooms for the kids and for them. They share a kitchen although only some of the meals are prepared collectively and there are two common rooms, one for quiet, one with a video screen. They each put in about 20 hours of care, shopping, and cooking for family meals, contributing to the collective maintenance, and talking with and helping their kids. They also each contribute care within their faith community for about three hours a week. The kids each do about nine hours a week of household tasks and laundry, and an hour or two helping neighbors.

Example 5. Beth is a 50-year-old lawyer and single mother of children 7 and 10. She periodically works so intensively on a particular case (for about six months) that she is unable to contribute much to her care responsibilities. She has close friends and family in her community of care, who are close to her children, and have children about the same age as hers. They take up a lot of the child-care responsibilities during these intense periods, with the kids often spending the night with the extended family and friends. During these periods, Beth also hires people to do cleaning, shopping, and cooking both for her and for the extended family helping with the kids. Once the case is finished, she takes time off from paid work for six months. Her firm is organized so that core clients have a group of lawyers they work with, some of whom will be available while she is on leave. She usually enjoys the intensity of the work, but she would like the intense periods to be less frequent. She doesn't like the sense of being out of touch with all the details of the lives of her kids and her community.

Example 6. Mohammed is a 55-year-old personal assistant for elderly people. His paid work is care work. His children are grown and no one in his immediate circle of friends and family requires a lot of care from him. He does his paid work 30 hours a week. He likes it, has the energy for it, and although it pays fairly well (about average wage rate), he does the full 30 hours because he wants sufficient income to support his passion for travel. He does about 24 hours of care tending to his own care and in his faith community of care and hiking club.

Example 7. Sharon is a 25-year-old single mother of three young children with no significant financial support from their fathers. She had her first child when she was 19 and is now going to community college part time. She doesn't like the idea of communal housing, but she lives in a subsidized high rise that has a good child-care facility in it. It is easy for her to drop off the youngest two children there four mornings a week when she has classes. Her older child is in public school for full days. She is able to do paid work 15 hours a week. With the stipend she receives as a parent and a student, this is sufficient to support her children on a tight budget. The high rise also has a good communal kitchen and two days a week she cooks dinner with two other families with young children. During this period most of her time for care is devoted to her kids and maintaining their home. Nevertheless, she has created a community of care in her building, and she provides and receives babysitting, occasional meals (when a parent is sick), and regularly brings her oldest son to visit an 85-year-old man who enjoys telling stories and showing magic tricks to him. She usually does some tidying and shopping for him each week.

These imagined examples are meant to suggest both the flexibility of the norms and the range of choices they would enable.

V. Benefits of the Work Norms of Part-Time for All

There is now substantial empirical evidence evaluating the impacts of part-time work. In this section we describe this evidence, which generally points to a range of benefits likely to accompany the reduction in paid work from PTfA. In particular there are benefits in terms of environmental sustainability, work–life balance, health, a transformed experience of time, and more time for what really matters in life.

A. Environmental Sustainability

Can part-time work help to protect the environment? It appears so. The last decade has seen the publication of a number of empirical studies investigating the impact of reduced hours on emissions, the bulk of which find that part-time work does indeed reduce emissions. Schor studied 18 OECD nations and found that working hours are positively associated with their ecological footprints.[36] Rosnick and Weisbrot compared working hours and energy consumption in the United States and Western Europe and found that if the United States were to reduce its working hours to Western European levels, energy consumption would decline by 20 percent.[37] Hayden and Shandra performed a cross-sectional analysis examining the impact of working hours on the ecological footprints of 45 countries, and found a positive association.[38] Knight, Rosa, and Schor find that changes in working hours for OECD nations from 1970–2007 are positively correlated with changes in ecological footprints, carbon footprints, and carbon emissions.[39] Nässén & Larsson find that "a decrease in working time by 1% may reduce energy use and greenhouse gas emissions by about 0.7% and 0.8%, respectively."[40] Fitzgerald, Jorgenson, and Clark perform a longitudinal study of 52 developed and developing nations.[41] They find that working time increases energy consumption, that the relationship between working hours and energy consumption is intensifying through time, and that there is evidence for both scale and compositional impacts. King and van den Bergh investigate how five different scenarios for reducing working hours affect carbon emissions differently; they found that while all scenarios reduce carbon emissions, implementing a four-day workweek is most effective.[42] Fitzgerald et al. examine the relationship between state-level working hours and carbon emissions for all 50 US states.[43] They find that working time is positively associated with higher state-level carbon emissions. In terms of the scale effect, they find that "longer hours of work increase emissions through their contribution to GDP, net of labor productivity and the employment to population ratio."[44] In terms of the composition effect, they find that "the relationship between working hours and carbon emissions holds net of GDP as well. This is likely due to longer hours of work leading to more carbon-intensive lifestyles due to lower levels of time affluence."[45] Fremstad et al. study household data from the United States, and find that longer work hours are indeed correlated with larger carbon footprints (they demonstrate evidence for both the scale effect and the compositional effect), though they find a more modest impact than other studies.[46]

It should be pointed out, however, that the literature is not completely unanimous. The only contrary studies that we are aware of are from Shao and Rodríguez-Labajos who confirm a significant relationship between hours of work and environmental impact in developed countries but not for developing ones,[47] and Shao and Shen who find that, below a certain threshold, hour reductions are no longer associated with lower carbon emission and energy use.[48]

In sum, the bulk of the evidence indicates that good part-time work does indeed appear to be an important component of environmental sustainability. The attraction of good part-time work is that it offers a way to achieve the reductions in emissions that historically have only occurred through unemployment and recession, without actually having to suffer the misery of unemployment and recession. The major caveat is that even if necessary, part-time work is clearly not *sufficient* for environmental sustainability.[49] A good many other complementary policies—such as global and national agreements on carbon caps, massive state investment into decarbonization (such as shifting towards clean energy and building new public transit infrastructure), the immediate banning of coal, and so on—are vitally necessary as well.

B. Work–Life Balance and Health

In terms of work–life balance, there is now a significant body of research showing that longer work hours are associated with heighted work–life conflict.[50] Indeed, White et al.,[51] Crompton and Lyonette[52] and Burchell et al.[53] find that working hours are the most significant predictor of work-life conflict, and this seems to be true in contexts where part-time work is better quality (such as the Nordic countries) as well as worse quality (such as the UK).

More specifically, researchers have found that part-time work leads to less work-life conflict (or more "balance") in five European countries,[54] in four European countries and Australia,[55] in four East-Asian countries,[56] and in 22 European countries.[57]

That said, there are some interesting caveats. It appears that shorter part-time hours provide more work-life balance than longer part-time hours.[58] Roeters and Craig find little support for the expectation that part-time work reduces work-life conflict more in countries where it is more prevalent and protected.[59] Grönlund and Öun find that moving to part-time is helpful in mitigating work-life conflict for mothers, but not fathers.[60] Similarly, Beham et al. find that women in marginal part-time work are more satisfied than men in a similar situations, while men in full-time work report higher satisfaction with work-life balance than women.[61]

Turning to the issue of health, Sparks et al. carried out a literature review of 21 studies;[62] the authors find small but significant correlations between the number of hours worked and overall health symptoms (psychological and physiological), with longer hours associated with worse health. Boisard et al. find that across Europe longer working hours are significantly correlated with a number of health problems including backache, headache, stomach pain, shoulder and neck muscular pain, overall fatigue and stress, insomnia, anxiety and irritability.[63] Burchell et al. find that regularly working over 20 hours a week (and especially working more than 48 hours a week) contributes to an increased risk of work-related health effects.[64] Chandola et al. find that chronic work stress is associated with coronary heart disease and that this association is greater for individuals under the age of 50.[65] In their comprehensive review of the evidence, Fagan et al. conclude that, "Long working hours and schedule inflexibility . . . have a direct effect on physiological and psychological health indicators, as well as indirect effects, such as reduced recovery time and a tendency for long hours of work to be associated with an unhealthy lifestyle (poor diet, insufficient exercise, high levels of alcohol consumption."[66]

Of course, hours are not the only factor that impacts one's health. Fagan et al. highlight a number of moderating influences discussed in the literature, such as the prevailing organizational culture, the amount of financial compensation, the match or discrepancy between actual and preferred working hours, social support, and the degree of job control and autonomy over work schedules.[67]

C. Time for What Really Matters

One of the key underlying benefits of PTfA would be the transformation of people's experience of time. With everyone doing unpaid care and paid work part-time, there will be Time for All. This would have many dimensions to it. The first would be a reduction in the now pervasive sense of time scarcity, and thus in the stress, anxiety, pressure, and pinched, guarded, and even ungenerous disposition that scarcity generates in so many. Some of this shift would come directly in people's experience of work; other dimensions of the transformation would emerge as the role of work itself shifts in their lives. The rhythms and demands of work would no longer dominate their lives, invading the different rhythms of care and recreation.[68]

The reduction in work hours means there would be more time for relationships, which we have good reason to believe are important for well-being and a sense of a satisfying life. There is a lot of evidence about the importance of relationships for happiness.[69] As we have argued, care is a vital part of building and sustaining relationships. Reduced work hours would create time for this care, as well as for the direct pleasures of friendship and leisure time shared with friends, family, and colleagues. Being relieved of long hours of work would make people feel more able to be generous with their time in being responsive to the needs of friends and family, as well as to co-workers and community members.

The priority given to work in many segments of society in high-income countries has often meant that the "clock time" of the work-place, with deadlines and pressure for speed and efficiency, comes to dominate people's sense of time more generally. But these are relationships with time that are not suitable to caring for young children or supporting an unhappy friend or even mentoring anxious young co-workers or students. Booking an hour appointment for any of these purposes may shape the nature of the time together in ways that interfere with connection and thus undermine the purpose of coming together. When people spend fewer hours at work, and their lives are shaped and defined by a range of very different activities of care, leisure, and community participation, they are less likely to have the norms of work time invade the other spheres of their lives.

Putting work in its place would, thus, generate an increased scope or "spaciousness" for people's identities. When people first hear about PTfA they often focus on being "forced" to care and to reduce work hours. But, as we see it, the new norms would provide a great deal more choice about which dimensions of life matter most (and might shift over the course of one's life). The ability to draw a sense of purpose and contribution from multiple sources also would mean that setbacks in one area could be buffered by a deep sense of meaning rooted in other areas.

Before we turn to some of the benefits to be had within the work-place itself, we want to address a basic puzzle about why we say there will be a reduction in the experience of time scarcity: Why will there be more time if the reduction in work hours is combined with an increase in care hours? The total is after all 52 hours a week, which is less than the hours required in many high-end jobs, but significantly more than the 40 hours some men who do little care are putting into paid work. For them, the hours of social contribution would increase.

Of course, the question will resonate differently depending on one's gender. Women who work full time and have children generally are already doing, or at least organizing, a lot of care as well as paid work. They will get both a reduction in work hours and a much greater contribution to their care responsibilities available to them from (especially male) partners and from their communities of care. Their combined hours of work and care will almost certainly go down. Having people to share their care responsibilities will also reduce their stress. Women working multiple precarious jobs, with all the costs of transportation time and difficulty of scheduling childcare, will see the biggest improvement from the increased number of good part-time jobs and better labor laws—but this will take some time to be fully implemented. They, too, will of course benefit from expanded communities of care.

We expect that men with high prestige, high-income jobs with long hours may believe that the new demands of care would undo the benefit of reduced work hours (which they may see as questionable in the first place). Imagine such a man, Bill, who has young children, but whose female partner has taken most of the care responsibility. He might find a reduction to 30 hours a shock at many levels. His income would be reduced, and having done very little care previously, he might at first find spending "22 hours" a week doing care leaves him feeling that he is "working" just as hard, but with no money or status as a reward. He might find himself wondering (or imagining in advance) why he would trade 25 hours of demanding, but often exciting, rewarding, and high-status work for "22 hours" of household work and child-care. He might not experience this as a freeing up of time, but as giving up demanding hours that he experienced as rewarding for tasks that were also demanding, sometimes repetitive, even tedious, and only occasionally rewarding in any way he recognizes. At least at the outset, he may not feel like his experience of time has improved. He might not even feel less stressed. His partner, Zihan, a professional who had previously worked 45 hours a week as well as taking primary responsibility for managing the household, might experience a great deal less time scarcity by reducing work hours to 30 and receiving about 20 hours more in care contribution. One might hope that her increased happiness would come to be a source of satisfaction for Bill and lead to an improvement in their relationship. One might also hope that as Bill developed experience with the rhythms of care, and competence in it, he would come to feel the joys of better relationships with his children, and the satisfaction of contributing to the nurture as well as to the finances of the family.

This example highlights the gendered dimension of the transformation of time, as well as pointing to the scope of cultural and personal change that will be required, particularly for men but also for women currently finding jobs with high pressure, high status, high income, and long hours stimulating and rewarding.

We expect that even those very attached to the power, prestige, and stimulation of high-paying professional and managerial jobs would be happy for a significant reduction in the stress of long hours, increasing workloads, and relentless expectations that one should be doing more, performing better and faster. They will need to be persuaded that important creative and productive parts of their jobs can be done in the context of 30 hours. We expect they would come to enjoy their work more with reduced hours and to recognize the benefits of care not as an additional drain and demand, but as assets to their lives.

Men who have enjoyed the power and privilege of elite jobs and comfortably taken advantage of gender norms that insulate them from care responsibilities will need to be persuaded by a combination of arguments about justice and fairness, and a persuasive picture of a better, more balanced and rewarding life. Such persuasion has to take place in the context of collective changes in norms so that their personal changes are supported by those of others. We are not naïve about people's willingness to give up privilege. And, indeed, one reason this book still needed to be written is that the success of the feminist movement in getting middle-class women into the professions and management did not come with a transformation of care norms—despite arguments for such a transformation in the 1970s. We strongly believe that losses (for upper income earners) in consumption capacity and in the ability to bring a singled minded focus to work, together with giving up the "comforts" of being cared for without reciprocation will be more than compensated by the multiple benefits of a life rich in relationships and diverse forms of contribution and enjoyment.

Perhaps the greatest benefit from work-time reduction is that of increased time for what really matters. In 2009 Bronnie Ware, an Australian nurse, wrote an extraordinary blogpost which became a book, *The Top Five Regrets of the Dying*, based on her many conversations with elderly people nearly the end of life with whom she worked as a palliative carer.[70] She found that people's top regrets were:

1. I wish I'd had the courage to live a life true to myself, not the life others expected of me.
2. I wish I hadn't worked so hard.
3. I wish I'd had the courage to express my feelings.
4. I wish I had stayed in touch with my friends.
5. I wish that I had let myself be happier.

There is good reason to believe that PTfA would significantly help lessen the second and fourth of these regrets since less work allows more time for friends. In the Care Chapter we discussed how the norms of caregiving could help men in particular develop the skills for acquiring, and cherishing, friendship. Interestingly, Ware elaborates that the regret of having worked so hard, "came from every male patient that I nursed. They missed their children's youth and their partner's companionship. . . . All of the men I nursed deeply regretted spending so much of their lives on the treadmill of a work existence."

There are few thoughts more terrifying than the possibility that on that day that we come to die we will be struck with the realization that we have not lived well. A society of PTfA cannot, of course, prevent this, but in providing everyone with the material and temporal bases for free time and caring relationships, it expands our opportunities to expend much more of our lives in those activities that truly do matter in the end.

VI. Transforming Work and Its Meaning

The discussion above points to the ways in which significantly reducing hours of work must also entail a transformation of the meaning of work in people's lives—as well as new ways of thinking about success and excellence.

We are not, of course, intending to reject the value of work, which we have defined here as paid or market-based work. Work can bring a sense of contribution, fulfillment, the joy of exercising talents, an opportunity to cooperate in producing valuable goods and services, a source of social recognition, an important site of human relationships, and a source of satisfaction of "providing for one's family" and helping others. We think that under the new norms, work would bring these benefits more fully and more widely. At the same time, work would be put in its place: It would be just one source of the important satisfactions of life. Under the new norms, people would increasingly recognize that there are many sources of these values.

Similarly, in contemporary Western cultures, work is an important source of identity and sometimes prestige and power. But even in the best cases where people love the work they do, paid work is—or should be—only one source of core values of contribution and meaning. The new norms would foster "a healthy sense of resistance to work's tendency (especially when it is fulfilling) to colonize other parts of life."[71] And, of course, for many people, their employment provides little beyond (often inadequate) monetary reward. The relation between work and identity may, for them, be a sense of low prestige, inadequacy, or failure. When the role of work in defining identity is reduced, those who remain in unsatisfying jobs will have the compensation of being recognized for their contributions to care, community, and for their participation in leisure activities such as arts or sports. It will be widely recognized that people provide support to their communities of care and "support their families" by providing care as well as income. People who are unable to do paid work will no longer feel as though they cannot be "a provider."

One form the new norms might take to reflect (and advance) this shift would be a shift in customary forms of greeting. When one is introduced in a social setting, people would expect multiple answers to the question, "what do you do?" One would expect to hear about the nature of one's care commitments, which would reveal interesting information about family and/or about one's chosen community of care. One would also expect to hear about the person's community involvement and the kind of leisure activities that are important to her. And one would expect to hear about the person's work, and whether it is some combination of paid and unpaid work, as might often be the case for artists and activists. In a brief encounter, people would expect answers that focus on different dimensions of the person's life, depending on the context and the importance of those dimensions at that stage of the person's life. The default expectation would not be that the answer would be about paid work.

We want to reiterate that to put work in its place as only one dimension of life is not to deny the value of work. We agree with Muirhead, that "any democratic culture must in some way affirm the value of work."[72] We must recognize, however, the deeply arbitrary ways in which people's ability to work—their efforts as well as their skills and talents—are shaped by all kinds of factors beyond their control.[73] The important point for PTfA is to examine whether there is any reason the benefits of work could not continue in this reduced status and, in particular, when the normal hours of work do not exceed 30 per week. Ultimately, the claim is that individuals' lives will be better and society will function better, if people find their rewards and identity from care, from community participation, from leisure and friendship, as well as from work. But we must also expect changes at many levels.

For example, the much-vaunted North American work ethic would not disappear (as some might fear), but it would be transformed. The short version of our argument is that the existing version has troubling dimensions, but nevertheless has some important value. That value can be consistent with the diminished importance and reduced hours of work under PTfA.

Muirhead offers a helpful perspective on the protestant work ethic that has shaped existing American (and Canadian) norms. He says, it "functioned as a moral tool that facilitated the exploitation of workers in the Industrial Age. Its residue today supports a lingering compulsion to work, regardless of what the work is for or where the profits go."[74] Pugh offers another helpful perspective. She makes a compelling argument about the widespread asymmetry of commitment in which the contemporary work ethic is embedded.[75] Generally, in the US today, employees expect, and get, no loyalty or commitment from their employers. Nevertheless, they retain a strong work ethic. She suggests that the character trait of willingness and ability to work hard, to do one's best is what matters for the sense of dignity and pride in one's work. Even if employers do not deserve such an ethic, and even if it permits exploitation, we share her sense that the willingness to work hard and do one's best can be valuable to those who cultivate such a character trait. And, of course, even if the employers don't deserve it (because they do not reward it with any kind of loyalty or adequate compensation or socially valuable product), all those who consume the goods and services of such workers benefit.

Our view is that the new work ethic would be different from the existing one in two ways. First, the idea would be that one should work responsibly (that is, with focus, attention, and often, creativity) and try to do one's work well. But working long hours would not be part of that ethic. Coming in early and leaving late (often mentioned as a way of showing what a dedicated worker one is) would no longer be seen as desirable traits. The real point is that one's commitment to work well and responsibly is independent of the hours one puts in.

The second change would be a norm of some level of critical scrutiny about one's work environment. As work becomes only one source of identity and contribution, as jobs multiply with the norm of part-time work for all, and as the value of care and community contribution is increased, we think one can expect an increased capacity and willingness to inquire into the quality and purpose of one's work. People who are attentive to the value of care will be better able to ask questions about harsh work environments and to advocate for attention to care within their workplace. Strong norms of community participation may foster attention to the impact of one's work, say on the environment or on the working conditions of people who provide some of the components of the products they produce. A good work ethic will not be seen as uncritical commitment to the existing work practices.

In short, the idea that one should do one's work well would be fostered as part of the new norms of PTfA but that commitment would not be uncritical, and it would not be mistaken for a willingness to work long hours. It would also not put the quality of one's work as automatically of higher priority than the energy one has available for other forms of contribution such as care or community participation. That means that there would be times in people's lives when they should not "give their all" or even do their very best at work. Their very best might be required elsewhere.

VII. What Will Make Deep Transformation Possible?

Let us turn now to considerations of different feminist models for moving towards a more egalitarian and more care-sensitive society. It is helpful to compare our model of PTfA with those advanced by other prominent thinkers. We begin by looking at the work of Anne Marie Slaughter in *Unfinished Business*,[76] widely known from the earlier *Atlantic* article, "Why Women Still Can't Have It All."[77] We then, more briefly, consider Wages for Housework and the ideal of universal breadwinning.

A. Anne Marie Slaughter

We agree with Slaughter about the need to revalue care, and we agree that both men and women "are responsible for providing the combination of income and nurture that allows those who depend on them to flourish."[78] We disagree about the kind and extent of the transformation of work that could accomplish the kind of revaluation of care that we both advocate. It is important to remember that feminists have been making impassioned, articulate, and well-reasoned arguments about the value of care from at least 1869 to the present.[79] Those pleas and arguments seem to have had little effect. We think only a radical restructuring of work and care can accomplish this vital shift in the culture. Our claim is that her plan for structural change is actually at odds with the revaluation of care she advocates.

Slaughter offers many insights about the ways work and care are interconnected. Her objective is to make it easier for women (and others with care responsibilities) to hold high-level positions, to revalue care, and to shift the long-standing link between care and gender. These are also goals of PTfA. Here we point to a few of the characteristics of her approach that matter for a contrast with PTfA. First, she talks about two powerful drives, competition and care. Competition is often a term that she uses to refer to work. For her, both can play an important and fulfilling role in people's lives and both are important for society. She wants people (both men and women) to be able to experience the benefits of both competition and care. She sees that work must be restructured in order to accomplish these goals.

The key to her solution is much greater flexibility on the part of employers and the structures of workplaces. First, there is the now often mentioned flexibility of working from home, accommodating urgent care responsibilities, and more flexible work schedules in terms of when one does one's work. She also thinks that it is important to measure what people accomplish, not how many hours they spend in the office. All of these involve significant revisions to the contemporary ideal worker.

The other, more novel, form of flexibility she suggests is her proposal for an "interval" approach to work (like interval training in exercise, shifting between intense and moderate exercise). Slaughter basically accepts that high-level jobs involving important managerial and decision-making functions must inevitably involve long hours of intense work. Working in this way is incompatible with significant care responsibilities, even with the more modest kinds of flexibility she endorses. These will accommodate the occasional emergency, but on an ongoing basis a person with children who wants to hold one of those jobs needs to have someone else be "the lead parent." The problem is that many women either do not have someone willing to take on that role, or they want to do it themselves. This then has the effect of permanently cutting them off the fast track. The interval model would allow for both men and women to climb the ladder of success in the early years of their career (before major care commitments), and then step off it for a while, and then re-enter with a decent chance of being able once again to occupy the fast track. The problem with the fast track for Slaughter is that in the absence of such flexibility, many women step off for family reasons and can never get back on.

Under the norms of PTfA there will be no such fast track. No one will spend years of their lives in exhilaratingly powerful, high-paying jobs, working 50–70 hours a week and thus having virtually no time for care (or community participation or leisure). Of course, to dispense with the fast track would be to radically restructure work at the high end. It is a common belief in law, finance, and high levels of management in both the public and private sector, that the really important jobs cannot be done well except on this fast-track model. And at a somewhat more modest scale, to climb the ladder of success in many corporate (and government) contexts means to move up the management scale: to have greater decision-making authority and greater control over a larger number of other employees. (This is a model Slaughter repeatedly refers to.) It is widely assumed that such jobs require at least 40 hours a week, if not the 50–70 hours of the really high-end positions. This mid-level fast track would also be incompatible with the maximum of 30 hours.

Meeting the goals of PTfA requires transforming the structures of the workplace such that all work can be done part-time (or through job sharing or short-term intensity rotation, e.g., six months on, six months off). This will, as we noted earlier, require significant creativity in rethinking the definitions of traditional "jobs." Maybe each manager oversees fewer employees or projects, or manages teams of two to three job-sharers doing the work that had previously been done by one. In jobs where personal relations with clients are particularly important—such as doctors and lawyers—clients may need to get to know and trust a small team, one of whom can reliably be available.

Of course, the underlying purpose for such restructuring is to transform the meaning and practices of both work and care; in particular, to make it possible for everyone to provide care throughout their lives. But the more immediate reason it is important not to settle for the improvements of Slaughter's plan is the danger of creating two categories of workers, (1) those who more-or-less comply with the current ideal worker—work comes first, they are available 24/7 whenever "necessary", and (2) those who take care responsibilities seriously as a major and ongoing priority in their lives. Slaughter admits that as long as those ideal workers exist, employers are going to prefer them.

There are two ways these categories of workers would continue, even after many of the accommodations and innovations Slaughter suggests. The first is that without a norm of regular unpaid care from all, there will be those who see that being without care responsibilities will give them a fast track to rising on the ladder of success. Ambitious people may decide that they would prefer a sustained fast track to commitments to care. They may decide not to have children, to structure their intimate relationships around an agreed priority for work, and to generally signal to friends and family of origin that their works comes first. They may be available to contribute to exceptional care needs when it doesn't interfere with something important at work. They may be happy to contribute money to help hire others to provide care for friends or family in need. But they will not contribute time, and thus will rarely be present for hands-on or face-to-face emotional care. These are people who may envision themselves as virtually life-long ideal workers. (A predictable risk of this approach is that their own care needs in old age, sickness, or accident may not seem very real to them. They may think that they will have the money to buy care, so it won't be a problem.) Perhaps they envision an active retirement from paid work, but again, free from the encumbrance of care obligations.

The other way such workers would be available to be preferred by employers is on the interval model Slaughter proposes. People might "slow down," or even step off the path of advancement while their children were young, or during a period when an aging parent needs a lot of care. But then, on her model, they could return, eager to ramp up to the fast track. These are people who have experienced serious care commitments to people (children in particular) who are likely to continue to need their care and attention, if not as much of their time. We think there is some ambiguity in Slaughter's description of people diving back into intense commitment to work and her repeated invocation of the importance of relationship and the care it calls for. Perhaps these people will never quite return to being the old form "ideal workers" in that they will never simply treat work as the absolute priority. But to return to the fast track, they will need to minimize the interruptions they permit care to make in their commitment to work. Thus, while employers might still prefer the first group (the permanent fast track folks), once people are committed to getting back on the fast track for another invigorating interval, (at least traditional) employers are going to prefer them to those who have major (and inevitably unpredictable) care commitments.

Of course, there is an underlying question we will return to of the picture of work as competition, of success as climbing a management ladder that gives one ever greater authority over others and a larger scope of decision-making authority. This is not everyone's picture of fulfilling or creative work or success, nor surely that of a genuinely democratic society.[80] But for the moment, let us admit that it describes the structures of many workplaces and their definition of success. PTfA would prevent (or at least resist) the creation of these three classes of workers: (1) the permanent fast-trackers; (2) the interval fast-trackers; and (3) those who spend their lives with very significant care commitments in combination with work commitments. Without a radical restructuring of work and care beyond what Slaughter suggests, it is clear what the workplace hierarchy would be among these three categories. It is hard to see how it would foster the serious revaluing of care that she says she advocates. Money and power would be accorded along the standard ideal worker hierarchy. Care would be something "nice" people do some of the time, and really nice (and "unambitious" or "untalented") people do a lot of the time. People with serious talent and ambition will be keen to get back to the fast interval because that will still be what really counts as success in the workplace and in society more broadly as well as what gives them the maximum scope for creative ambition. Her vision may allow for somewhat more flexibility in the workplace but it is unlikely to shift the fundamental priority accorded to power and money over care.

Thus, we think Slaughter's greater flexibility would be an improvement over existing practices, but we doubt that it could possibly solve the problems that PTfA is aimed at, and it is very unlikely to seriously advance her own call for revaluing care. It will also not make a sufficient difference for the care/policy divide. It is true that despite the lure of the advantages given to the permanent fast-trackers there will be some significant group of people (probably disproportionately women) who become interval fast-trackers. That means that when they return to high-level policy positions, they will have had some significant experience of care. They will bring that knowledge with them. But they will no longer be involved in much daily care for others. Indeed, they will come to rely on others to care for them so they can sustain the grueling work hours. This will make sense to them since they see their work as so important and pressing. They will live in a work environment that still marks work as what matters for power, status, money, and social recognition of contribution. After a while, it will be hard to sustain a sense that care matters as much as work. Their policy judgments will come to reflect the superior value of work, and probably the superior value of the people who do the intense work that requires a virtual abandonment of care. The hierarchy of work over care will assert itself even for them. Thus, the care/policy divide will not be quite as bad as before the interval option, but it will still play a role for both the permanent fast-trackers and the interval fast trackers. And those who choose to combine work and care will still not have access to high-level policymaking positions.

For the culture at large, the model of power, prestige, money, and social recognition accorded to intense work that precludes care will be largely untouched. Ideas about the importance of care will be given lip service and reflected in romantic movies, but the hierarchy between work and care—and those who do it—will remain ominously in place, like an iceberg in the path of the vessel of our lives. In short, we do not see how a serious revaluation of care will be advanced by the kind of flexibility that Slaughter recommends. Deep structural changes for all will be needed to redress the long-standing devaluation of care.

Moreover, the gender hierarchy involved in the distribution of care is unlikely to be deeply affected by the interval model—even if some women choose to be permanent fast trackers, and some men become one of the other two categories of workers. More generally, the value accorded to care will remain low. Unless everyone does care, both the care and those who do it will continue to be devalued. And, as noted in Chapter 2 on Care, not just gender is at stake. Slaughter's model will not undo the distribution of care along other kinds of hierarchy—race, class, ethnicity, citizenship status.

Slaughter's model would ease the stresses of family life. Even the more modest forms of flexibility are desperately needed, especially in the United States. But it is a superficial not systemic solution. It will not give most people adequate time for both work and care, as well as the community involvement important for democracy and the leisure important for health and well-being. It will not end the desperate sense of time scarcity that afflicts so many in North America. And for those who aim for the fast track, or live with someone who does, their family will rely on a division of labor—even if it is not as deeply gendered as current North American patterns.

In sum then, of the basic objectives of PTfA, Slaughter's model will improve the stress on families, but not deeply enough. It will have little impact on the way care is organized around categories of hierarchy, thus sustaining inequality. And it will improve the care/policy divide, only in a limited way. Each of these limitations is connected to our view that the structure she advocates will not seriously challenge or change the devaluation of care.

B. What About Other Alternatives?

Of course, people have been thinking about these problems for a long time. Other prominent suggestions include: Wages for Housework; pensions for homemakers; improved part-time work or shorter work hours (but without the requirement of care from everyone); a universal breadwinner model in which both men and women do full-time work; excellent, publicly funded childcare (and sometimes eldercare) to enable gender equality in the universal breadwinner model; and to uniformly provide young children with excellent care (redressing the current class differences in children's preparation for and success in school). Would any of these accomplish the goals of PTfA?

We do not believe that any of these alternatives could solve all of the core problems—family stress, equality, the care-policy divide, and time scarcity. State-supported wages for housework and pensions could improve women's equality and security (and thus freedom) and could reduce stress in households, because care givers/homemakers (who are overwhelmingly women) would have less need to supplement the household income (and their own retirement income). Lowering the numbers of households in which all adults are doing both full-time work and significant care, would reduce the current acute sense of time scarcity. But the equality improvements would be small, as those who were working would continue to enjoy higher incomes as well as power and prestige. And, of course, offering (almost certainly low) wages to those who do the care, would do nothing to redress the care-policy divide. And it would do nothing to shift the value of care.[81]

Another alternative, improving part-time work, as the Dutch have done, but without significantly changing the gender norms around who works and who cares, would reduce family stress, but do little for equality or for the care-policy divide or shifting the value of care.

The "solution" of the universal breadwinner, with norms that encourage/coerce everyone into full-time participation in the paid labor force, faces the inevitable question of who is going to do the care. Of course, a universal breadwinner norm "frees" women to choose to work full time and have increasing access to jobs that were once reserved for men. But this freedom for some women has usually had a price for others:

Labor includes reproductive labor: the labor of reproducing life; the labor of reproducing the conditions that enable others to live. Black women and women of color; working-class women; migrant women; women who have worked in the factories, in the fields, and at home; women who care for their own children as well as other children; such women have become the arms for other women whose time and energy has been freed. Any feminism that lives up to the promise of that name will not free some women . . . by employing other women to take their place. Feminism needs to refuse this division of labor, this freeing up of time and energy for some by the employment of the limbs of others. If the freeing up of time and energy depends on other people's labor, we are simply passing our exhaustion on to others.[82]

Of course, as Nancy Fraser showed us, it is wise to compare the best possible version of "the universal breadwinner" with proposed alternatives.[83] That version would include excellent, publicly supported child-care and presumably elder care, with good pay and benefits for the care workers. But it is difficult to believe that would happen without a change in the value accorded to care. Moreover, the presence of publicly supported childcare would, in itself, do nothing to shift the existing hierarchy of work and care, or the existing norms around who does the remaining unpaid care. As has already been happening in the wealthy countries, some women would have greater access to the professional and managerial jobs, but paid care work would probably continue to be relegated to low paid jobs and thus to the women and minorities who are disproportionately funneled into those jobs. Important parts of the unequal structure of care would therefore remain. The equality problem would not be adequately addressed by the "universal breadwinner" model, without trying to import some parts of the norm shift around the value and distribution of care advocated by PTfA.

What about family stress? Excellent, widely available, subsidized daycare would remove one important cause of family stress. But it would not substantially change the stresses that arise when all the adults in a household are working long hours. The well-off could buy additional paid care to help with household demands, but even they would still face the challenges of meeting family care needs when children are in formal care eight or nine hours a day and parents are working as many or more hours. In the most equitable version of the universal breadwinner model, where the structure of work remained similar to what it is currently, but care workers were paid decently, one might say that instead of "passing our exhaustion on to others," everyone would be equally exhausted. There is growing evidence that such stress and exhaustion harms the workplace as well as the family.[84]

Finally, under the universal breadwinner model, the care-policy divide would be largely sustained. Even if more women held high-level policymaking positions, they would be women who were able to hold those jobs because someone else was doing the care for their family and friends. Policymakers would remain ignorant of care.

There is a separate question of whether PTfA is best from the perspective of benefits for children in particular. In the opening essay of their important book, *Gender Equality: Transforming Family Divisions of Labor*, Gornick and Meyers note that there has sometimes been a tension between policies aimed at improving the care of children and those aimed at creating gender equality in work and politics.[85] Their own view, advocating a dual-earner/dual-care giver society, is that there need not be trade-offs between these goals. We agree. But in thinking about alternatives, it is worth noting that those whose primary focus is on benefits of formal child-care (particularly for poor children), might be opposed to a strong norm of parents providing a significant amount of care for their children.[86] What matters here is, first, the acknowledgment that excellent, affordable full time daycare would certainly be an improvement over the existing situation in the Anglo countries. But providing child-care without any restructuring of work, still leaves children facing stressed and exhausted parents. What we advocate is high quality, flexible (including part time) preschool offered through public schools, thus making it available to children from all income groups. This formal care would supplement care provided by families and communities of care. Families would make judgments about how much time, and at what age, formal care was beneficial for their children. But since this would be publicly funded childcare, we would expect a wide range of families to take advantage of it. Thus, we expect that reduced stress, increased time for people to care for their children, and the availability of formal care would be to the benefit of all children.[87]

In sum, we think only the sort of fundamental change in norms and structures of work and care that we advocate here can meet the pressing problems of family stress, equality, the care/policy divide, and time scarcity while advancing a fundamental revaluing of care. There are alternatives (some of which would be less demanding for those attached to current norms) that could address some parts of the problem, but they could not address all of the core problems.

VIII. Division of Labor Under PTfA: An Equal Role for Work and Care for All?

We turn now to the question of the division of labor under the new norms of PTfA. There are two big, related, questions here. The first is whether in addition to the basic norms of a maximum of 30 hours a week of work and a minimum of "22 hours" of care, there should be a (weaker but still significant) norm of everyone doing roughly equal amounts of work and care over a lifetime. Would people who from youth on, choose to do the maximum of work and the minimum of care be seen as less than model community members, or should everyone feel entirely free to choose within the basic norms?

The related question is whether there should be a norm of economic independence. Should family units (however constituted) avoid arrangements in which one person (or group of people) does mostly care work for, say 15 years, and is thus economically dependent on the others in her family? What if a woman is involved with care responsibilities for three children and wants to spend 15 years doing only 10 hours of work (and 25 hours of care)? Should this be treated as well within the norms, or an undesirable asymmetry that is of collective concern in part because of the vulnerabilities that arise from economic dependence?

Feminists have long pointed out the dangers of economic dependence, including the link between susceptibility to Intimate Partner Violence, power imbalances in the family, and poverty later in life.[88] Of course, an argument against economic dependence is, in essence, an argument against a division of labor between work and care. Some version of the division is so common that a sub-norm of equal work and care for all requires additional justification. The basic norms of PTfA—10–30 hours for work and at least "22 hours of care"—offer quite a wide range of implementation. Indeed, sometimes we have defended PTfA on the basis that there is a great deal of flexibility built into those norms, both for individual preference and for change over time. But here, we want to argue for a sub-norm of *equal work and care*, which would not have the stringency or social force of the basic norms, but would be norms nevertheless.

We chose the minimum of "22 hours" because we thought that would be necessary (and sufficient) for the basic knowledge and experience of care that the norms aim at. Still, someone who consistently chose the maximum of work and the minimum of care would not model an equal valuation of these modes of contribution. If the justification were that this preference matched the reverse preference of a partner, who wanted to do the minimum of work and significantly more than "22 hours" of care, the concerns would be about economic dependence, about possible gendered patterns, and whether existing preferences (especially during the transition) are a good enough reason not to promote a norm of everyone contributing through both care and work. In addition, someone who never engaged in paid work for more than 10 hours a week would have a limited understanding of employment—of both the difficulties and the rewards of earning a living and contributing to society through paid work.

Ultimately, optimal compliance with the new norms would probably be seen to be an average of 20–25 hours a week each for care and work. This average would allow for periods of longer hours at one or the other. But the norm would best be maintained if none of those periods were very long.

People might want to reduce their work hours when their children were young. If all of the primary care givers are to have a central relation with their children, they are not likely to want to work more than 20–25 hours a week. We currently define economic security as able to support a person and a child with 30 hours a week of paid work, but the aspiration is to reduce those hours over time. Since PTfA is not expected to eliminate large variation in wages and salaries, family members with widely different earning capacity might be tempted, as often happens now, to have most of the work done by the high earner, and the care done by the lower earner. The new norms should discourage this. Otherwise, it could become a way of using the flexibility of the norms to perpetuate the care/policy divide and threaten to reinforce existing gender norms around care, as well as the devaluation of care.

What about those who want to spend as much time with a new baby as possible? The norms of PTfA would best be fostered by a policy of parental leave for both parents for the first couple of months so that both can bond with the baby, support each other, and avoid one becoming the "expert" care giver and the other the "helper." Then, there should be parental leave for an additional year or so that could be divided between the parents. We would encourage a roughly equal division. (Additionally, during a transition, policies that incentivize fathers to take parental leave and then shift to part-time work would be desirable.) But what if one parent would still rather only work 10 hours a week as long as they had children under three? Should that be discouraged? Since it would often only be six years or so, it seems to us that it could be seen as compatible with a life-long norm of equal work and care. If that preference were to extend to children under six, it might extend to nine years, and if finances required that partner(s) work maximum hours, this would tend toward an undesirable division of labor. Again, it would be important for everyone to pay attention to gendered patterns.

IX. Challenges of a Maximum of 30 Hours a Week

When people first hear about the proposed norms for PTfA, they are often as troubled by the limit of 30 hours a week of paid work as they are by the requirement of care from all. Here we consider a variety of ways of thinking about the challenges of norms that limit hours of paid work.

When looking at an "average implementation," we suggested that after one's basic commitments are met (including self-care and community participation), most people would have somewhere in the ballpark of 32 hours for leisure plus 18 hours per week that were not allocated.[89] This raises the troubling issue of whether (at least during the transition to the new norms) the use of those extra hours for work should normally be discouraged. In other words, our view is that the norm of a maximum of 30 hours of work should hold even if people are doing all the other things they should. Why? Our concern is that it will take a gigantic effort to shift the dominant associations of work (rather than care) with identity, contribution, status, and dignity. In addition to the adjustment to a lowered income and thus consumption ability (for the well-off), we expect that anxiety over losing status (both on and off the job) with lower work hours will drive many people to be inclined to exceed the 30 hours. The key here is to ensure that the norms constrain employers not to prefer and reward workers who are willing to work more than 30 hours. Under the current norms and practices, at the high-income end of employment (the professional/managerial workers) there is a strong association between power, status, income, and long hours. Thus, there will be a strong residual belief that to succeed, to be at the top, involves long hours. Norms need to be able to resist the resulting urge to extend one's working hours.

At the low-income end, it is currently the absence of economic security and decent part-time work that usually drives people into working long hours, often in multiple jobs. Their identity as people who can support their family and the sense of dignity that accompanies this may play a role in their willingness to work long hours. The promise of PTfA is that given options of economic security and good part-time jobs, identity and dignity would no longer drive people to exceed the 30-hour norm. The transformation would, however, have to address the concern that people still might want to take advantage of the improved options to enhance their income (and thus status), or their future prospects, by working longer hours. To avoid such choices, there would need to be good paths of advancement, for people to "move up" to more challenging, more skilled work, without the requirement of long hours. But, at least during the transition, that might not be enough. To overcome the inclination to take on more work, there would need to be a shift in the relationship between status and consumption power, as well as the overall shift in the role of work in identity, status, power, and contribution.

Before turning to that transition, let us consider what legitimate exceptions there might be to the norm of a maximum of 30 hours. What might be good reasons people would want to expand their work hours?

First, to clarify, periods of long hours of work that are followed by a comparable time spent focused on care are not what we mean by an exception to the upper limit of 30 hours. As we noted above, some jobs, like being a lawyer or an international aid worker, may require the worker to be away (either geographically or in their focus) from their care responsibilities for stretches of, say, six to nine months. But under the new norms, their routine would then be to return "home" to their other responsibilities and not to do paid work for the following six to nine months. These people are, in any given 18-month period, not exceeding the 30-hour maximum.

But there may be other circumstances in which people actually want to exceed that limit. For example, young people who are learning a new trade or profession, facing a steep learning curve, might want to be able to have time to master the basics more intensively than 30 hours would allow.[90] The norms might allow for a year of 40–45-hour work weeks. Here, too, the expectation might be that such a person had some catching up to do in the other dimensions of his life, but less formally than the month-by-month trade-off of the lawyer or aid worker mentioned above. Her friends and family might express sympathy that she does not feel able to abide by the norms during this period. But the new norms would bring disapproval if the training year spread into a longer period.

People who change jobs might face something similar; they might need some intense time to get up to speed after a promotion or transfer or move to a new job. But we don't think the norm should be that every new employee is expected to spend a year exceeding the norm of 30 hours of work.

Something less intense, but similar might happen when people shift from a model of 30 hours of care and 22 hours of work to the reverse. Maybe there is some catching up on the new terms of their expanded job that is most effectively done with a period of more intense work. However, this objective might be counter-balanced by the question of whether a more gradual shift to longer hours would make the transition easier and more effective. In cases like this, we think normally one would not want to exceed 6 months of work time that was in excess of 30 hours.

New immigrants who are trying to find jobs and adjust to a new culture, including a new culture of work, might be understood to require a year or two during which some combination of multiple jobs and more intense work in one or more of them would bring them outside the norm of 30 hours. Of course, employers should be aiming not to exceed the 30-hour norm, and thus to find ways to integrate new workers without excessive hours.

Remember that in these examples, the excessive hours that we are suggesting should be treated as exceptions still generally only amount to 40 hours—the current average in North America. (Remembering that there are large variations around that average.) The key is not to let the exceptions creep into an erosion of the norm that capable, responsible adults do not do paid work more than 30 hours a week.

Finally, there is another reason we can imagine people wanting to exceed the norm: time as compensation for ability. Some people read faster, write faster, and learn faster than others. It is a common-place with regard to students that those who are slower (not necessarily less intelligent, imaginative, or thoughtful), compensate by working harder—by which people generally mean working longer hours. One law student to whom the study of law came easily commented that he noticed other students struggling and working long hours in order to do what was relatively easy and quick for him. He suggested that "they were in the wrong game." They should do something that wasn't so hard for them. But, of course, sometimes students struggle with the pedagogy of law schools and then turn out to be excellent and fulfilled lawyers. Should they be excused from the PTfA norms during their education so they can find out if the actual practice of law is something that they can do within the norm? (This, of course, leaves aside the ways the model of legal education would have to change if most students were expected to limit themselves to 30 hours of work—class preparation and class time.) Maybe, within some (now routinely violated) extremes, we should treat education as an example of the need to accommodate intense learning curves at the beginning of a career. But here, as in all cases of exception, people would need to examine closely what the assumptions are (and what the evidence for them is) about long-standing patterns of education and professional training. In legal education, long hours and intense work are sometimes described as good preparation for life as a lawyer. It has been said that if students can't cut the workload at law school, that is probably a good indication that they would not make it as lawyers. But that assumes no changes in the work norms for lawyers.

Education and early training thus raise two questions. First, is whether early career learning curves justify exceptions to the 30-hour maximum. Here people should take seriously that long-standing patterns may actually have little justification. The fact that it has been done that way for a century doesn't mean it's a good idea. The second question is the one we started with: What if some students and early practitioners can keep up if they spend longer hours than most of their colleagues and not otherwise? Here, we think the first inquiry should be whether there is any harm in providing accommodation for such students' different learning styles. Suppose it was an easy option to take fewer courses. (Perhaps tuition could be by the course so that the students who take longer are not having to pay more.) Of course, some students who just don't want to work as hard/long as the school's norm, but could keep up if they wanted to, might also take advantage of such a system. Under the new norms, what would be wrong with that? We will return shortly to the issue of the link between hard/long work, competition, and excellence. But it is worth mentioning here that in the law school contexts that we are familiar with, there is a huge pre-occupation with whether accommodation might give some students a competitive advantage over others. Similarly, part-time studies are often disparaged not only in terms of some image of the intrinsic wholeness of the first-year curriculum, but with the argument that future employers need to know if students were able to get their "A" while taking five courses in competition with other students taking five courses, or if they had it "easier" by taking a reduced load. (One hears these arguments even if the reason for permitting a part-time load is that the student has major care responsibilities.)[91]

A. Excellence

This brings us to another reason why people might want to re-sist an equal balance of work and care, and even to exceed 30 hours of work: a deeply held belief among many elite workers (including scientists, academics, and artists) that excellence and success intrinsically requires long hours. Hence Elon Musk's insistence that "nobody ever changed the world on 40 hours a week."[92]

Success, of course, could just be the result of conventions in workplaces that need to change. The belief that excellence requires intensity and long hours is a more substantive view. We see this as a cherished belief that is attached to excellence in sports and musical performance as well as many spheres of work. If people feel attached to their work (that is, they are lucky enough to have very good jobs), they may also be very attached to the idea of their being excellent at doing it. If a maximum of 30 hours looks to them as though they would be less than excellent at their work, they might well resist—even in the face of other benefits of a less pressured, more balanced life. Such people might also believe that no one could do their kind of job really well without devoting long hours to it.

Sometimes this has to do with the structure of the work, in particular, the idea that to be a high-level manager of people doing complex work requires someone putting in long hours in order to stay on top of all the different levels of decision-making and production taking place within their sphere of responsibility. Indeed, one might hope for a radical transformation in the contemporary managerial structure of work so that the existing nexus between power, status, and long hours is shifted. For example, with norms of collaborative work, where collaboration is the primary strategy for planning, organizing, and delegating, one might expect a dwindling of the idea that success is about rising to positions of controlling others. It would then also not be essential that there is always one person at the top of each (large) pyramid who puts in the long hours to monitor everyone.

These changes would have many benefits, but the idea of achieving some kind of exceptional mastery as a result of consistent long hours of work needs to be addressed in some other way. Sometimes it will be a direct challenge to whether the added "excellence" of long hours is really something that matters enough to justify the long hours. Of course, it is often harder to identify exactly what would be lost in say, the reduction of the cumulative knowledge of a scholar or experience of a medical clinician or experimental physicist if they put in only 30 hours of work a week over their long careers. Here, we think the most helpful evidence is around creative productivity being enhanced by lower work hours, or put the other way, declining creative productivity after 30 hours a week. It might well be that there are important periods of intense creativity that should not be interrupted. But these are, of course, easily handled with the periods of time off we have in mind for other kinds of intense periods of work. (It would be interesting to track what kinds of "breaks" intense young mathematicians or physicists currently take, and whether there is any reason these breaks couldn't include forms of care, both for themselves and others.)

We can envision occasional exceptions for individuals passionately committed to their creative work, whether that is art or science or something else. But we resist the idea that there are whole categories of work that should be exceptions. We think that communities would have to see some stronger evidence of the necessary link between a valuable excellence and long hours than we have yet seen to adopt categorical exceptions to the norms.

What will matter most is the emergence of new conceptions of excellence in life that are not tied to the exclusive focus on one thing. Those people who are passionately committed to a single-minded focus might be accommodated as a form of neurodiversity, but in ways that did not undermine the norm of limited hours of paid work.

B. What About Immigrant Care Givers?

An important concern with PTfA is how it would impact the lives of poor immigrants who currently engage in care work. Will PTfA continue to rely on an exploitative system of immigrant labor?[93] Millions of poor people around the world currently rely on care work for employment.[94] Indeed, in low-income countries one often hears the argument that the well-off have an obligation to hire servants to provide employment. If large numbers of people were to take up the norms proposed here, the demand for paid care in private homes would be reduced. In higher-income countries (to whom our argument is addressed), the most obvious form of such an impact would be on the global care chain, which provides employment for poor women all over the world. Opinion among both scholars and advocates is divided on whether this pattern of importing poor women to provide care (thus enabling more affluent women to work full-time) causes more harm than good. Because of global economic inequality, the need for employment is urgent (sometimes in part because economies, such as the Philippines, have come to be organized around the export of care givers).[95] But there are also serious harms: great costs to the families of these care givers, as well as the terrible conditions of work many of them have to endure.[96]

Our expectation is that under the new norms, the significant decrease in demand for paid care in private homes would be balanced by a significant increase in decent, publicly funded care jobs in childcare, elder care, disability care, and care services in currently under-resourced institutions. In most rich countries, there is a need for more such workers, but the funds have not been allocated. With a new recognition of the importance of care, we think it is reasonable to expect that these resources would be forthcoming. Publicly funded care jobs are more likely to be properly paid and regulated than the existing jobs in private homes.

X.   Conclusion

Our proposal for new norms of work and care arises from our conviction that the structures of work and care are intertwined. The harms of these structures cannot be fixed without attending to both. This chapter has outlined the harms of the existing structure of work and presented the rationale for a norm of a minimum of 10 and a maximum of 30 hours of paid work for all capable adults until retirement. Without such a fundamental shift in how work is organized, care cannot be revalued and reorganized in a way consistent with equality. Equality and the revaluing of care are the bedrock of the norms we propose. Together with the need to fix the care-policy divide and reduce the stress in families, this bedrock is the justification for constraint on individual preference. In addition, we are confident that in the long run restructuring new norms will work to the benefit of everyone, individually and collectively.

In this chapter, we have tried to address the concerns we have heard about the limits on work combined with the demands for care. We argue that the "constraint" of the norms, while real (as with all norms), should be seen in light of the benefits, which we see as freeing. Putting work in its place would generate an increased scope or "spaciousness" for people's identities. The new norms would provide a great deal more choice about which dimensions of life matter most, even though care would be a responsibility for everyone. Part of the "spaciousness" would be a changed relationship with time. Not only would time scarcity be greatly decreased (with many important benefits),[97] but the rhythms of work-time, of clock-time, would no longer dominate so much of life.

We have tried to give a sense of the scope of diversity in how people would enact the new norms, as well as thinking through some of the grounds for fierce resistance to the upper limit of 30 hours from people devoted to their work and to conceptions of success and excellence that seem to require long hours.

In particular, we argue that to really shift the current hierarchy or work over care, it will not be enough to make it easier for women and men and non-binary people with care responsibilities to step off and then return to the fast track of long hours for high-powered jobs. A deep transformation will require the elimination of the current form of the "fast track" with all of its time demands and its rewards of status and money. We argue that there is little danger of the best of human excellence and ambition being thwarted by removing the inhumane demands and rewards that exacerbate inequality.

Finally, we advocate a "sub norm" of roughly equal hours of work and care to avoid economic dependence and divisions of labor that might slow the dismantling of the hierarchy of work over care.

Is all of this economically feasible? To that fundamental question we now turn.

3

Transitioning

"No, not less of a man, but maybe more human"
—A Dutch doctor on being asked if part-time work made
him less of a man.[1]

What kind of concrete economic institutions would be necessary to foster and facilitate an equitable division of caregiving work? These final two chapters examine the big picture viability of Part-Time for All. In this chapter, we discuss *transition*. In other words, what is necessary to help societies move toward PTfA? The next and final chapter discusses *feasibility*. Presuming we could get there, would an economy based on secure, flexible, quality, part-time work really function? Would such an economy be stable in an era of globalization, and could we afford it?

As soon as we think about the question of transition toward PTfA we immediately recognize two interconnected issues. On the one hand, there is the question of how we can reform our economic institutions so that everyone has the *option* of working a high-quality, flexible, part-time job. This is the issue of expanding the availability of good part-time work so that all those who want such jobs can actually get them. On the other hand, there is the question of how we can enhance *desire* for such jobs in the first place. After all, it is not enough to simply create available options for part-time work. Unless there is a corresponding change in norms, values, and desires, many people (particularly men) will refuse to undertake part-time work, preferring the status and financial rewards associated with full-time work. In this chapter we examine these two basic questions in turn. Of course, in the real world, we expect that transition will involve both components developing simultaneously in messy and overlapping ways. The new

Part-Time For All. Jennifer Nedelsky and Tom Malleson, Oxford University Press.
© Oxford University Press 2023. DOI: 10.1093/oso/9780190642754.003.0004

institutions, and the norms regarding their desirability, need to shift in tandem. Nevertheless, for the sake of clarity we discuss these two components one at a time.

Section 1 discusses the changes needed in rich economies to create more options for part-time work; this can happen through two basic mechanisms: expanding the availability of part-time jobs and/or reducing the hours that constitute normal full-time work. Section 2 examines a host of policies and institutions that could motivate people to take up the options of part-time work. Specifically, we look at public policies that can shift gender norms; policies that can shift norms of what constitutes a "career"; policies that can enhance economic security; policies that can dampen the obsession with consumption; and helpful changes to the tax code. All of which are crucial aids for fostering a transition to new norms of PTfA.

I. Creating Opportunities for Part-Time Work

If people desire shorter hours of work, is there any difficulty in achieving this? One might think that employees can simply bargain with employers for the number of hours they desire. However, this turns out not to be case. In fact, market systems typically contain important biases against work time reduction, that is, biases in favor of longer hours, which need to be understood if they are to be overcome. Scholars of working time tend to point to five main systemic biases against work time reduction.[2] First, fixed employment costs (such as those associated with training and recruitment) make it cheaper for firms to hire fewer workers on longer hours. Second, reducing hours can require costly shifts in work reorganization as job bundles need to be split and reassigned in sometimes complex ways. Third, firms will be resistant to reducing hours if they fear that it will be difficult to find additional workers of comparable skill and experience. Fourth, benefit payments often bias firms against reducing hours because if they must make such payments on a per person rather than a per hour basis (as is commonly the case in the United States and Canada) then it is significantly more expensive for firms to have two employees working 20 hours than one employee working 40 hours. Finally, firms often use long hours as a way of identifying work commitment and loyalty. For all these reasons, to the extent that employers are forced by their employees to reward productivity increases, they will almost always prefer to do so in the form of increased wages rather than decreased hours. Consequently, workers are usually only able to achieve a reduction in work hours in times of strength (due to strong union membership, tight labor markets, or a broad national consensus in terms of the need for sharing work hours as a strategy to reduce unemployment).[3]

That said, work time reduction is not an entirely negative prospect from the perspective of business; it offers some potential advantages too. Work time reduction can increase productivity by reducing worker fatigue or boredom.[4] It can attract and retain talented labor, particularly from women, who are often only willing to work reduced hours.[5] And it can be combined with the reorganization of production and sometimes the intensification of work to allow for enhanced productivity (for example, by rearranging shifts so that machines can be run longer).[6] The historical record indicates that attempts to reduce work time are most likely to be successful when there is strong pressure from legislation or unions, and when the costs borne by businesses are minimized (for instance, when the costs associated with reorganizing production for shorter shifts are offset by wage freezes, or government subsidies, or rolled out slowly enough that they are effectively paid for through the productivity gains that normally occur with passing time).

For our purposes, the key question is this: What would be necessary to allow everyone who wants good part-time work to be able to get it? A moment's reflection reveals that there are two basic pathways for governments to promote work time reduction. A government can aim directly at increasing the number of good part-time jobs. Alternatively, a government can strive to reduce the number of hours of standard "full time" jobs, so that they come to resemble part-time jobs more and more. We discuss these two mechanisms in turn.

II. Creating Quality Part-Time Work

There are two main avenues for enhancing the number of available part-time jobs.[7] The first is the ability for parents to work part-time after the birth or adoption of a child. Reduced hours with job protection is available as part of parental leave in 12 out of 15 EU member states and in Norway.[8] For example, since 1978, parents in Sweden have had the right to reduce their daily work hours by 25 percent until the child is eight years old. In Norway, parents are entitled to work 50, 60, 75, 80, or 90 percent of their usual hours (at proportional pay) for up to two years, as well as being able to formally request reduced hours until the child is ten. Similarly, in Austria, both parents may reduce their hours or change the scheduling of hours until the child is seven years old, with a right to return to full-time work thereafter.[9] In general, these options are much more frequently taken up by women than men (fathers increasingly do take paternity leave, but only for a small amount of time, before reverting to full-time work, not usually ever switching to part-time work).

A second mechanism for increasing the availability of part-time work is the introduction of a right to adjust hours. While most European countries allow adjustments to hours for new parents, three countries—France, Germany, and the Netherlands—have actually introduced a right for all employees to adjust their hours for any reason they like.[10] Employees must provide a reasonable notification period, and such changes cannot be altered sporadically (they represent permanent contractual changes), but when employees do make such a request the employer cannot refuse on a whim, but only if she can show that there would be serious business costs associated with providing the hour adjustment. Courts in these countries, and especially in the Netherlands, have not accepted minimal costs as adequate grounds for refusal, but have expected businesses to shoulder a certain amount of costs in order to adjust hours to employees' needs.

For example, the Netherlands has made use of both of these mechanisms. In terms of parental leave, the law is explicitly aimed at creating a more equal division of domestic and paid work between parents. Though governments sometimes claim to be aiming for a 150 percent arrangement, where each parent works "three-quarter time," instead the reality is that most fathers work full-time and mothers work half-time.[11] In terms of rights to time sovereignty, in 2000 the Netherlands passed the Working Time Adjustment Act, which Graaf and Batker called, "perhaps the most important piece of time-balance legislation ever."[12] This legislation provides employees who have worked at a firm of more than 10 workers for at least one year with a legal right to change their hours irrespective of the reason for such change and also to remain in the same occupational position.[13] Employers must show serious business, organizational, or health and safety objections before they are able to reject a claim to adjust hours (LaJeunesse, 2009, p. 223).[14]

The Netherlands is proof that transition to part-time work can happen quickly and effectively. The country has witnessed an astronomical increase in part-time work, from about 20 percent to 50 percent of the workforce in thirty years (and these are generally secure, quality jobs, as we discuss next chapter). A large part of this is attributable to the policies just mentioned. But part of its success is surely due to its ability to make part-time work attractive, by enhancing economic security, increasing the prominence of part-time careers, and other such things that we discuss below.

III. Reducing Full-Time Hours

There are profound differences in the total number of hours that are worked across the industrialized world. Average annual hours per employee in France and the Netherlands are 1402 and 1399 respectively, which is far less than in the United States (at 1767 hours). Germany has the world's shortest hours—at 1332—which is 25 percent, or the equivalent of eleven full working weeks, shorter than the United States (OECD, 2020). Of course, employment hours are only part of total working hours. It should not be forgotten that when we consider the total work being done—the paid and the unpaid—it is everywhere women who work the most. If you combine paid and unpaid work, the average man in a heterosexual couple with children (youngest child under seven) does 60 hours of work per week; the average woman in the same situation does 71 hours.[15]

Throughout industrial history there have been two major aims of work time reduction: as a defensive policy to reduce unemployment through worksharing (that is, reducing the hours of full-time work in order to share the work around), and as a progressive policy to increase leisure, dignity, and in more recent years, work-life balance and gender equality. Since the 1980s the former concern has been particularly prominent in France, Germany, and Italy, whereas the latter concern has been most visible in Denmark, Sweden, and the Netherlands. How have major reductions in hours been accomplished? We saw above that in the case of the Netherlands a major part of the story was the increase in part-time work. Whereas in Germany and the Nordic countries, as well as France, work time reduction has been achieved mainly via a reduction in full-time hours, such as through the famous 35-hour week.[16]

In Germany and the Nordic countries, work time reduction has been achieved via union negotiation. The German model is a particularly instructive model for us, especially the core idea that unions aim for a particular kind of bargain, which is that workers agree to keep their wages constant (or accept lower than normal raises) in exchange for reduced hours. What is so powerful about this bargaining strategy is that it can go on indefinitely, whereby workers cumulatively work shorter and shorter hours, without ever losing any pay. This is not to say that this kind of arrangement in Germany has been totally costless for workers; the typical pattern has been that where workers won reduced hours they usually were only able to do so in exchange for wage moderation and flexibilization.[17] For instance, IG Metall (the metalworkers union, and the largest union in Europe) succeeded in reducing hours through collective agreement from 40-hour weeks in 1985 to 35-hour weeks by 1995 through this kind of exchange.[18]

In France, the 35-hour week came into being through two pieces of legislation introduced by the center-left government under Lionel Jospin.[19] Its main aim was not work time reduction specifically, but reducing unemployment through worksharing. The first legislation, Aubry I (named after Martine Aubry, the Minister of Labor), introduced in June 1998, had three main aspects. First, a mandatory reduction of the standard workweek from 39 to 35 hours by January 1, 2000 (2002 for firms with 20 or fewer employees); after this period, employers would be forced to pay overtime rates for longer hours (we can think of this as the government's "stick"). Second, a call to labor unions and employers to launch sector-wide and firm-level negotiations on work time reduction. Third, the introduction of financial incentives for firms to reduce their hours (these incentives took the form of lower payroll taxes offered for a period of five years to firms that reached an agreement with a union or employee representative to reduce work time by at least 10 percent and create at least 6 percent additional jobs. The quicker a firm reduced its hours, the more generous the aid it received; we can think of this as the government's "carrot").[20]

Even though Aubry I was quite generous in its aid to business, the main business association, MEDEF, was nevertheless strongly opposed. The central economic issue with work time reduction is whether it will increase unit labor costs. If work time reduction is accompanied with full wage compensation, as the French unions were demanding, this would mean that fewer hours would be worked for the same total pay, hence labor costs would rise significantly (assuming they are not offset in other ways, such as by productivity gains). This is problematic because increased labor costs reduce profit, which causes some firms to go under, and can also hurt the competitiveness of French firms internationally—both of which would end up hurting rather than helping the employment situation. So, while there was much agreement across the political spectrum that *in theory* increased labor costs can be economically damaging, the debate in France centered around whether, in practice, labor costs would actually rise, with MEDEF predicting dangerous rises and the government promising no rises. Unsurprisingly, MEDEF also opposed the 35-hour legislation on the political grounds of being opposed to any "interference" into what they saw as "their" domain.

The business opposition led to Aubry I being watered down with the introduction of Aubry II, introduced in the autumn of 1999. Aubry II specified that working hours could be measured as an average of the whole year, as opposed to a weekly average (provided that weekly hours did not exceed 48 or an average of 44 over 12 weeks). Such annualization meant that firms could make their employees schedules more "flexible" by reducing hours some weeks, when demand was lower, and increasing hours during periods of high demand. Aubry II also eliminated the need to create a minimum number of jobs in return for payroll tax cuts. The aid became available to any firm that reached a 35-hour agreement as long as it simply expressed a commitment to creating or saving jobs. For these reasons Aubry II was somewhat disappointing for the Left—it was less tied to increasing employment (which undermined an important social justification for the subsidies), and it promoted employer-centered flexibility that increased the risk of intensification of work and created less predictable schedules, which threatened the quality-of-life and gender equality aspect of work time reduction.

Nevertheless, comprehensive reviews of the evidence suggests that the 35-hour week was relatively successful in achieving its aims.[21] There were significant overall reductions in hours: from 1997 to 2002, the average workweek of full-timers in firms with more than ten employees fell by 3.2 hours to 35.6 hours—an impressive reduction of 8.2 percent of overall working time. The measures were likely responsible for a significant portion of the employment boost (although the exact number of jobs generated has been hotly debated). Income cuts were rare but wage moderation was frequent (52 percent of those who moved to 35 hours before 2000 experienced a wage freeze, averaging 26 months, 22 percent saw lower than usual wage gains, and 27 percent felt no effect on their incomes). However, many complained that the reduced hours were accompanied with intensified work. For our purposes, one notable change is that the 35-hour week gave men and women more time for parenting—63 percent of women, and 52 percent of men, with children under 12, said that the legislation allowed them to spend more time with their children. When asked how work time reduction affected their daily lives, both at work and outside, 59 percent of workers said their lives had improved, while only 13 percent said their quality of life had deteriorated. Female managers were the most satisfied with the changes—73 percent of whom said that their daily lives had improved. The least satisfied were unskilled female workers; but even here more than double the number (40 percent compared to 20 percent) thought the changes had improved rather than worsened their daily lives. Employed women with children under the age of 12 were among the biggest winners: 71 percent said their daily life improved, while only 4.8 percent said it had worsened.[22] Moreover, men who reduced their work reported being significantly more involved in caring, indicating a modest change in gender roles.[23]

IV. Overtime

Across the OECD significant numbers of people work more than 48 hours per week—in Europe it's 15 percent of the population (Eurofound, 2017, p. 54). Such long hours make caregiving very difficult. They also result in the social absurdity of high levels of overtime side-by-side millions of people unemployed and desperate for work.[24] Reducing overtime is an important mechanism for work time reduction (thereby encouraging PTfA), as well as potentially redistributing work to reduce unemployment. Hence reduction of overtime can be a win-win strategy as it makes employees work less and employers hire more.

Countries typically regulate overtime by a mixture of three strategies mandated either by legislation or through collective agreement. The first is to set a threshold for standard working hours (such as 40 or 48 hours per week), after which point overtime compensation must be paid; in Europe the increased compensatory rates for overtime pay are highly varied, ranging from 10 percent on top of the normal pay rate up to 150 percent.[25] The second strategy is to require employees to sign consent forms to working overtime (with protections that they may not be punished for refusing to sign). The third strategy is to simply set a legal limit on the total number of overtime hours that may be worked in a week or a year. In practice, the social democratic countries tend to have stricter regulation about maximum hours, whereas the more liberal countries tend to make it easier for employers to extend hours. For instance, although the EU Directive on Part-Time Work establishes a right for employees to refuse to work more than 48-hour week, employers in the United Kingdom routinely flaunted this.

So a country wishing to engage in work time reduction to transition to PTfA should undoubtedly follow the first two strategies.[26] Probably the most successful route would be to raise the compensation rate that businesses must pay overtime workers so that firms face a significant disincentive to offering overtime. This rate could then be raised incrementally for the extra hours worked. Finland is a good example. It imposes high overtime compensation rates of up to 100 percent so as to restrict overtime work. Moreover, the compensation rate rises progressively with extra hours worked (as it does in France, Greece, Norway, Poland, and Portugal).[27]

V. The Wage-Leisure Tradeoff

In practice, reforms for work time reduction have been most successful when they have not overly threatened the bottom line. As we have seen, the fundamental resistance to work time reduction from business is the worry that it will increase labor costs (and therefore threaten profits which in turn will threaten future investment and employment), so this is the real-world constraint that has to be faced. It is important to emphasize that, empirically, where we have seen successful examples of work time reduction, they have occurred without raising labor costs.[28] When work time reduction is implemented in such a way that is neutral for labor costs, business will still likely object, but such objections are likely to be more ideological and less detrimental to the actual functioning (i.e., the investment and employment level) of the economy.

So for us the key question is this: how can a society reduce its full-time hours in a viable manner, that is, without increasing labor costs and damaging employment levels? There are three main ways, which are often combined in practice.

First, workers could take a pay cut, thereby simply working less and earning less. This is what we advocate for workers at the top ten or twenty percent of the income spectrum; but the bulk of workers will be highly resistant to pay cuts, for obvious reasons. Second, workers can offer wage moderation, freezing wages or accepting lower-than-usual pay raises, thereby allowing the increased leisure to be paid for by increased productivity gains (part of which comes from the natural productivity increases that occur regularly but slowly in a market economy, part of which comes from the productivity increases that tend to accompany reduced fatigue and boredom from reduced hours, and part of which might come from workers agreeing to demands for enhanced employer-oriented flexibility and the intensification of work). Germany has been the model here. Psychologically speaking, this route is far more promising. The evidence is strong that most people are far happier to accept a wage *freeze* (in exchange for more leisure) than they are to accept a pay *cut*, regardless of the leisure they get for it. Once people attain a certain income they are usually very resistant to giving it up.[29] This means that proponents of PTfA will have far more luck persuading workers to forego future wage increases than they will in persuading them to reduce the money in their pocket. The third possibility is for the state to offer financial support to firms that increase employment through reduced work time, meaning that the state is essentially subsidizing business and so helping to absorb the increased labor costs. The French 35-hour law made significant use of this technique.

So while each of these strategies is plausible, Hayden rightly points out that none of them are costless for workers.[30] The first can hurt workers' income; the second can increase the intensity of work, or worsen time sovereignty; and the third can increase taxes. In addition, Bosch and Lehndorff emphasize that successful work time reduction requires that the other major disincentives identified above need to be accommodated.[31] In particular, changing the benefit payment structure from a "per worker" to a "per hour" basis, and at least partially socializing the costs of training workers (since business will be resistant to work time reduction if there are insufficient additional skilled workers to hire, meaning they have to pay for the training themselves).

The bottom line is that significant work time reduction is entirely feasible. The historical record shows that it is possible to collectively reduce hours by 4–8 percent, the equivalent of two or three hours of a week's work, in a five-year period, without increasing labor costs or damaging economic competitiveness.[32]

The German case provides the general model: wide-spread collective bargaining that is based, fundamentally, on an exchange of work-time reduction for wage moderation. Such an exchange means that workers agree to stay at the same income level by taking their share of future productivity gains not in wages but in reduced hours. In other words, hours are reduced but labor costs do not rise since they are paid for by slowly improving productivity. The French model of occasional large, state-led jumps forward in work time reduction is also useful; here the strategy involves a national campaign to encourage wide-spread union negotiation across the economy simultaneously, and most importantly, financial compensation to firms who reduce hours (with added incentives for those firms who reduce hours and increase employment particularly quickly).

In sum, this model of collectively agreeing to wage moderation in exchange for work time reduction is the model that rich industrialized countries should follow toward PTfA. Such a process would mean that full-time workers would not lose any income; they would stay at their current income, which at least in Europe allows for a very comfortable level of material existence (indeed an extremely rich one by any historical or global standard), and, over time, work less and less, and thus be able to contribute more and more care. Since workers' standard of living remains constant, this is the process that could be—and, given the fact that continual growth looks to be an ecological catastrophe, we think *should* be—carried on indefinitely.

However, from a PTfA perspective, there is one important problem, or at least caveat, with the reduction of full-time hours. The issue is that shorter hours have often been achieved in practice in exchange for more "flexibility" (from the employer's point of view), such as annualization, increased on-call time, night or weekend shifts, or more frequent schedule changes. From a care giver's perspective there is a difficult tradeoff here. Care givers get more time off work, which is deeply important, but simultaneously they may lose some control over their schedules. This allows us to see that time sovereignty is not simply a matter of the *quantity* of time off, but it is also a measure of its *quality*. Care givers require both.

Taking a step back now, we have seen that there are two general strategies that a country may follow toward the goal of quality part-time work for all. One route is to directly increase the amount of quality part-time jobs that exist. The Dutch case is a rough example of this route. The alternative route is to aim for full-time work for all, while simultaneously reducing full-time hours. France, to a certain degree, and Germany, Sweden, and Denmark more specifically, are approximate examples of this route. In terms of transitioning to Part-Time for All, both strategies have substantial merit, but also risks. The former is more direct, but it's also more individualized and less successful at challenging gender norms; the danger of this strategy is that men don't take up part-time work thereby reinforcing severe gender segregation;

so this method should only be adopted if it's supplemented with complementary reforms to incentivize men to take up part-time work too (as discussed below). The latter is a more collective approach and somewhat more successful at challenging gender roles, though only asymmetrically (breadwinning for all becomes the idealized norm instead of caregiving for all, which we favor); and this route is more circuitous and risks maintaining long, care-unfriendly hours. So neither road is perfect and both have their dangers. Hence whatever is chosen must be done carefully. Ideally, we would advocate for governments to adopt both strategies simultaneously, since there is no reason not to use all the tools at the government's disposal for fostering work time reduction.

VI. Creating Desire for Part-Time Work

In the Netherlands, people have nearly all the options for part-time work that one could possibly want. Yet still men generally do not avail themselves of such options. Only 23 percent of employed men work part-time (compared to 73% of women).[33] This perpetuates gender segregation in that men consistently work more hours, make more money, have better careers, are less financially dependent, and do less caregiving. Across Europe as a whole in 2019, women engaged in part-time work at almost four times the rate of men (29 percent of employed women are part-time compared to only 8 percent of men).[34] Much the same could be said of Sweden: even though fathers have had the right to take paternity leave since 1974, by 2005, 30 years later, men still took only 21 percent of total leave days.[35]

Unless men are motivated to take up part-time work, it will invariably remain women's work. This will maintain gender segregation and reinforce gender stereotypes in both the workplace and the home. More generally, without changes in motivation and desire, people will not take up part-time work in large numbers, men will not take up part-time work in equal proportion to women, and time sovereignty options may well be used, again particularly by men, to increase rather than decrease hours. Hence for PTfA to be realized, institutional options by themselves are not enough.

We also need to build the *desire* to take up such options. The crux of the issue is whether we can motivate men to provide more care. Their reluctance to provide equal care is the asymmetry at the heart of the gender system that maintains patriarchal inequality and makes PTfA so difficult to achieve. This will be no easy feat—many men are resistant to working less and caring more because doing so means relinquishing financial wealth and cultural status in exchange for unpaid and devalued (but in many ways just as demanding) caregiving. Less obviously, and probably less frequently, some women may resist giving up their control over the sphere of care. Whether that control is justified in terms of belief in men's incompetence, fears around their violence, or an attachment to the one sphere where they can possess authority, for many women fully sharing responsibility for care will not look like an unqualified good. For women, however, the rewards are likely to come more quickly. They will have help with their care responsibilities as well as societal recognition of the value of care. As they gain confidence in men's competence, these benefits are likely to outweigh the previous desire for control. Well-grounded fears of violence are, of course, a different matter, and women should never be asked to share care where their safety or their children's is at risk.

The central argument of this section is that it is indeed possible to make the new norms of PTfA an attractive option, even for men. Doing so will require a number of changes to our economic structures and cultural ways of life. As we have indicated before, sometimes the norm changes will precede economic changes, sometimes the other way around. The important point is that for PTfA to become a reality there must be reciprocal change in both these areas so that new norms support new economic possibilities and vice-versa. In particular, we require changes in the following areas: a transformation of gender norms around work and care, a new model of a career, enhanced economic security, reduced consumerism, and changes to the tax structure.

A. Changing Gender Norms

Our central argument throughout this book has been that we need significant changes in contemporary norms about who works and who cares. The zombie norms of male breadwinners and female care givers continue to exert tremendous influence. They prove particularly consequential when heterosexual couples get pregnant and start making decisions (consciously or subconsciously) about how to split up to the care and labor market work that must be done.

In thinking about how to change these norms it is important to remind ourselves why they exist in the first place. That is a complicated issue, of course, but there are at least four factors which seem particularly prominent. First, men in general have significantly more bargaining power in their relationships with women, and more power in general. Second, there are still strong cultural expectations about gender roles.[36] Third, and deeply connected to cultural expectations, are the personal desires of individuals. Bjørnholt argues that a major reason why men don't change their priorities about work and care is the straightforward reason that they like the current set up.[37] England concurs.[38] Why would men voluntarily choose to work less and care more if that means losing the money and status that work brings only to suffer the cultural stigma that "female" tasks bring? Fourth, the current institutional options tend to reinforce people's sense of what is possible or normal. In a patriarchal society these four factors coincide. Male power is inscribed, enforced, and reinforced through cultural expectations, individual male desire, and institutional possibilities. Shifting norms is so difficult because it requires shifting these four things simultaneously.

Let us restate some of new norms the project of PTfA aims to bring about. The most important one is the assumption that all should take part in care: that women are just as capable breadwinners as men, and men are just as capable care givers as women, and gender-nonconforming people are just as capable as anyone else. Additionally, we need a new norm about long hours of work. Overwork should not be seen as heroic, but as narrow-minded and sad—evidence that one doesn't value spending time and building relationships with kids, family, and friends.

There are three basic tools for shifting norms. The first is grassroots organizing and informal education, such as we noted earlier in the context of first wave feminism, smoking, drinking and driving, and same sex relationships. Much of the discussion in the first two chapters could be taken as the kinds of arguments that should be promoted in thousands of informal conversations and grassroots projects. Activists and academics need to shift norms by injecting new discourses, new narratives, new ideas, and new ideals into the mainstream. We need regular conversations at dinner tables, coffee shops, places of worship, and union meetings about what it is to be a "real man." This is the slow pedagogical work that feminists have been doing for a long time, but it needs a PTfA twist.

While the idea of female breadwinners is slowly and surely becoming accepted, we need to push harder to promote the idea (among women as well as men) that men are capable care givers. We should be more emphatic and provocative in insisting that there are two types of men: flourishing men—those who know how to cook and clean, who are nurturing and loving, who center relationships and emotional intelligence in their lives—and stunted men. We need to be more vocal in our praise of flourishing men, and more forthright in our disdain for men who have allowed these abilities to atrophy—those who see their care giver role as trips to sporting events, or occasional "babysitting," or doling out angry discipline. Disdain can be an antidote to the approval this male relation to care still receives. We might feel more compassion for those whose failure to develop caring abilities has *not* been rewarded with power, money, and prestige. (There are class differences in the forms this care-free masculinity takes.)[39] But in all cases, the failure is a harm to men as well as to their families and societies. One positive example is the FNV, the federation of Dutch unions, which launched a campaign in the 1990s to encourage men to work part-time by explicitly attempting to change cultural values, developing slogans like, "Good morning, I'm your father."[40] We need to show men the evidence amassed by Bronnie Ware that, for men in particular, among the top regrets of their lives was the wish they had not spent so much time at work.[41]

Another pedagogical approach to shifting norms is through encouraging and highlighting new role models. After all, role models are simply living, walking exemplars of new norms. They are norms enfleshed. So it is important to tell and retell stories like the one of the Dutch cabinet member who excused himself from a parliamentary debate to get home to his daughter's birthday, the successful part-time law partners and senior managers, and the doctor who said that part-time work didn't make him less of a man "but maybe more human".[42]

The second tool is formal education. Gender stereotypes need to be challenged in curricula and classrooms throughout the schooling system.[43] As we noted earlier, it might also be helpful if all students received instruction in care giving.

The third major tool to change norms is that of public policy. Indeed, we know that providing new institutional options for people can by itself go some of the way to changing norms. Consider the fascinating study by Pedulla and Thébaud.[44] The authors took a representative sample of 18–32 year-old unmarried, childless individuals from the United States, and surveyed them on their preferred division of labor while randomly placing them in different situations of more or less workplace supportiveness. What they found is that institutional constraints significantly influence young men and women's work-family preferences. The number of college-educated women who want an egalitarian division of labor jumps by over 30 percent when the institutional options for that become available.[45] This is strong evidence for the possibility of norm change. What people want changes dramatically based on the institutional options available to them.[46]

Let us now describe six public policies that would be particularly useful in helping to galvanize a shift in gender norms.

(i) Fostering Part-Time Work

There is good reason to hope that expanding opportunities for part-time work can be useful in furthering gender norm changes. For instance, there is evidence that when fathers work less, they tend to do more caregiving.[47] This is partly due to the increased spare time, and partly due to the fact that part-time work for men tends to even out the bargaining power between partners, giving women more influence over the division of labor. In addition, there is evidence that part-time work can itself foster changes in values. Wielers and Raven find that increased options for part-time work in the Netherlands has led to changing values in that part-time fathers adhere to the work obligation norm (the idea that work is a duty) less than full-time working fathers. It seems reasonable to infer that a reduced sense of work obligation is being replaced, at least partially, with an increased interest in caregiving.[48] The authors conclude that "in the new organization of family life, fathers are expected to contribute to household chores and the upbringing of the children. Fathers can only meet these expectations by trading-off work and family norms."[49]

(ii) Fatherhood-Friendly Parental Leave

It is well known that the arrival of the first child is an incredibly important event for the setting of gendered patterns. Women typically take more time off, they then become the parenting "experts," whereas fathers are relegated to the role of "helpers," which then motivates them to fall back on traditional gender roles of being breadwinners not genuine care givers. Women then face a significant economic penalty for taking more time out of the labor market (the typical penalty that women suffer for having a child is close to 20 percent of earnings in the long run).[50] Then later if the couple have a second child, it will be economically rational for the woman to take time off again—thus further segregating their economic positions and reinforcing gender stereotypes. The result is that most heterosexual couples, even those who see themselves as progressive and want to be egalitarian, tend to become significantly *more* traditional and gendered with the arrival of a child.[51]

This means that policies impacting caregiving over the early years of a new child's life will play a significant role in either reinforcing traditional gender roles or fostering more egalitarian ones. How should parental leave be structured so as to promote new norms of universal caregiving? The evidence shows that the most important factor is encouraging fathers to take as equal a share of the caregiving as possible. This means that they need to take a relatively longer leave than is typical (several months at least, not several weeks).[52] There is also some suggestive evidence that solo or "home alone" time, where the mother is back at work and the father is solo parenting, is useful for gender equality, as it upsets the normal division of "expert" vs "helper".[53] More generally, for all parenting couples, it is important not to build in a division of labor between one person primarily responsible for economic contribution and the other for care contribution.

Additionally, it is important to structure parental leave in a such a way as to motivate men to take more of it. Most high-income states often provide paid leave just to the woman, or to the couple as transferable leave, allowing the couple to divide it as they see fit. The problem with this laissez-faire approach is that it has a boomerang effect in that women end up taking the overwhelming majority of the leave. Across the OECD, few men, less than 16 percent, exit the labor market to care for children, and when they do it is usually for very short periods (less than 2 percent take full-time leave).[54] We know that parental leave policies which lead to women taking significantly more leave than men are deeply problematic; they create an unequal division of labor that over time sediments into different gender roles, penalizing women's position in the labor market and reinforcing conventional gender stereotypes.

However, we also know that when men can be induced to take more leave, positive consequences follow. Perhaps most importantly, increased leave can change men's attitudes and desires. For instance, the Swedish sociologist Thomas Johansson notes that "fathers describe the experience [of parental leave] as life changing. They become more involved in housework and childcare. Their relationships are closer. And many have time to rethink the meaning of their lives".[55] Haas and Hwang found that the amount of leave taken by fathers had a positive effect on their participation in childcare as well as on their satisfaction with contact with children.[56] Similarly, Nepomnyaschy and Waldfogel found that fathers who take longer leave after the birth of a child are more involved in childcare nine months later.[57] Aldous et al. found much the same.[58]

As more and more men start taking leave, this also has the effect of slowly shifting broader cultural expectation. Recall the anecdote of our Swedish colleague who insisted that if he didn't take paternity leave his colleagues would look down on him as a money grubber. This is just one anecdote, but even so it illustrates how far the cultural expectations have shifted from the North American norm where paternity leave is still seen as a strange, unusual, and unwise career move. A high rate of paternity leave is very useful because it undermines the traditional basis for employers preferring male employees over female. If any employee is just as likely as anyone else to request time off, then women will be hired just as frequently as men, and the gender pay gap will erode. Relatedly, enhanced paternity leave is beneficial for married women for the straightforward reason that the more caring the father does the less the mother has to do, allowing her to return to work. Elly-Ann Johansson finds that each month the father stays on parental leave results in mothers being able to work more thereby increasing maternal earnings by 6.7 percent.[59] So paternity leave can help the economic position of women, and therefore their bargaining position, which will likely spill over into other positive gender changes in a virtuous cycle.

How can parental leave be structured so as to motivate men to take more? Most studies point to several key factors: statutory entitlement to paid leave;[60] an entitlement pay level that is high enough to mostly replace lost earnings;[61] an organizational culture at work such that there is no discrimination or career penalty for men who take leave;[62] flexible work arrangements;[63] and a quota of non-transferable days reserved for men, usually called "daddy days" or "use-it-or-lose-it".[64]

Sweden is the exemplar here. All parents have the right to take 480 days of leave between the couple. This leave is paid at about 80 percent of earnings.[65] The leave can be shared between the couple as they want, except for two months which cannot be transferred—these are reserved for the "minority care giver," in most cases the father. Such days must be taken by the father or they are lost. In addition to these policies, Sweden has even introduced an "Equality Bonus," which awards parents who share their leave allowance equally an extra SEK3,000 ($350) per month.[66]

The "use-it-or-lose-it" policy is particularly important for cultivating new gender norms. Since the policy provides incentives for fathers to take more leave it has been called "fatherhood by gentle force".[67] The most generous use-it-or-lose it policy is in Iceland, where three months are guaranteed for fathers at 80 percent of salary.[68] Finland offers 12 days at 66 percent earnings. Belgium and Slovenia offer more days (6 months and 90 days respectively), but at a low flat-rate.[69]

The policy has proven highly successful in increasing paternity leave. In Iceland, the number of fathers who took parental leave skyrocketed from less than 1 percent in 2002 to 90 percent of fathers in 2011 taking the full three months that they were entitled to.[70] In Sweden, the policy is credited with helping to increase the amount of leave taken by fathers from 11 percent of the total leave in 1994 to

19 percent in 2004.[71] In Denmark, during the short period of time that the "daddy quota" was in operation, the percentage of fathers who took leave went from 7 percent to 24 percent. Moreover, the evidence shows that the longer the quota reserved for fathers, the higher the total share of father's leave becomes: so the highest proportion of leave days taken is found in Iceland (32.7 percent) and Sweden (20.5 percent), and lower levels in Denmark (5.9 percent) and Finland (5.5 percent) where leave arrangements are more limited.[72]

Before moving on, we want to suggest two more policies connected to parental leave that are important for changing gender norms. We advocate a policy whereby new fathers receive a financial bonus when they take solo leave, that is, leave when the mother is back at work. In addition, we would limit full-time parental leave, of either partner, to about a year. Leave policies that are overly long end up backfiring by keeping people (usually women) out of the labor market for too long with the result that they irrevocably damage their human capital and employment possibilities.[73]

(iii) Encouragement of Part-Time Work for Parents (Particularly Fathers)

Incentivizing fathers to take paternity leave has been a crucial gender innovation, as even relatively short periods of leave can end up having profound effects upon men, their connection to their children, their identity, and their self-perception as care givers. The problem is that most men still take only very small amounts of parental leave before returning to full-time work. In other words, the current situation is that parental leave is simply a small break in the regular routine—having a child does not radically change male work patterns. Even in Sweden—arguably the most gender-egalitarian country in the world—only 6 percent of fathers change from full-time to part-time work.[74] The briefness of paternity leave means that it does not have a fundamental impact on the labor market; the labor market everywhere remains a man's labor market, and a deeply anti-caregiving labor market.

The key lesson from the use-it-or-lose-it policies is that getting men to change their behavior requires strong incentives to do so. This suggests to us that an important policy innovation would be to incentivize men to switch to part-time work after the birth of a child, and importantly, to do so for a substantial length of time. Hence we suggest that countries should adopt a proposal of this general sort, whereby all parents of children under the age of, say, five are legally entitled to shift to part-time work (with no penalty, and the right to return to full-time if they so choose). Moreover, the "minority care giver" (i.e., the partner who works longer hours, typically the father) should be eligible to receive financial wage-based compensation for shifting to part-time work, lasting up to five years. For example, if a father chooses to reduce his hours to 75 percent (from 40-hours per week to 30), the state might subsidize his income to 90 percent; or if he reduces to 50 percent (from 40-hours per week to 20), the state might subsidize his salary to 66 percent.

A policy of this sort would be immensely powerful because if large numbers of men started taking five full years of part-time work, it would shift the entire labor market.[75] Every workplace across the entire economy would immediately gain experience with shifting workloads and re-creating schedules to create new part-time positions; everyone would immediately become familiar with the phenomenon of good part-time jobs; and there would be an explosion of new role models and new patterns for doing things differently, all of which would make it much easier for other people to request part-time options as well. Having senior male managers take five years of part-time would make it vastly easier for junior employees to do the same, as HR would become familiar with the process, and everyone would see part-time work as normal, standard employment, not a sign of being "unmotivated" or "unloyal" or "unambitious." The shape of the entire economy would change.

With policies like these in place, we would hope that the norms about having children would shift substantially. From a PTfA perspective, the model that we would encourage is that of a couple both taking off the first month or two of the child's life; this should be followed by a year or 18-months of leave divided up between the parents, one at a time (so both experience some time as the solo care giver), while the other returns to work. Of course, the hours of solo care giving would be modest given a return to work limited to 30 hours per week. After this, both parents would continue to work part-time until the child is five, and ideally for much of their careers beyond that.

(iv) Universal Daycare

We share with other feminists the conviction of the importance of accessible daycare to allow women to enter and re-enter the labor market more easily. We note, however, that even excellent, accessible daycare cannot alone solve the problems that PTfA addresses and that, under the norms of PTfA, it would be possible (and common) for mothers to work even if their children were not in formal care. Nevertheless, especially in the transition, universal day care will allow women to work in the same proportion as men thus eroding gender stereotypes and augmenting women's bargaining power vis-à-vis their male partners. According to Jennifer Hook's analysis of twenty countries, the level of employment of mothers is the most important factor influencing men's contributions to childcare and domestic work.[76] Even once the norms of PTfA are fully adopted, many parents who are both working part-time and engaging in a lot of childcare, might want their children to spend regular time in formal care. As noted earlier, we advocate integrating flexible pre-school into the public school system.

In sum, universal daycare would advance gender equality, benefit many children, and provide all parents with more flexibility for work, leisure, and for contributions to community participation.

(v) Quotas

Governments can attempt to shift gender norms by legally enforcing gender quotas for certain positions. Quotas are particularly important for political parties in order to get equal numbers of women into government as men.[77] This matters because there is substantial evidence that female politicians tend to support legislation on women's issues more so than men.[78] For instance, Lambert finds that having more women in power is consistently associated with more generous childcare and parental leave policies: an increase of 10 percent of women in parliament corresponds to a 5 percent increase in maternity employment policy.[79] Hence quotas can help to address the care/policy divide.

A number of countries have followed Norway's lead in introducing quotas for corporate boards—where now 40 percent of all board positions must, by law, be female. The hope here is that such quotas will shift cultural expectations of women's roles and also shift bargaining power of women as they slowly gain more power in the economy. Norway has also introduced quotas for men in the childcare profession, as a way to create more gender equality in an overwhelmingly female profession and shift cultural expectations of who does caring work. Since 1998 there has been a system of quotas for men to enter pre-primary teacher colleges, as well as campaigns aimed at getting more men employed in preschool and school. The quotas have been successful: between 2003 and 2007 the number of men employed by preschools has risen by half (whereas the numbers have stagnated in other Nordic countries).[80]

(vi) Public Prizes for Feminist Leaders and Role Models

A final public policy possibility is that of public prizes for feminist leaders. These can be ways to celebrate role models and publicly affirm new gender norms that government is hoping to encourage. For instance, in 2009 the Netherlands introduced a "Modern Man Prize," which is awarded for three categories: men who are considered role models in combining work and family tasks, an organization that is actively involved in the debate on male and female roles, and a company that enables its personnel to maintain a healthy work-life balance.[81] To give one example, the businessman Rutger Groot Wassink won the prize in 2011 for his work in cofounding a campaign that promotes "Papadag" (Daddy Days), which are days off for working fathers to be with their kids.[82]

B. Toward A Modern Career

A workplace is not simply a place where people work. It is also an institutionalization, a cultural reification, of what a worker *is*. Workplaces in the Global North remain, by and large, products of an earlier era. Their structure, rules, and regulations are permeated with a notion of the actor within them. This is the mythical norm of the "ideal worker." As we have seen, the ideal worker is, among other things, one who is able to devote continual, uninterrupted, perpetually available labor to the workplace, year after year. The ideal worker certainly does not work part-time and most definitely does not take parental leave. The ideal worker, around which our workplaces are organized, is, in essence, a 1950s man. This is the person who can devote full and uninterrupted attention to the workplace, precisely because he has a wife at home who relieves him of the bulk of caregiving and domestic work. The conventional workplace thereby assumes in its very structure, its very DNA, a gendered division of labor. This is why contemporary workplaces so often feel like evil time machines. As soon as one enters, you are thrust back in time into an outdated and patriarchal set of gender roles.

One consequence of the ideal worker norm is that employers tend to judge commitment, loyalty, and ambition (and thereby determine career advancement) based on how closely one resembles this ideal. That is, advancement is tied to one's ability and willingness to put in long hours of continual uninterrupted work.[83] Another consequence of the ideal worker norm is the tacit belief that "good workers" have no or only very minimal care obligations. Consider that fact that if a person in the United States takes only one year off from work over a 15-year period, their annual earnings will end up being 39 percent lower than those who don't take time off.[84] This is a massive financial penalty that care givers (and others) suffer if they deviate from the ideal working norm.

The problems with the ideal worker norm are obvious. The norm is extremely biased against care givers who obviously do require significant interruptions for childcare and other forms of caregiving, and who need significant reductions and flexibility in their work time. It is an extraordinary thing that our workplaces are modeled on a kind of life that is simply not possible for half of the population.

Given that the ideal worker norm is a patriarchal and anachronistic ideal for a twenty-first century career, what should be the ideal? The norm should be that of a part-time, flexible career. This is a vision of a career that is marked by dedication but not by full-time or inflexible work. It is a vision of a career where working time ebbs and flows around the major contours of life and caregiving responsibilities. It is a kind of career that allows for emotional coherence, work-life integration, as well as the equal participation of all in the full scope of life's activities.

Achieving this, of course, is no easy task. It faces all the usual obstacles: old-fashioned norms; recalcitrant preferences of individuals (particularly men who enjoy the status quo); the bargaining power of the men at the top versus the relatively disempowered position of women and men lower down who want to do things differently; and competition from other firms who don't care about being family friendly.

What is needed to shift the ideal worker norm to a new norm of part-time, flexible work? We emphasize four important ingredients: narratives, powerful women, role models, and rights.

First, we need to try to create new narratives about work. We need to talk about workaholism not as pride but pathology. We should depict single-minded attention to work not as "ambition" but as narrow-mindedness and uncaring selfishness. We should repeat at our dinner tables, coffee shops, and work meetings that the 60-hour week is a stunted form of life. It is not sexy or impressive, but unhealthy, old-fashioned, patriarchal, and, ultimately, sad for people to spend so little time in caring relations. Connected to this, heterosexual women need to embrace a shift in what counts as attractive masculinity. There is still a widespread feeling that men in heterosexual relationships should be stronger, taller, richer, more powerful, and more financially successful than their female partners; women can feel embarrassed if their male partner "falls short" on any of these terms.[85] The link between economic success and sexual attraction is both long standing and long contested. Since care has been feminized for so long, seeing caring as an attractive form of masculinity may challenge many current images of heterosexual masculinity. This is one more way in which PTfA faces challenges of changing not just norms and institutions, but desire.

In place of the old career norms, we should celebrate the importance of care for a full, dignified life, and one that is truly rich. We should talk of modern ambition as desire to contribute in family, community, and work (including artistic contribution, paid or unpaid). In particular, we should measure work commitment by contributions at the workplace not hours worked per week.

An important part of creating new narratives about careers is highlighting examples of organizations where careers look very different. Examples include the law firm in the Netherlands, where 14 of the 33 lawyers work part-time.[86] Or the jobs in the Norwegian caring sector, which are characterized by part-time work as well as part-time attitudes and expectations about mothers' employment patterns.[87] Or Daimler Chrysler, in Germany, which promotes part-time work in leading positions, and has a "Diversity and Equal Chances" scheme, in which employers promote different working time options, such as part-time work, work on call, reduced daily, monthly and yearly working time, job sharing, and so on. The scheme provides sabbaticals, long-term working time accounts, partial retirement, and care leave (with a maximum of one year and the subsequent choice to end the working contract with the guarantee to be re-employed later). Moreover, a variety of practices have been developed to keep parents on leave integrated in the company (such as offering them participation in trainings and workshops, and other human resource development).[88]

A second important ingredient for shifting the norms of careers is to get more women into management positions. Haas and Hwang, for instance, show that a significant and independent predictor of company support for work-family balance is the female share of management positions.[89] Board quotas may well be useful here to speed this process up.

Third, the evidence shows again and again that a vital ingredient in changing workplace culture is having role models of people who do things differently. Haas and Hwang show that men are much more likely to ask for leave if top managers have done so.[90] Smithson et al. similarly find that flexible working policies are most successful when they are taken up by senior staff, particularly senior men.[91]

Fourth and finally, changes in career norms require legislative support. On the one hand, there needs to be an expansion of flexible and part-time working rights. Good real-world practice in this regard includes Denmark, where work reviews from employers often include work-life balance.[92] And Sweden, where all companies with at least 25 employees must file annual action plans for gender equality, developed in collaboration with union representatives.[93] The fact that 47 percent of firms in the Netherlands offer highly qualified part-time positions, is at least partial evidence of the plausibility of changes in this direction.[94]

In addition to positive rights, there is a need for negative protections. In particular, care givers who are attempting to pursue alternative kinds of careers need to be protected from discrimination.[95] So a new model of a part-time career would be well aided by tough legislation against any promotion discrimination suffered by part-time workers. A good example is the Swedish Discrimination Act (2008), which states that employers must facilitate the ability of both male and female employees to combine work and parenting.[96] These rights and anti-discrimination protections need to be legal rights, which apply to workers across the economy, because if they are simply left as voluntary practices for individual companies to pick up or leave aside, there will always be the risk of competitive pressure leading to a race-to-the-bottom to undermine care-friendly practices.

C. Economic Security

New norms of PTfA are far more attractive in a context of economic security. Indeed, for many people, the single greatest worry about part-time work is that it would threaten one's economic livelihood. While it may seem obvious that part-time work will generate less income than full-time work, this would only be the case for the wealthy under PTfA (middle-income people will see their income stay relatively constant in exchange for reduced hours, while the poor will see their total income rise due to increased state supports). Nevertheless, the idea of part-time work produces two kinds of fear. The first, and for many, the main one, is the fear of economic insecurity. This is the fear of poverty and deprivation. The other is the fear of not being able to consume as much as one wants (we discuss issues of consumerism below).

Fear of economic insecurity is a common and well-founded fear. Most of us can only feel secure when we have regular and predictable access to essential goods and services, such as housing, transportation, food, childcare, healthcare, and a pension. Without these things, without basic security, one cannot live a fully human life because one is unable to step back from material necessity to plan broader goals or cultivate diverse aspirations, and then go about accomplishing them. Without security every moment is crushed under the weight of necessity, and freedom is consumed by the relentless drive to acquire basic bodily and cultural needs. Insecure people are unfree.

In contemporary Anglo countries, insecurity is rampant. For instance, in the United States, 40 million people rely on food stamps,[97] 33 million people do not have health insurance, even after Obamacare,[98] millions lack affordable childcare, and there is not one state or city in the whole country where a full-time worker on minimum wage can afford a modest two-bedroom apartment.[99] The major reason for this is that much of the basic necessities of life can only be acquired through the market. Very few essentials are guaranteed to all as an entitlement on the basis of citizenship. In the United States, basic needs must either be purchased on the market or provided as employment benefits, but the benefits themselves are often linked to full-time employment. Good healthcare and pension coverage, for instance, are usually linked to employment (as they are funded in large part by employer contributions), and usually to full-time employment, which means that part-time work is deeply threatening to economic security. So to the extent that part-time work reduces one's income below the ability to buy life's essentials (or deprives one of the benefits linked to full-time work), it directly threatens one's security. It is no mystery why part-time work will look far less attractive to someone who has to save up for health insurance, save up to avoid old-age penury, or save up for childcare, than for someone who knows that such things will be provided freely by the state no matter what.

Although we cannot fully defend it here, we agree with those who see economic security as a basic right that should be guaranteed by all rich countries.[100] Theoretically, economic security could be provided via a guaranteed wage (such as an unconditional basic income), a guaranteed job (such as having the government be the employer of last resort), guaranteed universal basic services (through a robust welfare state), or some combination thereof. A vital research program for the twenty-first century will be figuring out which combination of these approaches works best.[101] We consider this an open and live question. For PTfA to be truly available to everyone, for the norms to be shared by all because they can actually be put into practice, some version of economic security is necessary.

Historically, what we have seen is that by far the most progress has been made toward economic security through the method of guaranteeing universal services. In practice, where economic security has been achieved to the greatest extent, it has been through decommodifying essential goods, that is, delinking them from the market in order to make them simply rights of permanent residents.[102] So perhaps the most promising path for advocates of PTfA is to build a comprehensive welfare state that provides the essential goods and services necessary for a secure and dignified life. What exactly are these goods? In the rich countries, it is hard to conceive of security without at least healthcare, childcare, housing, transport, and some kind of minimum income guarantee to buy food and clothing and other basic items. It is no accident that these five things form the heart of most living wage campaigns.[103]

What are examples of this in practice? All contemporary welfare states have gone a significant way down this road. Europe has gone the furthest, and the Nordic states in particular are exemplars. The Nordic countries, through their high taxes and generous public services, have been very successful in providing high levels of security for practically all their citizens.[104] Consider the case of Sweden (the facts are quite similar for Denmark, Norway, and Finland). Sweden has total tax revenues of 43 percent of GDP.[105] This enables it to provide universal healthcare and universal childcare; subsidized public housing accounts for 20 percent of the entire housing stock, about half the rental market;[106] there is highly subsidized public transport system with a number of cities offering transportation services for free, as well as free lunches for school children; there is also an income guarantee in the form of a generous welfare system, disability insurance, and pension.

Sweden has gone beyond providing basic security to all its citizens. It also guarantees certain vital opportunities. Undergraduate study is basically free; there is generous parental leave at highly subsidized rates; there is also significant job support in the form of Active Labor Market Policies (Denmark spends 1.96 percent of its GDP on such policies and Sweden spends 1.25 percent, whereas the United States and Canada spend 0.1 percent and 0.22 percent respectively).[107] For instance, the Swedish state provides retraining programs to help people find jobs, and will even provide subsidies for people to relocate to different areas. In addition, Sweden provides all kinds of publicly subsidized amenities, from parks to museums to swimming pools. We fully endorse such public programs. This approach of decommodifying basic opportunities is an important complement to PTfA because it makes life on the moderate income of part-time work much more appealing. With enhanced security, part-time work will be more attractive. Universal public services will not make one rich, but they will diminish the fear of deprivation. This is important because without the fears of poverty and insecurity clouding one's perceptions, the joys and ethical advantages of PTfA are much more compelling. Opting for part-time work so as to care more is much more attractive when one knows that whatever transpires in one's life, there is a broad infrastructure of support to fall back on. Unsurprisingly, the empirical evidence bears this out. Studies show that security does indeed make part-time work more appealing. Rosenfeld and Birkelund compare women's part-time work across countries.[108] They find that decommodification and family transfers have strong, positive correlations with female part-time employment, with the Nordic countries having the highest levels of both. Stier and Lewin-Epstein find that among employed people, "the rate of public assistance significantly affects men and women's preferences for working time. In countries with a high rate of decommodification, working men and women prefer to reduce their hours of work in exchange for a reduction in payment."[109] Klammer and Keuzenkamp conclude their study with this: "the general finding is that universalistic and individualised social security schemes (e.g. healthcare systems or pension systems based on citizenship, rather than on the individual work record) give people some freedom to make use of different time schemes and options offered."[110]

D. A Brief Note on Housing

Almost invariably when we discuss PTfA, someone will express the worry that part-time work is not feasible because of the difficulties in finding affordable housing. For example, a minimum-wage worker (such as a single parent) can afford the average price of a one-bedroom apartment—meaning they spend no more than 30 percent of their income on rent—in only 9 percent of Canadian neighborhoods. In Vancouver, a minimum-wage worker would have to work an astounding 84 hours per week to afford the average one-bedroom apartment.[111] Clearly an essential part of the economic security that is required for PTfA is that of affordable housing.

How can this be provided? The answer is both straightforward and incredibly complicated. At the most basic level, it is obvious that affordable housing requires governments to spend more and enhance regulations aimed at alleviating the financial pressure of housing, particularly for low-income people. The difficulty, of course, is persuading governments to pay these costs, and knowing which of the many possible policy tools will be most effective. Possible tools include the traditional social-democratic ones of public or nonprofit provision of social housing, rent control, and housing benefits. With the ascent of neoliberalism, there has been a shift toward less universal and more targeted, market-friendly policies, such as subsidies to builders of rental units, subsidies to homeowners, subsidies to private homebuilders, as well as all kinds of zoning liberalizations.[112]

This is not the place to engage in comparative housing policy in any depth. Suffice to say that the places which have gone the furthest in treating affordable housing as a right for all, have been, unsurprisingly, the Northern European welfare states. Austria (particularly Vienna) as well as Denmark and Sweden are instructive examples, with 38 percent of housing in Vienna being social housing, and 22 percent in Denmark.[113] In Denmark, for instance, social housing is not seen as second-tier housing, but is often the housing of choice for the middle-class too. It accommodates one million people in more than 8,500 housing estates, owned by 550 non-profit housing associations, with roles for tenants in management ("tenant democracy"), and funding from the state via the Danish Housing Investment Bank.[114] In the mid-1960s, the Swedish Social Democratic Party launched a program to build one million affordable homes in ten years. This was an extremely ambitious program, given that at the beginning of the launch the entire population of the country was only eight million. Though not without its problems, the program did successfully meet its target, successfully building 1,006,000 homes in a decade. Even in the United Kingdom, in the 1950s—not long after the most devastating war in the country's history had decimated the state's finances—roughly half of all the new houses built were publicly funded council homes.[115] We suspect that a society aiming at PTfA would want to emulate many of the affordable housing policies practiced in these places.

Not only is affordable housing crucial for PTfA, but we agree with those insisting that housing is a basic human right, and so should not be treated as an investment vehicle, since doing so turns a fundamental need—a secure shelter—into an asset for wealthy people to speculate on. What is required is guaranteed affordable housing, or what is sometimes called a "public option for housing."[116]

E. Reduced Consumerism

Consumerism is a central pillar of contemporary culture. Since World War II, the rich countries have engaged in the largest consumer binge in the history of our species. If everyone on the planet were to live like an average American, we would require five planets.[117] Not only are we consuming more than human beings ever have, we are consuming more and more with each passing year. The average American today spends 20 percent more than in 1990 (in real, inflation-adjusted terms) on cars, housing, and food; 80 percent more on clothes; and 300 percent more on furniture and household goods.[118] With stagnating household wages, much of this increase has come in the form of growing private household debt.[119] Many people find PTfA difficult to imagine because they cannot envision a happy life that doesn't contain a large, detached house with two-car garage in the suburbs, or perhaps a spacious condo in an exciting urban neighborhood.[120] The psychoanalyst Erich Fromm said this of our culture:

> Modern man [sic], if he dared to be articulate about his concept of heaven, would describe a vision which would look like the biggest department store in the world . . . He would wander around open-mouthed in this heaven of gadgets and commodities, provided only that there were ever more and new things to buy, and perhaps, that his neighbors were just a little less privileged than he.[121]

There are a number of problems with this consumerism. Not only is it devastating for the planet, but it fuels a desire for ever longer working hours to be able to pay for ever more consumption. As long as people measure the success of their lives according to their ability to consume, part-time work will remain an unattractive and stigmatized option. Part-time work, in other words, will only be attractive to broad numbers of people to the extent that consumerism is not the overriding goal in people's lives. So part of the goal of contemporary feminists (and greens and others) is to construct a vision of a good life, with caring at its centre, that possesses a firm sense of when "enough is enough."[122] Our position is not that we must all become Zen monks. But that once basic economic security is assured, then there are other things in life, such as relationship building and caregiving, which should take priority over the endless pursuit of increased wealth. As comedian Lily Tomlin liked to say, "the trouble with the rat race is that even if you win, you're still a rat."[123]

Winning these cultural battles will not be easy. Is there anything that public policy can do to help temper consumerist desires? The issues here are too complex for any simple policy mechanism to easily shift such deeply ingrained values. Nevertheless, the scholarship on comparative working time provides us with two important suggestions.

First, it is noteworthy that some high-income societies have successfully bucked the trend, and are in fact starting to value more time over more money. Across the rich countries, if you ask people if they would like to work more and earn more, or work less and earn less, the majority of people prefer the money. But not everywhere. The Nordic countries are the exception. Slightly more people there would prefer the free time.[124] Bosch and Lehndorff found that in Britain 62 percent prefer more money versus 32 percent who prefer fewer hours, compared to Denmark, where the numbers are practically reversed, 32 percent want the money, and 66 percent prefer fewer hours.[125] So, if there is anywhere in the rich world that is becoming less consumerist (or what is sometimes called "postmaterialist"), it is the Nordic countries. It is not totally clear why this is so, but it is hard to ignore the fact that it is the Nordic countries which value more money the least, followed by the continental European countries, followed by the Anglo countries who value it the most.[126] Given this pattern, a sensible hypothesis is that having a more generous welfare state may well reduce the flames of consumerism. Intuitively this makes a lot of sense: the more economically secure you are, the less money needs to be the center of your life. Indeed, when we look at the evidence there is, in fact, a correlation (though granted no proof of causation) between countries with greater economic security and reduced consumerism.[127]

A second important pattern in the literature is that societies with more inequality also appear to have more consumerist desire. Some scholars have argued that this is because the more unequal a society is, the more intense the pressure will be to work long hours in order to "keep up with the Joneses." This is the practice of conspicuous consumption that Veblen famously identified.[128] For example, Clark and Oswald found that the satisfaction levels of British workers varied *inversely* with the wages of their peers—the more inequality, the more unhappiness there was with one's own situation.[129] Likewise, Bowles and Park find a clear correlation between inequality and average annual work hours. Their conclusion is that "inequality is a predictor of work hours; . . . its effects are large, and estimates are robust across a variety of specifications".[130]

In sum, there is good evidence to suggest that enhancing economic security and reducing inequality may both help to reduce consumerism, and thereby make PTfA a more attractive prospect. Once again, the Nordic countries are models about how to practically go about doing this. Enhancing security and reducing inequality both require a robust welfare state. The core ingredients are no mystery; they are those of a strong union movement, high taxes, and universal services.[131]

There is also reason to hope that when work is no longer the center of people's identity and status, the importance of income from work and its corresponding consumption power will also be reduced in importance. Under the new norms of PTfA the increase in the benefits of other spheres of people's lives will be simultaneous with the reduction of consumption (and the compulsions that accompany it). Indeed, PTfA seems a particularly painless path toward the reduction in consumption in wealthy countries that the planet requires.

F. Tax System

We know that tax systems can have significant effects on people's working and caring patterns. To take an extreme example, Prescott believes that almost all of the differences in work hours between Europe and the United States can be attributed to higher taxes in Europe.[132] This is unlikely since other factors, like the extent of union power, surely play an important role.[133] Nevertheless, it is likely true that high tax rates, at least at very high levels, will tend to demotivate work, and therefore can provide an indirect incentive to engage in more unpaid work, such as caregiving.[134]

Part-time work would be more attractive if the tax system were used judiciously to demotivate overconsumption and long hours of work. The hope is that if men, in particular, see work as becoming marginally less attractive, there is a better chance of caregiving being seen as marginally more attractive. We suggest four kinds of tax reform that would be useful in promoting PTfA.

The first and most important way to demotivate long work is to offer tax relief to firms who reduce hours, in the French manner discussed above. This should go hand-in-hand with stiffer overtime regulations so that overtime pay commences at a lower threshold.

A second policy is increasing the marginal income tax rate. This would mean that every additional hour of work pays marginally less.

A third important device would be to increase the progressivity of income taxes, so higher incomes pay a higher rate. Since part-timers earn less, other things equal, the effect of this reform would be that part-timers would pay less than proportional tax compared to full-timers, thereby encouraging part-time work over full-time.

A fourth innovation would be a progressive consumption (or luxury) tax in order to cool the flames of conspicuous consumption (which often drives long working hours).[135]

All of these taxes need to apply to individuals, not families, because when taxes apply to families they often create incentives for the lower earner (usually the woman) to stop working altogether, thereby enhancing labor market segregation.[136] Germany is often cited as an example of this negative effect.[137]

Overall, the point of redistributive taxation is twofold. It makes part-time work more affordable by enhancing economic security. And it reduces the pressures to work harder to keep up with the rich.

This is an area where there is no real issue of feasibility. No economist would doubt the possibility of using tax incentives to reduce long

222 PART-TIME FOR ALL

hours of work. Indeed, every proposal from the Left involving more taxes tends to be met by mainstream economists with a hysterical chorus of "we can't do that because it will decrease work!" But for us, reducing paid work (at least for men) is no undesirable consequence, but the actual policy goal.

VII. Recap

The transition to PTfA will look different for different societies, and also for different classes in society. At the most general level, we should differentiate between three broad strategies of transition for three different social groups. For the poor, the central task is to enhance their economic security (by way of increased public services and minimum wage hikes) so that part-time work provides a living wage. The material well-being of those who are now poor would thus increase. For the middle classes, by which we mean those whose earnings exceed a living wage, the main strategy should be to collectively bargain for decreased hours in exchange for moderation in wage increases. For the rich, say, the top 20 percent of earners, we advocate an immediate, voluntary reduction of wages in exchange for significant reductions in hours.[138]

We have said that PTfA requires robust economic security, as exists in the Nordic countries, or ideally even more. Without such security, part-time work will be too scary for many to contemplate. In Canada, Australia, and the United Kingdom, part-time work at minimum wages usually will not constitute a living wage. For instance, a Briton on part-time work at the minimum wage would earn £13,900 per year, whereas the living wage is, roughly, £18,500 (see next chapter for a further discussion of the living wage figures).[139] So it is plausible to imagine countries like this passing some moderate reforms, such as enhanced subsidies for childcare or increased minimum wages, that could take them over the threshold of making part-time work genuinely feasible for all.

Nevertheless, there is one very clear and evident aberration in the high-income world: the United States. Here, the poorest workers are nowhere near being able to live decently on part-time work. Such workers (often racialized women), would need to increase their current income by a jaw-dropping 3.5-times in order to obtain a living wage.[140] The lack of guaranteed public services (particularly the lack of free healthcare and childcare), mean that the wage required to make ends meet is dramatically higher than elsewhere. If this is American exceptionalism, it is of the worst kind.

Does this mean there can be no progress toward PTfA? Must we wait until the United States transforms into Germany or Sweden—a potentially long wait—for gender equality to be a real possibility? Yes and no. It is true that for a sizable segment of the population, part-time work is not imminently feasible, and it is therefore harder to envision men opting to work less and care more, which will continue to force care labor onto women, reinforcing the train of problems and inequities which that entails. On the other hand, there are still many avenues where progress can be made. Feminists can and will continue to critique traditional gender roles as they strive to popularize new caring forms of masculinity. New norms of PTfA can still be taken up by pockets of people—such as groups of middle-class and richer workers bargaining for reduced hours, or progressive firms expanding their care-friendly policies to attract female employees, or parts of the public sector where there is significant female employment and unionization. In some places, municipal governments could model part-time employment at a living wage. Nevertheless, without the public funding for basic needs like healthcare, education, and childcare, and without strong unions or an interventionist state to regulate the markets in favor of care givers, progress will inevitably be slow.

VIII. Conclusion

Moving toward a society of PTfA requires changes on two interconnected levels: we require more institutional options for part-time work for everyone, and there also needs to be enhanced cultural desire to choose such jobs. Expanding options for part-time work can be done by increasing the amount of quality part-time jobs, as the Netherlands has done, or reducing the number of hours of full-time work, like France and Germany and other places have done. It is possible to foster the desire for part-time work by changing norms of who is supposed to care, challenging the model of what constitutes a career and the role of work in one's life, strengthening economic security, reducing consumerism, and adapting the tax structure. None of this is easy, of course, but as the real world examples have shown, all of it is possible.

4

Feasibility

Is it feasible to have an entire economy based on part-time work? Is it affordable for individual workers and for society as a whole? Could such an economy generate the resources for the kind of economic security we advocate? The aim of this chapter is to address these fundamental questions by analyzing the economic institutions that would be required to sustain and underlie a society committed to PTfA.

The central argument is that an economy which provides options for secure, flexible, quality, part-time work for all is indeed economically viable. Although the society envisioned here is profoundly different from the current reality, at least in North America, it is not at all utopian. PTfA is compatible with modern, complex, capitalist economies; it can survive globalization, and it can flourish in the twenty-first century. At its base, PTfA requires a basic institutional framework like that of any European social democracy. This is significant change for many countries, no doubt, but it is plausible, reformist change. PTfA can be thought of as a deepening of social democratic reforms in a gender-egalitarian direction; but it does not require revolution or the creation of never-before-tried institutions; it does not require a leap into the unknown.

Before we begin, let us recall the basic political and economic components of PTfA.[1]

- *Good Part-Time Work.* Most of the jobs in the economy would be quality, part-time jobs, with benefits (such as pension and health care) significantly delinked from employment.
- *Time Sovereignty.* Workers would enjoy a series of negative protections—standardized hours, a standardized workweek, protection from unpredictable hours, and the right to refuse overtime. They would also possess a number of positive rights,

Part-Time For All. Jennifer Nedelsky and Tom Malleson, Oxford University Press.
© Oxford University Press 2023. DOI: 10.1093/oso/9780190642754.003.0005

including the right to take flexible parental leave for a number of years, flextime, and, importantly, the right to adjust hours.

- *Economic security.* At current levels of economic development, a part-time job of roughly thirty-hours per week would be sufficient to guarantee every worker a living wage. We anticipate the main sources of this security being a robust public sector with high minimum wages. In particular, a caring state would provide all its residents with guaranteed rights to healthcare, childcare, education, a pension, affordable housing, affordable transportation, as well as basic amenities, from parks to pools.

- *Care-Friendly Policies.* A caring state would also pursue a number of supplementary policies to encourage the new norms of PTfA. These include but are not limited to: strong anti-discrimination protections for part-time and flexible work; fatherhood friendly parental leave (including a use-it-or-lose-it policy, bonuses for equal sharing of leave and perhaps also for solo male leave, and, during the transition, the right for parents to shift to part-time for up to five years after the birth of a child with subsidies for the minority care giver); quotas for women on corporate boards, political parties, administrative boards, and courts, and for men in caring professions; and public prizes for feminist role models and feminist workplaces that embody the new norms.

Clearly such a society is not on the immediate horizon. In the most optimistic scenario it is a decade or so away in Europe, somewhat more than that in Canada, the United Kingdom, and Australia, and further still in the United States. Nevertheless, having a medium to long-term model is still useful because it gives us something clear to aim for. It provides a target which clarifies our goals and orients our activism.

The question then, is whether such a model is feasible. Assuming the political will necessary to implement such changes, it's important to think carefully about two kinds of feasibility, which we do in turn. First, *institutional feasibility*. By this we mean, are each of the individual components of the model viable in contemporary complex economies? And is the model holistically sound in the sense that the components are compatible with each other? Second, *economic feasibility*. Can society afford PTfA? Is it compatible with wide prosperity?

And is it possible given the realities of globalization? (We address the issue of political feasibility in the conclusion).

For readers wishing to skim over the nitty-gritty empirical details, the basic conclusions that we reach are as follows:

- Good part time work is possible, even at high levels of management. The Netherlands and Denmark demonstrate its feasibility.
- In a number of European countries, the level of economic security is already such that a single mother on part-time work earns a living wage; in other words, PTfA is already feasible in such places.
- Time sovereignty policies (such as flextime) are also possible, not overly costly, and already widely implemented, particularly in Sweden and Finland.
- Providing the infrastructure of care—particularly economic security for all—will not be cheap. But it is affordable, even with concurrent reductions in work time, if governments are willing to raise taxes on the rich.
- There is nothing impossible about having a market economy which consistently reduces its working hours (indeed, this has been the norm for much of Europe over the last 150 years). Market economies typically grow over time, which means that there is an open choice about what to do with that increased economic potential. Often the choice is made to channel it into greater income, but it's just as possible for workers to take productivity increases as reduced hours instead of increased pay. That is the ideal trajectory for PTfA.
- PTfA is also compatible with high and rising levels of material prosperity. Not only does productivity tend to increase when hours drop (due to reduced levels of fatigue, boredom, stress, etc.) but recent evidence shows that levels of inequality are actually a drag on growth, which is good news for societies like PTfA, which are substantially more egalitarian.
- While globalization does pose some challenges to PTfA, they are not nearly as debilitating as often thought. The race-to-the-bottom is only a problem for specific industries, and corporate mobility has not reduced countries' overall abilities to raise

revenue (though the revenue raising has become more regressive). The welfare state is manifestly not being undermined by globalization, or if it is, it is happening incredibly slowly, and reforms to protect it are entirely feasible.

I. Institutional Feasibility

In order to assess the feasibility of each component of the model, we investigate the best practices that currently exist (which are mainly from Western Europe) and pay close attention to their economic viability. Since we already discussed security and care-friendly policies last chapter, we focus here on the other two components: good part-time work and time sovereignty.

A. The Feasibility of Quality Part-Time Work

The situation at present is that in the neoliberal countries, particularly the United States and United Kingdom, part-time work constitutes a growing part of the labor force, now about a quarter of total employment. Generally speaking, part-time work is inferior work. It is associated with lower wages;[2] long-term financial scarring;[3] reduced benefits;[4] reduced training opportunities and possibilities for promotion;[5] precariousness;[6] it is everywhere highly gendered,[7] and in the United States highly racialized as well.[8]

In New York City, a family composed of two adults, both working 30-hour weeks, would earn a median income of $74,400.[9] This is slightly less than a living wage for the family (assuming two children), which is estimated to be $88,800.[10] So universal caregiving is not currently possible for the bottom half of the population. This is emphatically the case for the poorest individuals. For instance, a single mother in New York City working 30 hours per week at a minimum wage job, will earn only $19,500.[11] This is in brutal contrast to a living wage, which for such a person is more than three-times greater, at $71,400.[12] As a matter of principle, we insist on the right of every person to receive a living wage, that is, a wage sufficient to acquire economic security—the basic necessities of food, healthcare, housing, transportation, childcare, and other basic necessities (such as clothing and personal care items) required to live a modest but dignified life. Since PTfA requires that everyone, even the poorest, be able to survive adequately on part-time work, it is not currently possible in the United States.

The situation is still bad, but not nearly so dire in the other neoliberal countries. In Ontario, Canada, a person on part-time minimum wage will make CAD$22,400, whereas a living wage for that person (with a child) child is roughly CAD$37,000.[13] In the United Kingdom, a person on part-time minimum wage will make £13,900,[14] whereas the living wage is, roughly, £18,500.[15] And in Australia, a part-time minimum wage will earn AUD$29,500,[16] compared to a living wage of, roughly, AUD$41,200.[17]

In Europe, part-time work is becoming more common as well; the number of part-timers has gradually increased from 15 percent in 2002 to 19 percent in 2017.[18] However, here the situation is somewhat different. At a very general level it is fair to say that part-time work is usually somewhat worse than full-time work, for the reasons listed above.[19] Yet, there are a couple of important caveats. First, part-time work, while worse on average, tends to be not nearly as bad as in the neoliberal countries (due to things like the 1997 European Union Directive on Part-Time Work, which aimed to "eliminate discrimination against part-time workers and to improve the quality of part-time work," as well as increased union strength). Second, there are a number of important examples, particularly the Netherlands and the Nordic countries, where part-time work is typically just as high-quality as full-time work.

In order to create quality part-time work, two main ingredients are necessary.[20] The first is that part-time work offer pay and benefits (including pensions, sick leave, vacations, and so on) that are proportional to their full-time counterparts. This practice of pro-rating pay and benefits for part-time work is common in Europe. Since the 1997 European Union Directive on Part-Time Work most European countries have made discrimination against part-time workers illegal.[21] Ideally, key benefits such as health care and pensions should be delinked as much as possible from employment (as is already quite common in European countries). This means that individuals can be sure of receiving such crucial resources, regardless of the number of hours they work. The second key requirement for making part-time jobs good jobs is that they pay at least a living wage so that, in combination with the state's public services, such jobs provide robust economic security.

Probably the best example demonstrating the feasibility of good part-time work is the Netherlands; indeed, it has been called the world's first "part-time economy",[22] with the largest number of part-time jobs in the world. In the early 1980s the Netherlands had very high levels of unemployment (reaching 12 percent). The Wassenaar agreement of 1982 strove to reduce this through worksharing. The idea was that workers would agree to reduce their demands for pay raises, which would restore profitability, in exchange for a shorter workweek. From the 1990s, the motivation for work time reduction shifted from reducing unemployment to other aims, such as improving productivity by granting employers more "flexibility," providing workers with more free time and time sovereignty, and improving work-family balance to further gender equality. Work time reduction in the Netherlands has been accomplished in recent years by a reduction of full-time hours, but more importantly by a dramatic increase in the prevalence of part-time work.[23] From 1983–1996 the fraction of employees working part-time (i.e., less than 35-hours) went from 21 percent to 36.5 percent.[24] By 2019, a remarkable 47 percent of the labor force was engaged in part-time work (compared to the EU27 average of 18 percent).[25] In other words, part-time work is no longer a marginal phenomenon but has become standard, mainstream employment.

However, it is important to note that in many ways the Netherlands remains quite traditional in its gender norms,[26] at least compared to the Nordic countries. Part-time work is very highly gendered, with 73 percent of women working part-time and only 23 percent of men.[27] There is still a strong motherhood norm that women should not work more than three days per week. Similarly, there is a strong norm for men to be the primary breadwinner (only 12 percent of men desire to work part-time compared to 78 percent of women[28]). Dutch men have one of the worst records in Europe in terms of the amount of paternity leave that they take.[29] The standard employment pattern for Dutch heterosexual families is a 1.5 model, whereby the man works full-time and the woman works half-time.

Part-time work is only useful for gender equality if men begin to do it too (indeed, if men don't do it, then part-time work is actually positively harmful for gender equality as it segregates women into worse jobs and can lead to economic dependence).[30] Is this happening? Yes and no. Most men continue to work full-time. Where there is male part-time work, it is overwhelmingly among the young and the elderly. Among men aged 25–54, i.e., core fatherhood age, only 7 percent of men work part-time.[31] This is somewhat better than other places, but not much.[32] Nevertheless, there are some positive signs. The Netherlands has the highest incidence of part-time work for fathers in Europe.[33] It is becoming increasingly common for men to work part-time or to squeeze a full-time job into four days per week, in order to have a "daddy day," now a standard part of Dutch vocabulary. To give one example, when a Dutch lawyer, Jan Henk van der Velden, joined his firm over twenty years ago, there were no female partners and none of the men worked part-time. Today, two-thirds of the partners are part-timers.[34] This is not an isolated incident. Across the country, the proportion of men with children working part-time tripled from 1992 to 2009 (going from 2.1 percent to 6.5 percent), reaching 9 percent by 2016, which is the right trajectory for universal caregiving even if the absolute numbers remain small.[35]

Not only does the Netherlands have a large number of part-time jobs, but such jobs are, for the most part, quality jobs. Since the passage of the Equal Treatment (Working Hours) Act in 1996, it has been illegal for employers to discriminate between full and part-time workers in the provision of pay, benefits, holidays, and employment opportunities.[36] Part-time jobs are mostly open-ended contracts, not a precarious form of non-standard employment.[37] Part-time workers are not significantly more likely to work unsocial hours (evenings, nights, or weekends).[38] Additionally, the National Old Age Pension provides every citizen with a flat-rate pension by 65 irrespective of previous employment or earnings. The Netherlands also has the highest proportion in Europe of firms with part-time positions at high levels of qualification (47 percent of firms offer this).[39] The result of all this is that the gap between hourly part-time and full-time wages is only about 5 percent,[40] with very little part-time work being involuntary (only 5 percent of women and 10 percent of men working part-time would prefer to be full-time).[41]

A single mother working 30 hours per week on minimum wage in the Netherlands would earn about €17,000[42] (whereas a living wage is, roughly, €13,700).[43] A Dutch family composed of two adults, both working 30-hour weeks, would earn a median income of €54,800.[44] While a living wage for the whole family (two adults, two kids) requires €40,600.[45] Note that the living wage is much lower here than in the United States, largely because the robust welfare system means that individuals do not have to privately pay nearly as much for healthcare, childcare, transport, or housing. In other words, PTfA is perfectly feasible here.

The same is true for Germany. In Berlin, a part-time worker on the minimum wage would earn €14,800,[46] while a living wage is approximately €13,700.[47]

Part-time work is also high quality in Denmark.[48] For years, unions have been successful at achieving parity in working conditions for part-time work vis-à-vis full-time work.[49] In 2001, Denmark implemented the EU Directive on Part-Time Work, and in 2002 a new Part-Time Law made it easier for workers to get part-time jobs.[50] Unlike the United Kingdom and United States, part-time work is not an employment trap. Gash showed that the transition rates from part-time to full-time employment were equally high as the transitions from full-time to a second full-time job.[51] Danish part-timers enjoy robust benefits and pensions; when comparing two typical workers, one who works full-time throughout her working life, versus one who works part-time (at 75 percent for ten years then full-time for rest of career), the part-timers end up with 98 percent of the pension of the full-timer.[52] Part-time work is also well paid. Whereas the hourly wage gap between full-time and part-time women is greater than 20 percent in Germany, Italy, Spain, and the United Kingdom, it is 5–7 percent in Finland, the Netherlands and Norway, and not significantly different from zero in Denmark.[53] Moreover, the percentage of women who find that part-time work makes life economically "difficult" is very low, at only 2.5 percent. Overall, Danish part-timers appear to be very happy with their situation. The percentage of part-time women who say they are "dissatisfied" with their job is only 4 percent, while the percentage of part-time workers who are dissatisfied with their life as a whole is only 0.4 percent.[54]

A single mother working at the lowest wage (there is no official minimum wage in Denmark since wages are set through collective bargaining) for 30 hours per week in Denmark earns €22,500,[55] whereas a living wage is, roughly, €14,200.[56] So while in the United States a worker earning minimum wage would only earn a third of what would be needed for a living wage, in Denmark people earning the lowest wages would earn fifty percent more than is needed for a living wage. Indeed, a worker in McDonald's in the United States will earn about $8.90 per hour, but in Denmark will earn $20 for doing the same job.[57] A family with two adults both working part-time would earn, on average, €78,000.[58] A living wage for such a family (assuming two kids) would be €42,200.[59] So here too we see that PTfA is perfectly feasible.

In sum, PTfA requires economic security. Achieving this does require a market system that is more regulated and equitable than the current United States. But it does not require radical or revolutionary changes. Social democracy will suffice. PTfA is not immediately plausible in the United States, but it definitely is in Europe, and it is certainly conceivable in the near future in countries like Canada, the United Kingdom, and Australia, which are halfway houses between United States and Europe.

The major lesson here is that the European example clearly demonstrates the feasibility of establishing quality part-time work. The key ingredients are establishing proportional pay and benefits, and providing economic security through publicly supported basic goods.

B. Time Sovereignty

For workers to have flexibility in their jobs, and in their lives, they require control over their time—time sovereignty. This is the final economic pillar of PTfA. There are both negative and positive dimensions to this, negative in the sense of "protections" and positive in the sense of "opportunities."

Beginning with the negative protections, there are four that stand out: standardized hours, a standardized workweek, protection from unpredictable hours, and the right to refuse overtime.

First, standardized hours, such as a fixed 35- or 40-hour week (or, we hope, shorter), are important in preventing firms from competing with each other by lengthening work hours. This is one of many results of free market competition that are undesirable. Indeed, it's important to keep in mind that the general point of all market regulation is to acquire the social benefits of competition while mitigating the social costs that competition can bring.[60] In countries with interventionist governments or widespread union coverage, like most of Europe, workers have been able to set a framework for standard hours so that there is no direct competition over working time: firms cannot increase profits by making employees work longer and longer hours. Without such a framework, unregulated market competition between firms tends to lead to longer and more unsociable hours. This is part of the reason why hours in non-unionized labor markets, like Japan and the United States, remain so long.[61] Hochschild captures the dilemma well in one of her interviews in a large American firm, when a senior manager declares that, "Fifty or sixty hours a week. *That's what other corporations are doing*. To be competitive, that's what we need to do. In my gut, I can't believe we can do it very differently".[62]

Second, standardized hours in the form of a regular workweek—such as 9am–5pm, Monday to Friday—is vital for preventing the emergence of anti-social working patterns, such as late nights, weekends, extremely long or extremely short hours, all of which wreak havoc on the ability of care givers to balance work and care.[63] Of course, different schedules are sometimes necessary, but there is an important difference between a workplace that requires irregular hours for its very purpose (such as hospitals open during evenings and weekends), and workplaces that do not (such as fast-food restaurants).

Unsurprisingly, there is significant evidence that atypical working hours increase work–life conflict—and this is true above and beyond the length of the working hours.[64] La Valle et al. found that 75 percent of mothers in the United Kingdom who regularly worked at atypical times did so because it was a job requirement rather than a deliberate choice.[65] Almost half of the mothers who usually work shifts would prefer different or regular hours, two-thirds of those who work Saturdays would prefer not to, and over three-quarters of those who work every Sunday would prefer not to. Researchers in Spain found that a work schedule that finishes no later than 6 p.m. significantly increases the time that parents devote to childcare.[66] Fagan and Burchell show that across Europe, for both men and women, the proportion of people reporting work-family incompatibility is almost double if they work nights compared to days, or work shifts.[67]

An example of best practices in this regard is the Swedish Working Hours Act of 1982. This act, which can be overridden by collective agreement, sets out the minimal standards for work time, thereby preventing Swedish firms from attempting to outcompete each other by lengthening or worsening work hours. The act specifies that normal working hours must not exceed 40 hours per week; that night work between midnight and 5 a.m. is prohibited (with some exceptions); that an employee must have continuous weekly rest of 36 hours per seven-day period; that a rest break must be taken after five hours of work; and that overtime must not exceed 48–50 hours every four-week period or 200 hours per year.[68] More recently, the Swedish Discrimination Act of 2008 mandates that employers must facilitate the ability of both male and female employees to combine work and parenting.[69]

Third, unpredictable hours are extremely disruptive of caregiving because they undermine care givers' ability to plan, or to respond to changes in the needs of the cared for. To take one example, without scheduling regulations firms in the United Kingdom have been competing with each other to offer ever more "flexible" hours, culminating in the phenomenon of zero-hour contracts. These are contracts where workers are not guaranteed a single hour of work per week, but are perpetually on call, allowing the boss to call them in and send them home at a moment's notice. Roughly 6 percent of all British workers are on zero-hour contracts.[70] In European firms (of more than ten employees), 17 percent give less than four days' notice of schedule changes, 24 percent give between four days and two weeks, and 53 percent give more than two weeks' notice.[71] So the current best practice is two weeks or more. A notification period of this length is an important ingredient for PTfA.

A fourth important negative right is the right to refuse overtime for care reasons. Presently eight countries in Europe provide a right in this regard. This has been the case in Switzerland since 1964 where employees with caregiving responsibilities have the right to refuse overtime. Similarly, in Norway, employees may refuse overtime if it clashes with childcare needs. Likewise, in France employees have the right to refuse a change in scheduling, or overtime, if the schedule conflicts with family responsibilities.[72]

What about the positive dimensions of time sovereignty, that is, the ability of workers to actually exercise choice and autonomy over their time? Last chapter we discussed two positive aspects of time sovereignty—the right to flexible parental leave, and the right to adjust hours. Here we add one further aspect which is necessary to enable care givers to balance their work and caregiving responsibilities in an ongoing and continual way: flextime.[73] Flextime is the ability of employees to actually *choose* their preferred start and end times (within a standard "time corridor"). It is usually defined as the ability of employees to "vary the beginning and end of their daily working time, in order to adapt it to their personal needs and preferences".[74]

Flextime, sometimes called "flexitime," is very widely desired. In the United States a massive 87 percent of all employees report that if they were looking for a new job, flextime would be "extremely" or "very" important.[75] Likewise, in Europe, employees identify flextime as their single top priority in terms of their firms' working-time policies.[76] Unfortunately, it is still relatively rare. In the United States only 27 percent of firms offer the bulk of employees access to flextime.[77]

Again, we find the best practices of flextime in various Western European countries. The European Establishment Survey on Working Time and Work–Life Balance (ESWT), the authoritative survey in the field, surveying over 21,000 firms, found managers report that the main driving force behind the introduction of flextime is employee desire for it. However, they also recognize that there can be benefits for the firm too, such as better adaptation of working time to the workload, lower absenteeism, and a reduction of paid overtime hours.[78]

Currently, the best practices of flextime are found in Sweden and Finland. In Sweden, roughly 68 percent of workplaces offer flextime to 82 percent of their employees, and in Finland roughly 64 percent of workplaces provide flextime to 78 percent of their employees. Furthermore, the ability to adjust start/end times is only one aspect of flextime. Another kind of flextime is the establishment of systems of "annualized working hours" or "working time accounts." These are schemes that allow overtime hours to be banked for use as periods of time off work—often with the whole year (or even longer) as the reference period within which the time account has to be settled. These currently exist in 13 percent of European firms, with best practices in Austria (where 28 percent of firms provide such accounts) and Sweden (where 27 percent of firms provide it).[79]

What can be said of the institutional feasibility of flextime? The effects of flextime on firm efficiency are widely debated. On the one hand, there are a range of possible costs, including scheduling complications, new hires required to fill in staffing gaps, disruptions from temporary absences, disruptions from scheduling changes, increased difficulty of managerial supervision, administrative costs of deciding who is eligible, and so on. For example, Hochschild describes how the large firm she was studying,[80] which was renowned in the United States for its Work-Life Balance program, felt compelled to dismantle the program when it hit hard economic times—demonstrating that the firm clearly felt that the program was a drag on its efficiency and competitiveness.

On the other hand, there are a range of possible economic benefits of flextime. The main ones are the reduction of overtime pay, the decreased absenteeism, the lower staff turnover (which results in lower training costs), enhanced commitment, motivation, and loyalty from employees, the retention and better recruitment possibilities of highly skilled workers (mainly women) who value flexibility.[81] For example, HSBC bank claimed that introducing flextime resulted in a tripling of the number of women who returned to work after maternity leave, saving the bank millions of pounds in recruitment costs.[82] Research from PricewaterhouseCoopers shows that work–life balance, rather than income, was the main factor in choice of employer for 45 percent of new graduates worldwide.[83]

Empirical attempts to measure the effect of flextime on business performance have produced mixed results.[84] Gray finds that firms which allow for reduced visibility of employees (e.g., part-time work or working from home) have worse performance.[85] On the other hand, Chung et al. find that high-flexibility firms have a better economic situation, more employment growth, slightly more problems finding skilled staff, slightly fewer problems retaining staff, equal motivation, less strained relations, and more work–life balance than low-flexibility firms.[86] Similarly, Dex and Scheibl find largely positive effects on productivity, turnover, quit rates and work performance measures.[87] Lee and DeVoe find that flextime increases profitability when implemented through a strategy centered on employees, but decreases profitability when implemented with a strategy focused on cost reduction.[88] The comprehensive ESWT survey concludes that the majority of managers—i.e., the group who might be thought to be the most resistant to flextime—are actually largely supportive of it. Sixty-one percent of managers said introducing flexible work led to higher job satisfaction; 54 percent said it led to a better adaptation to the workload; 27 percent said it led to lower absenteeism; 22 percent said it led to reduction in paid overtime; 20 percent said it led to other positive effects; whereas only 10 percent said it led to communication problems; 5 percent said it led to increased costs; and 4 percent said it led to other negative effects.[89]

The most sensible conclusion is that flextime will affect different firms differently. It will be harder for small firms, where scheduling constraints are tighter, but it will be more beneficial for larger firms, where absenteeism, loyalty, and retaining skilled female staff are more important issues. The fact that flextime has not spread easily or naturally throughout the business world, the fact that it exists more commonly in the public sector than the private, and more commonly in highly regulated market economies than laissez-faire ones, suggest that it is not inherently profitable for business. That said, neither does it seem hugely costly. On balance we conclude that flextime is likely to impose some costs on business, but these are likely to be minor. A good deal of managerial resistance to introducing flextime seems to be nothing more than the standard institutional conservativeness of sticking with the status quo.[90] Hochschild quotes one particularly candid administrator declaring, "I need 15 percent core workers who work regular hours or longer." The other 85 percent could work part-time or flextime. "If benefits for part-timers were prorated there would be no cost—in money or efficiency—to splitting one job into two, or two jobs into three. . . . It would probably increase the plant's efficiency."[91]

We therefore support the introduction of a general right to flextime for workers, at least in larger firms. As long as businesses are given significant notification periods, and are allowed to refuse requests on serious grounds of cost or health-and-safety, then we are persuaded that granting such a right would not hurt firms very much at all, and may in fact benefit them.

Let us sum up this section. Time sovereignty requires negative protections and positive opportunities. On the protection side, care givers require standardized hours, a standardized workweek, protection from unpredictable hours, and the right to refuse overtime. On the positive side, they require flextime (in addition to flexible paternity leave, and the right to adjust working hours).

There is, however, a tension here. On the one hand, standardization is crucial for preventing downward competition that erodes time sovereignty. As Hinrichs pointed out, the establishment of standardized working-hours has been "one of the major achievements of the working class."[92] On the other hand, standardization itself is a form of inflexibility, which may be disliked by employees just as much as employers. Contemporary populations often have diverse desires when it comes to ideal working hours so the conventional union goal of a standardized full-time workweek for all may be increasingly unattractive for a pluralistic workforce.

From the perspective of PTfA, the ideal to aim for, we believe, is a collective framework of regulated work time, like the Swedish Working Hours Act, *within which* workers acquire a high degree of time sovereignty. We need a new framework; one that we might call "standardized time sovereignty." This would enable care givers to schedule their work hours in a variety of ways to suit their respective needs, without such flexibility undermining the overarching protective nature that standardization provides.

Whether it is feasible to combine the standardization of work-time typical of Western European labor markets in the 1970s and 1980s, with the time sovereignty desired by a contemporary pluralistic workforce (not to mention the desire of employers for increased corporate

"flexibility" in competitive global markets), is yet to be seen.[93] We see
no inherent reason why standardized time sovereignty (i.e., time sovereignty within overarching standardized hours) would be unworkable
or overly costly for business. The real obstacle, which is true for most of
the reforms that we have advocated, is not primarily an economic one,
but is a practical and political one of whether progressive forces will be
strong enough to acquire this given the reality of weakening unions,
heterogeneous desires around work time, and the continued election
of neoliberal governments across the world.

II. Holistic Institutional Feasibility

So far we have been looking at the feasibility of the individual economic components of PTfA. But this raises the question of whether the
individual pillars would work together. Is it feasible to combine part-
time work with time sovereignty, economic security, and care-friendly
parental leave and quotas?

Intuitively it seems like the answer is yes. Denmark already has most
of these things (with less developed policies on part-time work). The
Netherlands has most of them as well (though with less development
of parental leave). Obviously different countries will prioritize different aspects of the package, but at least at first glance there is no obvious reason why Denmark couldn't, for example, expand its policies
on the availability of part-time work, or the Netherlands enhance its
paternal leave rights.

Let us look a bit deeper. The best way to answer this question of
holistic feasibility is to ask what kind of background institutions are
required to support the four pillars of PTfA (Good Part-Time Work,
Time Sovereignty, Economic Security, and Care-Friendly Policies).
Then we should be able to see if such institutions are compatible
or not.

Dutch- and Danish-style part-time work required a strong union
movement to ensure that part-time work is quality work,[94] an interventionist state to prohibit discrimination against part-time workers
and to increase the availability of part-time work (through legislation
like the Equal Treatment (Working Hours) Act and the Working Time

Adjustment Act), and to establish wages and public services so that part-time work always provides economic security.

Similarly, French-style work-time reduction required an interventionist state to subsidize firms that reduce hours, and a strong union movement to engage in broad collective agreements for exchanging reduced hours for wage moderation, as well as being able to sustain a national campaign to reduce hours across the economy. More generally, Bosch and Lehndorff report evidence from the OECD showing that "in those countries in which collective bargaining is more highly developed, working time falls more quickly".[95]

Flextime is perhaps somewhat easier to institute since it may actually be cost-effective for many businesses (particularly larger ones). No specific institutions are essential, but the fact that it is most advanced in Nordic countries suggests that strong union movements[96] and a large public sector (where most flexible jobs are located) are important advantages.

Nordic-style economic security requires high taxes and a robust welfare state. Those things in turn require strong social democratic political parties, and, probably more importantly than anything else, a strong union movement.[97] Probably the most important factor for unions is the sheer number of workers covered by collective agreement. But the structure matters too. Historically, Nordic countries, more so than continental Europe, had strong institutions for centralized bargaining, where the major unions would bargain across a whole industry or geographical region with the major employer bodies, which added to union strength. With the rise of neoliberalism, bargaining has become more decentralized everywhere, somewhat weakening the union position.

Care-friendly labor market policies, such as use-it-or-lose-it and quotas, likewise seem to have required strong unions to fight for them at a workplace level as well as a state that is willing to be interventionist and regulatory across the economy.[98]

Putting the pieces together we see that the main institutional prerequisites necessary for achieving PTfA are (1) a welfare state that is generous in its public services and interventionist in the market (such as in protections for part-time work), (2) high taxes, and (3) a strong union movement.

Since Western Europe possesses these features already, it could, conceivably, build an economy to sustain PTfA in the short to medium term, say, a decade or so in the Nordic countries, and perhaps two in continental Europe. Since the United States lacks all of these features, PTfA is considerably further off. It is difficult to imagine in less than a 30-year framework.[99] (Countries like Canada and the United Kingdom are somewhere in between). It is important to recall that in the United States, working people over the last thirty years have not even been strong enough to acquire *any* of the enormous increases in the economy's productivity gains—these have almost entirely been appropriated by the rich (the 1 percent and in particular the 0.1 percent). Even though the economy has become more productive, wages have flatlined.[100] Since working people in the United States have not been able to exercise either political power or organized labor power sufficiently to acquire any of the productivity gains in the economy for themselves, they are clearly even further away from being able to dictate the *form* that such gains should take, such as reduced work as opposed to raises.[101] These facts are no argument against the normative value of PTfA, but they do highlight the difficulty of its implementation in the near term, at least in the United States.

Nevertheless, the bottom line is that PTfA is institutionally feasible. The economic pillars of a universal caregiving society are fully realizable within the institutional structures that already undergird European social democracy.

III. Economic Feasibility

The question of economic feasibility is a complex one, with a number of different aspects. To begin with, one might wonder whether it's possible for taxes to be high enough to pay for the institutions underlying PTfA (in particular, the major costs of providing economic security so that part-time work becomes affordable for all). The answer to this is clearly yes. The Nordic countries show the possibility of raising taxes sufficiently to provide generous public services and a significant level of economic security. To do so, their taxes are 40–50 percent of GDP (compared to about 25 percent in the United States).[102]

No one doubts that high taxes are possible. The standard worry is whether high taxes will lead to inefficiency and slower growth. Mainstream economists tend to frame this as a tradeoff between equity and efficiency.[103] Is it true that there is a simple tradeoff here? This is a complicated debate, but at a broad level the basic answer must be no. Generous Nordic welfare states have now existed for over 40 years. They show no sign of disappearing or being significantly less efficient than more unequal countries. On the contrary, in recent years there has been a renewed interest in imitating the model elsewhere.[104] Indeed, it is the brutal inequality and disparity of the United States, fanning the flames of xenophobia and white supremacy, as well as its increasingly obvious incompatibility with environmental sustainability that makes the neoliberal model look increasingly unstable and unlikely to continue indefinitely.

On an empirical level, we doubt that high taxes and a robust welfare state will bring much if any economic costs in terms of growth. The basic fact is that, over the last thirty years Nordic growth rates, at an average of 1.98 percent per year, have been almost as high as neoliberal rates (2.59 percent per year).[105] In 2015, the GDP per capita of the Nordic countries was $55,000, a little higher than the neoliberal average of $47,000.[106] The basic reason for this is that whatever losses the Nordic countries may suffer from high taxes and substantial regulations, seem to be compensated by the economic advantages of their system. One such advantage is that high levels of public spending, such as free education from preschool to undergraduate, serve to increase the human capital of the working population, which increases productivity. Another advantage is that the public spending creates a valuable social infrastructure, from roads to high-speed internet, that increases business profit. A final advantage is that social spending on childcare and care-friendly policies enhance female participation in the labor market, which also increases GDP.[107]

On a normative level, we think that even if raising taxes to pay for universal caregiving does somewhat slow economic growth, it may well still be worth it because, broadly speaking, gender equality is more important than never-ending growth, at least in the rich countries, and especially given the reality of contemporary ecological constraints. Nancy Folbre is right to warn us against being too quick to dismiss

244 PART-TIME FOR ALL

normative aspirations on the ground of economic cost: "We should never be intimidated by accusations that improved care is too costly to consider. What's the economy for, anyway, if not to help us realize our vision of a good society?"[108]

Nevertheless, one might well wonder whether it is possible to increase government spending at the same time as reducing work. Is this fiscally possible? Once again, the answer seems to be yes. The countries that have gone the furthest with work time reduction—Germany, the Netherlands, the Nordic countries—are also the countries that spend much more on public services than their neoliberal counterparts.

Another worry is whether there would be significant fiscal consequences if large numbers of the richest 20 percent reduced their workloads (as we advocate), since these people pay a high proportion of total taxes.[109] It is difficult to predict what the consequences of this would be since presuming that the total demand in the economy is stable, voluntary reductions in work hours at the top will be offset by creation of *new* highly paid jobs. For every two or three senior managers, doctors, and lawyers reducing to 75 percent, a new part-time position would presumably be created (indeed, increasing the number of good, high-paid jobs in the economy is an important side benefit of PTfA). That said, it's hard to predict how many new jobs would be created, and since the new jobs would be earning less income, they would be paying somewhat lower tax rates.

To the extent that PTfA does lead to fiscal shortfalls these should be compensated through increased taxation. Indeed, part of the hope of raising income taxes to pay for the infrastructures of care is that this will encourage the superrich to work less anyway. In addition to increasing the rates and progressivity of income tax, governments can and should also look to other kinds of taxation. While there are a number of possibilities here (from luxury taxes to "robin hood" financial transaction taxes[110]), two are of particular importance. Green taxes—such as carbon taxes—are clearly of fundamental importance for all societies to set limits on pollution and prevent catastrophic climate change. Wealth taxes (on inheritance, property, or on total wealth itself) are also deeply important. Since the largest economic inequalities in our societies today are actually not those of income, but of total wealth, we need to develop better tools for addressing this.[111]

We suspect that just as the income tax was a fundamental tool underlying the social democratic projects of the twentieth century, wealth taxes will need to be a major tool for serious egalitarian projects of the twenty-first century.[112]

The countries of the Global North are clearly rich enough that they could easily provide excellent levels of public services requiring very few working hours, if the powers that be were willing to radically redistribute work and income. Consider this stunning thought-experiment: if the United States magically transformed itself into a feminist-socialist country with the desire to share out work and income evenly, it would be possible for every adult to have the median income that exists today, while benefiting from even better public services than exist in Sweden, with each worker only needing to work three hours per day![113] (At 30 hours a week this equalized income would be roughly $43,000 per worker). This is, of course, not a political possibility any time soon, but the numbers don't lie: our societies are rich enough that high taxes and reduced work are completely possible. Rich societies are already rich enough. With sufficient redistribution there is enough to provide for everyone to live flourishing lives with modest hours of paid work, without any more growth needed. And given the ecological realities, growth for growth's sake is a recipe for disaster. What we require is not more growth per se, but a more equitable distribution of wealth, work, and care.

Another worry is whether universal caregiving is viable over the long term. Is it sustainable to have a market economy that consistently reduces working time? Wouldn't PTfA mean less growth, and therefore higher unemployment in the future?

It is true that market economies tend to require growth for stability and high employment. When growth stops, the economy falls into recession, people lose their jobs, and society starts to fall apart. However, economic growth does not require increasing hours of work. On the contrary, over the last 150 years, GDP has grown hugely *at the same time* as working hours have fallen dramatically. This is because as productivity grows, society can either produce more resources, or reduce working hours, or both. Juliet Schor points out that from 1950–1990 US productivity doubled.[114] This meant that society collectively had a choice about whether to take the increased productivity as more consumption, or as more time off (for example, to stay at 1950s levels of material prosperity and work only half time). In fact, 100 percent of the productivity gains were taken as increased consumption; average working hours actually increased. From a PTfA perspective, as well as a green perspective, this was an absurd choice. What is needed, therefore, is a social mechanism to channel productivity growth into reduced hours. That is the central importance of the German and French model of collective agreements exchanging wage moderation for time off. In this way a market economy can grow indefinitely with stable employment (and stable environmental impact), and with hours of work steadily decreasing.

As we have said before, this is the ideal trajectory for PTfA. As time goes by, productivity increases are taken mostly as more time off. This allows for a steady-state economy, with constant levels of employment, growing free time for caregiving, but without growth in pollution.[115] After all, this is the only kind of trajectory that is possible over the long term, as every economy must exist within its ecological boundaries, and those do not grow. This need not mean that there can no GDP growth whatsoever. Some amount of growth is ecologically sustainable as long as it is based on clean production and consumption (such as green technology and renewable energy), that is, as long as it is delinked from a growth of pollution.

Furthermore, there are also good reasons for thinking that PTfA is perfectly compatible with high, and even rising levels of material prosperity. The first reason is that productivity tends to increase when hours drop. The evidence for this is now abundant: It has been found for munitions workers,[116] construction workers,[117] nurses,[118] medical residents,[119] 18 different manufacturing industries in the United States,[120] and more broadly across OECD countries.[121] The major reason cited for this effect is fatigue (though reduction of boredom, frustration, and stress undoubtedly plays a role too). Fatigue affects 38 percent of American workers and is estimated to cost employers $101 billion annually in health-related lost productive time (compared to workers without fatigue).[122] However, it should be pointed out that these studies tend to focus on the productivity gains that happen from reductions of long hours. It may well be that this trend continues the shorter hours go, but that is not clear (it might be that productivity gains cease when hours get very short). Nevertheless, it seems reasonable to cautiously expect there to be productivity gains from PTfA, as the reduced hours mean that workers are less fatigued, stressed, and bored.

Recall the examples of many European countries. For instance, France, Germany, Sweden and Denmark work far less than the United States—in the range of 20 percent less. Yet their levels of productivity, and hence, potential for future well-being, have continued to grow just as fast as that of the United States. As of 2019, the productivity of the US economy (measured in terms of GDP per person per hour worked) was $77.1, whereas it was $84.6 in Denmark, $77.1 in France, $76.4 in Sweden, and $74.8 in Germany.[123] In other words, there are no major differences in productivity even though working hours have been diverging for more than 30 years.

A second reason to be optimistic about the economic prospects of PTfA is that having less inequality is actually better for productivity (at least to a certain point). As inequality has skyrocketed in the neoliberal countries the evidence has become clearer and clearer that such disparities are actually a drag on economic growth.[124] For instance, in their influential paper, Berg et al. conclude that "inequality is a robust and powerful determinant both of the pace of medium-term growth and of the duration of growth spells, even controlling for the size of redistributive transfers: more equal societies grow faster and more sustainably than less equal ones."[125] There are several reasons for this. First, inequality typically leads to weaker aggregate demand. (The rich spend a smaller fraction of their income than the poor. So the more that a country's total income is controlled by the top, the less of it will be spent, and thereby the economy will be stimulated that much less). Second, inequality of outcome reduces equality of opportunity for the next generation; when those at the bottom lack good opportunities to learn and develop their capabilities, the economy suffers. Third, societies with greater inequality also tend to be low-tax societies, and that means that there are less resources available for public investments into productivity-enhancing areas of public goods which can fuel long-term growth, such as infrastructure, public transportation, education, investing into research and new technologies, and so on.[126] Since a PTfA society would be significantly more equal than a neoliberal one

(due to the higher levels of taxation, and the more robust public services), we can expect it to do comparatively better on this score.[127]

A third and final reason for optimism is that PTfA is much more
compatible with the changing demographic realities of our populations
which are living longer. The old "male breadwinner" model of women
not working outside the home, and men working continuously and
full-time from the age of 25 to 65, and then completely stopping at 65
is not a viable model. If many people start regularly living to 85 that
would mean that each man's 40 years of work would have to be enough
to support 130 years of non-work (45 years of men's non-work and 85
of women's). That seems unlikely. It is far easier to imagine a sustainable economy, with people living long and happy lives, where both
men and women are working, in a flexible and part-time manner, from
their 20s all the way up to their 70s, but with far more ebbs and flows;
perhaps working 30 hours per week until one is 60, with significant
reductions for several years around childbirth, then perhaps 20 hours
in their 60s, then even 10 hours in their early 70s. A lifetime of flexible
part-time work makes far more economic, not to mention psychological sense, than the "extreme go" followed by "complete stop" model
that currently exists.

A. Globalization

Globalization is often portrayed as an inexorable obstacle to all progressive goals.[128] What is the concern for PTfA? One possibility is that
globalization makes it difficult for states to regulate business (making
it difficult to force firms to provide quality part-time work or work
time reduction or flextime or parental leave, or anything else) because
these regulations will increase the firms' operating costs, which will
mean they cannot compete internationally and will be driven under
by competition from sweatshops in the Global South, particularly
in China. This is the threat of the race to the bottom. Another possibility is that globalization renders it impossible for states to raise
taxes on corporations because they can threaten to leave. The ability
of corporations to move—"capital mobility"—could create downward
pressure on taxation levels which, so the argument goes, will make it

impossible for states to afford robust welfare states or PTfA. Although both worries are plausible, they are in fact significantly exaggerated. Consider first the issue of the race to the bottom. There is some evidence that these pressures are real,[129] but the full story is much more complicated. The reality is that most businesses in the Global North are not in any kind of direct competition with unregulated sweatshops in the South. The fact is that over 75 percent of imports into the Northern countries are actually from other Northern countries.[130] Most trade remains North to North (the exception is for products like clothing and cheap manufactured products). And perhaps even more importantly, a larger and larger portion of the economy is nowadays in services, which by their nature are mostly not threatened by international trade (your haircut or restaurant meal or doctor or therapist or lawyer cannot easily be imported from China). Indeed, non-tradable economic activity is estimated to represent 70 percent or more of the US economy.[131]

Some worry that firms adopting part-time work might be driven under by international competitors willing to work long hours. But this is unlikely. As we saw earlier, it is true that firms typically have transition costs moving to part-time work, such as the costs associated with hiring and training new workers and re-arranging schedules, and it's also true that firms will be resistant to part-time work if it costs them more in terms of benefit payments (which is why benefits should be delinked from employment—which should be in employers interest). However, it is not at all clear that workplaces in a PTfA society (with part-time work, flextime, and so on) would be less productive than foreign competitors overall, given the advantages that such firms would enjoy in terms of reduced fatigue, reduced burnout, reduced absenteeism, enhanced retention, increased loyalty, increased ability to attract the top female talent (who prefer flexible workplaces), and so on.

Of course, we should not be naively pollyannaish about this—it may be that more humane, balanced firms are less profitable (in the narrow sense of the word) than sweatshop-like firms, even if they produce all kinds of other benefits (or "positive externalities" as the economists like to refer to the benefits of social life). Indeed, this is frequently the case for all manner of progressive regulations—forbidding child labor, ensuring rights to breaks and vacations, allowing pregnant women to take leave, forcing companies to follow health-and-safety or environmental regulations—all of these things, like PTfA reforms, may well place some costs on the workplace (even if there are all kinds of other benefits to society in terms of gender equality, reduced stress, improved health outcomes, and so on). In which case there is an inevitable tradeoff to make. Our position, unsurprisingly, is that in general the benefits of PTfA are likely to outweigh the costs. We doubt that the kind of firms we have been describing will be significantly less productive than competitors, but even if they are, some costs are worth it.

The final point to make is that to the extent that odious competition from care-unfriendly firms in the South really does undermine decent domestic firms, it is entirely possible to protect them. Countries can always implement tariffs to protect themselves. Indeed, Ha-Joon Chang's research has powerfully shown that tariffs have been used by practically every rich country in the world at some point of their own economic development.[132] Protectionism is how practically every rich country got rich in the first place. This is not the place to engage in a detailed analysis of the relative costs and benefits of tariffs.[133] Suffice to say that the fact that practically every prosperous nation on the planet depended on tariffs, often for decades if not centuries at a time, gives us good reason to doubt that they are prohibitively costly.

What about the second issue of capital mobility and tax competition? The problem here is that mobile capital allows corporations to move, or at least threaten to do so, if corporations feel that their tax burden is "too high," which they always do. Capital mobility should therefore drive down tax rates making it harder for countries to pay for the public services they want. This argument is logically coherent, but it is not the whole story.

One countervailing force is that globalization may actually produce a desire among citizens for *increased* taxes in order to provide more welfare to compensate them for the insecurity that globalization brings (this is called the "compensation thesis"[134]). A second factor is that countries with higher taxes also tend to have more educated and healthy workers, as well as a more developed public infrastructure—all of which is attractive for corporations deciding where to set up shop.

The empirical evidence shows that corporate tax rates do indeed seem to be falling. Between 1981–2017, the average statutory corporate tax rate in the OECD has fallen by half from 42 percent to 23 percent.[135] However, there is overwhelming agreement that globalization has not significantly reduced the *total* amount of money that governments can raise from taxation.[136] What seems to be happening is that capital mobility is putting downward pressure on corporate tax rates, causing states to respond by shifting tax away from mobile corporations to immobile sources (mainly income from labor but also things like sales tax, which are often more regressive forms of taxation). Yet since corporate taxes have never been the major source of government revenue (in 2013 in the OECD corporate tax accounted for an average of only 8 percent of total tax revenue[137] and since governments have just shifted to placing more taxes elsewhere, total revenues have not been harmed.

What this means is that governments today have just as much money, and so have just as much fiscal autonomy, as they did in the past, even if they have somewhat less choice about who exactly to tax. The fundamental fact to keep in mind is this: as a percentage of GDP, total tax revenues for the major industrial countries were about 10 percent before World War I, around 30 percent in the 1960s (the era of the building of the welfare state), and up to 40 percent by the 2000s.[138] This means that governments today have actually have *more* fiscal freedom to fund the welfare state in general, or PTfA in particular, than they did in the 1960s and 1970s when no one doubted that such a possibility existed.

So while the fact that corporations routinely avoid tax is not a death sentence to the welfare state, it is nevertheless a clear and present danger to a public's democratic ability to tax the economic actors that we want at the levels we desire (it is simply wrong and unfair that it's easier for rich people to avoid taxes than anyone else). Thankfully, we are not at all helpless. Individual countries can protect themselves by increasing audits and imposing penalties on companies that are tax avoidant. They can also shift how taxes are calculated, for instance by levying taxes on the basis of sales within the country (since firms cannot easily manipulate where their consumers are located).[139]

Similarly, individual shareholders could be taxed on their capital income based on their residency as opposed to the source of their income (in this way rich individuals living in the country would have to pay tax on their total income, regardless of whether that income is from domestic or international sources).[140]

Over the longer term, the goal should be to reduce tax competition through coordination among countries in order to agree on global minimum tax rates. It will of course be difficult to get everyone to go along, but the large economies are the ones that matter most, and they have strong incentive to do so (large economies like France and Germany, for example, have no incentive to indefinitely allow their corporations to relocate to Luxemburg for the tax breaks). And though progress has been slow on this front, the last couple of years has finally seen some breakthroughs in this direction. In 2021, 130 countries and jurisdictions finally agreed to plans for a global minimum corporate tax rate (including China, India, Brazil, Russia, all the other large G20 economies, as well as a number of the most important, and notorious, tax havens such as the Cayman Islands and Gibraltar). The underlying principle of the agreement is that multinationals will be forced to pay a minimum of 15 percent tax in each country they operate in; it also includes plans to prevent the shifting of profits into tax havens by tech giants and other multinationals by enabling signatory countries to tax the world's largest companies based on the revenues generated within their borders.[141]

In sum, globalization does pose some challenges to PTfA, but they are not nearly as debilitating as they are often thought to be. Odious competition is only a problem for specific industries, and corporate mobility has not reduced countries' overall abilities to raise revenue (though the revenue raising has become more regressive). The welfare state is manifestly not being undermined by globalization, or if it is, it is happening incredibly slowly, and reforms to protect it are eminently feasible.[142]

In sum, PTfA will undoubtedly be expensive—particularly due to the costs of providing economic security. But the major obstacles to its creation are largely domestic ones—such as the cultural battles over gender roles and the political battles about how much taxation we want to pay. They are not mainly due to globalization.

IV. Conclusion

Once we recognize that the inflexible, eight-hour day of the present is no more sacred or immutable than the twelve-hour day of the past, we will be free to build a society in which men and women and nonbinary people equitably share the joys and labors of work and care. Achieving such a society will clearly require immense changes to our cultural strictures and economic structures. Yet doing so is inherently feasible.

We have argued that a society of PTfA could be robustly built on four main pillars: quality part-time work, time sovereignty, economic security, and care-friendly policies (including but not limited to: anti-discrimination, fatherhood friendly parental leave, including a use-it-or-lose-it policy and bonuses for equal sharing of leave, as well as solo paternity leave, rights for parents [and incentives for fathers or other minority care givers] to switch to part-time work for the five years after the birth of a child; quotas of women on boards [corporate and government] and in legislatures, and of men in caring professions, and public prizes for feminist role models). Such a society does not yet exist anywhere in the world. However, it cannot be stressed enough that each and every one of its components do. We know that each pillar is feasible, as it already exists in some form, and we see no reason why the pillars could not be combined. This is a vital element of the realism of the project. We are not advocating institutions that are unknown or untried. Rather the task before us is to weave together the best practices that already exist in various parts of Western Europe into a coherent whole. This will be no easy task. But if we can overcome the standard political obstacles of getting care-friendly governments elected, PTfA is an entirely viable project: it is institutionally sound, economically affordable, ecologically sustainable, and capable of withstanding the pressures of globalization.

Conclusion

The heart of this project is the importance of care, its links to core values, and the way that care is structured and institutionalized throughout society. Care is not a "cost" of sustaining life which, with luck and privilege, we can get others to bear for us. Being care-free is not a mark of freedom. Care is the foundation of our relations with others—human and non-human—and those relations are at the heart of our most important values.

We enjoy freedom insofar as we are part of relations of freedom. We express our freedom in choices about our deepest values, in our judgments about what makes life worth living, what endows it with meaning, joy, dignity—all of which involve connection to others. We constitute meaning, including the meaning of dignity, in our relations with others. We experience joy in relation to our fellow humans and their vast capacity for love and creativity, and in relation to the earth community that we are embedded in. All of these relations require care to sustain them. And care is itself an expression of freedom. It is the creative interplay of human capacities, physical, emotional, intellectual, and spiritual.

Equality requires a just organization of care, and justice requires substantial equality in care giving. No society can achieve equality as long as responsibilities for care are organized on the basis of hierarchies, such as gender, race, class, and immigration status.

Democracy requires the end to the divide between high-status policymakers and lowly care providers. Competent policymakers, and those competent to assess those policies, need to have the knowledge, skills, and dispositions learned by doing regular care. In order for everyone to regularly provide care, the structure of work must change, and change dramatically. It is thus vital that the norms of work and care become the subject of vast, widespread, and ongoing democratic deliberation, in playgrounds, grocery stores, gyms, cafes, factories, board

Part-Time For All. Jennifer Nedelsky and Tom Malleson, Oxford University Press.
© Oxford University Press 2023. DOI: 10.1093/oso/9780190642754.003.0006

rooms around water coolers, and in online conversations. In every place we gather we need to begin more conversations about how work and care are structured in our lives.

A society that devalues care is making a fundamental mistake about what fosters happiness, well-being, dignity, satisfaction in life, and the capacity for freedom for all. This mistake will inevitably distort priorities that shape all areas of public policy as well as the values that guide individual lives.

These claims about equality, democracy, and the importance of care must be seen in the context of the paradoxical situation of rich societies today. In aggregate terms, they are already very prosperous and growing steadily richer with each passing decade. And yet this immense wealth—as well as the market work and care which are its foundations—is divided among the population with extreme unfairness and inequality. Instead of providing the conditions for universal flourishing for all, our societies are riven with deep social harms and locked in intractable conflict. Although we live in a context of material abundance, many people feel the cold fear of insecurity, and practically everyone suffers from a manic pace of life and acute scarcity of time. Given the scale of the reigning inequalities (particularly in the Anglo countries), the overwhelming demands of work and care, as well as the spectre of looming climate catastrophe, it is hard not to feel a sense of dread for the future. A strange predicament indeed for the richest societies that humanity has ever known.

Recall first the economic side of the problem. Inequality has worsened in most countries over the last several decades, particularly in the United States. Per-person productivity has more than doubled over the last fifty years, meaning society as a whole has acquired twice the economic power.[1] This could have been used to eradicate poverty, guarantee the basic material conditions for everyone to lead good lives, as well as substantially reduce average working hours. Alas, this did not happen. Instead, basically all of the immense economic gains were used to produce more wealth, instead of reducing hours. Moreover, this new wealth went almost entirely into the hands of the already very rich.

Over the last five decades in the United States the lives of the poor did not improve; the real value of the minimum wage has actually dropped from its peak (in 1968) by nearly 30 percent, standing now at $7.20 per hour. If the minimum wage had kept pace with productivity growth it would be over $24 per hour today.[2]

Similarly, the median income has scarcely improved. In 1968, the inflation adjusted male median income was $32,844, while in 2010 it was $32,137.[3]

Inequality has skyrocketed. In 1970, the average income of the poorest 50 percent of the population was $15,200 per year per adult, while that of the richest 1 percent was $403,000—a ratio of 1:26. By 2015 it was $16,200:$1,305,000, a ratio of 1:81.[4]

This pattern is similar, if somewhat less drastic, in the United Kingdom, Ireland, Canada, and Australia (Piketty, 2014).

Furthermore, we have seen throughout that inequality is not simply a matter of the distribution of dollars and cents; it is just as fundamentally about the distribution of care. The current organization of care is built on and interwoven with hierarchies of gender, race, class, and immigration status. The degradation of care and of those who do it is mutually reinforcing. And the availability of care to those who need it is also unequally distributed. Poor children, elderly people, those with disabilities, with mental health problems (really anyone whose

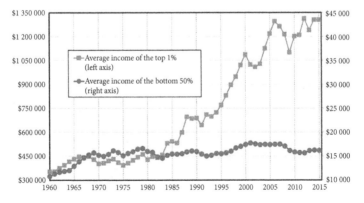

Figure C.1 Average income of the top 1 percent versus bottom 50 percent in the United States.[a]

[a] Piketty, *Capital and Ideology*, 526.

physical, cognitive, and emotional functioning is deemed to be outside the "normal") often lack adequate care.

Moreover, those who are scrambling to provide that (unpaid) care within their households are often severely stressed. Indeed, family stress and conflict has actually worsened over the last several decades. For instance, the percentage of mothers in dual-earner families reporting significant work-life conflict rose from 34 percent in 1977 to 43 percent in 2008 (it worsened even more dramatically for men, from 34 percent to 49 percent).[5] In a 2012 National Study in Canada, 40 percent of Canadian employees noted experiencing high levels of work-life conflict.[6] The fact that the last fifty years has seen women massively enter the paid workforce, while still being expected to perform the bulk of the unpaid care, has led some women to the bitter conclusion that "all feminism ever got us is more work."[7] Those who provide paid care suffer from the low status of care, with low pay, poor benefits and working conditions, and in the case of paid work in homes, sometimes abuse.

Taken together, these facts are greatly disheartening. The Anglo system is broken; or perhaps, it is fixed. In Europe, particularly the Nordic countries, the situation is better, but nowhere do we see anything approaching real equality in terms of the distribution of wealth and care responsibilities.[8]

As we have seen throughout this book, the dominant patterns of work and care create fundamental problems. We have focused on four primary ones. First, the inequality that stems from the fact that women (and increasingly racialized women) are expected to perform the bulk of societal care, and thereby end up poorer, more vulnerable, and more precarious, than those (mainly men but also increasing numbers of professional women) who are able to escape or offload their care obligations. Second, the stress and endemic "work-life conflict" that so many families are suffering through, as they struggle to balance the incompatible demands of care and full-time work. Third, the pervasive feeling of time scarcity. And finally, the care/policy divide, whereby those with lived experience of care are so often excluded from policy making, while those empowered to make policy are so often ignorant of care—a problem which then reinforces all the others. In addition to these four main issues, we have sought to emphasize that the dominant patterns of work and care are not just disastrous from an interpersonal perspective; they are destructive of environmental sustainability as well. The drive to work long hours—fueled by economic insecurity as well as consumerist cravings to buy ever more and ever bigger things—is deeply deleterious of environmental sustainability. Since 1950, total CO_2 emissions in the United States have more than doubled.[9] Such a trajectory is an unmitigated disaster for our collective future.

Why are these work and care patterns maintained given that they cause so much harm? The simple (and simplistic) answer is that those with power benefit from them and so resist any change. But the more fundamental answer is that they are maintained by the complementary reinforcing action of dominant norms (of feminized caregiving and masculinized work) and workplace structures (built on the ideal worker norm of continuous, inflexible, full-time work). It is the mutually-reinforcing nature of these norms and economic structures which makes it so hard to change the gendered division of labor, since any attempt to reform the work structures runs into the wall of norms ("this is just the way men and women naturally are!") and any attempt to shift the norms, runs into the wall of workplace convention ("it just can't be done differently in my workplace!") To put the point another way: there can be no real solution to the problems unless we manage to tackle both dimensions of the problems simultaneously and at their roots. This is why the booming self-help industry claiming that it can help middle-class women "get it all"—through leaning in, changing their demeanor, teleconferencing into work, hiring a nanny, or bargaining more aggressively—are all so woefully insufficient. Without dealing with the heart of the issue, the devaluation of care and the inflexible work structures, such solutions will remain little more than fairy dust.

This central purpose of this book has been to offer a real solution that could actually solve the aforementioned problems, precisely because it seeks to transform the very roots of the issue by shifting the dominant norms towards universal caregiving and simultaneously shifting the dominant workplace structures to secure, quality, part-time work. This is the project of PTfA.

We have demonstrated that the benefits of PTfA would be immense. In particular, a society that moved towards PTfA would significantly reduce inequality, family stress and work-life conflict, ameliorate the care/policy divide, and help facilitate a shift towards a sustainable economy. The value of such benefits is hard to exaggerate. PTfA is not primarily designed to fix the gigantic problems of economic inequality—other complementary policies will be necessary for that. Nevertheless, it would clearly be helpful. Under the new norms of PTfA, care in publicly funded settings such as child and elder care centers would be better paid, with better working conditions than we currently see. Voluntary reductions of working hours by the rich will somewhat reduce top incomes. The reduced importance of work in defining identity would also reduce the social impact of income inequality. Most important is the required groundwork for PTfA: the expansion of economic security to all, paid for by increased taxes on the rich, both dimensions of which will significantly redress inequality. Moreover, the new norms will impact equality profoundly, across many hierarchical divides, by the revaluing of care and the celebration of those who do it. When everyone shares responsibility for the essential function of care, a fundamental dimension of inequality will be dismantled. Care responsibility will stop being a barrier to economic, social, and political equality.

Of course, PTfA will not be costless. Affluent families will be somewhat less well-off; society as a whole will have somewhat slower rates of growth; and some individuals (particularly men) will feel their preferences constrained (though this constraint will be markedly less burdensome than that which women have suffered for many centuries). Nevertheless, it seems clear that the benefits—both for individuals and for societies—outweigh these costs by an enormous margin. PTfA is not costless, but it is worth it—overwhelmingly so.

In addition to the overarching desirability of PTfA, we have endeavored to persuade the reader of its viability. We have seen that it is entirely feasible to shift cultural norms in a progressive direction, and best practices from around the world show that it is also feasible to shift modern, complex economies towards secure, quality, flexible, part-time work for all.

What, then, are the general prospects for PTfA?

Although the project is economically viable, the major open question, as always, is the degree of political feasibility. Will coalitions of activists and social movements and progressive political parties be strong enough to actually implement a PTfA agenda? That is impossible to predict. The political feasibility of such a project is different in every country, and oscillates with each passing year. Clearly it is more plausible in the short-term in the European, particularly Nordic countries, where both the strength of the Left and the basic economic prerequisites (such as strong unions, interventionist states, high tax regimes, and so on) already exist. In the Anglo countries, particularly the United States, the obstacles are extreme: the lack of a robust welfare system; the still-dominant neoliberalism; the rise of patriarchal, white-supremacist nationalism; the deeply embedded culture of consumerism and possessive individualism; the deep economic insecurity generating continual fear of any policies that might dampen economic growth; the erosion of democracy in favor of plutocracy, and so on.

That said, if we take a step back and look at the broader changes to society that are slowly taking place everywhere, including the United States, the prospects for PTfA look considerably brighter. One particularly important shift is the broad evolution of gender norms. Almost everywhere gender norms are evolving in an egalitarian direction; this is happening slowly and haphazardly, of course, but the cumulative effect on society is profound. As traditional norms around "men's work" and "women's work" continue to erode, it seems inevitable that a growing proportion of the female population will no longer put up with the expectation that they work a second shift, and will increasingly call for arrangements like PTfA to balance their care and work. Another shift is the increasing automation of the economy, and the accompanying specter of unemployment. Whether automation really will usher in massive waves of unemployment, we do not know; but the threat is already motivating a marked increase in calls for economic security (witness the rapid growth of interest in basic income), which is a vital component of PTfA. A third important shift is demographic: the fact that the share of the "ultra-aged" (80+) is more or less doubling every twenty years in Europe, and is expected to represent almost 10 percent of total population by mid-century. Since this is when frailty and dependency intensify, we are likely to face a huge increase in the demand for elder care in the years to come.[10] As baby-boomers retire, the issue of who will be responsible for providing decent and dignified elder care will grow ever more pressing. A fourth broad change is that the environmental crisis—in particular the increasing frequency with which storms, fires, floods, hurricanes, and other natural disasters batter the rich cities of the world. As such environmental problems get worse and worse, it seems impossible for business as usual to continue. As many others have noted, the requirements of ecological sustainability—such as massive state investment in renewables, long-term economic planning, extensive market regulation, and so on—are completely incompatible with the core tenets of neoliberalism.[11] So, if anything is going to displace the neoliberal paradigm, the environmental crisis seems a likely candidate.[12] This, in turn, could greatly expand the space of possibility for a fundamental restructuring of work and care.

Lastly, consider the COVID-19 crisis. Over a mere twelve months, from mid-2020 to mid-2021, as we completed this book, there was a truly staggering change to work norms. In a flash of the eye, the old certainty that work had to be done from the office, that teleconferencing and flextime were impossible for most workplaces—these old verities simply vanished. In London, for example, a remarkable 43 percent of the entire local workforce worked from home.[13] Clearly COVID-19, and working from home, has not led to a revolution in gender relations. For many women, unfortunately, the situation has actually worsened.[14] Nevertheless, what we must never forget is how unbelievably fast the change to working from home occurred. In an instant the old dogmas about the essential nature of office work simply evaporated. This reminds us of a vital truth: that work patterns are always fundamentally malleable. If huge swathes of the population, millions and millions of people, in practically every part of the economy, can more-or-less instantly shift from office work to home work, is it really impossible to imagine a slower, more incremental shift from full-time to part-time work? Is it really impossible to imagine men as devoted to their children as they currently are to their office? We think not.

This book has attempted to outline many of the changes that are needed to make PTfA a reality. We have seen that we require deep norm shifts across society as well as profound economic transformation, particularly in North America. The size of these changes can feel daunting. But there is much that each of us can do in our own individual lives, here and now, to help galvanize movement towards bigger collective changes.

First and foremost, we can initiate conversations again and again with our colleagues, friends, family, and life partners about the care labor in our lives: the importance of it, who does it and who receives it, who benefits and who suffers. When young couples plan to get pregnant, we can urge them to remember the importance of dividing the new care responsibilities as equally as possible as this can set patterns for the rest of their lives (recognizing of course the very real constraints of inflexible workplaces and uncaring bosses). We can gently, and with compassion, remind our friends and colleagues of the overwhelming value of nurturing relationships, and the sad pathology of workaholism.

In our workplaces, we can advocate for more experimentation with flexible and part-time careers, more women in leadership, and for senior men to model leave taking and a balanced working life. As much as possible, in small ways and in large, we can refuse to normalize standard work practices, calling out as sexist, misogynistic, discriminatory, and anti-caring the standard biases towards long-hours, inflexibility, and always-in-the-office "presentism."

As Susan Okin remarked long ago, "only when a new flexibility develops, and it is conceded that the eight-hour day is no more sacred than the ten-hour or twelve-hour day was once held to be, will we be able to achieve a society in which both men and women [and nonbinary people] share in the pleasures and burdens of the tasks that are now so arbitrarily divided between them."[15]

Part-Time for All offers that flexibility as well as greater equality, a deep revaluing of care as the foundation of the relationships that matter in life, leadership informed by the knowledge and dispositions of care, and a new relationship with time that fosters freedom, generosity, and creativity.

Notes

Preface

1. Jennifer Nedelsky, "Dilemmas of Passion, Privilege and Isolation: Reflections on Mothering in a White, Middle Class Nuclear Family," in *Mother Troubles: Rethinking Contemporary Maternal Dilemmas*, ed. Julia Hanigsberg and Sara Ruddick (Boston: Beacon Press, 1999), 320–21.

Introduction

1. Perhaps the most pressing problem of all is climate change, which we see it as intimately linked to the devaluation of care. Revaluing care will be part of the necessary transformation from seeing the earth as an extractive resource to recognizing a mutual relation of care between earth (in all of her dimensions) and human beings.
2. We use the terms "men" and "women" here not to endorse a binary understanding of gender, which we reject, but because of their continued prevalence in society. The current norms of how one is expected to behave in terms of work and care (and much else) are typically articulated and enforced according to the categories of "men" and "women." The binary gendering of these norms is part of what we aim to transform. Throughout, we will use "women" as a shorthand for all women, regardless of whether cis or trans (and similarly for men).
3. This project builds on the work of many care theorists and scholars of gender equality. First and foremost, we recognize the many queer and disabled (and often racialized) people who have been at the forefront of imagining, inventing, and slowly building new understandings of relationships of care, that provide much of the inspiration for this book (we're thinking here of people like Leah Lakshmi Piepzna-Samarasinha, Loree Erickson, Eva Kittay, and many, many others). In terms of the scholars that we

have been particularly shaped by, we want to acknowledge in particular the following: Joanne Conaghan and Kerry Rittich, *Labour Law, Work, and Family: Critical and Comparative Perspectives* (Oxford University Press, 2005); Daniel Engster, *Justice, Care, and the Welfare State* (Oxford University Press, 2015); Nancy Folbre, *For Love and Money: Care Provision in the United States* (New York: Russell Sage Foundation, 2012); Nancy Folbre, *The Invisible Heart: Economics and Family Values* (New York: New Press, 2001); Nancy Folbre, *Valuing Children: Rethinking the Economics of the Family*, The Family and Public Policy (Cambridge, MA: Harvard University Press, 2010); Nancy Fraser, "After the Family Wage: Gender Equity and the Welfare State," *Political Theory* 22, no. 4 (1994): 591–618; Nancy Fraser, *Fortunes of Feminism: From State-Managed Capitalism to Neoliberal Crisis* (Verso Books, 2013); Janet C. Gornick and Marcia Meyers, *Gender Equality: Transforming Family Divisions of Labor*, vol. 6 (Verso Books, 2009); Frigga Haug, "The 'Four-in-One Perspective': A Manifesto for a More Just Life," *Socialism and Democracy* 23, no. 1 (March 2009): 119–23; Frigga Haug, *Die Vier-in-einem-Perspektive: Politik von Frauen für eine neue Linke* (Hamburg: Argument Verlag, 2008); Susan Himmelweit, ed., *Inside the Household: From Labour to Care*, Capital and Class Series (London: Palgrave Macmillan, 2000); Eva Feder Kittay, *Love's Labor: Essays on Women, Equality and Dependency* (New York: Routledge, 1998); Kerry Rittich, "Families on the Edge: Governing Home and Work in a Globalized Economy," *North Carolina Law Review* 88, no. 5 (2010): 1527–58; Joan C. Tronto, *Moral Boundaries: A Political Argument for an Ethic of Care* (New York: Routledge, 1993); Joan C. Tronto, *Caring Democracy: Markets, Equality, and Justice* (New York University Press, 2013); Allison Weir, "The Global Universal Care Giver: Imagining Women's Liberation in the New Millennium," *Constellations* 12, no. 3 (2005): 308–30.

4. For example, see Kathleen Gerson and Jerry A. Jacobs, *The Time Divide: Work, Family, and Gender Inequality* (Cambridge, MA: Harvard University Press, 2009), 161–62. There are important work-family, occupational, aspirational, parenting, and gender divides. Of course, there are even greater differences across countries.

5. Lyn Craig et al., "Is It Just Too Hard? Gender Time Symmetry in Market and Nonmarket Work and Subjective Time Pressure in Australia, Finland, and Korea," in *Gender and Time Use in a Global Context: The Economics of Employment and Unpaid Labor*, ed. Rachel Connelly and Ebru Kongar (New York: Palgrave Macmillan US, 2017), 465–94.

In Europe, 64.1 percent of the female population were employed in 2019 compared to 53.6 percent in 2000. See European Commission,

"Employment and Activity by Sex and Age—Annual Data," Eurostat, April 20, 2020, http://appsso.eurostat.ec.europa.eu/nui/show.do?dataset= lfsi_emp_a&lang=eng. Australia has found that as of 2020, the participation rate of females was 61.4 percent, up from 53.9 percent in 1999. See Commonwealth of Australia, "Labour Force, Australia, January 2020," Australian Bureau of Statistics, February 20, 2020, https://www.abs.gov.au/statistics/labor/employment-and-unemployment/labor-force-austra lia/jan-2020; Commonwealth of Australia, "Australian Social Trends, 2000," Australian Bureau of Statistics, July 4, 2000, https://www.abs.gov.au/ausstats/abs@.nsf/2f762f95845417aeca25706c00834efa/1b34567b9 e041927ca2570ec000e3c1e!OpenDocument. In Canada, "women's participation in the labor market increased by 60.4 percentage points between 1950 and 2015, from 21.6% to 82.0%." See Melissa Moyser, "Women and Paid Work," Women in Canada: A Gender-Based Statistical Report (Statistics Canada, March 8, 2017), 4. The US also saw the labor force participation rate of women increase to 57.1 percent in 2018 compared to 32.7 percent in 1948. See "Women in the Labor Force: A Databook" (U.S. Bureau of Labor Statistics, December 2019), https://www.bls.gov/opub/reports/womens-databook/2019/pdf/home.pdf.

6. Wayne Lewchuk et al., "The Precarity Penalty: The Impact of Employment Precarity on Individuals, Households and Communities—and What to Do about It" (PEPSO: Poverty and Employment Precarity in Southern Ontario, 2015), http://www.deslibris.ca/ID/246690. People in precarious jobs are also likely to live in areas where there are few childcare institutions, thus requiring longer travel time to drop off and pick up children. See also Martin Marchiori-Wong, "Taking Care of the Temporal Imbalance in Child Care Policies" (unpublished manuscript, April 29, 2017), Microsoft Word file. Statistics on work hours often fail to include information about long hours put in by people combining multiple part-time jobs. For an example of unpredictable part-time hours, see Jodi Kantor, "Starbucks to Revise Policies to End Irregular Schedules for Its 130,000 Baristas," The New York Times, August 14, 2014, https://www.nytimes.com/2014/08/15/us/starbucks-to-revise-work-scheduling-policies.html.

7. The popular press in most Anglo countries have published some variation of the narrative that dual-income families are "necessary" to afford a "good" life. See, e.g., Steve Doughty, "£40k-a-Year Is Cost of a Happy Family Life with 2 Children," Daily Mail, July 5, 2017, https://www.dailym ail.co.uk/news/article-4669190/40k-year-cost-happy-family-life-2-children.html; Samantha Maiden, "Aussie Dream of Owning Your Own Home Is Impossible without Two Incomes, Social Services Minister Scott

Morrison Says," *Herald Sun*, September 6, 2015, http://www.heraldsun. com.au/news/news-story/59f2acf39e4dfd50d4dd66e5a9c7d60e; Tara Siegel Bernard & Karl Russell, "The Middle-Class Crunch: A Look at 4 Family Budgets," *The New York Times*, October 3, 2019, https://www.nyti mes.com/interactive/2019/10/03/your-money/middle-class-income. html; "2-Income Families Nearly Doubled from 1976 to 2014," *CBC News*, June 24, 2015, sec. Business, https://www.cbc.ca/news/business/2-inc ome-families-nearly-doubled-from-1976-to-2014-1.3125996.

8. Sylvia Ann Hewlett and Carolyn Buck Luce, "Extreme Jobs: The Dangerous Allure of the 70-Hour Workweek," *Harvard Business Review* 84, no. 12 (2006): 49–59; Anna S. Burger, "Extreme Working Hours in Western Europe and North America: A New Aspect of Polarization," *London School of Economics and Political Science*, LSE "Europe in Question" Discussion Paper Series, no. 25 (2015): 27. For similar information on extreme work hours in other Anglo countries, see George Bangham, "The Times They Aren't A-Changin': Why Working Hours Have Stopped Falling in London and the UK" (London: Resolution Foundation, January 2020); Thomas Lemieux and W. Craig Riddell, "Who Are Canada's Top 1 Percent?," in *Income Inequality: The Canadian Story*, ed. David A. Green, W. Craig Riddell, and France St-Hilaire, The Art of the State 5 (Montreal: Institute for Research on Public Policy, 2016); Joshua Byrd et al., "Can You Guess Where You Sit on Australia's Income Ladder?," *ABC News*, May 21, 2019, https://www.abc.net.au/news/2019-05-21/inc ome-calculator-comparison-australia/9301378.

9. Lawrence Mishel and Alyssa Davis, "Top CEOs Make 300 Times More than Typical Workers: Pay Growth Surpasses Stock Gains and Wage Growth of Top 0.1 Percent," *Economic Policy Institute* (blog), June 21, 2015, http://www.epi.org/publication/top-ceos-make-300-times-more-than-workers-pay-growth-surpasses-market-gains-and-the-rest-of-the-0-1-percent/.

10. Nancy Folbre, *The Invisible Heart: Economics and Family Values* (New York: New Press, 2001).

11. Anne-Marie Slaughter, *Unfinished Business: Women Men Work Family* (Oneworld Publications, 2015); Cynthia Fuchs Epstein et al., *The Part-Time Paradox: Time Norms, Professional Lives, Family, and Gender.* (New York: Routledge, 1999); Louise Marie Roth, *Selling Women Short: Gender Inequality on Wall Street* (Princeton: Princeton University Press, 2006); Cynthia Thomas Calvert, *Flex Success: The Lawyer's Guide to Balanced Hours* (CreateSpace Independent Publishing Platform, 2011);

Pamela Stone, *Opting Out?: Why Women Really Quit Careers and Head Home* (Berkeley, CA: University of California Press, 2007).
12. We would like to thank Hoy Mun Carmen Loh for reminding us of this issue.
13. Gerson and Jacobs, *The Time Divide*, 50. Sixty percent of dual earning couples work more than 80 hours a week, while 13 percent work more than 100 hours a week.
14. Stone, *Opting Out*, 83–86, 220.
15. Wayne Lewchuk et al., "It's More than Poverty: Employment Precarity and Household Well-being" (PEPSO: Poverty and Employment Precarity in Southern Ontario, 2013) at 60.
16. Lewchuk et al., "The Precarity Penalty."
17. There has been a steady increase in the proportion of single-parent households among households with children across both North America and Europe. For statistical data see United States Census Bureau, "The Majority of Children Live With Two Parents, Census Bureau Reports," news release no. CB16-192, November 17, 2016, https://www.census.gov/newsr oom/press-releases/2016/cb16-192.html; "Number of Private Households by Household Composition, Number of Children and Age of Youngest Child (1 000)," Eurostat, European Commission, April 20, 2020, http:// appsso.eurostat.ec.europa.eu/nui/show.do?dataset=lfst_hhnhtych&lang= en; Sharanji Uppal, "Employment Patterns of Families with Children," Statistics Canada, catalogue no. 86-006-X, June 24, 2015, https://www150. statcan.gc.ca/n1/pub/75-006-x/2015001/article/14202-eng.htm.
18. See Linda C. McClain, "The Other Marriage Equality Problem," *Boston University Law Review* 93, no. 3 (2013): 921–70; Margaret Wente, "Marriage Is the New Class Divide," *The Globe and Mail*, March 21, 2015, https://www.theglobeandmail.com/opinion/marriage-is-the-new-class-divide/article23545818/.
19. Evelyn Nakano Glenn, *Forced to Care: Coercion and Caregiving in America* (Cambridge, MA: Harvard University Press, 2010).
20. Adelle Blackett, *Everyday Transgressions: Domestic Workers' Transnational Challenge to International Labor Law* (Ithaca, NY: Cornell University Press, 2019).
21. Barbara Ehrenreich and Arlie Russell Hochschild, eds., *Global Woman: Nannies, Maids, and Sex Workers in the New Economy*, A Holt Paperback (New York: Owl Books, 2004).
22. Jennifer Nedelsky, "The Gendered Division of Household Labor: An Issue of Constitutional Rights," in *Feminist Constitutionalism: Global Perspectives*,

ed. Beverly Baines, Daphne Barak-Erez, and Tsvi Kahana (New York: Cambridge University Press, 2012), 15–47.

23. Joan C. Tronto, *Caring Democracy: Markets, Equality, and Justice* (New York: New York University Press, 2013).

24. Susan Thistle, *From Marriage to the Market: The Transformation of Women's Lives and Work* (Berkeley, CA: University of California Press, 2006).

25. In some countries, like Canada, some of those who enter on in-home care giver visas are able to stay and move into higher paid, higher status work, though often in jobs like nursing that are still in the care sector. This is due to programs that allow such individuals to apply for permanent residency. See Government of Canada, "Hire a Home Child Care Provider or Home Support Worker," Work in Canada, March 23, 2020, https://www.canada. ca/en/immigration-refugees-citizenship/services/work-canada/hire-fore ign-worker/in-home-care giver.html.

26. Laura Addati et al., "Care Work and Care Jobs for the Future of Decent Work." (Geneva: International Labour Organization, 2018), https://www. ilo.org/global/publications/books/WCMS_633135/lang—en/index.htm.

27. In most OECD countries fathers devote fewer than one-quarter of the hours devoted by their female counterparts to routine housework, and less than half to care giving. Gornick & Meyers, *Gender Equality*, 10.

28. Stephen J. Rose and Heidi I. Hartmann, "Still a Man's Labor Market," (Washington, D.C.: Institute for Women's Policy Research, 2018).

29. It is unclear where this phrase first originated. It is now common in economics discourse, e.g., J. Quiggin, *Zombie Economics: How Dead Ideas Still Walk Among Us*. (Princeton: Princeton University Press, 2010).

30. Arlie Russell Hochschild, *The Commercialization of Intimate Life: Notes from Home and Work* (University of California Press, 2003).

31. Stone, *Opting Out*, 215.

32. For example, 49 percent of women earning more than $100,000/year are childless. Laura D'Andrea Tyson, "New Clues to the Pay and Leadership Gap," *New York: Bloomberg Businessweek*, October 27, 2003.

33. A recent census of Fortune 500 companies in the US found that in 2013 women held only 17 percent of corporate board seats and 15 percent of Executive Officer positions. In Europe, women hold only 23.3 percent of membership on boards of directors, despite being 45 percent of the labor force. Judith Warner, "The Women's Leadership Gap" (Center for American Progress, March 7, 2014); Marianne Bertrand et al., "Breaking the Glass Ceiling? The Effect of Board Quotas on Female Labor Market Outcomes in Norway," Working Paper (National Bureau of Economic Research, June 2014).

34. Colette Fagan et al., "The Influence of Working Time Arrangements on Work-Life Integration or 'Balance': A Review of the International Evidence" (Geneva: International Labour Office, 2012).
35. Hochschild, *The Time Bind*, 70.
36. Hochschild, *The Commercialization of Intimate Life*, xiii.
37. Sendhil Mullainathan and Eldar Shafir, *Scarcity: Why Having Too Little Means So Much* (New York: Macmillan, 2013).
38. Rosa Brooks, "Recline, Don't 'Lean In' (Why I Hate Sheryl Sandberg)," *Washington Post*, February 25, 2014, https://www.washingtonpost.com/blogs/she-the-people/wp/2014/02/25/recline-dont-lean-in-why-i-hate-sheryl-sandberg/.
39. Jessica Stillman, "Why Working More Than 40 Hours a Week Is Useless," *Inc.Com* (blog), March 22, 2012, https://www.inc.com/jessica-stillman/why-working-more-than-40-hours-a-week-is-useless.html.
40. Lyndall Strazdins et al., "Time Scarcity: Another Health Inequality?" *Environment and Planning A* 43, no. 3 (2011): 545–59.
41. Schulte, *Overwhelmed*, 254–78.
42. "Stop and Smell the Roses—Wiktionary," Wiktionary: The Free Dictionary, October 14, 2019, https://en.wiktionary.org/wiki/stop_and_smell_the_roses.
43. James Joyce, "A Painful Case," in *Dubliners* (London: Grant Richards, 1914).
44. Of course, poor women have long had to both earn income and provide care for their families. And prior to the industrial revolution, which brought us the current divide between public and private, work and home, many women were involved in family economic activity—such as farming—as well as care. The new problem is that far more women across classes are now working in the paid labor force, without a significant shift in their care responsibilities.
45. See Joan C. Williams, *Reshaping the Work-Family Debate: Why Men and Class Matter* (Cambridge, MA: Harvard University Press, 2010); Cynthia Fuchs Epstein et al., *The Part-Time Paradox: Time Norms, Professional Lives, Family, and Gender* (New York: Routledge, 1999); Linda Duxbury and Christopher Alan Higgins, *Something's Got to Give: Balancing Work, Childcare, and Eldercare* (Toronto: University of Toronto Press, 2017).
46. Riikka Prattes, "'I Don't Clean up after Myself': Epistemic Ignorance, Responsibility and the Politics of the Outsourcing of Domestic Cleaning," *Feminist Theory* 21, no. 1 (January 2020): 25–45.
47. For instance, see Adelle Blackett's work on the mutual reinforcement between degradation on the basis of race and degradation of domestic work.

Everyday Transgressions: Domestic Workers' Transnational Challenge to International Labor Law (Ithaca, NY: Cornell University Press, 2019).
48. One might think this would be self-evident. There is, however, a lot of evidence that privileged men, in particular, take much of the care they receive—from intimate partners, staff assistants, and janitors—as entitlements and thus invisible to them. Prattes, "'I Don't Clean up after Myself,'" 25–45.
49. For beautiful articulations of the care we receive from the earth, see Robin Wall Kimmerer, *Braiding Sweetgrass: Indigenous Wisdom, Scientific Knowledge and the Teachings of Plants* (Penguin Books, 2020).
50. For example, the United States, with less than 5 percent of the global population, uses about a quarter of the world's fossil fuel resources—burning up nearly 25 percent of the coal, 26 percent of the oil, and 27 percent of the world's natural gas. Worldwatch Institute, "The State of Consumption Today."
51. Joan Tronto, *Caring Democracy: Markets, Equality, and Justice* (New York University Press: 2013); Robin Wall Kimmerer, *Braiding Sweetgrass: Indigenous Wisdom, Scientific Knowledge and the Teachings of Plants* (Penguin Books, 2020); The Care Collective, *The Care Manifesto: The Politics of Interdependence* (Verso, 2020).
52. See Chapter 4 for the calculations and sources of these figures.
53. Robert van het Kaar, Robert and Amber van der Graaf. "Working Life in the Netherlands." Eurofound, October 6, 2021, https://www.eurofound.europa.eu/country/netherlands.
54. Jelle Visser, "The First Part-Time Economy in the World: A Model to Be Followed?" *Journal of European Social Policy* 12, no. 1 (2002).
55. Later we address the concern that it is these norms themselves that people worry about: if people feel they "have to" provide care, will they do a good job of it? In advance, one important answer is that most of the women who provide most of the care are acting in accordance with strong norms that women should provide (free) care. The paid care is heavily driven by economic necessity to take those jobs. The norms of PTfA should not be compared to some ideal world of care offered free of norms or need.
56. Bonnie Honig, "Three Models of Emergency Politics," *Boundary 2* 41, no. 2 (June 1, 2014): 45–70.
57. Unfortunately, even in Sweden such norms are still quite rare. Linda Haas and C. Phillip Hwang, *Social Politics: International Studies in Gender, State & Society* 23, no. 1 (2016).
58. Schulte, *Overwhelmed*, 221.

59. *M v H*, [1999] 2 SCR 3; *Civil Marriage Act*, SC 2005 c 33. Canadian juris-
prudence does not generally treat court decisions as "government action"
for constitutional purposes. I (J. N.) have never thought this made sense,
and the Supreme Court of Canada decision was a clear example of how a
determination by an important institution of government advanced the
ongoing transformation of collective norms.

60. Benjamin Kline Hunnicutt, *Kellogg's Six-Hour Day* (Temple University
Press, 1996). This book details the failed experiment of Kellogg's attempt at shortening the workday from eight hours to six hours. Although
workers preferred six-hour days, pressure from the rest of the labor force
(working eight-hour days) and the new owners of the company forced a
return to the eight-hour working day. Interestingly, it appears that gender
was a major factor in ending the experiment. It was mainly male workers
who mobilized for a return to an eight-hour day since the six-hour day
decreased the centrality of work in their community and had thereby
somewhat undermined the position of the male in the family.

61. "Labours Lost," *The Economist*, June 15, 2002, sec. Finance & Economics,
https://www.economist.com/finance-and-economics/2002/06/13/labors-
lost; Bill Chappell, "4-Day Workweek Boosted Workers' Productivity By
40%, Microsoft Japan Says," *NPR*, November 4, 2019, sec. Business, https://
www.npr.org/2019/11/04/776163853/microsoft-japan-says-4-day-workw
eek-boosted-workers-productivity-by-40; Yuki Noguchi, "Enjoy The
Extra Day Off! More Bosses Give 4-Day Workweek A Try," *NPR*, February
21, 2020, sec. Business, https://www.npr.org/2020/02/21/807133509/
enjoy-the-extra-day-off-more-bosses-give-4-day-workweek-a-try.

Chapter 1

1. Linda Duxbury and Christopher Alan Higgins, *Something's Got to
Give: Balancing Work, Childcare, and Eldercare* (Toronto: University
of Toronto Press, 2017), xi. They also note (p. x) that "[e]ven though eldercare is likely to surpass childcare as a more pressing concern for organizations and their employees, management scholars have not
embraced the topic," quoting Lisa Calvano, "Tug of War: Caring for Our
Elders While Remaining Productive at Work," *Academy of Management
Perspectives* 27, no. 3 (2013): 205. See also Ai-jen Poo, with Marie Conrad,

The Age of Dignity: Preparing for the Elder Boom in a Changing America (New York: New Press, 2015).

2. Nancy Folbre, *The Invisible Heart: Economics and Family Values* (New York: New Press, 2001); Nancy Folbre, *Valuing Children: Rethinking the Economics of the Family*, The Family and Public Policy (Cambridge, MA: Harvard University Press, 2010); Nancy Folbre, *Greed, Lust & Gender: A History of Economic Ideas* (Oxford University Press, 2009).

3. For data on Canada, see Duxbury and Higgins, *Something's Got to Give*; Linda Duxbury and Christopher Higgins, "Revisiting Work-Life Issues in Canada: The 2012 National Study on Balancing Work and Caregiving in Canada" (Sprott School of Business, Carleton University, 2012).

4. See e.g. Jennifer Gollan, "Elder Care Homes Rake in Profits as Workers Earn a Pittance," *Associated Press*, May 19, 2019, sec. Christian Louboutin, https://apnews.com/8e852a9b2fd9459e9e7ca2412c7bcf47.

5. See Daniel Markovits, *The Meritocracy Trap: How America's Foundational Myth Feeds Inequality, Dismantles the Middle Class, and Devours the Elite* (New York: Penguin Press, 2019), 120–21.

6. Gabrielle Meagher and Marta Szebehely, eds., *Marketisation in Nordic Eldercare: A Research Report on Legislation, Oversight, Extent and Consequences*, Stockholm Studies of Social Work (Stockholm: Department of Social Work, Stockholm University, 2013).

7. "22 hours" a week is a shorthand for the minimum most people should treat as a norm. Putting it in quotation marks is meant to suggest that while specific, it is provisional. It is a well-grounded estimate (see note 176) but cannot be expected to work for everyone.

8. Evelyn Nakano Glenn, *Forced to Care: Coercion and Caregiving in America* (Cambridge, MA: Harvard University Press, 2010), 5. The full definition is:

> Caring labor involves three types of intertwined activities. First, there is direct caring for the person, which includes physical care (e.g., feeding, bathing, grooming), emotional care (e.g., listening, talking, offering reassurance), and services to help people meet their physical and emotional needs (e.g., shopping for food, driving to appointments, going on outings). The second type of caring labor is that of maintaining the immediate physical surroundings/milieu in which people live (e.g., changing bed linen, washing clothing, and vacuuming floors). The third is the work of fostering people's relationships and social connections, a form of caring labor that has been referred to as "kin work" or as "community mothering." An apt metaphor for this type of care labor is "weaving and reweaving the social fabric." All three types of caring labor are included to varying degrees in the job definitions of such occupations as nurses'

aides, home care aides, and housekeepers or nannies. Each of these positions involves varying mixtures of the three elements of care, and, when done well, the work entails considerable (if unrecognized) physical, social, and emotional skills.

9. This is even true for middle-class white women, although increasingly they have the opportunity of rejecting or delegating the care responsibilities the culture assigns them—although not without cost. See Jennifer Nedelsky, "The Gendered Division of Household Labor: An Issue of Constitutional Rights," in *Feminist Constitutionalism: Global Perspectives*, ed. Beverly Baines, Daphne Barak-Erez, and Tsvi Kahana (New York: Cambridge University Press, 2012), 15–47.

10. For a thoughtful comment on the skills (as well as demands and importance) of care giving see the opinion piece by Lorene Cary:

> Because we do not prioritize psychological well-being, we don't ask how keeping the elderly and disabled in good spirits could make us a stronger, better, happier country. Instead, we ask home care workers to provide, often for little more than minimum wage, very subtle, tailored companionship—call it care or friendship or even love. With longer life expectancies, the need for caregiving in later life is increasing. How we update care systems will affect not only this often hidden sector of American life but also our national debt, and, if we had one, our Gross National Happiness Index.

Lorene Cary, "My Family Cared for My Sick Aunt. Who's Caring for Us?," *The New York Times*, October 25, 2019, sec. Opinion, https://www.nytimes.com/2019/10/25/opinion/health-care-old-age-disability.html; Lorene Cary, "Who's Caring for the Care givers?," *The New York Times*, October 27, 2019, New York edition, sec. SR.

11. Glenn, *Forced to Care*. See also Duffy, *Making Care Count*.

12. Adelle Blackett, *Everyday Transgressions: Domestic Workers' Transnational Challenge to International Labor Law* (Ithaca, NY: Cornell University Press, 2019). See also Terri Nilliasca, "Some Women's Work: Domestic Work, Class, Race, Heteropatriarchy, and the Limits of Legal Reform," *Michigan Journal of Race and Law* 16, no. 2 (2011): 406.

13. Blackett, *Everyday Transgressions*, 78–79.

14. See the important work on vulnerability as a basic part of the human condition by Martha A. Fineman. See, e.g., Martha Albertson Fineman, ed., "The Vulnerable Subject: Anchoring Equality in the Human Condition," *Yale Law Journal* 20, no. 1 (2008): 1–23, https://doi.org/10.4324/978020 3848531-26; Martha Albertson Fineman, "Vulnerability and Inevitable Inequality," *Oslo Law Review* 4, no. 3 (2017): 133–49.

15. "We [would] go to work instead of to day programs. Our needs [would] become less 'special' and more like the ordinary needs that are routinely met
in society. In freedom, we can do our bit to meet the needs of others. We
might prove too valuable to be put away." Johnson, "The Disability Gulag."
16. Nancy Fraser and Linda Gordon, "A Genealogy of Dependency: Tracing a
Keyword of the U.S. Welfare State," *Signs* 19, no. 2 (1994): 309–36.
17. Chloe G. K. Atkins, "The Failure of Formal Rights and Equality in
the Clinic: A Critique of Bioethics," *Ethics & Medicine* 2, no. 3 (Fall
2005): 139–62.
18. See, e.g., Sonia Sodha, "Underfunded and Overstretched—the Crisis
in Care for the Elderly," *The Observer*, December 10, 2016, sec. Society,
https://www.theguardian.com/society/2016/dec/10/care-for-elderly-cri
sis-how-to-improve-quality-of-life; Johnson, "The Disability Gulag."
19. See the essays in Shelley A. M. Gavigan and Dorothy E. Chunn, eds.,
*The Legal Tender of Gender: Welfare, Law, and the Regulation of Women's
Poverty* (Oxford and Portland, Oregon: Hart Publishing, 2010).
20. Rosie Harding, *Duties to Care: Dementia, Relationality, and Law*,
Cambridge Bioethics and Law (Cambridge: Cambridge University Press,
2017), 197–98. "Nor, in the Act, are Carers understood to require care
themselves."
21. Linda C. McClain, "The Other Marriage Equality Problem," *Boston
University Law Review* 93, no. 3 (2013): 921–70; Kerry Rittich, "Families
on the Edge: Governing Home and Work in a Globalized Economy," *North
Carolina Law Review* 88, no. 5 (2010): 1527–58.
22. We are not suggesting that stable, paid care givers cannot provide love and
comfort. In this particular case, a new care giver without a previous relationship to the child would have had to be hired. More generally, under
good conditions, paid care givers can establish loving relationships with
those they care for. But even then, children may want a parent for particular forms of comfort, emotional support, and even physical care when
they are sick or hurt.
23. See, e.g., "Flourishing through Mutual Support," Harbourside
Cohousing: Senior Cohousing in Sooke, BC, accessed August 13,
2020, http://www.harbourside.ca/index.html; Alex Bozikovic, "That
Co-Housing Retirement Life: How Smart Design Gives This Seniors'
Community a Life-Changing Twist," Globe and Mail, March 9, 2019,
https://www.theglobeandmail.com/arts/art-and-architecture/article-for
get-institutional-living-smart-design-gives-this-seniors/.

24. Of course, some faith communities will resist the norms of PTfA if they see gendered division of labor as divinely ordained. But many will not and already constitute themselves as communities of mutual care, shared in by both men and women. Some people might naturally feel themselves to be members of more than one community, like both a neighborhood and a faith community. They would need to decide, together with both communities, if it makes sense for them to split their hours, or whether that would leave them unable to be responsive enough to the needs of their communities. Thanks to Maria Arabella Robles for raising this issue.

25. See, e.g., Jennifer Nedelsky, "Communities of Judgment and Human Rights," *Theoretical Inquiries in Law* 1, no. 2 (2000): 1–38.

26. Ed Kucerak and Daniellle Rolfe, *Blue Roses*, Documentary (Kublacom Pictures Inc., 2018), http://www.bluerosesdocumentary.ca/.

27. "Moms Stop The Harm," 2020, https://www.momsstoptheharm.com.

28. Sheila Kathleen Jennings, Personal Communication, n.d. Here is part of her own story:

> My son overdosed in Calgary four years ago in a Tim Hortons bathroom stall. He was subsequently carried out of the stall to the Tim's parking lot in the depths of the Alberta winter, where he was dumped on the ground. A woman waiting nearby saw this happen and she called 911. She went over and stayed with him, and she left a note inside his coat setting out what happened to him. His heart stopped during that overdose, and it was reportedly difficult to reverse the OD and bring him back. I always wanted to thank that woman and I in part dedicated my dissertation to her for her care. Makes me think about preservative love (Ruddick, 1995)–but in this instance, we're trying to preserve one another's kids in this crisis. It also makes me think of those of our children who become "undeserving" of any care at all. My son "fell" socially into that category. The son of an ER doctor and lawyer. If you are undeserving of care, you can become a body that gets dumped.

See also Sheila Kathleen Jennings, "The Right to Support: Severely Disabled Children & Their Mothers" (PhD Dissertation, Toronto, ON, York University, 2019), YorkSpace, http://hdl.handle.net/10315/36669.

29. For more a more detailed example of their work, see "On the Front Lines," *Social Change* (blog), June 18, 2018, http://socialchange.adler.edu/on-the-front-lines/.

30. Jenny Morris, *Pride against Prejudice: A Personal Politics of Disability* (London: Women's Press, 1991).

31. "In describing care receivers as citizens as they receive care, rather than as dependents, invalids, wards, we open the possibilities to restore proper forms of human agency and dignity to ourselves as receivers of necessary care. Too often, recipients of care are viewed simply as passive objects of the activities of others." Joan C Tronto, "Who Cares? Public and Private Caring and the Rethinking of Citizenship," in *Women and Welfare: Theory and Practice in the United States and Europe*, ed. Nancy J. Hirschmann and Ulrike Liebert (New Brunswick, NJ: Rutgers University Press, 2001), 79.

32. There are now many articulations of a relational understanding of autonomy. J. N.'s was first presented in Jennifer Nedelsky, "Reconceiving Autonomy: Sources, Thoughts and Possibilities," *Yale JL & Feminism* 1 (1989): 7–36. It was further elaborated in Nedelsky, *Law's Relations*. See also Tom Malleson "Interdependency: The fourth existential insult to humanity," *Contemporary Political Theory* 17, no. 2 (2018).

33. See Kittay, *Love's Labor*.

34. Daphne de Marneffe, *Maternal Desire: On Children, Love, and the Inner Life*, 2nd ed. (Scribner, 2004), 1, Preface to the Second Edition.

35. We will see later that Sara Ruddick, a deeply thoughtful investigator of mothering care, does not reject the language of control. J. N. thinks this a more a linguistic difference than a disagreement about the deeper issues. Riane Eisler also offers an alternative approach to control: Riane Eisler and Daniel Levine, "Nurture, Nature, and Caring: We Are Not Prisoners of Our Genes," *Brain and Mind* 3, no. 1 (2002): 9–52.

36. Of course, having no control over one's life is extremely anxiety provoking. The sense of being at the mercy of others is antithetical to the value of autonomy, even while we also believe that "being in control of one's life" is a poor way of describing the nature of autonomy. See Nedelsky, *Law's Relations*, chap. 3 and 7.

37. C Starla Hargita, "Care-Based Temporalities and Parental Leave in Australia," *Griffith Law Review* 26, no. 4 (2017): 511–31.

38. This comment invokes Hannah Arendt's conception of action in the public realm. See Arendt, *The Human Condition*.

39. Daphne De Marneffe notes that in this neoliberal era people feel "an anxiety about the value of private experiences and interpersonal bonds that can't be quantified." de Marneffe, *Maternal Desire*, 111.

40. For Ruddick, "to be a 'mother' is to take upon oneself the responsibility of childcare, making its work a regular and substantial part of one's working life." Sara Ruddick, *Maternal Thinking: Toward a Politics of Peace* (Boston: Beacon Press, 1989), 17. She makes clear that taking on such

responsibility is a choice, not an automatic biological imperative. Not every woman who gives birth makes this choice, and men, nonbinary people, and nonbiological parents can also make it. Then they, too, become mothers. In our discussion of her insights, we adopt her meaning of "mother" and her usage of not using quotation marks—even though that is not the language we choose for our own arguments.

41. Carlin Meyer is the author of this remark. And Joan Tronto points out that the same could be said for intimate relations with the elderly.

42. Ruddick, *Maternal Thinking*, 17.

43. Ruddick is, throughout the book, attentive to the ways the harms of poverty, racism, war, or natural disaster can so overwhelm a mother's efforts that she sometimes cannot learn what the demands of protective love, growth, or social acceptance require.

44. Ruddick, *Maternal Thinking*, 225.

45. Ruddick, *Maternal Thinking*, 227.

46. Ruddick, *Maternal Thinking*, 232.

47. Ruddick, *Maternal Thinking*, 233.

48. Ruddick, *Maternal Thinking*, 68.

49. See, for example, Antonio R. Damasio, *Descartes' Error: Emotion, Reason and the Human Brain*, 18. Druck (New York: Quill, 2004).

50. Ruddick, *Maternal Thinking*, 69–70.

51. Ruddick, *Maternal Thinking*, 83.

52. Ruddick, *Maternal Thinking*, 85.

53. Ruddick, *Maternal Thinking*, 90.

54. Niall Hanlon, *Masculinities, Care and Equality: Identity and Nurture in Men's Lives* (Palgrave Macmillan, 2012).

55. Hanlon, *Masculinities, Care and Equality*, 203.

56. Hanlon, *Masculinities, Care and Equality*, 207.

57. Hanlon, *Masculinities, Care and Equality*, 209–10, emphasis added.

58. See e.g. Hanlon, *Masculinities, Care and Equality*, 203–4.

59. Vrinda Dalmiya, *Caring to Know: Comparative Care Ethics, Feminist Epistemology, and the Mahabharata* (India: Oxford University Press, 2016), 1. The nature of Dalmiya's project is different from ours here. She is a philosopher building a theory of epistemology, of how we know. But there is important overlap.

60. Dalmiya, *Caring to Know*, 14–15. She also cites Kittay, *Love's Labor*, for making this point about dependencies.

61. Dalmiya, *Caring to Know*, 13. Theories of knowledge (building on the work of Lorraine Code) depend on the examples of knowledge they begin

with. If we shift our examples from knowing things to knowing selves, the conceptual structure of knowledge changes.

62. See Iris Marion Young, "Feminism and the Public Sphere," *Constellations* 3, no. 3 (1997): 340–63. Young notes, "Generally speaking, able-bodied people simply fail to understand the lives and issues of people with disabilities. When asked to put themselves in the position of a person in a wheelchair, they do not imagine the point of view of others; rather, they project onto those others their own fears and fantasies about themselves. Thus more often than not, well-meaning, able-bodied people seeking to understand and communicate with a disabled person express the patronizing attitudes of pity that so enrage many people with disabilities" (344).

63. Dalmiya, *Caring to Know*, 22.

64. Dalmiya, *Caring to Know*, 20.

65. Dalmiya, *Caring to Know*, 18.

66. As J. N. has explored in her work on Arendtian approaches to judgment. See e.g. Ronald Beiner and Jennifer Nedelsky, eds., *Judgment, Imagination, and Politics: Themes from Kant and Arendt* (Lanham, Md: Rowman & Littlefield, 2001).

67. Eisler and Levine, "Nurture, Nature, and Caring," 19.

68. Eisler and Levine, "Nurture, Nature, and Caring," 19.

69. Eisler and Levine, "Nurture, Nature, and Caring," 39, citing Riane Eisler, *The Chalice and the Blade: Our History, Our Future* (San Francisco: HarperCollins Publishers, 1987); Riane Tennenhaus Eisler, *Sacred Pleasure: Sex, Myth, and the Politics of the Body*, 1st ed. (San Francisco: HarperCollins Publishers, 1995).

70. Eisler and Levine, "Nurture, Nature, and Caring," 43.

71. Eisler and Levine, "Nurture, Nature, and Caring," 44. They continue, "Since supportive social attachments (in and out of families) tend to increase oxytocin levels and decrease levels of stress hormones such as cortisol, there is every reason to suspect the same biochemical effects from increasing the level of interpersonal support on a societal scale through institutions and policies that disinhibit rather than inhibit caring."

72. María Vicenta Mestre et al., *Are Women More Empathetic than Men? A Longitudinal Study in Adolescence* (Cambridge: Cambridge University Press, 2013).

73. Michael Kimmel, "Almost All Violent Extremists Share One Thing: Their Gender," *The Guardian*, April 8, 2018, https://www.theguardian.com/world/2018/apr/08/violent-extremists-share-one-thing-gender-michael-kimmel.

74. "Statistical Briefing Book," Office of Juvenile Justice and Delinquency Prevention. Accessed December 29, 2021. https://www.ojjdp.gov/ojsta tbb/crime/ucr.asp?table_in=1&selYrs=2019&rdoGroups=3&rdoData= c; Statista Research Department, "Number of Mass Shootings in the United States between 1982 and November 2021, By Shooter's Gender," Statista, December 1, 2021, https://www.statista.com/statistics/476445/ mass-shootings-in-the-us-by-shooter-s-gender/.

75. Mark L. Rosenberg et al., eds, "Interpersonal Violence," in *Disease Control Priorities in Developing Countries*, 2nd ed, ch. 40 (Washington, DC: The International Bank for Reconstruction and Development, 2006).

76. Angela Scarpa and Adrian Raine, "Violence associated with anger and impulsivity," in *The Neuropsychology of Emotion*, ed. J. C. Borod (Oxford: Oxford University Press, 2000).

77. Emma Fulu et al., "Why Do Some Men Use Violence Against Women and How Can We Prevent It?: Quantitative Findings from the UN Multi-Country Study on Men and Violence in Asia and the Pacific" (United Nations: UN Volunteers, UN Women, United Nations Development Programme, 2013), https://www.ncjrs.gov/App/Publications/abstr act.aspx?ID=265661; Ian DeGeer, "Give Love, Get Love: The Involved Fatherhood and Gender Equity Project" (Toronto: White Ribbon Campaign, 2014), https://www.whiteribbon.ca/uploads/1/1/3/2/ 113222347/fatherhood_report.pdf. See also Nikki Van der Gaag et al., "State of the World's Fathers: Unlocking the Power of Men's Care" (Promundo, 2019)

78. Van der Gaag et al., "State of the World's Fathers," 9.

79. Brittany Wong, "Are Men Really Having A 'Friendship Crisis'?" *Huffington Post*, November 6, 2019, https://www.huffpost.com/entry/ men-friendship-crisis_l_5dbc9aa7e4b0576b62a1e90f.

80. "Marriage and Men's Health," *Harvard Health Publishing*, June 5, 2019, https://www.health.harvard.edu/mens-health/marriage-and-mens-health.

81. Bronnie Ware, "Regrets of the Dying," http://bronnieware.com/regrets-of-the-dying/.

82. My (J. N.) commitment to adding a section on care for the earth emerged during my isolation during the first few months of the COVID-19 pandemic. It was a very personal response and so I am writing this section in the first person.

83. Dorothy Dinnerstein, *The Mermaid and the Minotaur* (New York: Harper and Row, Perennial Library, 1977).

84. For a kindred approach, Kheel notes, "A holist ecofeminist philosophy ... is not so much an ethic as a consciousness or ethos. It is a 'way of life' or a

mode of consciousness that invites us to be 'responsible,' not in the sense of conforming to obligations and rights, but in the literal sense of developing the ability for response. . . . It welcomes the larger scientific stories of evolutionary and ecological processes, but never loses sight of the individual beings who exist within these larger narratives. *Ecofeminist philosophy never transcends or denies our capacity for empathy and care, our most important human connection with the natural world.*" Marti Kheel, *Nature Ethics: An Ecofeminist Perspective* (Rowman & Littlefield, 2007), 251 [emphasis added].

85. Thomas Berry offers a very helpful account of how the importation of Christianity into North America fostered the degradation of earth centered spirituality. The idea of a living planet and nonhuman life forms imbued with spirit was treated as "primitive," and part of the grounds for seeing European settlers as fundamentally superior to the Indigenous peoples who had offered to cooperate with them. See Thomas Berry, *The Dream of the Earth* (San Francisco: Sierra Club Books, 1988)

86. Kheel, *Nature Ethics*, 212, offers these reflections from Carolyn Merchant: "the image of the earth as a living organism and nurturing mother has historically served as a cultural constraint restricting the actions of human beings. One does not readily slay a mother, dig into her entrails for gold, or mutilate her body. . . . As long as the earth was considered to be alive and sensitive, it could be considered a breach of human ethical behavior to carry out destructive acts against it." "Mining the Earth's Womb," on *Machina Ex Dea: Feminist Perspectives on Technology*, ed. Joan Rothschild (New York: Pergamon Press, 1983), 100. Kheel adds, "For a divergent view that contends that 'feelings for mothers are too complex for the mother-nature relation to function unequivocally as an environmental prod,' see Catherine M. Roach, Mother/Nature: Popular Culture and Environmental Ethics (Indiana University Press, 2003), 71."

87. Berry, *The Dream of the Earth.*

88. For a look into her many contributions, see Stephanie Kaza, ed., *A Wild Love for the World: Joanna Macy and the Work of Our Time*, First edition (Boulder, CO: Shambhala, 2020).

89. Robin Wall Kimmerer, *Braiding Sweetgrass: Indigenous Wisdom, Scientific Knowledge and the Teachings of Plants* (Penguin Books, 2020), 126.

90. See the many works of John Borrows, in particular "Earth-Bound: Indigenous Resurgence and Environmental Reconciliation," in *Resurgence and Reconciliation*, ed. Michael Asch, John Borrows, and James Tully (Toronto: University of Toronto Press, 2018), 49–82. See also,

Kimmerer, *Braiding Sweetgrass*; Leanne Betasamosake Simpson, "Land as Pedagogy: Nishnaabeg Intelligence and Rebellious Transformation," *Decolonization: Indigeneity, Education & Society* 3, no. 3 (2014): 1–25; C. F. Black, "On Lives Lived With Law: Land as Healer," *Law Text Culture* 20 (2016): 164–88; Kim TallBear, "Caretaking Relations, Not American Dreaming," *Kalfou* 6, no. 1 (2019): 24–41.

91. For example, Richard Louv, *Last Child in the Woods: Saving Our Children from Nature-Deficit Disorder* (London: Atlantic Books Ltd, 2010).

92. Robin Wall Kimmerer, *Gathering Moss: A Natural and Cultural History of Mosses* (Oregon State University Press, 2003).

93. I see the language of care for the earth and care for place as connected, but not identical. Some people have a strong sense of protecting place, which is integrally connected to a particular part of the earth, but which is about the whole human-earth ecology/culture/way of life that has evolved there. It is, for example, often not aimed (in the first instance) at climate change or other large-scale forms of harm to the earth. This sense of place is particular and claims passionate allegiance in its particularity. I think it is possible that most forms of love for the earth and the commitment to nurturing and protection that grows out of that love is grounded in connection to particular parts of our planet. Ozlem Aslan provides examples of a commitment to place, a "placial ethics," that can be seen in the resistance to hydropower dams in Turkey. See Ozlem Aslan, "Resistances against Hydropower Projects as Place-Based Struggles: The Case of Artvin, Turkey" (Dissertation, University of Toronto, 2019), https://tspace.library.utoronto.ca/handle/1807/96926.

94. See Kimmerer, *Gathering Moss*; Louv, *Last Child in the Woods*.

95. John Borrows, "Outsider Education: Indigenous Law and Land-Based Learning," *Windsor Yearbook of Access to Justice* 33, no. 1 (2016): 29.

96. Leanne Simpson, a Michi Saagiig Nishnaabeg writer, reflects on her own long, slow process of learning: "No matter what we were doing together, those Elders always carried their Ancestors with them. They were in constant communication with them as they went about their daily lives engaged in practices that continually communicated to the spiritual world that they were Nishnaabeg. I didn't understand this. I kept asking them about governance, and they would talk about trapping. I would ask them about treaties, and they would take me fishing. I'd ask them what we should do about the mess of colonialism, and they would tell me stories about how well they used to live on the land. I loved all of it, but I didn't think they were answering my questions. I could see only *practice*. I couldn't see their *theory* until decades later. I couldn't see intelligence

until I learned *how* to see it by engaging in Nishnaabeg practices for the next two decades."
Leanne Betasamosake Simpson, *As We Have Always Done: Indigenous Freedom through Radical Resistance*, Indigenous Americas (Minneapolis: University of Minnesota Press, 2017), 18–19.

97. See Louv, *Last Child in the Woods*, 1–2.
98. Kimmerer, *Braiding Sweetgrass*, 126–27.
99. For example, Simpson says, "I want my great- grandchildren to be able to fall in love with every piece of our territory." Simpson, *As We Have Always Done*, 7.
100. For a critique of animal rights and environmentalism based on abstractions that devalue personal and affective ties, and disregard the importance of empathy and care for individual beings, see Marti Kheel, *Nature Ethics: An Ecofeminist Perspective* (Rowman and Littlefield, 2007).
101. For an articulation of the importance of Indigenous-led integration of Indigenous research and methodology into projects for the well-being of the whole earth community, see Amanda Yates, Kelly Dombroski, and Rita Dionisio, "Wellbeing-Led Governance Frameworks as Transformative Tools for an Ecological Emergency," *Dialogues in Human Geography*, forthcoming.
102. Stone, *The Samaritan's Dilemma*.
103. Dalmiya, *Caring to Know*.
104. See Tronto, *Caring Democracy*.
105. Of course, market advocates argue that the fact that care is low paid is *evidence* that it is low skilled. Otherwise, a market would have developed to identify and pay higher wages to those gifted at care. Our response is (to oversimplify) that the existing labor market has not recognized these gifts because a complex system of beliefs, institutions, practices reinforces the idea that care is low skilled. Exactly how this form of market failure is sustained is a complex question beyond the scope of this book. One analogy is the argument that discrimination, whether racial or gender-based is irrational because it would deprive businesses of some of the most skilled. The conclusion of market purists is that discrimination must therefore not exist. Exactly how the benefits to the privileged function to overcome the real costs of discrimination, is a similarly complex story.
106. Martin Marchiori-Wong, "Taking Care of the Temporal Imbalance in Child Care Policies" (unpublished manuscript, April 29, 2017), Microsoft Word file.

107. Joanna V. Noronha, "Nuclear Fusion: Housing, Property and Care Arrangements Beyond the Nuclear Family" (Wainwright Postdoctoral Fellowship Research, McGill University, Faculty of Law, 2019).

108. One concern is that people who never envisioned themselves as carers (disproportionately men) will associate their difficulty and their boredom with the long-standing idea that women "naturally" are good at care, and thus that their difficulties are just an indication that they should not be doing tasks that really properly belong to others. The naturalness of female care can also support the idea that there is neither learning nor skill involved, just something like instinct. Such ideas can serve to prevent people from applying to the realm of care their general knowledge that learning new skills always requires effort and intention.

109. Ruth Fletcher, "Negotiating Strangeness on the Abortion Trail," in *Revaluing Care in Theory, Law and Policy: Cycles and Connections*, ed. Rosie Harding, Ruth Fletcher, and Chris Beasley (New York: Routledge, 2017), 23.

110. Elizabeth Peel, "'It Has Had Quite a Lot of Reverberations through the Family': Reconfiguring Relationships through Parent with Dementia Care," in *Revaluing Care in Theory, Law and Policy: Cycles and Connections*, ed. Rosie Harding, Ruth Fletcher, and Chris Beasley (Routledge, 2017), 200, 204–5.

111. Susan B. Garland, "At 75, Taking Care of Mom, 99: 'We Did Not Think She Would Live This Long'—The New York Times," *The New York Times*, June 27, 2019, https://nyti.ms/2KGtu5X.

112. See Glenn, *Forced to Care*; Duffy, *Making Care Count*.

113. Susan Thistle, *From Marriage to the Market: The Transformation of Women's Lives and Work* (Berkeley, CA: University of California Press, 2006), 143. Thistle finds that fathers of young children whose wives work full time spend 18h/week providing care. She finds that wives do about 1.5 times as much, so that amounts to 27 hours. The total between them is 27 + 18 = 45. So, we can estimate that each of two parents/care givers needs to provide 22.5 hours of housework and childcare, which we round to 22 hours.

114. We recognize that there are other forms of relationships with dynamics that vary significantly from the model used by Thistle. For example, in terms of childcare, parents in same-sex couples and women in heterosexual couples spend significantly more time—compared to men in heterosexual couples—with their children, and thus spend more time engaging in care for those children (including physical care, teaching, playing, and child-related activities such as driving them). That said,

these variances do not necessarily shift the "22 hour" minimum, but rather showcase the differences in the extent to which people may need to change under the new norms. See Kate C. Prickett, Alexa Martin-Storey, and Robert Crosnoe, "A Research Note on Time With Children in Different- and Same-Sex Two-Parent Families," *Demography* 52, no. 3 (2015): 905–18; Stephanie Coontz, "How to Make Your Marriage Gayer," *The New York Times*, February 13, 2020, https://www.nytimes.com/2020/02/13/opinion/sunday/marriage-housework-gender-happiness.html; Kenneth Matos, "Modern Families: Same- and Different-Sex Couples Negotiating at Home" (Families and Work Institute, 2015), https://www.familiesandwork.org/research/2015.

115. Though the initial 22 hours were calculated for a "nuclear" family, we have been able to determine that similar hours of care are needed for non-traditional families and care arrangements as well. For example, there have been studies that show that in single-parent households, parents spend between 11–14 hours per week on childcare and two hours per day (or 14 hours per week) on nonnurturant care, totaling at least 25 hours of care per week. Given that these single-parent households differ from the care obligations in the two-parent two-children model, the slight change in hours from the 22 hour minimum is expected. See Joanna R. Pepin, Liana C. Sayer, and Lynne M. Casper, "Marital Status and Mothers' Time Use: Childcare, Housework, Leisure, and Sleep," *Demography* 55, no. 1 (February 2018): 107–33; Yoonjoo Lee and Sandra L. Hofferth, "Gender Differences in Single Parents' Living Arrangements and Child Care Time," *Journal of Child and Family Studies* 26, no. 12 (December 2017): 3439–51.

116. Thanks to Genevieve Painter who first raised this point to us.

117. This is sometimes referred to as "domestic violence," but the phrase "intimate partner violence" is intended to avoid some of the trivialization associated with "domestic violence."

118. Deborah Stone, *The Samaritan's Dilemma: Should Government Help Your Neighbor?* (New York: Nation Books, 2008). At a conference panel on care, we once heard a moving story about a young male lawyer needing time with his hospitalized elderly mother, who would only eat when he was there to feed her. His colleagues at his law firm said several times, with apparent sympathy, "do whatever you have to do." But then he saw his colleagues' "dim bewilderment" about why it was taking him so long to get something organized so that he didn't have to miss time from work and realized that by "do whatever you have to do," they meant hire someone to do what needs doing. They could not imagine that in

this case, that was impossible. The care required included the personal connection.

119. As a colleague described this project.

120. Although in Canada those who clean people's homes are usually paid a higher hourly wage than that earned by people who care for their children. Here we think there is a divergence between status and income: cleaners have lower status but are paid more.

121. Using 2013 figures, Anne-Marie Slaughter concluded that the wage gap for women without children was 96 cents on the male dollar while for married mothers it was 76 cents. Slaughter, *Unfinished Business*, 54.

122. Beans on Toast, *On & On*, Song, 2019.

123. Tronto defines "caring for" as one of five steps in the processes of care that entails taking responsibility for meeting the identified needs of a person or group. See Tronto, *Caring Democracy*, 22–23.

124. Tronto, *Caring Democracy*, 33, 46–64.

125. Thanks to the MAPS discussion group at Osgoode Hall Law School for helping J. N. think through the issues around activism.

126. Sometimes activist groups do engage in direct care. T. M., for example, describes helping someone held on a security certificate with home visits, driving him places, etc. This work was organized by an activist organization for supporting immigrants, but the support-work would clearly meet our definition of direct care.

127. Female faculty at universities routinely complain that they spend a lot more of their scarce time providing care for their students than their male colleagues do. Racialized faculty are also called upon to do a tremendous amount of this sort of care and counseling, often in response to discrimination racialized students experience. The faculty who leave office hours promptly to go write their articles are usually the ones who are rewarded with recognition and pay. Because the care that many female and racialized faculty provide is not recognized as work, it is easy for white, male academics either to disparage their colleagues' inability to focus on what matters or, more sympathetically, to try to help them to get their priorities straight. We have witnessed both. Either way, when the caring colleague does not get promoted, the others can just shake their heads whether in contempt or compassion.

128. There are also contributions that seem like work that happen in the context of care. For example, someone who volunteers many hours working with school children at a particular school also sometimes helps with the filing in the school office. This might not seem like care, but it is being done as part of an ongoing role of someone providing care not

just to particular students, but to a neighborhood school. It is surely an act of care toward overburdened staff. It has the relationship building dimension that makes it count as care. I (J. N.) take this example from my cousin Elizabeth Nelson who has spent much of her life providing care to those in her community, but who is not sympathetic to PTfA. (I think because it looks too much like regulation and thus impingement on freedom.)

129. Audre Lorde, *A Burst of Light: Essays* (Ithaca, NY: Firebrand Books, 1988), 131.

130. In my (J. N.) experience, family members who felt I did not have enough time for them were especially likely to complain about the (very limited) time I took for exercise. Of course, it is never a good thing if one's family feels "time neglected."

131. Sometimes this kind of work is referred to as "emotional labor." See, for instance, the fantastic online conversation between women about this kind of work. "Emotional Labor: The MetaFilter Thread Condensed Version 2," Metafilter, October 2, 2015, https://docs.google.com/vie wer?a=v&pid=sites&srcid=ZGVmYXVVsdGRvbWFpbnxpbnRlZ3JhbHHd vbWVVufGd4OjMwMTBhNGU5MTAxNTE1Mjg.

132. Laura Davy, "People with Intellectual Disability and the Relational Self: Redrawing the Moral Boundaries of Personal Autonomy" (Thesis, Sydney, University of Sydney, 2017).

133. This is a term from Duffy, *Making Care Count.*

134. See, e.g., Glenn, Forced to Care. See also Duffy, Making Care Count.

135. Some members of a helpful discussion group were concerned that the language of nurturant/nonnurturant could serve to reinforce a hierarchy that the terms are meant to challenge.

136. For example, see Markovits's comparison of the resources of pre-schools: "ordinary and elite preschools are almost unrecognizably different." Markovits, *The Meritocracy Trap*, 122.

137. Annabelle Timsit, "Even Europe's Most Family-Friendly Countries Don't Invest Enough in Their Youngest Kids," *Quartz*, July 15, 2019, https://qz.com/1664782/europe-doesnt-invest-enough-in-kids-under-three/. For an example of the effects of the shortage of care available to the growing elderly population, see Liz O'Donnell, "The Crisis Facing America's Working Daughters," *The Atlantic*, February 9, 2016, https://www.theatlantic.com/business/archive/2016/02/working-daughters-eldercare/459249/.

138. Peter Dietsch, *Catching Capital: The Ethics of Tax Competition* (Oxford: Oxford University Press, 2005), 48–50.

139. These grants could be used to support care infrastructures in poor countries. Thanks to Kole Kilibarda for this suggestion.

Chapter 2

1. Frigga Haug, *Die Vier-in-einem-Perspektive: Politik von Frauen für eine neue Linke* (Hamburg: Argument Verlag, 2008); Frigga Haug, "The 'Four-in-One Perspective': A Manifesto for a More Just Life," *Socialism and Democracy* 23, no. 1 (March 2009): 119–23.
2. Russell Muirhead, *Just Work* (Cambridge, MA: Harvard University Press, 2004), 148.
3. For example, see "The Economy of Francesco," 2021, https://francescoeconomy.org/. They have made "Work and Care," one of their topics of focus.
4. Clare Coffey et al., "Time to Care: Unpaid and Underpaid Care Work and the Global Inequality Crisis" (Oxfam, January 20, 2020), 15. The report also comments that "Across the world unpaid and underpaid care work is disproportionately done by poor women and girls, especially those from groups who, as well as gender discrimination, experience discrimination based on race, ethnicity, nationality, sexuality and caste. Women undertake more than three-quarters of unpaid care and make up two-thirds of the paid care workforce" (13).
5. See Adelle Blackett, *Everyday Transgressions: Domestic Workers' Transnational Challenge to International Labor Law* (Ithaca, NY: Cornell University Press, 2019), 17–34; *Convention C189—Domestic Workers Convention, 2011 (No. 189)*, June 16, 2011, Geneva, 100th ILC Sess. (entered into force September 5, 2013).
6. In the largest research project of its kind, researchers from University College London reviewed 25 studies involving more than 600,000 men and women from across Europe, the United States, and Australia. The researchers found a clear pattern that the longer you work, the higher your risk for stroke and heart disease is—even when taking into account other known risk factors such as age, sex, and socioeconomic status, plus behavior modifiers such as smoking, alcohol consumption, and physical activity. Working between 41 to 48 hours gives you a 10 percent higher risk of stroke, which jumps to a 27 percent increased risk if you work 49 to 54 hours. See Peter Dockrill, "Working Long Hours Is Linked to a Significantly Higher Risk of Stroke," *Science Alert* (blog), August 21, 2015, https://www.sciencealert.com/working-long-hours-is-lin

ked-to-a-significantly-higher-risk-of-stroke. See also Mika Kivimäki et al., "Long Working Hours and Risk of Coronary Heart Disease and Stroke: A Systematic Review and Meta-Analysis of Published and Unpublished Data for 603 838 Individuals," *The Lancet* 386, no. 10005 (October 31, 2015): 1739–46.

7. Lawrence Mishel and Alyssa Davis, "Top CEOs Make 300 Times More than Typical Workers: Pay Growth Surpasses Stock Gains and Wage Growth of Top 0.1 Percent," *Economic Policy Institute* (blog), June 21, 2015, http://www.epi.org/publication/top-ceos-make-300-times-more-than-workers-pay-growth-surpasses-market-gains-and-the-rest-of-the-0-1-percent/.

8. Guy Standing, *The Precariat: The New Dangerous Class* (London: Bloomsbury Publishing, 2011).

9. Pugh, *The Tumbleweed Society*, 18–29; Standing, *The Precariat*.

10. Standing, *The Precariat*, 15, 35.

11. Standing, *The Precariat*, 57–58.

12. Gerson, "Changing Lives, Resistant Institutions," 736.

13. Susan Thistle, *From Marriage to the Market: The Transformation of Women's Lives and Work* (Berkeley, CA: University of California Press, 2006), 106.

14. Thistle, *From Marriage*, 66–72.

15. Thistle, *From Marriage*, 115.

16. Thistle, *From Marriage*, 100.

17. Thistle, *From Marriage*, 144.

18. Williams, *Reshaping the Work-Family Debate*, 26.

19. There has been a steady increase in the proportion of single-parent households among households with children across countries in both North America and Europe. For statistical data see United States Census Bureau, "The Majority of Children Live With Two Parents, Census Bureau Reports," news release no. CB16-192, November 17, 2016, https://www.census.gov/newsroom/press-releases/2016/cb16-192.html; "Number of Private Households by Household Composition, Number of Children and Age of Youngest Child (1 000)," Eurostat, European Commission, April 20, 2020, http://appsso.eurostat.ec.europa.eu/nui/show.do?dataset=lfst_hhnhtych&lang=en; Sharanji Uppal, "Employment Patterns of Families with Children," Statistics Canada, catalogue no. 86-006-X, June 24, 2015, https://www150.statcan.gc.ca/n1/pub/75-006-x/2015001/article/14202-eng.htm.

20. There is a particular concern about perpetuating cycles of poverty. In the United States, the poor are less likely to marry, but still have children,

despite fathers' initial intentions. Regarding marriage disparity and poverty, see Linda C. McClain, "The Other Marriage Equality Problem," *Boston University Law Review* 93, no. 3 (2013): 921–70.

21. Barbara Ehrenreich and Arlie Russell Hochschild, eds., *Global Woman: Nannies, Maids, and Sex Workers in the New Economy* (New York: Owl Books, 2004); Pierrette Hondagneu-Sotelo, *Doméstica: Immigrant Workers Cleaning and Caring in the Shadows of Affluence* (Berkeley, CA: University of California Press, 2007), 19.

22. I (J. N.) particularly remember a moving conversation I had with a recovering alcoholic, still unable to find steady work, who spoke of his pain at not being able to be a "provider" for his children.

23. For a deeper discussion of this, see Niall Hanlon, *Masculinities, Care and Equality: Identity and Nurture in Men's Lives* (London: Palgrave Macmillan, 2012), 95.

24. Jerry A. Jacobs and Kathleen Gerson, "Unpacking Americans' Views of the Employment of Mothers and Fathers Using National Vignette Survey Data: SWS Presidential Address," *Gender & Society* 30, no. 3 (2016), 435.

25. Jacobs and Gerson, "Unpacking Americans' Views," 436.

26. Gerson, "Changing Lives, Resistant Institutions," 743.

27. See Daniela Grunow and Gerlieke Veltkamp, "Institutions as Reference Points for Parents-to-Be in European Societies: A Theoretical and Analytical Framework," in *Couples' Transitions to Parenthood: Analysing Gender and Work in Europe* (Cheltenham, UK: Edward Elgar Publishing, 2016), 7–9; Jacobs and Gerson, "Unpacking Americans' Views," 421–23.

28. This phrase was first used by Bernhard Teriet. Hinrichs, "Working Time Development in West Germany," 41.

29. OECD, "Hours Worked: Average Annual Hours Actually Worked," 2019, https://data.oecd.org/emp/hours-worked.htm#indicator-chart; Laura Bridgestock, "Differences in Average Working Hours Around the World," *Top Universities* (blog), March 12, 2014, https://www.topuniversities.com/blog/differences-average-working-hours-around-world.

30. Robert A. Hart, "Women Doing Men's Work and Women Doing Women's Work: Female Work and Pay in British Wartime Engineering," *Explorations in Economic History* 44, no. 1 (2007): 114–30.

31. Cynthia Thomas Calvert and Joan C Williams, *Flex Success: The Lawyer's Guide to Balanced Hours* (CreateSpace Independent Publishing Platform, 2011). See also Epstein et al., *The Part-Time Paradox*.

32. Leslie A. Perlow, "Time to Coordinate: Toward an Understanding of Work-Time Standards and Norms in a Multicountry Study of Software Engineers," *Work and Occupations* 28, no. 1 (February 1, 2001): 91–111.

33. For an excellent historical analysis, see Guy Standing, "Labour, Work and the Time Squeeze," in *The Precariat: The New Dangerous Class* (Bloomsbury Publishing, 2011), 115–43.

34. Suzan Lewis, "Restructuring Workplace Cultures: The Ultimate Work-Family Challenge?" *Women in Management Review* 16, no. 1 (February 2001): 21–29.

35. In an important move, the International Labour Organization recognized the importance of protections for domestic workers. The preamble of the *Convention Concerning Decent Work for Domestic Workers* reads in part:

> Recognizing the significant contribution of domestic workers to the global economy, which includes increasing paid job opportunities for women and men workers with family responsibilities, greater scope for caring for ageing populations, children and persons with a disability, and substantial income transfers within and between countries, and
>
> Considering that domestic work continues to be undervalued and invisible and is mainly carried out by women and girls, many of whom are migrants or members of disadvantaged communities and who are particularly vulnerable to discrimination in respect of conditions of employment and of work, and to other abuses of human rights, and
>
> Considering also that in developing countries with historically scarce opportunities for formal employment, domestic workers constitute a significant proportion of the national workforce and remain among the most marginalized, and
>
> Recalling that international labor Conventions and Recommendations apply to all workers, including domestic workers, unless otherwise provided.

C189—Convention Concerning Decent Work for Domestic Workers, June 16, 2011, International Labour Organization, Geneva, 100th ILC Session (entered into force September 5, 2013), http://www.ilo.org/dyn/normlex/en/f?p=NORMLEXPUB:12100:0::NO::p12100_instrument_id:2551460.

36. Juliet B. Schor, "Sustainable Consumption and Worktime Reduction," *Journal of Industrial Ecology* 9, no. 1–2 (2005).

37. D. Rosnick and M. Weisbrot, "Are Shorter Work Hours Good for the Environment? A Comparison of US and European Energy Consumption," *International Journal of Health Services* 37, no. 3 (2007).

38. Anders Hayden and John M. Shandra, "Hours of Work and the Ecological Footprint of Nations: An Exploratory Analysis," *Local Environment* 14, no. 6 (2009).

39. Kyle W. Knight, Eugene A. Rosa, and Juliet B. Schor, "Could Working Less Reduce Pressures on the Environment? A Cross-National Panel Analysis of OECD Countries, 1970–2007," *Global Environmental Change* 23, no. 4 (2013).

40. J. Nässén and J. Larsson, "Would Shorter Working Time Reduce Greenhouse Gas Emissions? An Analysis of Time Use and Consumption in Swedish Households." *Environment and Planning C: Government and Policy* 33, no. 4 (2015), 726.

41. Jared B. Fitzgerald, Andrew Jorgenson, and Brett Clark, "Energy Consumption and Working Hours: A Longitudinal Study of Developed and Developing Nations, 1990–2008," *Environmental Sociology* 1, no. 3 (2015).

42. Lewis C. King and Jeroen. C. J. M. van den Bergh, "Worktime Reduction as a Solution to Climate Change: Five Scenarios Compared for the UK," *Ecological Economics* 132, no. C (2017).

43. Jared B. Fitzgerald, Juliet B. Schor, and Andrew K. Jorgenson, "Working Hours and Carbon Dioxide Emissions in the United States,. 2007–2013," *Social Forces* 96, no. 4 (2018).

44. Fitzgerald et al., "Working hours," 17.

45. Fitzgerald et al., "Working hours," 17.

46. Anders Fremstad et al., "Work Hours and CO_2 Emissions: Evidence from US Households," *Review of Political Economy* 31, no. 1 (2019).

47. Qing Long Shao and Beatriz Rodríguez-Labajos, "Does Decreasing Working Time Reduce Environmental Pressures? New Evidence Based on Dynamic Panel Approach," *Journal of Cleaner Production* 125 (2016).

48. Qing Long Shao and Shiran Victoria Shen, "When Reduced Working Time Harms The Environment: A Panel Threshold Analysis for EU-15, 1970–2010," *Journal of Cleaner Production* 147 (2017). Fitzgerald et al., "Working Hours," critique this study for its small sample size and modelling strategy.

49. Fremstad et al., "Work Hours."

50. Brendan Burchell et al., "Working Conditions in the European Union: The Gender Perspective," (Dublin: Eurofound, 2007); Rosemary Crompton and Clare Lyonette, "Women's Career Success and Work–Life Adaptations in the Accountancy and Medical Professions in Britain," *Gender, Work & Organization* 18, no. 2 (2011); Eszter Sándor, "European Company Survey 2009: Part-Time Work in Europe" (Dublin: European Foundation for the Improvement of Living and Working Conditions, 2011); Mia Tammelin et al., "Work Schedules and Work–Family Conflict Among Dual Earners in Finland, the Netherlands, and the United Kingdom," *Journal of Family Issues* 38, no. 1 (2017); Michael White et al., "'High-performance' management practices, working hours and work–life balance," *British Journal of Industrial Relations* 41, no. 2 (2003).

292 notes

51. "High Performance."
52. "Women's career success."
53. "Working conditions."
54. Barbara Beham et al., "Who's Got the Balance? A Study of Satisfaction with the Work–Family Balance among Part-Time Service Sector Employees in Five Western European Countries," *The International Journal of Human Resource Management* 23, no. 18 (2012).
55. A. Roeters and Lyn Craig, "Part-Time Work, Women's Work–Life Conflict, and Job Satisfaction: A Cross-National Comparison of Australia, the Netherlands, Germany, Sweden, and the United Kingdom," *International Journal of Comparative Sociology* 55, no. 3 (2014).
56. Akiko Sato Oishi et al., "Do Part-Time Jobs Mitigate Workers' Work–Family Conflict and Enhance Wellbeing? New Evidence from four East-Asian Societies," *Social Indicators Research* 121, no. 1 (2015).
57. Barbara Beham et al., "Part-Time Work and Gender Inequality in Europe: A Comparative Analysis of Satisfaction with Work–Life Balance," *European Societies* 21, no. 3 (2019).
58. Beham et al., "Who's Got the Balance?"; Linda van Breeschoten and Marie Evertsson, "When Does Part-Time Work Relate to Less Work-Life Conflict for Parents? Moderating Influences of Workplace Support and Gender in the Netherlands, Sweden and the United Kingdom," *Community, Work & Family* 22, no. 5 (2019).
59. Roeters and Craig, "Part-time work."
60. Anne Grönlund and Ida Öun, "Beyond the Mummy Track?: Part-time Rights, Gender, and Career-Family Dilemmas," *Nordic Journal of Working Life Studies* 8, no. 3 (2018).
61. Beham et al., "Part-time work."
62. Kate Sparks et al., "The effects of hours of work on health: a meta-analytic review," *Journal of Occupational and Organizational Psychology* 70, no. 4 (1997).
63. Pierre Boisard, Damien Cartron, Michel Gollac, and Antoine Valeyre, "Time and Work: Duration of Work" (Dublin: Eurofound, 2003).
64. Burchell et al., "Working Conditions."
65. Tarani Chandola et al., "Work Stress and Coronary Heart Disease: What Are the Mechanisms?" *European Heart Journal* 29, no. 5 (2008).
66. Fagan et al., "Influence of Working Time," 26.
67. Fagan et al., "Influence of Working Time."
68. See "Control, Rhythms of Care, and the Hierarchy of Freedom and Necessity" in Part V of the Care Chapter.

69. Liz Mineo, "Good Genes Are Nice, but Joy Is Better," *Harvard Gazette* (blog), April 11, 2017, https://news.harvard.edu/gazette/story/2017/04/over-nearly-80-years-harvard-study-has-been-showing-how-to-live-a-healthy-and-happy-life/.

70. "Regrets of the Dying," Bronnie Ware, accessed August 17, 2016, http://bronnieware.com/regrets-of-the-dying/.

71. Muirhead, *Just Work*, 165.

72. Muirhead, *Just Work*, 20.

73. Tom Malleson, "Is Meritocracy Ableist"? *Forthcoming*.

74. Muirhead, *Just Work*, 165.

75. Pugh, *The Tumbleweed Society*, 18–29.

76. Anne-Marie Slaughter, *Unfinished Business: Women Men Work Family* (Oneworld Publications, 2015).

77. Anne-Marie Slaughter, "Why Women Still Can't Have It All," *The Atlantic*, July 2012, https://www.theatlantic.com/magazine/archive/2012/07/why-women-still-cant-have-it-all/309020/.

78. Slaughter, *Unfinished Business*, 50.

79. "Although Catherine E. Beecher and Harriet Beecher Stowe in the late nineteenth century [1869], like feminists more recently, sought to valorize domestic activities (in both their paid and unpaid forms) as 'real work,' these efforts past and present have had little effect in the larger culture." Hondagneu-Sotelo, *Doméstica*, 9–10.

80. Slaughter appears unperturbed by the absence of democracy in the workplace or broader economy. Compare with Malleson, *After Occupy*.

81. Fraser, "After the Family Wage."

82. Sara Ahmed, *Living a Feminist Life* (Durham, NC: Duke University Press, 2017), 85–86.

83. Fraser, "After the Family Wage."

84. Linda Duxbury and Christopher Alan Higgins, *Something's Got to Give: Balancing Work, Childcare, and Eldercare* (Toronto: University of Toronto Press, 2017).

85. Gornick and Meyers, *Gender Equality*, 3–64.

86. Daniel Engster, *Justice, Care, and the Welfare State* (Oxford University Press, 2015).

87. The importance of formal preschool care for children from low-income families arises is in part an effort to redress the ways the stresses of poverty and precarious work exacerbate the difficulties of managing work and care. For example, Wilkinson and Pickett note: "A nationwide study in the UK found that, by the age of three years, children from disadvantaged

backgrounds were already educationally up to a year behind children from more privileged homes. Essential for early learning is a stimulating social environment. Babies and young children need to be in caring, responsible environments. They need to be talked to, loved and interacted with. They need opportunities to play, talk and explore their world, and they need to be encouraged within safe limits, rather than restricted in their activities or punished. All of these things are harder for parents and other caregivers to provide when they are poor, or stressed, or unsupported." Richard Wilkinson and Kate Pickett, *The Spirit Level: Why Equality is Better for Everyone* (Penguin Books, 2010), 110–11.

With economic security and the new norms of PTfA, most families would have the capacity to provide the needed care. Public preschool could be an important supplement for all families, not a special requirement for low-income families. We know also that norms of model behavior vary across class, and schools often model and require middle class norms. Many of the assessments of the value of preschool for the poor is based on their later performance in school. This performance is, of course, an important predictor of economic success, but it is also likely to shaped by the ability to adapt to middle class norms. The history of intervention in the child rearing of the poor should make us wary of concerns that enabling poor parents to have time to care for their children would be harmful to those children.

88. For example, see Sally F. Goldfarb, "Violence against Women and the Persistence of Privacy," *Ohio St LJ* 61, no. 1 (2000): 1–87. For a closer look at how economic dependence fosters women's poverty later in life, see Robyn I. Stone, "The Feminization of Poverty among the Elderly," *Women's Studies Quarterly* 17, no. 1/2 (1989): 20–34.

89. See page 91.

90. There might also be loans to be paid; extending the time for repayment increases the interest to be paid. This is the sort of spill-over issue that educational institutions, banks, and governments ought to consider when structuring educational loans under the new norms. These norms will need to be supported at many levels. Thanks to Maria Arabella Robles for pointing this out.

91. In some Canadian law schools, these arguments have been used to justify very limited access to part-time legal education. To gain access to part-time programs at some law schools, applicants must demonstrate that they are the sole support parent of young children (or some other demand on the rest of their time). Simply wanting to continue to earn an income (even to support one's family) while going to law school is not thought sufficient grounds for access to a part-time program at some law schools.

92. Rick Paulas, "Don't Work 80 Hours a Week for Elon Musk, or Anyone," Vice, November 29, 2018, https://www.vice.com/en/article/ev3b3p/dont-work-80-hours-a-week-for-elon-musk-or-anyone?utm_source=vicef buk&fbclid=IwAR13vUcKq0ZAEF7TX6UBT4WKCqPVui9zWXZE MGGDZaNWXufqYbJzh9YFohc&utm_content=1606300492&utm_ medium=social.

93. See Shireen Hassim's essay, "Whose Utopia," on the different, but related, proposal by Gornick and Meyers in Gender Equality: Transforming Family Divisions of Labor (Verso Books, 2009), 93–109.

94. "[W]orld wide, paid domestic work continues its long legacy as a racialized and gendered occupation." Hondagneu-Sotelo, Doméstica, 19. Also, "the really stinging injury is this: they themselves are denied sufficient resources to live with and raise their own children." Hondagneu-Sotelo, 25.

95. There is a huge variation in the conditions of work in different countries. For example, a study on migrant domestic workers in Singapore reveals the stigmatization and treatment faced by these workers. See Nicole Lim and Anju Mary Paul, "Stigma on a Spectrum: Differentiated Stigmatization of Migrant Domestic Workers' Romantic Relationships in Singapore," Gender, Place & Culture, January 20, 2020, 1–23.

96. We do not take a stand on the question of whether either individuals or governments should participate in the global care chain. But the core objectives of Part-Time for All cannot be achieved as long as care work is left to the poor, to those who have no other economic options. The inequalities—economic, social, and political—that are perpetuated by the degradation of care harm the very fabric of human societies. It then becomes a central challenge to the implementation of PTfA to redress that degradation and to transform the patterns of paid and unpaid care, in ways that avoid harm to those who currently survive by doing paid care—including the millions who leave their homes (near and far) to provide care for the relatively affluent. These are people whose livelihoods have been created in part by the hierarchies PTfA aims to dismantle. They bear some of the greatest personal costs of the existing system, but they are also most vulnerable to costs of transformation.

97. Mullainathan and Shafir, Scarcity.

Chapter 3

1. Anders Hayden, Sharing the Work, Sparing the Planet (Toronto: Between The Lines, 1999), 153.

2. Gerhard Bosch and Steffen Lehndorff, "Working-Time Reduction and Employment: Experiences in Europe and Economic Policy Recommendations," *Cambridge Journal of Economics* 25, no. 2 (2001); Hayden, *Sharing the Work*; Karl Hinrichs, William Roche, and Carmen Sirianni, eds, *Working Time In Transition* (Philadelphia: Temple University Press, 1991); Juliet B. Schor, *The Overworked American* (New York: Basic Books, 1991).

3. Karl Hinrichs, William Roche, and Carmen Sirianni, "From Standardization to Flexibility: Changes in the Political Economy of Work Time" in *Working Time In Transition*, ed. Karl Hinrichs, William Roche, and Carmen Sirianni (Philadelphia: Temple University Press, 1991).

4. Gilbert Cette, Samuel Chang, and Maty Konte, "The Decreasing Returns on Working Time: An Empirical Analysis on Panel Country Data," *Applied Economics Letters* 18, no. 17 (2011); Lonnie Golden, *The Effects of Working Time on Productivity and Firm Performance: A Research Synthesis Paper* (Geneva: International Labor Office, 2012).

5. Janneke Plantenga and Chantal Remery, *Reconciliation of Work and Private Life: A Comparative Review of Thirty European countries* (Luxembourg: Office for Official Publications of the European Communities, 2005).

6. Hayden, *Sharing the Work*.

7. Another avenue which we pass over here is that of increasing the availability of early and flexible retirement. Ute Klammer and Saskia Keuzenkamp, *Working Time Options over the Life Course: Changing Social Security Structures* (Dublin: European Foundation for the Improvement of Living and Working Conditions, 2005).

8. Ariane Hegewisch, *Flexible Working Policies: A Comparative Review* (Manchester: Equality and Human Rights Commission, 2009), 6.

9. Ariane Hegewisch and Janet C. Gornick, *Statutory Routes to Workplace Flexibility in Cross-National Perspective* (Washington, DC: Institute for Women's Policy Research, 2008), 11.

10. Compare this to the United States where only 6 percent of employees have the ability to move to part-time at the same position. Kenneth Matos and Ellen Galinsky, *2012 National Study of Employers* (Families and Work Institute, 2012), 13.

11. Hegewisch and Gornick, "Statutory Routes," 20.

12. J. De Graaf and D. K. Batker, "Americans Work Too Much for Their Own Good," Bloomberg, accessed September 20, 2013, http://www.bloomberg.com/news/2011-11-03/americans-work-too-much-for-their-own-good-de-graaf-and-batker.html.

13. It should be noted that 47 percent of all requests reported by employers in 2007 were for increased hours. These had virtually identical success rates as those for reduced hours. Hegewisch, "Flexible working policies," 23.

14. Robert LaJeunesse, *Work Time Regulation as a Sustainable Full Employment Strategy: The Social Effort Bargain* (London: Routledge, 2009), 223.

15. Eurofound, *Work-Life Balance: Solving the Dilemma* (Dublin: European Foundation for the Improvement of Living and Working Conditions, 2007), 117. Not only are women exploited in the sense that they work harder than others for less pay, they also have less free time. Robert Goodin argues powerfully that control over discretionary time is a fundamental part of social justice. He shows that there is "an absolutely huge inequality in discretionary time between lone mothers and DINKs [couples that have 'Double-Income-and-No-Kids'], wherever we look." "Temporal Justice," *Journal of Social Policy* 39, no. 01 (2010): 5. In the United States, the real outlier, the gap is an astounding 42-hours per week. Even in the best case, that of Sweden, single mothers have 26 hours per week less discretionary time than DINKs. Given that the ordinary workday is eight hours, what this means is that even in Sweden lone mothers have to work three full extra days every single week than do DINKs.

16. Stan De Spiegelaere and Agnieszka Piasna, *The Why and How of Working Time Reduction* (European Trade Union Institute, 2017).

17. Gerhard Bosch, "From 40 to 35 Hours-Reduction and Flexibilisation of the Working Week in the Federal Republic of Germany," *Int'l Lab. Rev.* 129, no. 5 (1990).

18. Hayden, *Sharing the Work*, 144.

19. The following account draws primarily from Anders Hayden, "France's 35-Hour Week: Attack on Business? Win-Win Reform? Or Betrayal of Disadvantaged Workers?" *Politics & Society* 34, no. 4 (2006) and LaJeunesse, *Work Time Regulation*; see also the French report from the Assemblée Nationale, "Rapport fait au nom de la Commission d'enquête sur l'impact sociétal, social, économique et financier de la réduction progressive du temps de travail" 2014, accessed October 5, 2021, https://www.assemblee-nationale.fr/14/rap-enq/r2436.asp.

20. Because the 35-hour project relied on tax cuts to incentive businesses, it was costly for the public purse. The total cost is difficult to estimate since it requires estimating not only losses from tax revenue but also the savings that accrued from individuals who would have been unemployed (and so receiving unemployment benefits) without the new measures. One estimate puts the net cost at roughly €8,000 per job. Spiegelaere and Piasna, "The Why and How of Working Time Reduction," 71.

21. Hayden, "France's 35-Hour Week"; Assemblée Nationale, "Rapport"; Spiegelaere and Piasna, "The Why and How."

22. Hayden, "France's 35-Hour Week."

23. Spiegelaere and Piasna, "The Why and How." In subsequent years, conservative governments have somewhat relaxed the working time requirements, allowing for more overtime, and in President Sarkozy's words, "more work for more money." François Michon, "From 'Working Less for More Jobs' to 'Working More for More Money'—Recent Developments and Issues on Working Time in France" in *Working Time—In Search of New Research Territories Beyond Flexibility Debates* (Tokyo: The Japan Institute for Labour Policy and Training, 2009). Nevertheless, working hours have not rebounded. According to Steffan Lehndorff, from 1998 to 2002, the actual hours "usually worked" per week dropped by two hours. "It's a Long Way from Norms to Normality: The 35-Hour Week in France," *ILR Review* 67, no. 3 (2014). Under the conservatives, from 2003 to 2008, weekly work hours rose by a total of 0.5 hours per week. Thus, roughly one quarter of the initial effect was reversed under the subsequent government.

24. For example, in the United States in the Great Recession, unemployment peaked at 10 percent, at the same time roughly 10 percent of all workers were working more than fifty hours per week. OECD, "Work-Life Balance," OECD, accessed November 5, 2016, http://www.oecdbetterlifeindex.org/topics/work-life-balance/.

25. Jacques Freyssinet and François Michon, *Overtime in Europe* (Dublin: European Foundation for the Improvement of Living and Working Conditions, 2003).

26. We leave it as an open question whether employees who want it should be legally prohibited from working very long hours, or whether in addition to the norms of PTfA there should simply be financial disincentives, in the form of taxation, to dissuade such work.

27. Freyssinet and Michon, *Overtime in Europe*.

28. Hayden, *Sharing the Work*; Hinrichs, Roche, and Sirianni, "From Standardization to Flexibility."

29. Karl Hinrichs, "Working-Time Development in West Germany: Departure to a New Stage" in *Working Time in Transition*, ed. Karl Hinrichs, William Roche, and Carmen Sirianni (Philadelphia: Temple University Press, 1991).

30. Hayden, *Sharing the Work*.

31. Bosch and Lehndorff, "Working-Time reduction."

32. The Dutch reduced their working hours from 1800 to 1397 over a 25-year period (the equivalent of a 4.4 percent reduction in each five-year period). In Germany, IG Metall workers went from a 40 to a 35-hour week over ten years (i.e., a 6.25 percent reduction in five years). Hayden, *Sharing the Work*, 144, 149. And French workers went from a 38.8 to a 35.6-hour week (i.e., a 8.2 percent reduction in five years). Hayden, "France's 35-Hour Week," 511. Of course, it goes without saying that these reductions are not necessarily permanent, but can be reversed, as indeed there has been a partial reversal in both the German and French cases under neoliberal pressure. Lehndorff, "It's a long way."

33. Robert van het Kaar and Amber van der Graaf, "Working Life in the Netherlands," Eurofound, August 11, 2021, https://www.eurofound.eur opa.eu/country/netherlands.

34. Van het Kaar and Van der Graaf, "Working Life in the Netherlands."

35. Collette Fagan, "Analysis Note: Men and Gender Equality" (Brussels: European Commission: Employment, Social Affairs and Equal Opportunities, 2010).

36. In psychological Implicit Association testing, 77 percent of men and 83 percent of women show strong subconscious bias for male = career, female = family. One psychologist described these results as "the thumbprint of the culture on our minds." Schulte, *Overwhelmed*, 90). Or, to take another example, a study of male childcare workers found that their career choices were often ridiculed by friends and family to get a "proper job." Fagan, "Men and Gender Equality," 32.

37. Margunn Bjørnholt, "Part-Time Work and the Career and Life Choices of the Men from the Work-Sharing Couples Study," *Equality, Diversity and Inclusion: An International Journal* 29, no. 6 (2010).

38. Paula England, "The Gender Revolution: Uneven and Stalled," *Gender & Society* 24, no. 2 (2010).

39. In 1964, the United States President's Commission Report remarked that "To become a fully functional adult male, one prerequisite is essential: a job." LaJeunesse, *Work Time Regulation*, 8. Today we must retort that if *all* one has is a job—with no ability to care or nurture—then one is not a real man at all, only a stunted one. The epithet "caveman" might once have been used to express disdain for this stunted version of masculinity. But there is a danger in echoing language of the "civilized" and the "primitive," given the role of gender in justifying colonization (as well as ongoing assumptions of Western/Northern superiority). And the language of "caveman" might be more quickly used for working class men, than for the suave masculinity

of the wealthy, who are probably even more ignorant of care. In addition, we now have evidence that actual, empirical, hunter gatherer societies were in many instances the original "affluent societies," in that they had far more leisure time than we do today, and more egalitarian, less gendered labour patterns. Marshall Sahlins, *Culture in Practice: Selected Essays* (New York: Zone Books, 2005). This was achieved not by creating ever more goods, but by maintaining a constant and low level of desires. These modes of life offer us some wisdom that has been lost, even though contemporary societies cannot emulate them.

40. Hayden, *Sharing the Work*, 153.
41. "Regrets of the Dying," Bronnie Ware, accessed August 17, 2016, http://bronnieware.com/regrets-of-the-dying/.
42. Hayden, *Sharing the Work*, 152–153.
43. Torben Iversen and Frances Rosenbluth find that education is a significant predictor of more gender equality in the division of household work. "The Political Economy of Gender: Explaining Cross-National Variation in the Gender Division of Labor and the Gender Voting Gap," *American Journal of Political Science* 50, no. 1 (2006).
44. David S. Pedulla and Sarah Thébaud, "Can We Finish the Revolution? Gender, Work-Family Ideals, and Institutional Constraint," *American Sociological Review* 80, no. 1 (2015).
45. Pedulla and Thébaud, "Can We Finish the Revolution?" 127.
46. Similar evidence is found in Germany, where the introduction of the right to adjust hours was followed by a 6 percent increase in the rate of part-time work. The rate for men increased by over 4 percent compared with a EU average increase of just 1.5 percent over the same time. Sándor, "European Company Survey," 33. This suggests that increased institutional options for time sovereignty can indeed increase male part-time work, as we would hope.
47. Assemblée Nationale, "Rapport"; Fagan, "Men and Gender Equality"; Scott Coltrane, "Fatherhood, Gender, and Work-Family Policies" in *Gender Equality: Transforming Family Divisions of Labour*, ed. Janet C. Gornick and Marcia K. Meyers (London: Verso, 2009); Jennifer. L. Hook "Care in Context: Men's Unpaid Work in. 20 Countries, 1965–2003," *American Sociological Review* 71, no. 4 (2006).
48. Rudi Wielers and Dennis Raven, "Part-Time Work and Work Norms in the Netherlands," *European Sociological Review* 29, no. 1 (2013).
49. Wielers and Raven, "Part-Time Work," 111.
50. Henrik Kleven, Camille Landais, and Jakob Egholt Søgaard, "Children and Gender Inequality: Evidence from Denmark," *American Economic Journal: Applied Economics* 11, no. 4 (2019).

51. Janeen Baxter, Belinda Hewitt, and Michele Haynes, "Life Course Transitions and Housework: Marriage, Parenthood, and Time on Housework," *Journal of Marriage and Family* 70, no. 2 (2008); Daniela Grunow, Florian Schulz, and Hans-Peter Blossfield, "What Determines Change in the Division of Housework over the Course of Marriage?" *International Sociology* 27, no. 3 (2012); Laura Sanchez and Elizabeth Thomson, "Becoming Mothers and Fathers: Parenthood, Gender, and the Division of Labor," *Gender & Society* 11, no. 6 (1997).

52. Joan Aldous, Gail M. Mulligan, and Thoroddur Bjarnasson, "Fathering Over Time: What Makes the Difference?" *Journal of Marriage and the Family* 60, no. 4 (1998); Francine M. Deutsch, Julianne B. Lussier, and Laura J. Servis, "Husbands at Home: Predictors of Paternal Participation in Childcare and Housework," *Journal of Personality and Social Psychology* 65, no. 6 (1993); Tina Miller, "Falling Back into Gender? Men's Narratives and Practices around First-Time Fatherhood," *Sociology* 45, no. 6 (2011).

53. Erin M. Rehel, "When Dad Stays Home Too: Paternity Leave, Gender, and Parenting," *Gender & Society* 28, no. 2 (2013); Karin Wall, "Fathers on Leave Alone: Does it Make a Difference to their Lives?" *Fathering* 12, no. 2 (2014).

54. Iversen and Rosenbluth, "The Political Economy of Gender."

55. Schulte, *Overwhelmed*, 219.

56. Linda Haas and C. Phillip Hwang, "The Impact of Taking Parental Leave on Fathers' Participation in Childcare and Relationships with Children: Lessons from Sweden," *Community, Work and Family* 11, no. 1 (2008).

57. Lenna Nepomnyaschy and Jane Waldfogel, "Paternity Leave and Fathers' Involvement With Their Young Children," *Community, Work and Family* 10, no. 4 (2007).

58. Aldous, Mulligan, and Bjarnasson, "Fathering over Time?"

59. Elly-Ann Johansson, *The Effect of Own and Spousal Parental Leave on Earnings* (Uppsala: The Institute for Labour Market Policy Evaluation, 2010).

60. Ray et al. cite OECD figures from 2002 showing that providing paid parental leave goes some way to encouraging fathers to take the leave. For instance, in 2000, parental leave was unpaid in Portugal and so fewer than 150 men took it. Three years later, after the law was changed to give fathers two weeks of paid leave, the number of men taking it had risen to 27,000. Rebecca Ray, Janet C. Gornick, and John Schmitt, "Who Cares? Assessing Generosity and Gender Equality in Parental Leave Policy Designs in 21 Countries," *Journal of European Social Policy* 20, no. 3 (2010): 206.

61. Plantenga and Remery find, unsurprisingly, that the level of paternity leave payment is positively correlated with take-up rates. *Work and Private Life*, 48.

62. In Ireland, for example, there is higher take-up of parental leave in the public sector, where there are stronger return-to-work guarantees. Eurofound, "Work-Life Balance," 12.

63. As mentioned earlier, in Norway, paternity leave can be taken on a part-time basis of 50 percent, 60 percent, 70 percent, 80 percent, or 90 percent—until the child is two years old. Hegewisch and Gornick, "Statutory Routes," 11.

64. Dominique Anxo et al., *Parental Leave in European Companies* (Dublin: European Foundation for the Improvement of Living and Working Conditions, 2007); Eurofound, "Work-Life Balance"; Plantenga and Remery, *Work and Private Life*.

65. Anxo et al., "Parental Leave in European Companies," 7.

66. Fagan, "Men and Gender Equality," 27.

67. Arnlaug Leira, quoted in Ray, Gornick, and Schmitt, "Who Cares?" 199.

68. Svala Jonsdottir, "National Report on the Icelandic Experience of Parental Leave Provision" in *Reports: The Parental Leave System In Iceland* (Reykjavik: Focus Consultancy and GOPA-Cartermill, 2008), 8.

69. Anxo et al., "Parental Leave in European Companies," 6.

70. Carl Cederström, *State of Nordic Fathers* (Nordic Council of Ministers, 2019), 19.

71. Kathrin Zippel, "The Missing Link for Promoting Gender Equality: Work-Family and Anti-Discrimination Policies" in *Gender Equality: Transforming Family Divisions of Labour*, ed. Janet C. Gornick and Marcia K. Meyers (London: Verso, 2009), 213.

72. Ulla Agerskov, ed., *Nordic Statistical Yearbook*, Vol. 45 (Copenhagen: Nordic Council of Ministers, 2007), 104.

73. Gøsta Esping-Andersen, *The Incomplete Revolution: Adapting to Women's New Roles* (Cambridge: Polity, 2009); Plantenga and Remery, *Work and Private Life*; Mara Yerkes, "Part-Time Work in the Dutch Welfare State: The Ideal Combination of Work and Care?" *Policy & Politics* 37, no. 4 (2009).

74. Grönlund and Öun, "Beyond the Mummy Track?"

75. We fully agree with Haas and Hwang that "perhaps reducing work hours for a longer period during children's preschool years constitutes a more serious challenge to the male model of work than taking full-time parental leave for a few months." Haas and Hwang, " 'It's About Time!' " 154.

76. Hook, "Care in Context."

77. Countries with the highest proportions of women in government include Bolivia, Rwanda, New Zealand, and the Nordic countries.

78. Michael B. Berkman and Robert E. O'Connor, "Do Women Legislators Matter? Female Legislators and State Abortion Policy," *American Politics*

Quarterly 21, no. 1 (1993); K. A. Bratton and L. P. Ray, "Descriptive Representation, Policy Outcomes, and Municipal Day-Care Coverage in Norway," *American Journal of Political Science* 46, no. 2 (2002); Michele Swers, *The Difference Women Make: The Policy Impact of Women in Congress* (Chicago: University of Chicago Press, 2002); Sue Thomas, "The Impact of Women on State Legislative Policies," *The Journal of Politics* 53, no. 4 (1991).

79. P. A. Lambert, "The Comparative Political Economy of Parental Leave and Child Care: Evidence from Twenty OECD Countries," *Social Politics* 15, no. 3 (2008).

80. Fagan, "Men and Gender Equality."

81. Fagan, "Men and Gender Equality."

82. Claire Ward, "How Dutch Women Got to be the Happiest in the World," Macleans, August 19, 2011, http://www.macleans.ca/news/world/the-feminismhappiness-axis.

83. Consider the study by Rudman and Mescher, which asked participants to rate a fictitious employee named Kevin Dowd. The study compares two scenarios in which Mr Dowd requests leave for caregiving (one to care for a sick daughter, one to care for a sick mother), versus a scenario where he does not take leave. Everything else was identical. The participants rated the caregiving Mr. Dowd as a poorer worker and thought that he deserved more punishments and less rewards than the control. Female participants actually judged the caregiving Mr. Dowd more harshly than men did. Laurie A. Rudman and Kris Mescher, "Penalizing Men Who Request a Family Leave: Is Flexibility Stigma a Femininity Stigma?" *Journal of Social Issues* 69, no. 2 (2013).

84. Stephen J. Rose and Heidi Hartmann, *Still a Man's Labor Market* (Institute for Women's Policy Research, 2018).

85. Female students have kindly shared moving stories of themselves, their friends, their sisters who ended otherwise satisfying relationships with men who didn't meet these standards. One particularly sad story was of a man whose care responsibilities prevented him from ambitiously trying to advance himself at work. The woman telling the story said that she admired his commitment to care and felt bad as she ended the relationship, but she just could not see him as attractive enough in the absence of professional ambition.

86. Katrin Bennhold, "Working (Part-Time) in the 21st Century," *The New York Times*, December 29, 2010.

87. Ida Drange and Cathrine Egeland, *Part-Time Work in the Nordic Region II* (Copenhagen: Nordic Council of Ministers, 2014).

88. Dominique Anxo et al., *Working Time Options over the Life Course: New Work Patterns and Company Strategies* (Dublin: European Foundation for the Improvement of Living and Working Conditions, 2006), 99.

89. Linda Haas and C. Phillip Hwang, "Is Fatherhood Becoming More Visible at Work? Trends in Corporate Support for Fathers Taking Parental Leave in Sweden," *Fathering* 7, no. 3 (2009).

90. Haas and Hwang, "Is Fatherhood Becoming More Visible at Work?"

91. Janet Smithson et al., "Flexible Working and the Gender Pay Gap in the Accountancy Profession," *Work, Employment & Society* 18, no. 1 (2004).

92. Schulte, *Overwhelmed*.

93. Karin Allard, Linda Haas, and C. Phillip Hwang, "Family-Supportive Organizational Culture and Fathers' Experiences of Work–Family Conflict in Sweden," *Gender, Work & Organization* 18, no. 2 (2011).

94. Sándor, "European Company Survey," 27.

95. Discrimination against female care givers is currently rampant. In the United Kingdom, three in four mothers (77 percent) report they had a negative or possibly discriminatory experience during pregnancy, maternity leave, and/or on return from maternity leave. Lorna Adams et al., *Pregnancy and Maternity-Related Discrimination and Disadvantage* (London: IFF Research, 2015). For one notorious example, Len Fenwick (CEO of Bloomberg LP, the global financial services and media company) once said, "I'm not having any pregnant bitches working for me." Schulte, *Overwhelmed*, 75.

96. Allard, Haas, and Hwang, "Family-Supportive Organizational Culture."

97. USDA, *Supplemental Nutrition Assistance Program Participation and Costs* (USDA: Food and Nutrition Services, 2020).

98. CDC, "Health Insurance Coverage," 2019, Centers for Disease Control and Prevention, accessed October 8, 2021, https://www.cdc.gov/nchs/fastats/health-insurance.htm.

99. NLIHC, "Affordable Housing is Out of Reach for Many American Workers," National Low Income Housing Coalition, May 25, 2016, http://nlihc.org/press/releases/6845.

100. Guy Standing, *The Precariat* (London: Bloomsbury Academic, 2011); Cass R. Sunstein, *The Second Bill of Rights* (New York: Basic Books, 2004); Phillipe van Parijs, *Real Freedom for All* (Oxford: Clarendon Press, 1995).

101. Tom Malleson and David Calnitsky, "Which Way Forward for Economic Security: Basic Income or Public Services?" *Basic Income Studies* 16, no. 2 (2021); Phillipe van Parijs and Yannick Vanderborght, *Basic Income* (Cambridge, MA: Harvard University Press, 2017); Mark Paul, William

Darity Jr., and Darrick Hamilton, *The Federal Job Guarantee: A Policy to Achieve Permanent Full Employment* (Washington, DC: Center on Budget and Policy Priorities, 2018); J. Portes, H. Reed, and A. Percy, *Social Prosperity for the Future: A Proposal for Universal Basic Services* (London: Institute for Global Prosperity, 2017).

102. Gøsta Esping-Andersen, *The Three Worlds of Welfare Capitalism* (Cambridge: Polity Press, 1990). We prefer to talk of permanent "residents" rather than "citizens," so as to avoid excluding the large nonstatus populations of contemporary countries.

103. Richard Anker, *Estimating a Living Wage: A Methodological Review* (Geneva: International Labour Office, 2011).

104. Esping-Andersen, *Three Worlds*; Jonas Pontusson, *Inequality and Prosperity: Social Europe vs. Liberal America* (Ithaca, NY: Cornell University Press, 2005).

105. OECD, "Labour productivity levels—most recent year," OECD, 2019, accessed October 18, 2021, https://stats.oecd.org/Index.aspx?DataSetCode=PDB_LV.

106. SABO, "Public Housing in Sweden," Sveriges Allmännytta, 2016, http://www.sabo.se/om_sabo/english/Sidor/Publichousing.aspx.

107. OECD, "Active Labour Market Policies: Connecting People with Jobs," OECD, 2017, accessed October 18, 2021, https://www.oecd.org/employment/activation.htm.

108. Rachel A. Rosenfeld and Gunn Elisabeth Birkelund, "Women's Part-Time Work: A Cross-National Comparison," *European Sociological Review* 11, no. 2 (1995).

109. Haya Stier and Noah Lewin-Epstein, "Time to Work: A Comparative Analysis of Preferences for Working Hours," *Work and Occupations* 30, no. 3 (2003): 320.

110. "Working Time Options," 78.

111. David Macdonald, *Unaccommodating: Rental Housing Wage in Canada* (Canadian Centre for Policy Alternatives, 2019).

112. Angelica Salvi Del Pero et al., "Policies to Promote Access to Good-Quality Affordable Housing in OECD Countries," *OECD Social, Employment and Migration Working Papers*, no. 176 (2016).

113. Rory Hearne, "A Home or a Wealth Generator? Inequality, Financialisation and the Irish Housing Crisis," in *Cherishing All Equally*, ed. James Wickham (Dublin: TASC, 2017); Kathleen Scanlon, Christine Whitehead, and Melissa Fernández Arrigoitia, eds, *Social Housing in Europe* (Chichester: Wiley Blackwell, 2014).

114. Hearne, "A Home or a Wealth Generator?"
115. Rowan Moore, "Housing in Crisis: Council Homes Were the Answer in 1950. They Still Are," *The Guardian*, April 30, 2016, https://www.theg uardian.com/cities/2016/apr/30/housing-crisis-council-homes-are-the-answer.
116. A. D. Cohen et al., "A National Homes Guarantee" (People's Action, 2019). In the American context, Gowan and Cooper argue that the US federal government should financially support local governments to build large numbers of affordable, mixed-income, publicly-owned, rental-housing. The hope being that public-ownership will allow increasing land value to benefit the public coffers in general, not simply wealthy property owners; and mixed-income housing will reduce the concentration of poverty, fostering class and racial integration. Peter Gowan and Ryan Cooper, *Social Housing in the United States* (People's Policy Project, 2018).
117. Erik Assadourian, "The Rise and Fall of Consumer Cultures," in *State of the World. 2010: Transforming Cultures* (New York: W. W. Norton & Company, 2010).
118. Juliet B. Schor, *Plenitude* (New York: Penguin Press, 2010), 25–26.
119. Goodin et al. point out that although on the surface it looks like most men have only small amounts of "spare time," meaning time in which they are not doing any kind of labor, they actually have far larger amounts of "discretionary time," (typically about four times more hours) meaning time that is left over after all *necessary* work (paid work, unpaid work, self-care) is done. Robert Goodin et al., *Discretionary Time: A New Measure of Freedom* (Cambridge: Cambridge University Press, 2008), 95–96. The reason for this is that men are typically engaging in far more hours of paid work than is strictly necessary for meeting life's necessities. Partly this is because many men have little choice over their hours, but in part it reflects the power of consumerism. Few people desire to have basic security only, most desire riches.
120. There is enormous pressure from society (particularly from business) to prioritize consuming over leisure. Think of the constant bombardment of advertisements that rain down on us every single day. Yet there are never any ads encouraging us to take time off. As GA Cohen once pointed out, "there are no 'leisure ads' because firms have no interest in financing them, nor in paying for public reminders of the unpleasant side of labor which buys the goods." LaJeunesse, *Work Time Regulation*, 67. There is thus a deep asymmetry in our societies in terms of the pressure put on individuals to prefer more things instead of more time.

121. John De Graaf, David Wann, and Thomas H. Naylor, *Affluenza: The All-Consuming Epidemic* (San Francisco: Berrett-Koehle, 2005), 146.

122. Tom Malleson, "A Community-Based Good Life or Eco-Apartheid," *Radical Philosophy Review* 19, no. 3 (2015); Robert Skidelsky and Edward Skidelsky, *How Much Is Enough? Money and the Good Life* (New York: Other Press, 2012). Roberts and Brandum put the point well when they argue that we need a vision of the good life that is less concerned with "keeping up" with the Joneses as it is with "spending time" with them. Hayden, *Sharing the Work*, 75.

123. QI, "Even If You Win The Rat Race, You're Still A Rat," Quote Investigator, September 28, 2014, http://quoteinvestigator.com/2014/09/28/rat-race/.

124. Stier and Lewin-Epstein, "Time to Work," 314.

125. Bosch and Lehndorff, "Working-Time Reduction," 221.

126. Stier and Lewin-Epstein, "Time to Work."

127. Robert Inglehart, "Changing Values among Western Publics from 1970 to 2006," *West European Politics* 31, no. 1–2 (2008); Robert Inglehart and Paul R. Abramson, "Economic Security and Value Change," *American Political Science Review* 88, no. 2 (1994).

128. Thorstein Veblen, *The Theory of the Leisure Class*, ed. Martha Banta (Oxford: Oxford University Press, [1918] 2007).

129. Andrew E. Clark and Andrew J. Oswald, "Satisfaction and Comparison Income," *Journal of Public Economics* 61, no. 3 (1996)

130. Samuel Bowles and Yongjin Park, "Emulation, Inequality, and Work Hours: Was Thorsten Veblen Right?" *The Economic Journal* 115, no. 507 (2005): 399.

131. Tom Malleson, *After Occupy: Economic Democracy for the 21st Century* (New York: Oxford University Press, 2014); Tom Malleson, *Against Inequality: The Practical and Ethical Case for Abolishing the Superrich* (Forthcoming); Jonas Pontusson, *Inequality and Prosperity*.

132. Edward C. Prescott, "Why Do Americans Work So Much More than Europeans?" *Federal Reserve Bank of Minneapolis Quarterly Review* 28, no. 1 (2004).

133. Alberto Alesina, Edward Glaeser, and Bruce Sacerdote, "Work and Leisure in the US and Europe: Why so Different?" in *NBER Macroeconomics Annual 2005, Volume 20*, ed. Mark Gertler and Kenneth Rogoff (Cambridge: MIT Press, 2005).

134. Interestingly, the weight of the empirical evidence to date actually indicates that higher taxes generally do *not* strongly reduce hours of

work, at least for men (though they do lead wealthy people to attempt to shift their portfolios around to avoid taxes). Malleson, *Against Inequality*. Nevertheless, it does seem likely that once rates get high enough, disincentives to work will start to kick in.

135. Bowles and Park, "Emulation, Inequality, and Work Hours."

136. Lisa Philipps points out that a gender equitable tax law would eliminate tax relief to breadwinners for supporting dependent partners. Instead there should be increased taxation on those who have more involvement in paid work (and are thereby benefitting, or free riding, from unpaid care work), which can then be used to directly support care givers. "There's Only One Worker: Toward the Legal Integration of Paid Employment and Unpaid Caregiving" in *New Perspectives on the Public-Private Divide*, ed. the Law Commission of Canada (Vancouver: UBC Press 2003).

137. Klammer and Keuzenkamp, "Working Time Options."

138. This reduction in hours for the rich would not only be useful for the gender and time-scarcity reasons that we've been focusing on, but it would also have job-creation benefits, as more employment in these high-level jobs would be needed to compensate for the reductions in work hours.

139. This figure comes from the Living Wage Foundation. They calculate an hourly living wage to be £9.50, slightly higher in London, assuming 37.5 hours of work per week. The current minimum wage for those over 23 (as of 2021) is £8.91 per hour. Living Wage Foundation, accessed October 8, 2021, https://www.livingwage.org.uk/.

140. See page 193.

Chapter 4

1. We think of this as a real utopian model. The idea of "real utopia" is associated with the work of Erik Olin Wright, *Envisioning Real Utopias* (London: Verso, 2010). Real Utopias are institutional projects that are normatively hopeful and emancipatory, while simultaneously grounded in careful study of empirical possibilities, tradeoffs, and limitations.

2. Colette Fagan et al., *In Search of Good Quality Part-Time Employment* (Geneva: International Labour Office, 2013).

3. Didier Fouarge and Ruud Muffels, "Working Part-Time in the British, German and Dutch Labour Market: Scarring for The Wage Career?" *Schmollers Jahrbuch* 129, no. 2 (2009): 217–26.

4. In the United States, 46 percent of part-time employees report that they have access to personal health insurance offered by their employers, compared to 91 percent of full-time employees. Almost 8 in 10 full-timers have access to paid vacation compared to only 4 in 10 part-timers. Chiung-Ya Tang and Shelley Macdermid Wadsworth, *Time and Workplace Flexibility* (Families and Work Institute, 2010).

5. Sándor, "European Company Survey." For example, 24 of the 27 female managers interviewed by Durbin and Tomlinson had not been considered for or secured a promotion since switching to part-time work. A CEO of one of the interviewees explicitly declared that "part-time working is not acceptable for a senior position." Susan Durbin and Jennifer Tomlinson, "Female Part-Time Managers: Careers, Mentors and Role Models," *Gender, Work & Organization* 21, no. 4 (2014): 314.

6. Standing, *The Precariat*.

7. Sándor, "European Company Survey."

8. Linda A. Bell, "The Incentive to Work Hard: Differences in Black and White Workers' Hours and Preferences" in *Working Time: International Trends, Theory and Policy Perspectives*, ed. Deborah M. Figart and Lonnie Golden (London: Routledge, 2000).

9. Based on a median hourly wage of $23.84 in 2020. Bureau of Labor, "May 2020 State Occupational Employment and Wage Estimates: New York," *US Bureau of Labor Statistics*, accessed October 8, 2021, https://www.bls.gov/oes/current/oes_ny.htm#00-0000.

10. All living wage figures should be taken with a grain of salt since they inevitably contain ineliminably subjective elements of what exactly to include and different sources often make quite different estimates. Anker, "Estimating a living wage." This specific living wage estimate comes from Doctor Glasmeier at MIT. Amy K. Glasmeier, "Living Wage Calculation for New York," Massachusetts Institute of Technology, accessed October 8, 2021, https://livingwage.mit.edu/states/36. It is a rather conservative estimate; compare, for instance, the Economic Policy Institute's estimate of a living wage for a 4-person family in New York metro area of $124,129. EPI, "Family Budget Calculator," Economic Policy Institute, accessed October 8, 2021, https://www.epi.org/resources/budget/. Second, the figure the author gives ($102,583) is for two adults with two children, with the assumption that the adults are working full-time and then paying for full-time

childcare. We modify this to assume that the adults are working 75 percent time (i.e., 30 hours), and so are only paying for 50 percent childcare. Reducing childcare costs by 50 percent, and assuming the same rate of tax, gives the figure cited above.

11. This is based on working 52 weeks at the 2021 minimum wage in New York of $12.50 per hour. The minimum wage is scheduled to rise to $15 per hour in a couple of years, which would create an income of $23,400, still less than half a living wage.

12. Glasmeier gives a figure of $74,883 for one adult with one child. "Living Wage Calculation." As above, we modify this to assume that the adult is working 75 percent time (i.e., 30 hours), and so only paying for 75 percent childcare. Reducing childcare costs by 25 percent, and assuming the same rate of tax, gives the figure cited above.

13. Ontario living wage estimates come from Ontario Living Wage Network, "Living Wage by Region," Ontario Living Wage Network, accessed October 8, 2021, https://www.ontariolivingwage.ca/living_wage_by_region. The living wages differ depending on the city, from CAD$16.16 to CAD$22.08 per hour, and are based on an assumption of working 37.5 hours. The figure that we cite is based on a rough average for all of Ontario by using a middle figure of CAD$19/hour.

14. Based on the 2021 minimum wage of £8.91 per hour, for 30 hours per week, 52 weeks per year.

15. According to the Living Wage Foundation, the living wage (outside of London) is £9.50 per hour (based on an assumed 37.5-hour week). "Living Wage Foundation."

16. Based on the 2019 minimum wage of AUD$18.93 per hour, for 30 hours per week, 52 weeks per year.

17. There is no official calculation of the living wage for Australia, but the Australian Council of Trade Unions argues that it should be set at 60 per cent of the median wage of a full-time worker or AUD$20.84 per hour (i.e., AUD$41,184 per year). Anna Patty, "Labor's Living Wage Is Different to the Minimum Wage. Here's How," *The Sydney Morning Herald*, April 1, 2019, https://www.smh.com.au/business/workplace/labor-s-living-wage-is-different-to-the-minimum-wage-here-s-how-20190326-p517o0.html.

18. Eurostat, "Temporary and Part-Time Jobs on the Rise," accessed October 8, 2021, https://ec.europa.eu/eurostat/web/products-eurostat-news/-/WDN-20180813-1.

19. Eurofound, "Fifth European Working Conditions Survey" (Luxembourg: Publications Office of the European Union, 2012); Fagan et al., "Good Quality Part-Time Employment."

20. Fagan et al., "Good Quality Part-Time Employment"; Clare Lyonette, Beate Baldauf, and Heike Behle, *Quality Part-Time Work: A Review of the Evidence* (London: Government Equalities Office, 2010).
21. Janet C. Gornick and Marcia K. Meyers, eds, *Gender Equality: Transforming Family Divisions of Labour* (London: Verso, 2009), 34.
22. Jelle Visser, "The First Part-Time Economy in the World: A Model to Be Followed?" *Journal of European Social Policy* 12, no. 1 (2002).
23. De Spiegelare and Piasna, "The why and how."
24. LaJeunesse, *Work Time Regulation*, 225.
25. Van het Kaar and Van der Graaf, "Working Life in the Netherlands."
26. Eva Jaspers and Ellen Verbakel, "The Division of Paid Labor in Same-Sex Couples in the Netherlands," *Sex Roles* 68, no. 5–6 (2013).
27. Van het Kaar and Van der Graaf, "Working Life in the Netherlands."
28. Giovanni Russo, "Job and Life Satisfaction among Part-Time and Full-Time Workers: The 'Identity' Approach," *Review of Social Economy* 70, no. 3 (2012).
29. Ray et al., "Who Cares?"
30. Colette Fagan et al., *The Influence of Working Time Arrangements on Work-Life Integration or 'Balance': A Review of the International Evidence* (Geneva: International Labour Organization, 2012).
31. Fagan et al., "Good Quality Part-Time Employment."
32. Among employed men aged 15–24, 58 percent work PT; among 55–64 year olds, 27 percent; and among 65 and older, 74 percent. It is in these categories that part-time work is considerably more common that other European countries. Fagan et al., "Good Quality Part-Time Employment," 9.
33. Anxo et al., "Working Time Options," 39.
34. Bennhold, "Working (Part-Time)."
35. Van Breeschoten and Marie Evertsson, "Does Part-Time Work Relate," 610; Wielers and Raven, "Part-Time Work," 107.
36. Probably the most common form of discrimination against part-time work that still exists is that they receive less job-related training, which can impact future career opportunities. Wielers and Raven, "Part-Time Work."
37. Fagan et al., "Good Quality Part-Time Employment."
38. Jelle Visser, "Negotiated flexibility, working time and transitions in the Netherlands" in *Regulating Working-Time Transitions in Europe*, ed. Jacqueline O'Reilly (Cheltenham: Edward Elgar, 2003), 141.
39. Sándor, "European Company Survey," 27.
40. LaJeunesse, *Work Time Regulation*. Visser reports that median hourly earnings of female part-time workers at 93.1 percent of full-time

counterparts. Whereas in the United States, part-time female workers only make 63 percent of the hourly wages of full-timers. Visser, "The First Part-Time Economy," 33.

41. Van het Kaar and Van der Graaf, "Working Life in the Netherlands."
42. Based on the 2021 minimum wage of €10.91 per hour, for 30 hours per week, 52 weeks per year.
43. This figure comes from WageIndicator.org. They provide a range an estimate for 2019 of €910–€1140 for a monthly living wage for a single adult (they do not provide estimates for single parents). Since this figure is for a lone individual, we take the upper end of the estimate as a better approximation for the living wage for an adult with child. Our cited figure should probably still be taken as a low estimate.
44. According to the Dutch Central Plan Bureau, the median gross salary for 2020 in the Netherlands was €36,500. We double this and take 75 percent to obtain a part-time wage. Amsterdam Tips, "Salaries in Amsterdam, Netherlands," Amsterdam Tips, December 1, 2020, https://www.amsterdamtips.com/salaries-in-amsterdam-netherlands.
45. WageIndicator.org estimates a living wage (in 2019) for "two parents and two children, 1.5 working" to be between €1290–€1690 per month. Taking the upper estimate for each working parent provides the cited figure.
46. Based on the 2021 minimum wage of €9.50 per hour, for 30 hours per week, 52 weeks per year.
47. This figure comes from WageIndicator.org. They provide a range an estimate for 2019 of €980–€1140 for a monthly living wage for a single adult (they do not provide estimates for single parents). Since this figure is for a lone individual, we take the upper end of the estimate as a better approximation for the living wage for an adult with child. Our cited figure should probably still be taken as a low estimate.
48. In general, Denmark is less like the Netherlands than it is like Sweden in that its part-time sector is quite small; most workers, men and women, work full-time—so Denmark is well on its way to becoming a universal breadwinner society. Jens Lind and Erling Rasmussen, "Paradoxical patterns of part-time employment in Denmark?" *Economic and Industrial Democracy* 29, no. 4 (2008). However, since Denmark is also leading the way in terms of its reduction in full-time hours, it can be conceived as approaching PTfA via this indirect route.
49. Mikkel Mailand and Trine P. Larsen, "Trade unions and precarious work," FAOS Research paper no. 121 (2011).
50. Thomas Bredgaard et al., "Flexicurity and atypical employment in Denmark," Centre for Labour Market Research Paper no. 1 (2009).

51. Vanessa Gash, "Preference or constraint? Part-time workers' transitions in Denmark, France and the United Kingdom," *Work, Employment & Society* 22, no. 4 (2008).

52. Alma Wenneno Lanninger and Marianne Sundström, *Part-time work in the nordic region* (Copenhagen: Nordic Council of Ministers, 2014).

53. Eleanora Matteazzi, Ariane Pailhé, and Anne Solaz, "Does part-time employment widen the gender wage gap? Evidence from twelve European countries," Society for the Study of Economic Inequality Working Paper no. 293 (2013).

54. Lanninger and Sundström, "Part-Time Work."

55. Denmark does not have a statutory minimum wage. The lowest full-time wage in 2021 was roughly €2,500 per month. Live Scandinavia, "This Is the Minimum and Average Salary in Denmark [2021 Update]," Live Scandinavia, accessed October 8, 2021, https://livescandinavia.com/this-is-the-minimum-and-average-salary-in-denmark/. Taking 75 percent of this gives the cited figure.

56. There are no living wage estimates currently available for Denmark (living wages are not necessary as regular wages are already living wages). The figure here is calculated in the following way. According to Numbeo, the cost of living (averaging a large bundle of items) in Copenhagen is 104 percent that of Amsterdam. Numbeo, "Cost of Living Comparison Between Amsterdam and Copenhagen," Numbeo, Accessed October 8, 2021, https://www.numbeo.com/cost-of-living/compare_cities.jsp?count ry1=Netherlands&country2=Denmark&city1=Amsterdam&city2=Cop enhagen&tracking=getDispatchComparison. So applying this ratio gives the cited figure. The Study in Denmark Center estimates living costs in Copenhagen at roughly €1200 per month, which comes to a very similar annual estimate of a living wage. Study in Denmark Center, "Student living costs in Denmark," Study in Denmark, accessed October 8, 2021, http://www.studyindenmark.com/livingcosts.aspx.

57. Liz Alderman and Steven Greenhouse, *Living Wages, Rarity for U.S. Fast-Food Workers, Served Up in Denmark* (New York: New York Times, 2014).

58. According to Statistics Denmark (2019), average pre-tax income for all people in 2019 was DKK388,122, or roughly €52,000 per year. Statistics Denmark, "Personal and family income," Statistics Denmark, 2019, accessed October 8, 2021, https://www.dst.dk/en/Statistik/emner/arbe jde-og-indkomst/indkomst-og-loen/person-og-familieindkomster. Assuming each couple earns 75 percent of this gives the cited figure.

59. Applying the same method as footnote 494.

60. David Schweickart, *After Capitalism*, 2nd ed. (Lanham, Maryland: Rowman & Littlefield, 2011).
61. The Japanese case, which is well known for its very long hours, is instructive in this regard. See Christoph Deutschmann, "The Worker-Bee Syndrome in Japan: An Analysis of Working-Time Practices" in *Working Time In Transition*, ed. Karl Hinrichs, William Roche, and Carmen Sirianni (Philadelphia: Temple University Press, 1991).
62. Arlie Russell Hochschild, *The Time Bind* (New York: Metropolitan Books, 1997), 70 (emphasis added). This is not simply ideology. Hochschild further describes how the firm in question eventually came to the conclusion that its financial position required it to scrap its employee-flexibility and work-life balance initiatives in order to compete with non-unionized firms in southern US states.
63. In Europe, the majority of workers have regular schedules: 77 percent work the same number of days every week and 67 percent work the same number of hours every week. Yet there is significant irregularity. More than half of all workers work at least one day in the weekend. Night work is undertaken by 19 percent of workers and shift work is carried out by 17 percent of workers. Eurofound, "Fifth European Working Conditions," 41.
64. Jeanne Fagnani and Marie-Thérèse Letablier, "Work and Family Life Balance: The Impact of the 35-Hour laws in France," *Work, Employment & Society* 18, no. 3 (2004); for an overview of the evidence, see Fagan et al., "Working time arrangements."
65. Ivana La Valle et al, *Happy families?: Atypical work and its influence on family life* (Bristol: Policy Press, 2002), 15.
66. Fagan et al., "Working time arrangements," 33.
67. Colette Fagan and Brendan Burchell, "Gender, Jobs and Working Conditions in the European Union" (Dublin: European Foundation for the Improvement of Living and Working Conditions, 2002), 67.
68. Ulla Weigelt, "On the Road to a Society of Free Choice: The Politics of Working Time in Sweden" in *Working Time in Transition*, ed. Karl Hinrichs, William Roche, and Carmen Sirianni (Philadelphia: Temple University Press, 1991), 212.
69. Allard, Haas, and Hwang, "Family-Supportive Organizational Culture."
70. Richard Partington, "Number of zero-hours contracts in UK rose by 100,000 in. 2017—ONS," *The Guardian*, April 23, 2018, https://www.theguardian.com/uk-news/2018/apr/23/number-of-zero-hours-contracts-in-uk-rose-by-100000-in-2017-ons.
71. Arnold Riedmann et al., *Working Time and Work-life Balance in European Companies* (Dublin: European Foundation for the Improvement of Living and Working Conditions, 2006), 33.

72. Hegewisch and Gornick, "Statutory Routes."
73. In addition to flextime, the ability to work from home ("flexplace") would be an important advance for care givers. However, we pass over this issue here since there is less data on this practice.
74. Riedmann et al., "Working Time," 3.
75. Tang and Wadsworth, "Time and Workplace Flexibility," 1.
76. Riedmann et al., "Working Time," 49.
77. Matos and Galinsky, "2012 National Study," 14. In Europe, about 60 percent of workers have their schedules set by employer with no form of flextime. Eurofound, "Fifth European Working Conditions," 92.
78. Riedmann et al., "Working Time."
79. Riedmann et al., "Working Time," 4, 7.
80. *The Time Bind.*
81. Anxo et al., "Working time options."
82. Plantenga and Remery, "Work and private life."
83. Lyonette, Baldauf, and Behle, "Quality Part-Time Work," 67.
84. For a good overview, see Golden, "Effects of Working Time."
85. Helen Gray, "Family-Friendly Working: What a Performance!" (London: Centre for Economic Performance, 2002).
86. Heejung Chung, Marcel Kerkhofs, and Peter Ester, "Working time flexibility in European companies" (Luxembourg: EU Office for Official Publications, 2007).
87. Plantenga and Remery, "Work and private life," 75.
88. Byron Y. Lee and Sanford E. DeVoe, "Flextime and profitability," *Industrial Relations: A Journal of Economy and Society* 51, no. 2 (2012).
89. Riedmann et al., "Working Time," 9.
90. Hegewisch and Gornick see evidence for this in the European case law: "The case law confirms that one of the big barriers to greater workplace flexibility is a negative gut response from many managers—'it can't be done'—no matter what the actual evidence . . . [This leads to a situation where] employees will not make a request in the first place, either out of fear for their jobs or career progression or because they cannot imagine how their job might be done differently. This is the case as much in high-powered career jobs . . . as in low wage industries, particularly in those where men primarily work." "Statutory Routes," 25–26.
91. Hochschild, *The Time Bind*, 73.
92. "Development in West Germany," 37.
93. Part of the difficulty is that, in practice, work-time reduction was often bargained for in exchange for more flexibilization. Bosch, "From 40 to 35 hours." If workers do not want this flexibilization, they will likely have to accept further wage restraint.

94. Notice that the reason that British doctors have access to quality part-time work whereas British accountants do not, is largely attributable to the fact that the former but not the latter have a strong union. Crompton and Lyonette, "Women's career success."

95. Bosch and Lehndorff, "Working-time reduction," 220.

96. For instance, the study by Lyness et al. empirically demonstrates the significant role that unions play in helping workers gain control over their work schedules. Karen S. Lyness et al., "It's All about Control: Worker Control over Schedule and Hours in Cross-National Context," *American Sociological Review* XX, no. X (2012).

97. Jonas Pontusson, "Once Again a Model: Nordic Social Democracy in a Globalized World" in *What's Left of the Left: Democrats and Social Democrats in Challenging Times*, ed. James E. Cronin, George W. Ross and James Shoch (Durham: Duke University Press, 2011).

98. As long ago as 1972, Swedish Prime Minister Olof Palme insisted that, "the demand for equality . . . involves changes not only in the conditions of women but also in the conditions of men. One purpose of such changes is to give women an increased opportunity for gainful employment and to give men an increased responsibility for care of the children." Haas and Hwang, "Impact of taking parental leave," 88.

99. We do not mean to imply that the United States has *no* intervention in the market. Like every market system, it has enormous amounts. Dean Baker, *The End of Loser Liberalism: Making Markets Progressive* (Washington, DC: Center of Economic and Policy Research, 2011); Robert B. Reich, *Saving Capitalism* (New York: Alfred A. Knopf, 2015). We mean only that it does not have nearly so well established traditions of progressive pro-labor intervention.

100. Adjusted for inflation, the male median income in 1968 was $32,844 and in 2010 was $32,137. Joseph Stiglitz, *The Price of Inequality* (New York: W. W. Norton & Company, 2012), 296.

101. LaJeunesse, *Work Time Regulation*, 191.

102. OECD, "Table C. Tax Structures in the OECD area," OECD, August 22, 2016. http://www.oecd.org/tax/tax-policy/table-c-tax-structures-in-the-oecd-area.htm.

103. Arthur M. Okun, *Equality and efficiency: The big tradeoff* (Washington, DC: The Brookings Institution, 1975).

104. Pontusson, "Once Again a Model."

105. Authors calculations from 1986–2015 for Nordic countries (Sweden, Denmark, Norway, Finland) and neoliberal countries (United States, Canada, United Kingdom, Australia, New Zealand). World Bank,

"DataBank," The World Bank, accessed August 23, 2016, http://databank. worldbank.org/data/home.aspx.

106. The Nordic figure is somewhat skewed by the very high GDP of Norway, which is significantly affected by prevailing oil prices. If Norway is removed, the Nordic figure becomes $48,000—essentially identical to the neoliberal one. World Bank, "DataBank."

107. Ha-Joon Chang, *Bad Samaritans: The Guilty Secrets of Rich Nations & the Threat to Global* Prosperity (London: Random House Business Books, 2007); Pontusson, *Inequality and Prosperity*.

108. Nancy Folbre, "Reforming Care" in *Gender Equality: Transforming Family Divisions of Labour*, ed. Janet C. Gornick and Marcia K. Meyers (London: Routledge, 2009), 120.

109. In the United States, the top 1 percent paid 40 percent of total federal income taxes in 2018. Erica York, "Summary of the Latest Federal Income Tax Data, 2021 Update," Tax Foundation, February 3, 2021, https://taxfou ndation.org/publications/latest-federal-income-tax-data/.

110. "Robin Hood Taxes" or "Tobin Taxes" are taxes on financial transactions such as the buying or selling of stock. The idea is that such taxes would be too small to discourage useful long-term investment but large enough to discourage very short-term speculative practices, where huge amounts of money is flying across borders (in potentially damaging and destabilizing ways) in what amounts to high-stakes gambling. Barry Eichengreen, James Tobin, and Charles Wyplosz, "Two cases for sand in the wheels of international finance," *The Economic Journal* 105, no. 428 (1995). Several dozen countries have their own financial transaction taxes, and Europe has been close to implementing one for several years, though it has not yet become law.

111. Malleson, *Against Inequality*; Thomas Piketty, *Capital in the Twenty-First Century* (Cambridge: The Belknap Press, 2014). The superrich have incomes of many millions of dollars every year, which means that even at very high rates of income tax, their overall wealth will still increase year-in year-out. For example, even with an extremely unrealistic 90 percent effective income tax on Jeff Bezos, he would still accumulate $550 million more dollars every single year (assuming a modest 5 percent return on his wealth of $110 billion), far more than he is ever likely to consume. As long as one's income after tax is greater than what is consumed (as is likely for the super-rich), they will continue to grow richer, widening inequality ever further. And this is true even with income tax rates at far higher levels than those which currently exist. The key point is that even an inconceivable 100 percent effective income tax would only reduce the

great fortunes of the superrich at an extremely slow pace. For example, assuming a 100 percent effective income tax, and that Bezos spends $100 million every year, it would still take 1,000 years to reduce his total wealth to normal levels. This is the primary reason why relying on the income tax is insufficient to reduce inequality at the very top. To meaningfully reduce inequality, we require a wealth tax.

112. Although income taxes are the major source of government revenues in OECD countries today, it's useful to recall that in 1900 they only accounted for a very small percentage of GDP. For instance, in the United States from WW1 until 1940, the income tax raised only about 2.5 percent of GDP. Christopher Chantrill, "Federal Government Tax and Revenue Chart," US Government Revenue, accessed October 11, 2021, http://www.usgovernmentrevenue.com/revenue_chart_1792_2016U Sp_18s1li011lcn_10f. This is similar to the amount raised by the (not very effective) wealth taxes in existence today.

113. The median adult income in the United States in 2020 was $41,535. US Census, "Table a-6. Earnings Summary Measures by Selected Characteristics: 2019 and 2020," United States Census Bureau, https://www.census.gov/data/tables/2021/demo/income-poverty/p60-273.html. To get the disposable income, we reduce this figure by the effective tax rate, which for this income was roughly 25.5 percent. ITEP, "Who Pays Taxes in America in 2020?," Institute on Taxation and Economic Policy, https://itep.org/who-pays-taxes-in-america-in-2020/. This gives us a rough estimate for median personal disposable income of $30,944.

In 2020, average labor productivity in the United States was $80.5 per worker per hour (in current USD, PPP). OECD, "Level of Gdp Per Capita and Productivity," Organisation for Economic Co-operation and Development, https://stats.oecd.org/index.aspx?DataSetCode=PDB_LV. The US public sector is funded through taxation representing roughly 26 percent of GDP in 2020, whereas one of the world's most generous public systems is Sweden's at 43 percent. "Tax Revenue," Organisation for Economic Co-operation and Development, https://data.oecd.org/tax/tax-revenue.htm. This high level of taxation allows for universal daycare, free primary and secondary education, free university, an excellent system of public health care, good pensions, extensive public transport, sixteen months of parental leave, generous welfare and disability benefits, retraining programs for workers to find new work, etc. So let us imagine that a future feminist-socialist society funds its public sector at the rate of 55 percent of GDP. This represents a 12 percent improvement over Sweden's level of service provision, more than double current US spending on social services. This would be enough to fund to fund public services at a level even better than current Swedish levels in addition to a generous unconditional basic income. Karl Widerquist, "The Cost of Basic Income: Back-of-the-Envelope Calculations," *Basic Income Studies* 12, no. 2 (2017). PBO, "Costing a National Guaranteed Basic Income Using the Ontario Basic Income Model," (Ottawa: Office of the Parliamentary Budget Office, 2018). If for the sake of simplicity we assume that all taxation comes from a single income tax, then each worker would require an income of $69,000 pre-tax to end up with the basic amount of $31,000 post-tax. At prevailing rates of productivity, this income requires an average of only 857 hours of work, i.e., 18 hours of work per week or 3.6 hours per day (assuming four weeks' holiday and the same percentage of population in the labor force as currently).

114. *The Overworked American* (New York: Basic Books, 1991).

115. For growth to be ecologically sustainable it must be de-linked as much as possible from what ecologists call "throughput," that is, the amount of matter and energy moving through the economy. Herman E. Daly, "Allocation, Distribution, and Scale: Towards an Economics that is Efficient, Just, and Sustainable," *Ecological Economics* 6, no. 3 (1992): 186. Technological optimists think that delinking will happen as a matter of course, so we can continue to grow indefinitely. Most greens, however, point to the fact that over the last couple of decades, even though technology has become greener, total greenhouse emissions have actually *risen*. Tim Jackson, *Prosperity Without Growth: Economics for a Finite Planet* (London: Earthscan, 2009). This implies that green technology alone will not save us from catastrophic climate change, but must be accompanied by actual reductions in throughput right away. We need to slow our consumption now (particularly the rich who consume by far the most). Fitzgerald, et al., "Working hours"; Schor, *Plenitude*.

116. John Pencavel, "The productivity of working hours," *The Economic Journal* 125, no. 589 (2015).

117. Awad S. Hanna, Craig S. Taylor, and Kenneth T. Sullivan, "Impact of extended overtime on construction labor productivity," *Journal of Construction Engineering and Management* 131, no. 6 (2005).

118. Ann E. Rogers et al., "The working hours of hospital staff nurses and patient safety," *Health Affairs* 23, no. 4 (2004).

119. Rebecca Jeanmonod, Donald Jeanmonod, and Ryan Ngiam, "Resident productivity: does shift length matter?" *The American Journal of Emergency Medicine* 26, no. 7 (2008).

120. Edward Shepard and Thomas Clifton, "Are longer hours reducing productivity in manufacturing?" *International Journal of Manpower* 21, no. 7 (2000).

121. Cette, Chang, and Konte, "The decreasing returns." For a good overview of the evidence, see Golden, "Effects of Working Time."

122. Judith A. Ricci et al., "Fatigue in the US workforce: prevalence and implications for lost productive work time," *Journal of Occupational and Environmental Medicine* 49, no. 1 (2007).

123. OECD, "Labour productivity levels."

124. Andrew Berg et al., "Redistribution, inequality, and growth: new evidence," *Journal of Economic Growth* 23, no. 3 (2018); Siddhartha Biswas, Indraneel Chakraborty, and Rong Hai, "Income inequality, tax policy, and economic growth," *The Economic Journal* 127, no. 601 (2017); F. Cingano, "Trends in income inequality and its impact on economic growth," *OECD Social, Employment and Migration Working Papers*, no. 163 (2014).

125. Berg et al., "Redistribution, inequality, and growth," 292.

126. Joseph Stiglitz, "Inequality and Economic Growth" in *Rethinking Capitalism*, ed. Michael Jacobs and Mariana Mazzucato (Chichester: John Wiley & Sons, 2016).

127. Moreover, with reduced inequality, PTfA may well perform better on a wide range of health and social indicators, such as life expectancy, obesity, incarceration rates, teenage pregnancy, and so forth, that are all correlated with inequality. Karen Rowlingson, "Does income inequality cause health and social problems?" (London: Joseph Rowntree Foundation, 2011); Richard Wilkinson and Kate Pickett, *The Spirit Level: Why Equality is Better for Everyone* (London: Penguin Books, 2010).

128. This section draws on Malleson, *After Occupy*, 128–132; Malleson, *Against Inequality*.

129. Ronald B. Davies and Krishna Chaitanya Vadlamannati, "A race to the bottom in labor standards? An empirical investigation," *Journal of Development Economics* 103, no. C (2013).

130. Geoffrey Garrett and Deborah Mitchell, "Globalization, government spending and taxation in the OECD," *European Journal of Political Research* 39, no. 2 (2001): 153.

131. Giovanni Lombardo and Federico Ravenna, "The size of the tradable and non-tradable sectors: Evidence from input-output tables for 25 countries," *Economics Letters* 116 (2012): 560. This is smaller for smaller countries. Lombardo and Ravenna calculate the size of the non-tradability sector using a few different measurements, and give estimates for the

OECD ranging from 34 percent to 56 percent. "Tradable and non-tradable sectors," 560.

132. Ha-Joon Chang, *Kicking Away the Ladder: Development Strategy in Historical Perspective* (London: Anthem, 2002); Chang, *Bad Samaritans*.

133. For details, see Chang, *Kicking Away the Ladder*; Chang, *Bad Samaritans*; Erik S. Reinert, *How Rich Countries Got Rich—And Why Poor Countries Stay Poor* (London: Constable, 2007).

134. Garrett and Mitchell, "Government spending and taxation"; Dani Rodrik, *Has Globalization Gone Too Far?* (Washington, D.C.: Institute for International Economics, 1997).

135. Kimberly A. Clausing, "Does tax drive the headquarters locations of the world's biggest companies?" *Transnational Corporations* 25, no. 2 (2018): 38.

136. Lucas Bretschger and Frank Hettich, "Globalisation, capital mobility and tax competition: theory and evidence for OECD countries," *European Journal of Political Economy* 18, no. 4 (2002); Francis G. Castles, "A Race to the Bottom?" in *The Welfare State Reader*, 2nd ed., ed. Christopher Pierson and Francis G. Castles (Cambridge: Polity Press (2007); Axel Dreher, "The influence of globalization on taxes and social policy: An empirical analysis for OECD countries," *European Journal of Political Economy* 22, no. 1 (2006); Axel Dreher, Jan-Egbert Sturm, and Heinrich W. Ursprung, "The impact of globalization on the composition of government expenditures: Evidence from panel data," *Public Choice* 134, no. 3–4 (2008); Geoffrey Garrett, "Global Markets and National Politics: Collision Course or Virtuous Circle?" *International Organizations* 52, no. 4 (1998); Garrett and Mitchell, "Government spending and taxation"; Philipp Genschel, "Globalization and the transformation of the tax state," *European Review* 13, no. 1 (2005); Herwig Immervoll and Linda Richardson, "Redistribution policy and inequality reduction in OECD countries: What has changed in two decades?" *Forschungsinstitut zur Zukunft der Arbeit* Discussion Paper no. 6030 (2011); Duane Swank, *Global Capital, Political Institutions, and Policy Change in Developed Welfare States* (Cambridge: Cambridge University Press, 2002); Vera Troeger, "Tax Competition and the Myth of the 'Race to the Bottom,'" The CAGE-Chatham House Series no. 4 (2013).

137. OECD, "Work-Life Balance."

138. Genschel, "Globalization and the transformation," 55.

139. Gabriel Zucman, *The Hidden Wealth of Nations: The Scourge of Tax Havens* (Chicago: The University of Chicago Press, 2015).

140. Philipp Genschel and Peter Schwarz, "Tax competition: a literature review," *Socio-Economic Review* 9, no. 2 (2011).
141. Richard Partington, "Global tax reform: 130 countries commit to minimum corporate rate," *The Guardian*, July 1, 2021, https://www.theguard ian.com/business/2021/jul/01/global-tax-reform-130-countries-com mit-to-minimum-corporate-rate.
142. For additional discussion of the issue of tax havens vis-à-vis the welfare state see Emmanuel Saez and Gabriel Zucman, *The Triumph of Injustice* (New York, NY: W. W. Norton & Company, 2019); Malleson, *Against Inequality*.

Conclusion

1. Dean Baker, "The $24 an Hour Minimum Wage," Center for Economic and Policy Research, July 22, 2020, https://cepr.net/the-24-an-hour-mini mum-wage/.
2. Baker, "$24 an hour."
3. Stiglitz, *The Price of Inequality*, 296.
4. Thomas Piketty, *Capital and Ideology* (Cambridge, MA: The Belknap Press of Harvard University Press, 2020), 526.
5. Ellen Galinsky, Kerstin Aumann, and James T. Bond, *Times Are Changing: Gender and Generation at Work and at Home* (Families and Work Institute, 2009), 18.
6. Linda Duxbury and Christopher Higgins, *Something's Got to Give: Balancing Work, Childcare, and Eldercare* (Toronto: University of Toronto Press, 2017), 129.
7. Heidi I. Hartman, quoted in Steven A. Holmes, "Is This What Women Want?" *The New York Times*, December 15, 1996, accessed December 6, 2018, https://www.nytimes.com/1996/12/15/weekinreview/is-this-what-women-want.html.
8. For evidence that there is much work to be done even in the Swedish case, see Anita Nyberg, "Gender Equality Policy in Sweden: 1970s–2010s," *Nordic Journal of Working Life Studies* 2, no. 4 (2012); Haas and Hwang, "It's About Time!"; Jörgen Larsson and Sofia Björk, "Swedish Fathers Choosing Part-Time Work," *Community, Work & Family* 20, no. 2 (2017).
9. Hannah Ritchie and Max Roser, "CO_2 emissions," Our World In Data, last revised August 2020, https://ourworldindata.org/co2-emissions.

10. Esping-Andersen, *The Incomplete Revolution.*

11. E.g., Naomi Klein, *This Changes Everything: Capitalism vs. The Climate* (Toronto: Alfred A. Knopf Canada, 2014); Erik Olin Wright, *How to Be an Anti-Capitalist in the 21st Century* (London: Verso, 2019).

12. Another encouraging sign for the future is that contemporary Green Parties, which will undoubtedly expand in influence as the ecological situation worsens, are already naturally adopting policies very amenable to PTfA, such as universal childcare, four-day workweeks, and unconditional basic income.

13. Richard Partington, "Britons Working at Home Spend More Time on Job in Covid Crisis, ONS finds," *The Guardian*, April 19, 2021, accessed October 19, 2021, https://www.theguardian.com/business/2021/apr/19/working-at-home-job-covid-ons-off-sick.

14. The Guardian, "The Guardian View on Women and the Pandemic: What Happened to Building Back Better?" *The Guardian*, March 7, 2021, accessed April 14, 2021, https://www.theguardian.com/commentisfree/2021/mar/07/the-guardian-view-on-women-and-the-pandemic-what-happened-to-building-back-better.

15. *Women in Western Political Thought* (Princeton: Princeton University Press, 1979), 302–303.

Works Cited

Jurisprudence Cited

M v H, [1999] 2 SCR 3.

Legislation Cited

Civil Marriage Act, SC 2005 c 33.
Convention C189—Domestic Workers Convention, 2011 (No. 189), 16 June 2011, Geneva, 100th ILC Session (entered into force 5 September 2013).

Works Cited

"Cost of Living Comparison Between Amsterdam and Copenhagen." *Numbeo*. Accessed October 8, 2021. https://www.numbeo.com/cost-of-living/com pare_cities.jsp?country1=Netherlands&country2=Denmark&city1= Amsterdam&city2=Copenhagen&tracking=getDispatchComparison.

"Emotional Labor: The MetaFilter Thread Condensed Version 2." *Metafilter*. October 2, 2015. https://docs.google.com/viewer?a=v&pid=sites&srcid= ZGVmYXVsdGRvbWFpbnxpbnRlZ3JhdGVkbWVufGd4OjMwMTBh NGU5MTAxNTE1Mjg.

"Even If You Win The Rat Race, You're Still A Rat." *Quote Investigator*. September 28, 2014. http://quoteinvestigator.com/2014/09/28/rat-race/.

"Flourishing through Mutual Support." *Harbourside Cohousing*. Accessed August 13, 2020. http://www.harbourside.ca/index.html.

"Labours Lost." *The Economist*. June 15, 2002. https://www.economist.com/ finance-and-economics/2002/06/13/labors-lost.

"Marriage and Men's Health." *Harvard Health Publishing*. June 5, 2019. https:// www.health.harvard.edu/mens-health/marriage-and-mens-health.

"Moms Stop the Harm." 2020. https://www.momsstoptheharm.com.

"On the Front Lines." *Social Change* (blog). June 18, 2018. http://socialchange. adler.edu/on-the-front-lines/.

"Number of Private Households by Household Composition, Number of Children and Age of Youngest Child (1 000)." *Eurostat*. April 20, 2020. http:// appsso.eurostat.ec.europa.eu/nui/show.do?dataset=lfst_hhnhtych&lang=en.

"Statistical Briefing Book." *Office of Juvenile Justice and Deliquency Prevention*. Accessed DATE. https://www.ojjdp.gov/ojstatbb/crime/ucr.asp?table_in= 1&selYrs=2019&rdoGroups=3&rdoData=c.

"Stop and Smell the Roses—Wiktionary." *Wiktionary*. October 14, 2019. https://en.wiktionary.org/wiki/stop_and_smell_the_roses.

"The Economy of Francesco." 2021. https://francescoeconomy.org/.

Adams, Lorna, Mark Winterbotham, Katie Oldfield, Jenny McLeish, Alice Large, Alasdair Stuart, Liz Murphy, et al. *Pregnancy and Maternity-Related Discrimination and Disadvantage*. London: IFF Research, 2015.

Addati, Laura, Umberto Cattaneo, Valeria Esquivel, and Isabel Valarino. *Care Work and Care Jobs for the Future of Decent Work*. Geneva: International Labour Organization, 2018. https://www.ilo.org/global/publications/ books/WCMS_633135/lang—en/index.htm.

Agerskov, Ulla, ed. *Nordic Statistical Yearbook 2007, Vol. 45*. Copenhagen: Nordic Council of Ministers, 2007.

Alderman, Liz, and Steven Greenhouse. "Living Wages, Rarity for U.S. Fast-Food Workers, Served Up in Denmark." *New York Times*. October 27, 2014.

Aldous, Joan, Gail M. Mulligan, and Thoroddur Bjarnason. "Fathering over Time: What Makes the Difference?" *Journal of Marriage and the Family* 60, no. 4 (1998): 809–20.

Alesina, Alberto, Edwrd Glaeser, and Bruce Sacerdote. "Work and Leisure in the US and Europe: Why so Different?" In *NBER Macroeconomics Annual 2005, Vol. 20*, edited by Mark Gertler and Kenneth Rogoff, 1–100. Cambridge: MIT Press, 2005.

Allard, Karin, Linda Haas, and C. Phillip Hwang. "Family-Supportive Organizational Culture and Fathers' Experiences Of Work–Family Conflict in Sweden." *Gender, Work & Organization* 18, no. 2 (2011): 141–57.

Amsterdam Tips. "Salaries in Amsterdam, Netherlands." Amsterdam Tips. December 1, 2020. https://www.amsterdamtips.com/salaries-in-amster dam-netherlands.

Anker, Richard. *Estimating a Living Wage: A Methodological Review*. Geneva: International Labour Office, 2011.

Anxo, Dominique, Jean-Yves Boulin, Immaculada Cebrián, Colette Fagan, Saskia Keuzenkamp, Ute Klammer, Christina Klenner, Gloria Moreno, and Luis Toharía. *Working Time Options Over the Life Course: New Work Patterns and Company Strategies*. Dublin: European Foundation for the Improvement of Living and Working Conditions, 2006.

Anxo, Dominique, Colette Fagan, Marie-Thérèse Letablier, Corinne Perraudin, and Mark Smith. *Parental Leave in European Companies*. Dublin: European Foundation for the Improvement of Living and Working Conditions, 2007.

Arendt, Hannah. *The Human Condition*, 2nd ed. Chicago: University of Chicago Press, 2018.

Aslan, Ozlem. *Resistances against Hydropower Projects as Place-Based Struggles: The Case of Artvin, Turkey*. PhD Dissertation. University of Toronto, 2019. https://tspace.library.utoronto.ca/handle/1807/96926.

Assadourian, Erik. "The Rise and Fall of Consumer Cultures." In *State of the World 2010: Transforming Cultures: From Consumerism to Sustainability*, 3–20. New York: W. W. Norton & Company, 2010.

Assemblée Nationale. "Rapport fait au nom de la Commission d'enquête sur l'impact sociétal, social, économique et financier de la réduction progressive du temps de travail." 2014. Accessed October 5, 2021. https://www.assemblee-nationale.fr/14/rap-enq/r2436.asp.

Baker, Dean. *The End of Loser Liberalism: Making Markets Progressive*. Washington, DC: Center of Economic and Policy Research, 2011.

Baker, Dean. "The $24 an Hour Minimum Wage." *Center of Economic and Policy Research*. July 22, 2020. https://cepr.net/the-24-an-hour-minimum-wage/

Bangham, George. *The Times They Aren't A-Changin': Why Working Hours Have Stopped Falling in London and the UK*. London: Resolution Foundation, 2020.

Baxter, Janeen, Belinda Hewitt, and Michele Hayne. "Life Course Transitions and Housework: Marriage, Parenthood, and Time on Housework." *Journal of Marriage and Family* 70, no. 2 (2008): 259–72.

Beans on Toast. "On & On." Song, 2019.

Beham, Barbara, Sonja Drobnič, and Patrick Präg. "Who's Got the Balance? A Study of Satisfaction with the Work–Family Balance among Part-Time Service Sector Employees in Five Western European Countries." *The International Journal of Human Resource Management* 23, no. 18 (2012): 3725–41.

Beham, Barbara, Sonja Drobnič, Patrick Präg, Andreas Baierl, and Janin Ecker. "Part-Time Work and Gender Inequality in Europe: A Comparative Analysis of Satisfaction with Work–Life Balance." *European Societies* 21, no. 3 (2019): 378–402.

Beiner, Ronald, and Jennifer Nedelsky, eds. *Judgment, Imagination, and Politics: Themes from Kant and Arendt*. Lanham, Md: Rowman & Littlefield, 2001.

Bell, Linda A. "The Incentive to Work Hard: Differences in Black and White Workers' Hours and Preferences." In *Working Time: International Trends, Theory and Policy Perspectives*, edited by Deborah M. Figart and Lonnie Golden, 106–26. London: Routledge, 2000.

Bennhold, Katrin. "Working (Part-Time) in the 21st Century." *New York Times*. December 29, 2010.

Berg, Andrew, Jonathan D. Ostry, Charalambos G. Tsangarides, and Yorbol Yakhshilikov. "Redistribution, Inequality, and Growth: New Evidence." *Journal of Economic Growth* 23, no. 3 (2018): 259–305.

Berkman, Michael B. and Robert E. O'Connor. "Do Women Legislators Matter? Female Legislators and State Abortion Policy." *American Politics Quarterly* 21, no. 1 (1993): 102–24.

Bernard, Tara Siegel and Karl Russell. "The Middle-Class Crunch: A Look at 4 Family Budgets." *The New York Times.* October 3, 2019. https://www.nyti mes.com/interactive/2019/10/03/your-money/middle-class-income.html.

Berry, Thomas. *The Dream of the Earth.* San Francisco: Sierra Club Books, 1988.

Bertrand, Marianne, Sandra E. Black, Sissel Jensen, and Adriana Lleras-Muney. "Breaking the Glass Ceiling? The Effect of Board Quotas on Female Labor Market Outcomes in Norway." National Bureau of Economic Research Working Paper. June 2014.

Biswas, Siddhartha, Indraneel Chakraborty, and Rong Hai. "Income Inequality, Tax Policy, and Economic Growth." *The Economic Journal* 127, no. 601 (2017): 688–727.

Bjørnholt, Margunn. "Part-Time Work and the Career and Life Choices of the Men from the Work-Sharing Couples Study." *Equality, Diversity and Inclusion: An International Journal* 29, no. 6 (2010): 573–592.

Black, C. F. "On Lives Lived With Law: Land as Healer." *Law Text Culture* 20 (2016): 164–188.

Blackett, Adelle. *Everyday Transgressions: Domestic Workers' Transnational Challenge to International Labor Law.* Ithaca, NY: Cornell University Press, 2019.

Boisard, Pierre, Damien Cartron, Michel Gollac, and Antoine Valeyre. *Time and Work: Duration of Work.* Dublin: Eurofound, 2003.

Borrows, John. "Earth-Bound: Indigenous Resurgence and Environmental Reconciliation." In *Resurgence and Reconciliation*, edited by Michael Asch, John Borrows, and James Tully, 49–82. Toronto: University of Toronto Press, 2018.

Borrows, John. "Outsider Education: Indigenous Law and Land-Based Learning." *Windsor Yearbook of Access to Justice* 33, no. 1 (2016): 1–27.

Bosch, Gerhard. (1990). "From 40 to 35 Hours-Reduction and Flexibilisation of the Working Week in the Federal Republic of Germany." *Int'l Lab. Rev.* 129, no. 5 (1990): 611–27.

Bosch, Gerhard, and Steffan Lehndorff. "Working-Time Reduction And Employment: Experiences in Europe and Economic Policy Recommendations." *Cambridge Journal of Economics* 25, no. 2 (2001): 209–43.

Bowles, Samuel, and Yongjin Park. "Emulation, Inequality, and Work Hours: Was Thorsten Veblen Right?" *The Economic Journal* 115, no. 507 (2005): 397–412.

Bozikovic, Alex. "That Co-Housing Retirement Life: How Smart Design Gives This Seniors' Community a Life-Changing Twist." *The Globe and Mail.* March 9, 2019. https://www.theglobeandmail.com/arts/art-and-architect ure/article-forget-institutional-living-smart-design-gives-this-seniors/.

Bratton, K. A., and L. P. Ray. "Descriptive Representation, Policy Outcomes, and Municipal Day-Care Coverage in Norway." *American Journal of Political Science* 46, no. 2 (2002): 428–37.

Bredgaard, Thomas, Flemming Larsen, Per Kongshøj Madsen, and Stine Rasmussen. "Flexicurity and Atypical Employment in Denmark. Centre for Labour Market." *Research Paper* no. 1 (2009).

Bretschger, Lucas, and Frank Hettich. "Globalisation, Capital Mobility and Tax Competition: Theory and Evidence for OECD Countries." *European Journal of Political Economy* 18, no. 4 (2002): 695–716.

Bridgestock, Laura. "Differences in Average Working Hours Around the World." Top Universities (blog). March 12, 2014. https://www.topuniversit ies.com/blog/differences-average-working-hours-around-world.

Brooks, Rosa. "Recline, Don't 'Lean In' (Why I Hate Sheryl Sandberg)." *Washington Post.* February 25, 2014. https://www.washingtonpost.com/blogs/she-the-people/wp/2014/02/25/recline-dont-lean-in-why-i-hate-she ryl-sandberg/.

Burchell, Brendan, Colette Fagan, Catherine O'Brien, and Mark Smith. *Working Conditions in the European Union: The Gender Perspective.* Dublin: Eurofound, 2007.

Bureau of Labor. "May 2020 State Occupational Employment and Wage Estimates: New York." *US Bureau of Labor Statistics.* Accessed October 8, 2021. https://www.bls.gov/oes/current/oes_ny.htm#00-0000.

Bureau of Labor. "Women in the Labor Force: A Databook." *U.S. Bureau of Labor Statistics.* December 2019. https://www.bls.gov/opub/reports/wom ens-databook/2019/home.htm.

Burger, Anna S. "Extreme Working Hours in Western Europe and North America: A New Aspect of Polarization." *London School of Economics and Political Science "Europe in Question" Discussion Paper Series*, no. 25 (2015): 27.

Calvano, Lisa. "Tug of War: Caring for Our Elders While Remaining Productive at Work." *Academy of Management Perspectives* 27, no. 3 (2013): 204–18.

Calvert, Cynthia Thomas. *Flex Success: The Lawyer's Guide to Balanced Hours.* CreateSpace Independent Publishing Platform, 2011.

Calvert, Cynthia Thomas, and Joan C. Williams. *Flex Success: The Lawyer's Guide to Balanced Hours.* CreateSpace Independent Publishing Platform, 2011.

Cary, Lorene. "My Family Cared for My Sick Aunt. Who's Caring for Us?" *The New York Times.* October 25, 2019. https://www.nytimes.com/2019/10/25/opinion/health-care-old-age-disability.html.

Cary, Lorene. "Who's Caring for the Care givers?" *The New York Times.* October 27, 2019.

Castles, Francis G. "A Race to the Bottom?" In *The Welfare State Reader*, 2nd ed., edited by Christopher Pierson and Francis G. Castles, 226–44. Cambridge: Polity Press, 2007.

CBC News. "2-Income Families Nearly Doubled from 1976 to 2014." *CBC News*. June 24, 2015. https://www.cbc.ca/news/business/2-income-famil ies-nearly-doubled-from-1976-to-2014-1.3125996.

CDC. "Health Insurance Coverage." *Centers for Disease Control and Prevention*. 2019. Accessed October 8, 2021. https://www.cdc.gov/nchs/fast ats/health-insurance.htm.

Cederström, Carl. "State of Nordic fathers." Nordic Council of Ministers, 2019.

Cette, Gilbert, Samuel Chang, and Maty Konte. "The Decreasing Returns on Working Time: An Empirical Analysis on Panel Country Data." *Applied Economics Letters* 18, no. 17 (2011): 1677–82.

Chang, Ha-Joon. *Kicking Away the Ladder: Development Strategy in Historical Perspective*. London: Anthem, 2002.

Chang, Ha-Joon. *Bad Samaritans: The Guilty Secrets of Rich Nations & the Threat to Global Prosperity*. London: Random House Business Books, 2009.

Chandola, Tarani, Annie Britton, Eric Brunner, Harry Hemingway, Marek Malik, Meena Kumari, Ellena Badrick, Mika Kivimaki, and Michael Marmot. "Work stress and Coronary Heart Disease: What Are the Mechanisms?" *European Heart Journal* 29, no. 5 (2008): 640–48.

Chantrill, Christopher. "Federal Government Tax and Revenue Chart." *US Government Revenue*. Accessed October 11, 2021. http://www.usgovern mentrevenue.com/revenue_chart_1792_2016USp_18s1li011lcn_10f.

Chappell, Bill. "4-Day Workweek Boosted Workers' Productivity By 40%, Microsoft Japan Says." *NPR*. November 4, 2019. https://www.npr.org/2019/ 11/04/776163853/microsoft-japan-says-4-day-workweek-boosted-work ers-productivity-by-40.

Chung, Heejung, Marcel Kerkhofs, and Peter Ester. *Working Time Flexibility in European Companies*. Luxembourg: EU Office for Official Publications, 2007.

Cingano, F. "Trends in Income Inequality and Its Impact on Economic Growth." *OECD Social, Employment and Migration Working Papers*, no. 163 (2014): 1–65.

Clark, Andrew E., and Andrew J. Oswald. "Satisfaction and Comparison Income." *Journal of Public Economics* 61, no. 3 (1996): 359–81.

Clausing, Kimberly A. "Does Tax Drive the Headquarters Locations of the World's Biggest Companies?" *Transnational Corporations* 25, no. 2 (2018): 37–66.

Cohen, D. A., P. Gowan, S. Lopez, M. Weeks, M. Paul, T. Silverstein, K.. Simowitz, et al. *A National Homes Guarantee*. People's Action, 2019.

Coltrane, Scott. "Fatherhood, Gender, and Work-Family Policies." In *Gender Equality: Transforming Family Divisions of Labour*, edited by Janet C. Gornick and Marcia K. Meyers, 385–410. London: Verso, 2009.

Commonwealth of Australia. "Australian Social Trends, 2000." Australian Bureau of Statistics. July 4, 2000. https://www.abs.gov.au/ausstats/abs@.nsf/

2f762f95845417aeca25706c00834efa/1b34567b9e041927ca2570ec000e3
c1e!OpenDocument.

Commonwealth of Australia. "Labour Force, Australia, January 2020." Australian Bureau of Statistics. February 20, 2020. https://www.abs.gov.au/ statistics/labor/employment-and-unemployment/labor-force-australia/ jan-2020.

Conaghan, Joanne and Kerry Rittich. *Labour Law, Work, and Family: Critical and Comparative Perspectives*. Oxford: Oxford University Press, 2005.

Coontz, Stephanie. "How to Make Your Marriage Gayer." *The New York Times*. February 13, 2020. https://www.nytimes.com/2020/02/13/opinion/sunday/ marriage-housework-gender-happiness.html.

Craig, Lyn, Judith E. Brown, Lyndall Strazdins, and Jiweon Jun. "Is It Just Too Hard? Gender Time Symmetry in Market and Nonmarket Work and Subjective Time Pressure in Australia, Finland, and Korea." In *Gender and Time Use in a Global Context: The Economics of Employment and Unpaid Labor*, edited by Rachel Connelly and Ebru Kongar, 465–494. New York: Palgrave Macmillan, 2017.

Crompton, Rosemary, and Clare Lyonette. "Women's Career Success and Work–Life Adaptations in the Accountancy and Medical Professions in Britain." *Gender, Work & Organization* 18, no. 2 (2011): 231–54.

Dalmiya, Vrinda. *Caring to Know: Comparative Care Ethics, Feminist Epistemology, and the Mahabharata*. India: Oxford University Press, 2016.

Daly, Herman E. "Allocation, Distribution, and Scale: Towards an Economics that is Efficient, Just, and Sustainable." *Ecological Economics* 6, no. 3 (1992): 185–193.

Damasio, Antonio R. *Descartes' Error: Emotion, Reason and the Human Brain*. New York: Quill, 2004.

Davies, Ronald B. and Krishna Chaitanya Vadlamannati. "A Race to the Bottom in Labor Standards? An Empirical Investigation." *Journal of Development Economics* 103, no. C (2013): 1–14.

Davy, Laura. "People with Intellectual Disability and the Relational Self: Redrawing the Moral Boundaries of Personal Autonomy." Thesis. Sydney: University of Sydney, 2017.

De Graaf, John and D. K. Batker. "Americans Work Too Much for Their Own Good." Bloomberg. 2011. Accessed September 20, 2013. http://www. bloomberg.com/news/2011-11-03/americans-work-too-much-for-their- own-good-de-graaf-and-batker.html.

De Graaf, John, David Wann, and Thomas H. Naylor. *Affluenza: The All-Consuming Epidemic*. San Francisco: Berrett-Koehle, 2005.

De Marneffe, Daphne. *Maternal Desire: On Children, Love, and the Inner Life*, 2nd ed. Scribner, 2004.

De Spiegelaere, Stan and Aneiszka Piasna. "The Why and How of Working Time Reduction." European Trade Union Institute, 2017.

Del Pero, Angelica Salvi, Willem Adema, Valeria Ferraro, and Valérie Frey. "Policies to Promote Access to Good-Quality Affordable Housing in OECD Countries." *OECD Social, Employment and Migration Working Papers*, no. 176 (2016): 1–82.

DeGeer, Ian. *Give Love, Get Love: The Involved Fatherhood and Gender Equity Project*. Toronto: White Ribbon Campaign, 2014. https://www.whiteribbon.ca/uploads/1/1/3/2/113222347/fatherhood_report.pdf.

Deutsch, Francine M., Julianne B. Lussier, and Laura J. Servis. "Husbands at Home: Predictors of Paternal Participation in Childcare and Housework." *Journal of Personality and Social Psychology* 65, no. 6 (1993): 1154–66.

Deutschmann, Christoph. "The Worker-Bee Syndrome in Japan: An Analysis of Working-Time Practices." In *Working Time In Transition*, edited by Karl Hinrichs, William Roche, and Carmen Sirianni, 189–202. Philadelphia: Temple University Press, 1991.

Dietsch, Peter. *Catching Capital: The Ethics of Tax Competition*. Oxford: Oxford University Press, 2015.

Dinnerstein, Dorothy. *The Mermaid and the Minotaur*. Other Press, LLC, 2010.

Dockrill, Peter. "Working Long Hours Is Linked to a Significantly Higher Risk of Stroke." *Science Alert* (blog). August 21, 2015. https://www.scienceal ert.com/working-long-hours-is-linked-to-a-significantly-higher-risk-of-stroke.

Doughty, Steve. "£40k-a-Year Is Cost of a Happy Family Life with 2 Children." *Daily Mail*. July 5, 2017. https://www.dailymail.co.uk/news/article-4669 190/40k-year-cost-happy-family-life-2-children.html.

Drange, Ida and Cathrine Egeland. "Part-Time Work in the Nordic Region II." Copenhagen: Nordic Council of Ministers, 2014.

Dreher, Axel. "The Influence of Globalization on Taxes and Social Policy: An Empirical Analysis for OECD Countries." *European Journal of Political Economy* 22, no. 1 (2006): 179–201.

Dreher, Axel, Jan-Egbert Sturm, and Heinrich W. Ursprung. "The Impact of Globalization on the Composition of Government Expenditures: Evidence from Panel Data." *Public Choice* 134, nos. 3–4 (2008): 263–92.

Duffy, Mignon. *Making Care Count: A Century of Gender, Race, and Paid Care Work*. New Brunswick, NJ: Rutgers University Press, 2011.

Durbin, Susan, and Jennifer Tomlinson. "Female Part-Time Managers: Careers, Mentors and Role Models." *Gender, Work & Organization* 21, no. 4 (2014): 308–20.

Duxbury, Linda and Christopher Higgins. *Something's Got to Give: Balancing Work, Childcare, and Eldercare*. Toronto: University of Toronto Press, 2017.

Ehrenreich, Barbara and Arlie Russell Hochschild, eds. *Global Woman: Nannies, Maids, and Sex Workers in the New Economy*. New York: Owl Books, 2004.

Eichengreen, Barry, James Tobin, and Charles Wyplosz. Two Cases for Sand in the Wheels of International Finance. *The Economic Journal* 105, no. 428 (1995): 162–72.

Eisler, Riane. *The Chalice and the Blade: Our History, Our Future*. San Francisco: Harper Collins, 1987.

Eisler, Riane. *Sacred Pleasure: Sex, Myth, and the Politics of the Body*, 1st ed. San Francisco: Harper Collins, 1995.

Eisler, Riane and Daniel Levine. "Nurture, Nature, and Caring: We Are Not Prisoners of Our Genes." *Brain and Mind* 3, no. 1 (2002): 9–52.

England, Paula. "The Gender Revolution: Uneven and Stalled." *Gender & Society* 24, no. 2 (2010): 149–66.

Engster, Daniel. *Justice, Care, and the Welfare State*. Oxford: Oxford University Press, 2015.

Epstein, Cynthia Fuchs, Carroll Seron, Bonnie Oglensky, and Robert Sauté. *The Part-Time Paradox: Time Norms, Professional Lives, Family, and Gender*. New York: Routledge, 1999.

Esping-Andersen, Gøsta. *The Three Worlds of Welfare Capitalism*. Cambridge: Polity Press, 1990.

Esping-Andersen, Gøsta. *The Incomplete Revolution: Adapting to Women's New Roles*. Cambridge: Polity, 2009.

Eurofound. *Work–Life Balance: Solving the Dilemma*. Dublin: European Foundation for the Improvement of Living and Working Conditions, 2007.

Eurofound. *Fifth European Working Conditions Survey*. Luxembourg: Publications Office of the European Union, 2012.

Eurofound. *Sixth European Working Conditions Survey: Overview Report (2017 Update)*. Luxembourg: Publications Office of the European Union, 2017.

Eurostat. "Employment and Activity by Sex and Age: Annual Data." *Eurostat*. April 20, 2020. http://appsso.eurostat.ec.europa.eu/nui/show.do?dataset=lfsi_emp_a&lang=eng.

Eurostat. "Temporary and Part-Time Jobs on the Rise." *Eurostat*. 2018. Accessed October 8, 2021. https://ec.europa.eu/eurostat/web/products-eurostat-news/-/WDN-20180813-1.

Fagan, Colette. *Analysis Note: Men and Gender Equality*. Brussels: European Commission: Employment, Social Affairs and Equal Opportunities, 2010.

Fagan, Colette and Brendan Burchell. *Gender, Jobs and Working Conditions in the European Union*. Dublin: European Foundation for the Improvement of Living and Working Conditions, 2002.

Fagan, Colette, Clare Lyonette, C., Mark Smith, and Abril Saldaña-Tejeda. *The Influence of Working Time Arrangements on Work-Life Integration or 'Balance': A Review of the International Evidence*. Geneva: International Labour Organization, 2013.

Fagan, Colette, Helen Norman, Mark Smith, and Maria C. González Menéndez. *In Search of Good Quality Part-Time Employment*. Geneva: International Labour Office, 2013.

Fagnani, Jeanne and Marie-Thérèse Letablier. "Work and Family Life Balance The Impact of the 35-Hour laws in France." *Work, Employment & Society* 18, no. 3 (2004): 551–72.

Fineman, Martha Albertson, ed. "The Vulnerable Subject: Anchoring Equality in the Human Condition." *Yale Law Journal* 20, no. 1 (2008): 1–23. https://doi.org/10.4324/9780203848531-26.

Fineman, Martha Albertson, ed. "Vulnerability and Inevitable Inequality." *Oslo Law Review* 4, no. 3 (2017): 133–49.

Fitzgerald, Jared B., Andrew Jorgenson, and Brett Clark. "Energy Consumption and Working Hours: A Longitudinal Study of Developed and Developing Nations, 1990–2008." *Environmental Sociology* 1, no. 3 (2015): 213–23.

Fitzgerald, Jared B., Juliet B. Schor, and Andrew K. Jorgenson. "Working Hours and Carbon Dioxide Emissions in the United States, 2007–2013." *Social Forces* 96, no. 4 (2018): 1851–74.

Fletcher, Ruth. "Negotiating Strangeness on the Abortion Trail." In *ReValuing Care in Theory, Law and Policy: Cycles and Connections*, edited by Rosie Harding, Ruth Fletcher, and Chris Beasley, 14–30. Routledge, 2017.

Folbre, Nancy. "Reforming Care." In *Gender Equality: Transforming Family Divisions of Labour*, edited by Janet C. Gornick and Marcia K. Meyers, 111–28. London: Routledge, 2009.

Folbre, Nancy. *For Love and Money: Care Provision in the United States*. New York: Russell Sage Foundation, 2012.

Folbre, Nancy. *The Invisible Heart: Economics and Family Values*. New York: New Press, 2001.

Folbre, Nancy. *Valuing Children: Rethinking the Economics of the Family, The Family and Public Policy*. Cambridge: Harvard University Press, 2010.

Folbre, Nancy. *Greed, Lust & Gender: A History of Economic Ideas*. Oxford: Oxford University Press, 2009.

Fouarge, Didier and Ruud Muffels. "Working Part-Time in the British, German and Dutch Labour Market: Scarring for the Wage Career?" *Schmollers Jahrbuch* 129, no. 2 (2009): 217–26.

Fraser, Nancy. "After the Family Wage: Gender Equity and the Welfare State." *Political Theory* 22, no. 4 (1994): 591–618.

Fraser, Nancy. *Fortunes of Feminism: From State-Managed Capitalism to Neoliberal Crisis*. New York: Verso Books, 2013.

Fraser, Nancy and Linda Gordon. "A Genealogy of Dependency: Tracing a Keyword of the U.S. Welfare State." *Signs* 19, no. 2 (1994): 309–36.

Fremstad, Anders, Mark Paul, and Anthony Underwood. "Work Hours and CO_2 Emissions: Evidence from US Households." *Review of Political Economy* 31, no. 1 (2019): 42–59.

Freyssinet, Jacques and François Michon. *Overtime in Europe*. Dublin: European Foundation for the Improvement of Living and Working Conditions, 2003.

Fulu, Emma, Xian Warner, Stephanie Miedema, Rachel Jewkes, Tim Rosellii, and James Lang. *Why Do Some Men Use Violence Against Women and How Can We Prevent It? Quantitative Findings from the UN Multi-Country Study on Men and Violence in Asia and the Pacific*. United Nations: UN Volunteers,

UN Women, United Nations Development Programme, 2013. https://www. ncjrs.gov/App/Publications/abstract.aspx?ID=265661.

Galinsky, Ellen, Kerstin Aumann, and James T. Bond. "Times are Changing: Gender and Generation at Work and at Home." *Families and Work Institute*, 2009.

Garland, Susan B. "At 75, Taking Care of Mom, 99: 'We Did Not Think She Would Live This Long.'" *The New York Times*. June 27, 2019.

Garrett, Geoffrey. "Global Markets and National Politics: Collision Course or Virtuous Circle?" *International Organizations* 52, no. 4 (1998): 787–824.

Garrett, Geoffrey and Deborah Mitchell. "Globalization, Government Spending and Taxation In the OECD." *European Journal of Political Research* 39, no. 2 (2001): 145–77.

Gash, Vanessa. "Preference or Constraint? Part-Time Workers' Transitions in Denmark, France and the United Kingdom." *Work, Employment & Society* 22, no. 4 (2008): 655–74.

Gavigan, Shelley A. M. and Dorothy E. Chunn, eds. *The Legal Tender of Gender: Welfare, Law, and the Regulation of Women's Poverty*. Hart Publishing, 2010.

Genschel, Philipp. "Globalization and the Transformation of the Tax State." *European Review* 13, no. 1 (2005): 53–71.

Genschel, Philipp and Peter Schwarz. "Tax Competition: A Literature Review." *Socio-Economic Review* 9, no. 2 (2011): 339–70.

Gerson, Kathleen. "Changing Lives, Resistant Institutions: A New Generation Negotiates Gender, Work, and Family Change." *Sociological Forum* 24, no. 4 (2009): 735–53.

Gerson, Kathleen and Jerry A. Jacobs. *The Time Divide: Work, Family, and Gender Inequality*. Cambridge, MA: Harvard University Press, 2009.

Glasmeier, Amy K. "Living Wage Calculation for New York." Accessed October 8, 2021. https://livingwage.mit.edu/states/36.

Glenn, Evelyn Nakano. *Forced to Care: Coercion and Caregiving in America*. Cambridge, MA: Harvard University Press, 2010.

Golden, Lonnie. *The Effects of Working Time on Productivity and Firm Performance: A Research Synthesis Paper*. Geneva: International Labor Office, 2012.

Goldfarb, Sally F. "Violence against Women and the Persistence of Privacy." *Ohio St LJ* 61, no. 1 (2000): 1–87.

Gollan, Jennifer. "Elder Care Homes Rake in Profits as Workers Earn a Pittance." *Associated Press*. May 19, 2019. https://apnews.com/8e852a9b2 fd9459e9e7ca2412c7bcf47.

Goodin, Robert E. "Temporal Justice." *Journal of Social Policy* 39, no. 1 (2010): 1–16.

Goodin, Robert E., James Mahmud Rice, Antti Parpo, and Lina Eriksson. *Discretionary Time: A New Measure of Freedom*. Cambridge: Cambridge University Press, 2008.

Gornick, Janet C. and Marcia K. Meyers. "Institutions that Support Gender Equality in Parenthood and Employment." In *Gender Equality: Transforming Family Divisions of Labour*, edited by Janet C. Gornick and Marcia K. Meyers, 3–66. London: Verso, 2009.

Gornick, Janet C. and Marcia K. Meyers. *Gender Equality: Transforming Family Divisions of Labor*. New York: Verso Books, 2009.

Gowan, Peter, and Ryan Cooper. *Social Housing in the United States*. People's Policy Project, 2018.

Government of Canada. "Hire a Home Child Care Provider or Home Support Worker." *Work in Canada*. March 23, 2020. https://www.canada.ca/en/immigration-refugees-citizenship/services/work-canada/hire-foreign-worker/in-home-care giver.html.

Gray, Helen. *Family-Friendly Working: What a Performance!* London: Centre for Economic Performance, 2002.

Grönlund, Anne, and Ida Öun. "Beyond the Mummy Track?: Part-time Rights, Gender, and Career-Family Dilemmas." *Nordic Journal of Working Life Studies* 8, no. 3 (2018): 177–98.

Grunow, Daniela, Florian Schulz, and Hans-Peter Blossfeld. "What Determines Change in the Division of Housework over the Course of Marriage?" *International Sociology* 27, no. 3 (2012): 289–307.

Grunow, Daniela and Gerlieke Veltkamp. "Institutions as Reference Points for Parents-to-Be in European Societies: A Theoretical and Analytical Framework." In *Couples' Transitions to Parenthood: Analysing Gender and Work in Europe*. UK: Edward Elgar Publishing, 2016.

Haas, Linda and C. Phillip Hwang. "The Impact of Taking Parental Leave on Fathers' Participation in Childcare and Relationships with Children: Lessons from Sweden." *Community, Work and Family* 11, no. 1 (2008): 85–104.

Haas, Linda and C. Phillip Hwang. "Is Fatherhood Becoming More Visible at Work? Trends in Corporate Support for fathers taking parental leave in Sweden." *Fathering* 7, no. 3 (2009): 303–321.

Haas, Linda and C. Phillip Hwang. "'It's About Time!': Company Support for Fathers' Entitlement to Reduced Work Hours in Sweden." *Social Politics: International Studies in Gender, State & Society* 23, no. 1 (2016): 142–67.

Hanlon, Niall. *Masculinities, Care and Equality: Identity and Nurture in Men's Lives*. Palgrave Macmillan, 2012.

Hanna, Awad S., Craig S. Taylor, and Kenneth T. Sullivan. "Impact of Extended Overtime on Construction Labor Productivity." *Journal of Construction Engineering and Management* 131, no. 6 (2005): 734–39.

Harding, Rosie. *Duties to Care: Dementia, Relationality, and Law*. Cambridge Bioethics and Law. Cambridge: Cambridge University Press, 2017.

Hargita, C. Starla. "Care-Based Temporalities and Parental Leave in Australia." *Griffith Law Review* 26, no. 4 (2017): 511–31.

Hart, Robert A. "Women Doing Men's Work and Women Doing Women's Work: Female Work and Pay in British Wartime Engineering." *Explorations in Economic History* 44, no. 1 (2007): 114–30.

Hassim, Shireen. "Whose Utopia." In *Gender Equality: Transforming Family Divisions of Labor*, edited by Janet C. Gornick and Marcia K. Meyers, 93–109. London: Verso Books, 2009.

Haug, Frigga. "The 'Four-in-One Perspective': A Manifesto for a More Just Life." *Socialism and* Democracy 23, no. 1 (March 2009): 119–23.

Haug, Frigga. *Die Vier-in-einem-Perspektive: Politik von Frauen für eine neue Linke.* Hamburg: Argument Verlag, 2008.

Hayden, Anders. *Sharing the Work, Sparing the Planet.* Toronto: Between The Lines, 1999.

Hayden, Anders. "France's 35-Hour Week: Attack on Business? Win-Win Reform? Or Betrayal of Disadvantaged Workers?" *Politics & Society* 34, no. 4 (2006): 503–42.

Hayden, Anders and John M. Shandra. "Hours of Work and the Ecological Footprint of Nations: An Exploratory Analysis." *Local Environment* 14, no. 6 (2009): 575–600.

Hearne, Rory. (2017). "A Home or a Wealth Generator? Inequality, Financialisation and the Irish Housing Crisis." In *Cherishing All Equally*, edited by James Wickham, 61–94. Dublin: TASC, 2017.

Hegewisch, Ariane. *Flexible Working Policies: A Comparative Review.* Manchester: Equality and Human Rights Commission, 2009.

Hegewisch, Ariane and Janet C. Gornick. *Statutory Routes to Workplace Flexibility in Cross-National Perspective.* Washington, DC: Institute for Women's Policy Research, 2008.

Hewlett, Sylvia Ann and Carolyn Buck Luce. "Extreme Jobs: The Dangerous Allure of the 70-Hour Workweek." *Harvard Business Review* 84, no. 12 (2006): 49–59.

Himmelweit, Susan, ed. *Inside the Household: From Labour to Care, Capital and Class Series.* Palgrave Macmillan UK, 2000.

Hinrichs, Karl. "Working-Time Development in West Germany: Departure to a New Stage." In *Working Time In Transition*, edited by Karl Hinrichs, William Roche, and Carmen Sirianni, 27–60. Philadelphia: Temple University Press, 1991.

Hinrichs, Karl, William Roche, and Carmen Sirianni. "From Standardization to Flexibility: Changes in the Political Economy of Work Time." In *Working Time In Transition*, edited by Karl Hinrichs, William Roche, and Carmen Sirianni, 3–26. Philadelphia: Temple University Press, 1991.

Hinrichs, Karl, William Roche, and Carmen Sirianni, eds. *Working Time In Transition.* Philadelphia: Temple University Press, 1991.

Hochschild, Arlie Russell. *The Commercialization of Intimate Life: Notes from Home and Work.* University of California Press, 2003.

Hochschild, Arlie Russell. *The Time Bind*. New York: Metropolitan Books, 1997.

Holmes, Steven A. "Is This What Women Want?" *New York Times*. December 15, 1996. https://www.nytimes.com/1996/12/15/weekinreview/is-this-what-women-want.html.

Hondagneu-Sotelo, Pierrette. *Doméstica: Immigrant Workers Cleaning and Caring in the Shadows of Affluence*. University of California Press: 2007.

Honig, Bonnie. "Three Models of Emergency Politics." *Boundary 2* 41, no. 2 (June 1, 2014): 45–70.

Hook, Jennifer L. "Care in Context: Men's Unpaid Work in 20 Countries, 1965-2003." *American Sociological Review* 71, no. 4 (2006): 639–660.

Hunnicutt, Benjamin Kline. *Kellogg's Six-Hour Day*. Temple University Press, 1996.

Immervoll, Herwig and Linda Richardson. "Redistribution Policy and Inequality Reduction in OECD Countries: What Has Changed in Two Decades?" *Forschungsinstitut zur Zukunft der Arbeit*, Discussion Paper no. 6030 (2011). http://hdl.handle.net/10419/58948.

Inglehart, Robert. "Changing Values among Western Publics from 1970 to 2006." *West European Politics* 31, no. 1–2 (2008): 130–46.

Inglehart, Robert and Paul R. Abramson. (1994). "Economic Security and Value Change." *American Political Science Review* 88, no. 2 (1994): 336–54.

ITEP. "Who Pays Taxes in America in 2020?" *Institute on Taxation and Economic Policy*. https://itep.org/who-pays-taxes-in-america-in-2020/.

Iversen, Torben and Frances Rosenbluth. "The Political Economy of Gender: Explaining Cross-National Variation in the Gender Division of Labor and the Gender Voting Gap." *American Journal of Political Science* 50, no. 1 (2006): 1–19.

Jackson, Tim. *Prosperity Without Growth: Economics for a Finite Planet*. London: Earthscan. 2009.

Jacobs, Jerry A. and Kathleen Gerson. "Unpacking Americans' Views of the Employment of Mothers and Fathers Using National Vignette Survey Data: SWS Presidential Address." *Gender & Society* 30, no. 3 (2016): 413–41.

Jaspers, Eva and Ellen Verbakel. "The Division of Paid Labor in Same-Sex Couples in the Netherlands." *Sex Roles* 68, no. 5–6 (2013): 335–48.

Jeanmonod, Rebecca, Donald Jeanmonod, and Ryan Ngiam. "Resident productivity: does shift length matter?" *The American Journal of Emergency Medicine* 26, no. 7 (2008): 789–91.

Jennings, Sheila Kathleen. "The Right to Support: Severely Disabled Children & Their Mothers." PhD Dissertation. Toronto, ON: York University, 2019. YorkSpace. http://hdl.handle.net/10315/36669.

Johansson, Elly-Ann. *The Effect of Own and Spousal Parental Leave on Earnings*. Uppsala, NY: The Institute for Labour Market Policy Evaluation, 2010.

Johnson, Harriet McBride. "The Disability Gulag." *New York Times*, November 23, 2003.

Jonsdottir, Svala. "National Report on the Icelandic Experience of Parental Leave Provision." In *The Parental Leave System In Iceland*, 6–20. Reykjavik: Focus Consultancy and GOPA-Cartermill, 2008.

Joyce, James. "A Painful Case." In *Dubliners*, 119–30. London: Grant Richards, 1914.

Kaza, Stephanie, ed. *A Wild Love for the World: Joanna Macy and the Work of Our Time*, 1st ed. Boulder: Shambhala, 2020.

Kimmel, Michael. "Almost All Violent Extremists Share One Thing: Their Gender." *The Guardian*. April 8, 2018. https://www.theguardian.com/world/2018/apr/08/violent-extremists-share-one-thing-gender-michael-kimmel.

Kimmerer, Robin Wall. *Braiding Sweetgrass: Indigenous Wisdom, Scientific Knowledge and the Teachings of Plants*. New York: Penguin Books, 2020.

Kimmerer, Robin Wall. *Gathering Moss: A Natural and Cultural History of Mosses*. Oregon State University Press, 2003.

Kheel, Marti. *Nature Ethics: An Ecofeminist Perspective*. Rowman & Littlefield, 2007.

King, Lewis C. and Jeroen. C. J. M. van den Bergh. "Worktime Reduction as a Solution to Climate Change: Five Scenarios Compared for the UK." *Ecological Economics* 132, no. C (2017): 124–34.

Kittay, Eva Feder. *Love's Labor: Essays on Women, Equality and Dependency*. New York: Routledge, 1998.

Kivimäki, Mika, Markus Jokela, Solja T. Nyberg, Archana Singh-Manoux, Eleanor I. Fransson, Lars Alfredsson, Jakob B. Bjorner, et al. "Long Working Hours and Risk of Coronary Heart Disease and Stroke: A Systematic Review and Meta-Analysis of Published and Unpublished Data for 603 838 Individuals." *The Lancet* 386, no. 10005 (October 31, 2015): 1739–46.

Klammer, Ute and Saskia Keuzenkamp. *Working Time Options over the Life Course: Changing Social Security Structures*. Dublin: European Foundation for the Improvement of Living and Working Conditions, 2005.

Klein, Naomi. *This Changes Everything: Capitalism vs. The Climate*. Toronto: Alfred A. Knopf Canada, 2014.

Kleven, Henrik, Camille Landais, and Jakob Egholt Søgaard. "Children and Gender Inequality: Evidence from Denmark." *American Economic Journal: Applied Economics* 11, no. 4 (2019): 181–209.

Knight, Kyle W., Eugene A. Rosa, and Juliet B. Schor. "Could Working Less Reduce Pressures on the Environment? A Cross-National Panel Analysis of OECD Countries, 1970–2007." *Global Environmental Change* 23, no. 4 (2013): 691–700.

Kucerak, Ed and Danielle Rolfe. *Blue Roses*. Documentary. Kublacom Pictures Inc., 2018. http://www.bluerosesdocumentary.ca.

La Valle, Ivana, Sue Arthur, Christine Millward, James Scott, and Marion Clayden. *Happy Families? Atypical Work and Its Influence on Family Life*. Bristol: Policy Press, 2002.

LaJeunesse, Robert. *Work Time Regulation as a Sustainable Full Employment Strategy: The Social Effort Bargain*. London: Routledge, 2009.

Lambert, P. A. "The Comparative Political Economy of Parental Leave and Child Care: Evidence from Twenty OECD Countries." *Social Politics* 15, no. 3 (2008): 315–44.

Lanninger, Alma Wennemo and Marianne Sundström. *Part-Time Work in the Nordic Region*. Copenhagen: Nordic Council of Ministers, 2014.

Larsson, Jörgen and Sofia Björk. "Swedish Fathers Choosing Part-Time Work." *Community, Work & Family* 20, no. 2 (2017): 142–61.

Lawson, Max, Anam Parvez Butt, Rowan Harvey, Diana Sarosi, Clare Coffey, Kim Piaget, and Julie Thekkudan. "Time to Care: Unpaid and Underpaid Care Work and the Global Inequality Crisis." *Oxfam*, 2020.

Lee, Byron Y. and Sanford E. DeVoe. "Flextime and Profitability." *Industrial Relations: A Journal of Economy and Society* 51, no. 2 (2012): 298–316.

Lee, Yoonjoo and Sandra L. Hofferth. "Gender Differences in Single Parents' Living Arrangements and Child Care Time." *Journal of Child and Family Studies* 26, no. 12 (December 2017): 3439–51.

Lehndorff, Steffan. "It's a Long Way from Norms to Normality: The 35-Hour Week in France." *ILR Review* 67, no. 3 (2014): 838–63.

Lemieux, Thomas and W. Craig Riddell. "Who Are Canada's Top 1 Percent?" In *Income Inequality: The Canadian Story*, edited by David A. Green, W. Craig Riddell, and France St-Hilaire. Montreal: Institute for Research on Public Policy, 2016.

Lewchuk, Wayne, Michelynn Laflèche, Diane Dyson, Luin Goldring, Alain Meisner, Stephanie Procyk, Dan Rosen, John Shields, Peter Viducis, and Sam Vrankulj. *It's More than Poverty: Employment Precarity and Household Well-Being*. PEPSO: Poverty and Employment Precarity in Southern Ontario, 2013.

Lewchuk, Wayne, Michelynn Laflèche, Stephanie Procyk, Charlene Cook, Diane Dyson, Luin Goldring, Karen Lior, et al. "The Precarity Penalty: The Impact of Employment Precarity on Individuals, Households and Communities—and What to Do about It." PEPSO: Poverty and Employment Precarity in Southern Ontario, 2015. http://www.deslibris.ca/ID/246690.

Lewis, Suzan. "Restructuring Workplace Cultures: The Ultimate Work-family Challenge." *Women in Management Review* 16, no. 1 (February 2001): 21–29.

Lim, Nicole and Anju Mary Paul. "Stigma on a Spectrum: Differentiated Stigmatization of Migrant Domestic Workers' Romantic Relationships in Singapore." *Gender, Place & Culture* (January 20, 2020): 1–23.

Lind, Jens and Erling Rasmussen. "Paradoxical Patterns of Part-Time Employment in Denmark?" *Economic and Industrial Democracy* 29, no. 4 (2008): 521–40.

Live Scandinavia. "This Is the Minimum and Average Salary in Denmark [2021 Update]." *Live Scandinavia*. Accessed October 8, 2021. https://live scandinavia.com/this-is-the-minimum-and-average-salary-in-denmark/.

Living Wage Foundation. "Living Wage Foundation." *Living Wage Foundation*. Accessed October 8, 2021. https://www.livingwage.org.uk/.

Lombardo, Giovanni and Federico Ravenna. "The Size of the Tradable and Non-tradable Sectors: Evidence from input-output tables for 25 countries." *Economics Letters* 116 (2012): 558–561.

Lorde, Audre. *A Burst of Light: Essays*. Ithaca, NY: Firebrand Books, 1988.

Louv, Richard. *Last Child in the Woods: Saving Our Children from Nature-Deficit Disorder*. London: Atlantic Books Ltd, 2010.

Lyness, Karen S., Janet C. Gornick, Pamela Stone, and Angela R. Grotto. "It's All about Control: Worker Control over Schedule and Hours in Cross-National Context." *American Sociological Review* XX, no. X (2012): 1–27.

Lyonette, Clare, Beate Baldauf, and Heiki Behle. "Quality Part-Time Work: A Review of the Evidence." London: Government Equalities Office, 2010.

Macdonald, David. "Unaccommodating: Rental Housing Wage in Canada." Canadian Centre for Policy Alternatives, 2019.

Maiden, Samantha. "Aussie Dream of Owning Your Own Home Is Impossible without Two Incomes, Social Services Minister Scott Morrison Says." *Herald Sun*. September 6, 2015. http://www.heraldsun.com.au/news/news-story/59f2acf39e4dfd50d4dd66e5a9c7d60e.

Mailand, Mikkel and Trine P. Larsen. "Trade Unions and Precarious Work." *FAOS* Research paper no. 121 (2011).

Malleson, Tom. "Interdependency: The Fourth Existential Insult to Humanity." *Contemporary Political Theory* 17, no. 2 (2018): 160–86.

Malleson, Tom. "Is Meritocracy Ableist?" Forthcoming.

Malleson, Tom. *After Occupy: Economic Democracy for the 21st Century*. New York: Oxford University Press, 2014.

Malleson, Tom. "A Community-Based Good Life or Eco-Apartheid." *Radical Philosophy Review* 19, no. 3 (2015): 593–619.

Malleson, Tom. *Against Inequality: The Practical and Ethical Case for Abolishing the Superrich*. Forthcoming.

Malleson, Tom and David Calnitsky. "Which Way Forward for Economic Security: Basic Income or Public Services?" *Basic Income Studies* 16, no. 2 (2021): 125–67.

Marchiori-Wong, Martin. "Taking Care of the Temporal Imbalance in Child Care Policies." Unpublished manuscript. April 29, 2017. Microsoft Word file.

Markovits, Daniel. *The Meritocracy Trap: How America's Foundational Myth Feeds Inequality, Dismantles the Middle Class, and Devours the Elite*. New York: Penguin Press, 2019.

Martino, Matt, Ben Spraggon, Joshua Byrd, Matt Liddy, and Cristen Tilly. "Can You Guess Where You Sit on Australia's Income Ladder?" *ABC News*. May

21, 2019. https://www.abc.net.au/news/2019-05-21/income-calculator-comparison-australia/9301378.

Matos, Kenneth. "Modern Families: Same- and Different-Sex Couples Negotiating at Home." Families and Work Institute, 2015. https://www.fami liesandwork.org/research/2015.

Matos, Kenneth and Ellen Galinsky. "2012 National Study of Employers." Families and Work Institute, 2012.

Matteazzi, Eleonora, Ariane Pailhé, and Anne Solaz. "Does Part-Time Employment Widen the Gender Wage Gap? Evidence from Twelve European Countries." *Society for the Study of Economic Inequality.* Working Paper no. 293 (2013).

McClain, Linda C. "The Other Marriage Equality Problem." *Boston University Law Review* 93, no. 3 (2013): 921–70.

Meagher, Gabrielle and Marta Szebehely, eds. *Marketisation in Nordic Eldercare: A Research Report on Legislation, Oversight, Extent and Consequences.* Stockholm: Department of Social Work, Stockholm University, 2013.

Mestre, María Vicenta, Paula Samper, María Dolores Frías, and Ana María Tur. *Are Women More Empathetic than Men? A Longitudinal Study in Adolescence.* Cambridge: Cambridge University Press, 2013.

Michon, François. "From 'Working Less for More Jobs' to 'Working More for More Money': Recent Developments and Issues on Working TIme in France." In *Working Time: In Search of New Research Territories Beyond Flexibility Debates,* 3–20. Tokyo: The Japan Institute for Labour Policy and Training, 2009.

Miller, Tina. "Falling Back into Gender? Men's Narratives and Practices around First-Time Fatherhood." *Sociology* 45, no. 6 (2011): 1094–1109.

Mineo, Liz. "Good Genes Are Nice, but Joy Is Better." *Harvard Gazette.* April 11, 2017. https://news.harvard.edu/gazette/story/2017/04/over-nearly-80-years-harvard-study-has-been-showing-how-to-live-a-healthy-and-happy-life/.

Mishel, Lawrence and Alyssa Davis. "Top CEOs Make 300 Times More than Typical Workers: Pay Growth Surpasses Stock Gains and Wage Growth of Top 0.1 Percent." Economic Policy Institute (blog). June 21, 2015. http://www.epi.org/publication/top-ceos-make-300-times-more-than-workers-pay-growth-surpasses-market-gains-and-the-rest-of-the-0-1-percent/.

Moore, Rowan. "Housing in Crisis: Council Homes Were the Answer in 1950. They Still Are." *The Guardian,* April 30, 2016. https://www.theguardian.com/cities/2016/apr/30/housing-crisis-council-homes-are-the-answer.

Morris, Jenny. *Pride against Prejudice: A Personal Politics of Disability.* London: Women's Press, 1991.

Moyser, Melissa. "Women and Paid Work." In *Women in Canada: A Gender-Based Statistical Report.* Statistics Canada. March 8, 2017.

Muirhead, Russell. *Just Work.* Cambridge, MA: Harvard University Press, 2004.

Mullainathan, Sendhil and Eldar Shafir. *Scarcity: Why Having Too Little Means So Much*. Macmillan, 2013.

Nässén, J. and J. Larsson. "Would Shorter Working Time Reduce Greenhouse Gas Emissions? An Analysis of Time Use and Consumption in Swedish Households." *Environment and Planning C: Government and Policy* 33, no. 4 (2015): 726–45.

Nedelsky, Jennifer. "Communities of Judgment and Human Rights." *Theoretical Inquiries in Law* 1, no. 2 (2000): 1–38.

Nedelsky, Jennifer. "Dilemmas of Passion, Privilege and Isolation: Reflections on Mothering in a White, Middle Class Nuclear Family." In *Mother Troubles: Rethinking Contemporary Maternal Dilemmas*, edited by Julia Hanigsberg and Sara Ruddick, 304–34. Boston: Beacon Press, 1999.

Nedelsky, Jennifer. "Reconceiving Autonomy: Sources, Thoughts and Possibilities." *Yale Journal of Law and Feminism* 1 (1989): 7–36.

Nedelsky, Jennifer. "The Gendered Division of Household Labor: An Issue of Constitutional Rights." In *Feminist Constitutionalism: Global Perspectives*, edited by Beverly Baines, Daphne Barak-Erez, and Tsvi Kahana, 15–47. New York: Cambridge University Press, 2012.

Nedelsky, Jennifer. *Law's Relations: A Relational Theory of Self, Autonomy, and Law*. Oxford: Oxford University Press, 2011.

Nepomnyaschy, Lenna and Jane Waldfogel. "Paternity Leave and Fathers' Involvement With Their Young Children." *Community, Work and Family* 10, no. 4 (2007): 427–53.

Nilliasca, Terri. "Some Women's Work: Domestic Work, Class, Race, Heteropatriarchy, and the Limits of Legal Reform." *Michigan Journal of Race and Law* 16, no. 2 (2011): 377–410.

NLIHC. "Affordable Housing is Out of Reach for Many American Workers." National Low Income Housing Coalition. May 25, 2016. http://nlihc.org/press/releases/6845.

Noguchi, Yuki. "Enjoy The Extra Day Off! More Bosses Give 4-Day Workweek A Try." *NPR*. February 21, 2020. https://www.npr.org/2020/02/21/807133509/enjoy-the-extra-day-off-more-bosses-give-4-day-workweek-a-try.

Noronha, Joanna V. *Nuclear Fusion: Housing, Property and Care Arrangements Beyond the Nuclear Family*. Wainwright Postdoctoral Fellowship Research, McGill University, Faculty of Law, 2019.

Nyberg, Anita. "Gender Equality Policy in Sweden: 1970s–2010s." *Nordic Journal of Working Life Studies* 2, no. 4 (2012): 67–84.

O'Donnell, Liz. "The Crisis Facing America's Working Daughters." *The Atlantic*. February 9, 2016. https://www.theatlantic.com/business/archive/2016/02/working-daughters-eldercare/459249.

OECD. "Revenue Statistics—OECD countries: Comparative tables." OECD. 2016. https://stats.oecd.org/Index.aspx?DataSetCode=REV.

OECD. "Work-Life Balance." OECD. 2016. Accessed November 5, 2016. http://www.oecdbetterlifeindex.org/topics/work-life-balance/.

OECD. "Table C. Tax Structures in the OECD area." OECD. August 22, 2016. http://www.oecd.org/tax/tax-policy/table-c-tax-structures-in-the-oecd-area.htm.

OECD. "Active Labour Market Policies: Connecting People with Jobs." OECD. 2017. Accessed October 18, 2021. https://www.oecd.org/employment/act ivation.htm.

OECD. "Hours Worked: Average Annual Hours Actually Worked." 2019. https://data.oecd.org/emp/hours-workedited byhtm#indicator-chart.

OECD. "Labour Productivity Levels: Most Recent Year." OECD. 2019. Accessed October 18, 2021. https://stats.oecd.org/Index.aspx?DataSetC ode=PDB_LV.

OECD. "Tax Revenue." OECD. 2019. https://data.oecd.org/tax/tax-reve nue.htm.

OECD. "Level of GDP Per Capita and Productivity." OECD. 2020. Accessed January 2, 2022. https://stats.oecd.org/index.aspx?DataSetCode=PDB_LV.

OECD. "Tax Revenue." OECD. 2020. Accessed January 2, 2022. https://data. oecd.org/tax/tax-revenue.htm.

OECD. "Average Annual Hours Actually Worked Per Worker." OECD Stat. 2020. https://stats.oecd.org/Index.aspx?DataSetCode=ANHRS.

Oishi, Akiko Sato, Raymond K. H. Chan, Lillian Lih-Rong Wang, and Ju-Hyun Kim. "Do Part-Time Jobs Mitigate Workers' Work–Family Conflict and Enhance Wellbeing? New Evidence from Four East-Asian societies." *Social Indicators Research* 121, no. 1 (2015): 5–25.

Okin, Susan Moller. *Women in Western Political Thought*. Princeton: Princeton University Press, 1979.

Okun, Arthur M. *Equality and Efficiency: The Big Tradeoff*. Washington, DC: The Brookings Institution, 1975.

Ontario Living Wage Network. *Living Wage by Region*. OLWN. 2020. Accessed October 8, 2021. https://www.ontariolivingwage.ca/living_wage_by_ region.

Partington, Richard. "Number of Zero-Hours Contracts in UK rose by 100,000 in 2017—ONS." *The Guardian*, April 23, 2018. https://www.theguardian. com/uk-news/2018/apr/23/number-of-zero-hours-contracts-in-uk-rose-by-100000-in-2017-ons.

Partington, Richard. "Britons Working at Home Spend More Time on Job in Covid Crisis, ONS Finds." *The Guardian*, April 19, 2021. https:// www.theguardian.com/business/2021/apr/19/working-at-home-job-covid-ons-off-sick.

Partington, Richard. "Global Tax Reform: 130 Countries Commit to Minimum Corporate Rate." *The Guardian*, July 1, 2021. https://www.theguardian.com/ business/2021/jul/01/global-tax-reform-130-countries-commit-to-mini mum-corporate-rate.

Patty, Anna. "Labor's Living Wage Is Different to the Minimum Wage. Here's How." *The Sydney Morning Herald*, April 1, 2019. https://www.smh.com.

au/business/workplace/labor-s-living-wage-is-different-to-the-minimum-wage-here-s-how-20190326-p517o0.html.

Paul, Mark, William Darity Jr., and Darrick Hamilton. *The Federal Job Guarantee: A Policy to Achieve Permanent Full Employment*. Washington, DC: Center on Budget and Policy Priorities, 2018.

Paulas, Rick. "Don't Work 80 Hours a Week for Elon Musk, or Anyone." *Vice*. November 29, 2018. https://www.vice.com/en/article/ev3b3p/dont-work-80-hours-a-week-for-elon-musk-or-anyone?utm_source=vicefbuk&fbclid=IwAR13vUcKq0ZAEF7TX6UBT4WKCqPVui9zWXZEMGGDZaNWXufqYbJzh9YFohc&utm_content=1606300492&utm_medium=social.

PBO. *Costing a National Guaranteed Basic Income Using the Ontario Basic Income Model*. Ottawa: Office of the Parliamentary Budget Office, 2018.

Pedulla, David S. and Sarah Thébaud. "Can We Finish the Revolution? Gender, Work-Family Ideals, and Institutional Constraint." *American Sociological Review* 80, no. 1 (2015): 116–139.

Peel, Elizabeth. "'It Has Had Quite a Lot of Reverberations through the Family': Reconfiguring Relationships through Parent with Dementia Care." In *ReValuing Care in Theory, Law and Policy: Cycles and Connections*, edited by Rosie Harding, Ruth Fletcher, and Chris Beasley, 198–214. Routledge, 2017.

Pencavel, John. "The Productivity of Working Hours." *The Economic Journal* 125, no. 589 (2015): 2052–76.

Pepin, Joanna R., Liana C. Sayer, and Lynne M. Casper. "Marital Status and Mothers' Time Use: Childcare, Housework, Leisure, and Sleep." *Demography* 55, no. 1 (February 2018): 107–33.

Perlow, Leslie A. "Time to Coordinate: Toward an Understanding of Work-Time Standards and Norms in a Multicountry Study of Software Engineers." *Work and Occupations* 28, no. 1 (February 1, 2001): 91–111.

Philipps, Lisa. "There's Only One Worker: Toward the Legal Integration of Paid Employment and Unpaid Caregiving." In *New Perspectives on the Public-Private Divide*, edited by the Law Commission of Canada, 3–39. Vancouver: UBC Press, 2003.

Piketty, Thomas. *Capital in the Twenty-First Century*, translated by A. Goldhammer. Cambridge: The Belknap Press, 2014.

Piketty, Thomas. *Capital and Ideology*. Cambridge, MA: The Belknap Press of Harvard University Press, 2020.

Plantenga, Janneke and Chantal Remery. *Reconciliation of Work and Private Life: A Comparative Review of Thirty European Countries*. Luxembourg: Office for Official Publications of the European Communities, 2005.

Pontusson, Jonas. *Inequality and Prosperity: Social Europe vs. Liberal America*. Ithaca, NY: Cornell University Press, 2005.

Pontusson, Jonas. "Once Again a Model: Nordic Social Democracy in a Globalized World." In *What's Left of the Left: Democrats and Social*

Democrats in Challenging Times, edited by James E. Cronin, George W. Ross, and James Shoch, 89–115. Durham, NC: Duke University Press, 2011.

Portes, J., H. Reed, and A. Percy. *Social Prosperity for the Future: A Proposal for Universal Basic Services.* London: Institute for Global Prosperity, 2017.

Prattes, Riikka. "'I Don't Clean up after Myself': Epistemic Ignorance, Responsibility and the Politics of the Outsourcing of Domestic Cleaning." *Feminist Theory* 21, no. 1 (January 2020): 25–45.

Prescott, Edward C. "Why Do Americans Work So Much More than Europeans?" *Federal Reserve Bank of Minneapolis Quarterly Review* 28, no. 1 (2004): 2–13.

Prickett, Kate C., Alexa Martin-Storey, and Robert Crosnoe. "A Research Note on Time With Children in Different- and Same-Sex Two-Parent Families." *Demography* 52, no. 3 (2015): 905–918.

Pugh, Allison J. *The Tumbleweed Society: Working and Caring in an Age of Insecurity.* Oxford: Oxford University Press, 2015.

Quiggin, J. *Zombie Economics: How Dead Ideas Still Walk Among Us.* Princeton: Princeton University Press, 2010.

Ray, Rebecca, Janet C. Gornick and John Schmitt. "Who Cares? Assessing Generosity and Gender Equality in Parental Leave Policy Designs in 21 Countries." *Journal of European Social Policy* 20, no. 3 (2010): 196–216.

Rehel, E. M. "When Dad Stays Home Too: Paternity Leave, Gender, and Parenting." *Gender & Society* 28, no. 1 (2013): 110–32.

Reich, Robert B. *Saving Capitalism.* New York: Alfred A. Knopf, 2015.

Reinert, Erik S. *How Rich Countries Got Rich: And Why Poor Countries Stay Poor.* London: Constable, 2007.

Ricci, Judith A., Elsbeth Chee, Amy L. Lorandeau, and Jan Berger. "Fatigue in the US Workforce: Prevalence and Implications for Lost Productive Work Time." *Journal of Occupational and Environmental Medicine* 49, no. 1 (2007): 1–10.

Riedmann, Arnold, Harald Bielenski, Teresa Szczurowska, and Alexandra Wagner. *Working Time and Worklife Balance in European Companies.* Dublin: European Foundation for the Improvement of Living and Working Conditions, 2006.

Ritchie, Hannah and Max Roser. "CO_2 emissions." *Our World in Data.* 2020. Accessed April 11, 2021. https://ourworldindata.org/co2-emissions.

Rittich, Kerry. "Families on the Edge: Governing Home and Work in a Globalized Economy." *North Carolina Law Review* 88, no. 5 (2010): 1527–58.

Roach, Catherine M. *Mother/Nature: Popular Culture and Environmental Ethics.* Indiana University Press, 2003.

Rodrik, Dani. "Has Globalization Gone Too Far?" Washington, DC: Institute for International Economics, 1997.

Roeters, A. and Lyn Craig. "Part-Time Work, Women's Work–Life Conflict, and Job Satisfaction: A Cross-National Comparison of Australia, the

Netherlands, Germany, Sweden, and the United Kingdom." *International Journal of Comparative Sociology* 55, no. 3 (2014): 185–203.

Rogers, Ann E., Wei-Ting Hwang, Linda D. Scott, Linda H. Aiken, and David F. Dinges. "The Working Hours of Hospital Staff Nurses and Patient Safety." *Health Affairs* 23, no. 4 (2004): 202–12.

Rose, Stephen J. and Heidi I. Hartmann. *Still a Man's Labor Market.* Institute for Women's Policy Research, 2018.

Rosenberg, Mark L., Alexander Butchart, James Mercy, Vasant Narasimhan, Hugh Waters, Maureen S. Marshall, Dean T. Jamison, et al., eds. "Interpersonal Violence." In *Disease Control Priorities in Developing Countries*, 2nd ed., ch. 40. Washington, DC: The International Bank for Reconstruction and Development, 2006.

Rosenfeld, Rachel A. and Gunn Elisabeth Birkelund. "Women's Part-Time Work: A Cross-National Comparison." *European Sociological Review* 11, no. 2 (1995): 111–34.

Rosnick, D. and M. Weisbrot. "Are Shorter Work Hours Good for the Environment? A Comparison of US and European Energy Consumption." *International Journal of Health Services* 37, no. 3 (2007): 405–17.

Roth, Louise Marie. *Selling Women Short: Gender Inequality on Wall Street.* Princeton: Princeton University Press, 2006.

Rowlingson, Karen. "Does Income Inequality Cause Health and Social Problems?" London: Joseph Rowntree Foundation, 2011.

Ruddick, Sara. *Maternal Thinking: Toward a Politics of Peace.* Boston: Beacon Press, 1989.

Rudman, Laurie A. and Kris Mescher. "Penalizing Men Who Request a Family Leave: Is Flexibility Stigma a Femininity Stigma?" *Journal of Social Issues* 69, no. 2 (2013): 322–40.

Russo, Giovanni. "Job and Life Satisfaction among Part-Time and Full-Time Workers: The 'Identity' Approach." *Review of Social Economy* 70, no. 3 (2012): 315–43.

SABO. "Public Housing in Sweden." Sveriges Allmännytta. 2016. http://www.sabo.se/om_sabo/english/Sidor/Publichousing.aspx.

Saez, Emmanuel and Gabriel Zucman. *The Triumph of Injustice.* New York: W. W. Norton & Company, 2019.

Sahlins, Marshall. *Culture in Practice: Selected Essays.* New York: Zone Books, 2005.

Sanchez, Laura and Elizabeth Thomson. "Becoming Mothers and Fathers: Parenthood, Gender, and the Division of Labor." *Gender & Society* 11, no. 6 (1997): 747–772.

Sándor, Eszter. *European Company Survey 2009: Part-Time Work in Europe.* Dublin: European Foundation for the Improvement of Living and Working Conditions, 2011.

Scanlon, Kathleen, Christine Whitehead, and Melissa Fernández Arrigoitia, eds. *Social Housing in Europe.* Chichester: Wiley Blackwell, 2014.

Scarpa, Angela and Adrian Raine. "Violence Associated with Anger and Impulsivity." In *The Neuropsychology of Emotion*, edited by J. C. Borod, 320–39. Oxford: Oxford University Press, 2000.

Schor, Juliet B. "Sustainable Consumption and Worktime Reduction." *Journal of Industrial Ecology* 9, no. 1–2 (2005): 37–50.

Schor, Juliet B. *The Overworked American*. New York: Basic Books, 1991.

Schor, Juliet B. *Plenitude*. New York: Penguin Press, 2010.

Schulte, Brigid. *Overwhelmed*. New York: Sarah Crichton Books, 2014.

Schweickart, David. *After Capitalism*, 2nd ed. Lanham, MD: Rowman & Littlefield, 2011.

Shao, Qing Long and Beatriz Rodríguez-Labajos. "Does Decreasing Working Time Reduce Environmental Pressures? New Evidence Based on Dynamic Panel Approach." *Journal of Cleaner Production* 125 (2016): 227–35.

Shao, Qing Long and Shiran Victoria Shen. "When Reduced Working Time Harms the Environment: A Panel Threshold Analysis for EU-15, 1970–2010." *Journal of Cleaner Production* 147 (2017): 319–29.

Shepard, Edward and Thomas Clifton. "Are Longer Hours Reducing Productivity in Manufacturing?" *International Journal of Manpower* 21, no. 7 (2000): 540–53.

Simpson, Leanne Betasamosake. "Land as Pedagogy: Nishnaabeg Intelligence and Rebellious Transformation." *Decolonization: Indigeneity, Education & Society* 3, no. 3 (2014): 1–25.

Simpson, Leanne Betasamosake. *As We Have Always Done: Indigenous Freedom through Radical Resistance*. Minneapolis: University of Minnesota Press, 2017.

Skidelsky, Robert and Edward Skidelsky. *How Much Is Enough? Money and the Good Life*. New York: Other Press, 2012.

Slaughter, Anne-Marie. *Unfinished Business: Women Men Work Family*. Oneworld Publications, 2015.

Smithson, Janet, Suzan Lewis, ary Cooper, and Jackie Dyer. "Flexible Working and the Gender Pay Gap in the Accountancy Profession." *Work, Employment & Society* 18, no. 1 (2004): 115–35.

Sodha, Sonia. "Underfunded and Overstretched: The Crisis in Care for the Elderly." *The Observer*. December 10, 2016. https://www.theguardian.com/society/2016/dec/10/care-for-elderly-crisis-how-to-improve-quality-of-life.

Sparks, Kate, Cary Cooper, Yitzhak Fried, and Arie Shirom. "The Effects of Hours of Work on Health: A Meta-analytic Review." *Journal of Occupational and Organizational Psychology* 70, no. 4 (1997): 391–408.

Standing, Guy. "Labour, Work and the Time Squeeze." In *The Precariat: The New Dangerous Class*, 115–143. Bloomsbury Publishing, 2011.

Standing, Guy. *The Precariat*. London: Bloomsbury Academic, 2011.

Statista Research Department. "Number of Mass Shootings in the United States between 1982 and November 2021, By Shooter's Gender." *Statista*.

December 1, 2021. https://www.statista.com/statistics/476445/mass-shooti ngs-in-the-us-by-shooter-s-gender/.

Statistics Denmark. "Personal and Family Income." *Statistics* Denmark. 2019. Accessed October 8, 2021. https://www.dst.dk/en/Statistik/emner/arbejde-og-indkomst/indkomst-og-loen/person-og-familieindkomster.

Stier, Haya and Noah Lewin-Epstein. " Time to Work: A Comparative Analysis of Preferences for Working Hours." *Work and Occupations* 30, no. 3 (2003): 302–26.

Stiglitz, Joseph. *The Price of Inequality.* New York: W. W. Norton & Company, 2012.

Stiglitz, Joseph. "Inequality and Economic Growth." In *Rethinking Capitalism*, edited by Michael Jacobs and Mariana Mazzucato. Chichester: John Wiley & Sons, 2016.

Stillman, Jessica. "Why Working More Than 40 Hours a Week Is Useless." *Inc.* (blog). March 22, 2012. https://www.inc.com/jessica-stillman/why-work ing-more-than-40-hours-a-week-is-useless.html.

Stone, Deborah. *The Samaritan's Dilemma: Should Government Help Your Neighbor?* Nation Books, 2008.

Stone, Pamela. *Opting Out?: Why Women Really Quit Careers and Head Home.* Berkeley: University of California Press, 2007.

Stone, Robyn I. "The Feminization of Poverty among the Elderly." *Women's Studies Quarterly* 17, no. 1/2 (1989): 20–34.

Strazdins, Lyndall, Amy L. Griffin, Dorothy H. Broom, Cathy Banwell, Rosemary Korda, Jane Dixon, Francesco Paolucci, and John Glover. "Time Scarcity: Another Health Inequality?" *Environment and Planning A* 43, no. 3 (2011): 545–59.

Study in Denmark Center. "Student living costs in Denmark." *Study in Denmark.* 2021. Accessed October 8, 2021. http://www.studyindenmark. com/livingcosts.aspx.

Sunstein, Cass R. *The Second Bill of Rights.* New York: Basic Books, 2004.

Swank, Duane. *Global Capital, Political Institutions, and Policy Change in Developed Welfare States.* Cambridge: Cambridge University Press, 2002.

Swers, M. *The Difference Women Make: The Policy Impact of Women in Congress.* Chicago: University of Chicago Press, 2002.

TallBear, Kim. "Caretaking Relations, Not American Dreaming." *Kalfou* 6, no. 1 (2019): 24–41.

Tammelin, Mia, Kaisa Malinen, Anna Rönkä, and Melissa Verhoef. "Work Schedules and Work–Family Conflict among Dual Earners in Finland, the Netherlands, and the United Kingdom." *Journal of Family Issues* 38, no. 1 (2017): 3–24.

Tang, Chiung-Ya and Shelley Macdermid Wadsworth. *Time and Workplace Flexibility.* Families and Work Institute, 2010.

The Care Collective. *The Care Manifesto: The Politics of Interdependence.* London: Verso, 2020.

The Guardian. "The Guardian View on Women and the Pandemic: What Happened to Building Back Better?" *The Guardian*, March 7, 2021. https://www.theguardian.com/commentisfree/2021/mar/07/the-guardian-view-on-women-and-the-pandemic-what-happened-to-building-back-better.

Thistle, Susan. *From Marriage to the Market: The Transformation of Women's Lives and Work.* Berkeley: University of California Press, 2006.

Thomas, Sue. "The Impact of Women on State Legislative Policies." *The Journal of Politics* 53, no. 4 (1991): 958–76.

Timsit, Annabelle. "Even Europe's Most Family-Friendly Countries Don't Invest Enough in Their Youngest Kids." *Quartz*, July 15, 2019. https://qz.com/1664782/europe-doesnt-invest-enough-in-kids-under-three.

Troeger, Vera. "Tax Competition and the Myth of the 'Race to the Bottom.'" *The CAGE-Chatham House Series* no. 4 (2013): 1–12.

Tronto, Joan C. *Moral Boundaries: A Political Argument for an Ethic of Care.* New York: Routledge, 1993.

Tronto, Joan C. *Caring Democracy: Markets, Equality, and Justice.* New York: New York University Press, 2013.

Tronto, Joan C. "Who Cares? Public and Private Caring and the Rethinking of Citizenship." In *Women and Welfare: Theory and Practice in the United States and Europe*, edited by Nancy J. Hirschmann and Ulrike Liebert, 65–83. New Brunswick, NJ: Rutgers University Press, 2001.

Tyson, Laura D'Andrea. "New Clues to the Pay and Leadership Gap." New York: Bloomberg Businessweek. October 27, 2003.

United States Census Bureau. "The Majority of Children Live With Two Parents, Census Bureau Reports." News Release no. CB16-192. November 17, 2016. https://www.census.gov/newsroom/press-releases/2016/cb16-192.html.

United States Census Bureau. "Table a-6. Earnings Summary Measures by Selected Characteristics: 2019 and 2020." United States Census Bureau, https://www.census.gov/data/tables/2021/demo/income-poverty/p60-273.html.

Uppal, Sharanji. "Employment Patterns of Families with Children." *Statistics Canada*. Catalogue no. 86-006-X. June 24, 2015. https://www150.statcan.gc.ca/n1/pub/75-006-x/2015001/article/14202-eng.htm.

USDA. *Supplemental Nutrition Assistance Program Participation and Costs.* USDA Food and Nutrition Services, 2020.

Van Breeschoten, Leonie and Marie Evertsson. "When Does Part-Time Work Relate to Less Work-Life Conflict for Parents? Moderating Influences of Workplace Support and Gender in the Netherlands, Sweden and the United Kingdom." *Community, Work & Family* 22, no. 5 (2019): 606–28.

Van der Gaag, Nikki, Brian Heilman, Taveeshi Gupta, Ché Nembhard, and Gary Barker. *State of the World's Fathers: Unlocking the Power of Men's Care.* Promundo, 2019.

Van het Kaar, Robert and Amber van der Graaf. "Working Life in the Netherlands." *Eurofound.* October 6, 2021. https://www.eurofound.europa.eu/country/netherlands.

Van Parijs, Phillipe. *Real Freedom for All.* Oxford: Clarendon Press, 1995.

Van Parijs, Phillipe and Yannick Vanderborght. *Basic Income.* Cambridge, MA: Harvard University Press, 2017.

Veblen, Thorstein. *The Theory of the Leisure Class.* Oxford: Oxford University Press, [1918] 2007.

Visser, Jelle. "The First Part-Time Economy in the World: A Model To Be Followed?" *Journal of European Social Policy* 12, no. 1 (2002): 23–42.

Visser, Jelle. "Negotiated Flexibility, Working Time and Transitions in the Netherlands." In *Regulating Working-Time Transitions in Europe*, edited by Jacqueline O'Reilly, 123–69. Cheltenham: Edward Elgar, 2003.

WageIndicator.org. "Netherlands." 2016. Accessed August 6, 2016. http://wageindicator-wages-in-context.silk.co/page/Netherlands.

Wall, Kari. "Fathers on Leave Alone: Does It Make a Difference to Their Lives?" *Fathering* 12, no. 2 (2014): 196–210.

Ward, Claire. "How Dutch Women Got To Be the Happiest in the world." *Macleans.* Accessed August 15, 2016. http://www.macleans.ca/news/world/the-feminismhappiness-axis.

Ware, Bronnie. "Regrets of the Dying." *Bronnie Ware.* Accessed August 17, 2016. http://bronnieware.com/regrets-of-the-dying/.

Warner, Judith. *The Women's Leadership Gap.* Center for American Progress. March 7, 2014.

Weigelt, Ulla. *On the Road to a Society of Free Choice: The Politics of Working Time in Sweden.* In Karl Hinrichs, William Roche, and Carmen Sirianni, 203–30. Philadelphia: Temple University Press, 1991.

Weir, Allison. "The Global Universal Care Giver: Imagining Women's Liberation in the New Millennium." *Constellations* 12, no. 3 (2005): 308–30.

Wente, Margaret. "Marriage Is the New Class Divide." *The Globe and Mail.* March 21, 2015. https://www.theglobeandmail.com/opinion/marriage-is-the-new-class-divide/article23545818/.

White, Michael, Stephen Hill, Patrick G. McGovern, and Colin Mills. "'High-Performance' Management Practices, Working Hours and Work–Life Balance." *British Journal of Industrial Relations* 41, no. 2 (2003): 175–95.

Widerquist, Karl. "The Cost of Basic Income: Back-of-the-Envelope Calculations." *Basic Income Studies* 12, no. 2 (2017).

Wielers, Rudi and Dennis Raven. "Part-Time Work and Work Norms in the Netherlands." *European Sociological Review* 29, no. 1 (2013): 105–13.

Wilkinson, Richard and Kate Pickett. *The Spirit Level: Why Equality Is Better for Everyone.* London: Penguin Books, 2010.

Williams, Joan C. *Reshaping the Work-Family Debate: Why Men and Class Matter.* Cambridge, MA; Harvard University Press, 2010.

Wong, Brittany. "Are Men Really Having A 'Friendship Crisis'?" Huffington Post. November 6, 2019. https://www.huffpost.com/entry/men-friendship-crisis_l_5dbc9aa7e4b0576b62a1e90f.

World Bank. "DataBank." *The World Bank*. Accessed August 23, 2016. http://databank.worldbank.org/data/home.aspx.

Worldwatch Institute. "The State of Consumption Today."

Wright, Erik Olin. *Envisioning Real Utopias*. London: Verso, 2010.

Wright, Erik Olin. *How to Be an Anti-Capitalist in the 21st Century*. London: Verso, 2019.

Yates, Amanda, Kelly Dombroski, and Rita Dionisio. "Wellbeing-Led Governance Frameworks as Transformative Tools for an Ecological Emergency." *Dialogues in Human Geography*. Forthcoming.

Yerkes, Mara. "Part-Time Work in the Dutch Welfare State: The Ideal Combination of Work and Care?" *Policy & Politics* 37, no. 4 (2009): 535–52.

York, Erica. "Summary of the Latest Federal Income Tax Data, 2021 Update." Tax Foundation. Accessed October 8, 2021. https://taxfoundation.org/publications/latest-federal-income-tax-data/.

Young, Iris Marion. "Feminism and the Public Sphere." *Constellations* 3, no. 3 (1997): 340–63.

Zippel, Kathrin. "The Missing Link for Promoting Gender Equality: Work-Family and Anti-Discrimination Policies." In *Gender Equality: Transforming Family Divisions of Labour*, edited by Janet C. Gornick and Marcia K. Meyers, 209–30. London: Verso, 2009.

Zucman, Gabriel. *The Hidden Wealth of Nations: The Scourge of Tax Havens*. Chicago: The University of Chicago Press, 2015.

Index

For the benefit of digital users, indexed terms that span two pages (e.g., 52–53) may, on occasion, appear on only one of those pages.